Oak Island and the Arcadian Mysteries: Oak Island, Rennes le Chateau, and Shugborough Hall

Introduction. P. 2

Chapter 1: The True Story of Oak Island and Arcadia. P. 5
-*Philip Sidney and "Arcadia" - Drake's Oak Island Treasure?*

Chapter 2: Washington D.C., The Alexander Family and Nova Scotia. P. 22

Chapter 3: Arcadia in Scotland and "Sancto Claro." P. 31

Chapter 4: The Real Roseline of Rosslyn Chapel and the Prime Meridian of Orphir Round Kirk. P. 44

Chapter 5: Et in Orcadia Ego. The true story of Templars in America. P. 53

Chapter 6: Shugborough Hall and its follies: The Tower of the Winds and Shepherd's Monument. P. 62
-*The Shepherds of Arcadia Revealed. Admiral Anson's Moor Park.*

Chapter 7: Sir Francis Dashwood and his West Wycombe Estate. P.108

Chapter 8: Stirling Castle and the mystery of the Kings Knot. The Stewart Family and the Mysteries of Rennes le Chateau. P.120

Chapter 9: Edgar Allan Poe, Henry Wadsworth Longfellow, The Westford Knight, Oak Island, and Newport Tower. P.134

Chapter 10: Edgar Allan Poe and the Mystery of Rennes le Chateau. P.159

Chapter 11: The Frenchman's Tower of Palo Alto and the Legend of J.C. Brown. Arcadia in California. P.178

Chapter 12: Bonnie Prince Charlie's Legacy from Oak Island to the Frenchman's Tower. P.190
-*Bonnie Prince Charlie, Oak Island and the de La Tour family*
- *Rennes le Chateau, Rennes le Bains, and the de La Tour Auvergne family. Mystery solved?*
- *The Marquis de Lafayette and Chateau Villette*
- *Father Saunière and the de La Tour family.*

Chapter 13: The Paris and St. Sulpice Meridians. P. 214

Chapter 14: The White House Meridian. P. 228
-*The John Ericsson National Memorial and the White House Meridian*

Chapter 15: Chico California and the Arcadian Mysteries. P. 241
-*The "Little Washington D.C." of Chico California*
- *The Axis of John Bidwell at Chico. The Hooker Oak and the legacy of Hartford Connecticut.*
-*Overview of the street plan and significant components of Chico architecture.*

Chapter 16: The Knights Tombstone of Jamestown Virginia, The Beale Treasure, and the Mysteries of North America. P. 286
-*William and Mary, The House of Orange, and Mary Magdalene*
-*The Bruton Parish Church and the Page Family*

Chapter 17: The Other Sir Francis Bacon and Washington D.C. P. 310

Chapter 18: St. Paul's Chapel and Pierre L'Enfant. The Mystery of the Montgomery Memorial. P. 317

Appendix: *Google Earth Imagery of Oak Island Associations and more. P. 332*

Introduction:

"Visita Interiora Terrae Rectificando Invenies Occultum Lapidem Veram Medicinam"
Visit the interior of the Earth; by rectification thou shalt find the hidden stone.
    – Christian Rosenkreuz (according to some sources)

This short volume reveals some of my thoughts on the true meaning of the Shepherds Monument at Shugborough Hall and how it does relate to the imagery of Nicoals Poussin at Rennes le Chateau. Amazingly this information also led to the discovery of some information related to Oak Island that solidly links the stories of Stirling Castle, Shugborough Hall, Washington D.C., Chico California, The Frenchman's Tower of Palo Alto, Rennes le Chateau and Oak Island Nova Scoita via the Arcadian theme. A distinct group of families extending from old word gentry to the early colonial era seem to have been involved over the entire span of post medieval history including the development of the United States and Canada.

Each of these places contains artwork and octagonal forms that indicate a directional scheme in the tradition of the Prime Meridian and Axis Mundi. In the Greek and Roman world the Axis Mundi and associated temple were normally the domain of a priesthood known as Augurs. Over time these priesthoods evolved into many of the orders of Monks and Nuns that we see today. Some of the tradition of defining a domain for a ruler or spiritual concept was applied in many practical ways that helped to define the arts of navigation, cartography, and geodesy. Many times later people would value much older axes. As the art of navigation progressed associations were made with places in the New World that harkened back to these more ancient axes.

Through history temporal control over a given region or colony may have included the construction of a temple from which ephemeris or star charts could be collected. These observations allowed points on the earth to be compared to each other thus beginning a true and accurate definition of the spatial attributes of the planet that continues today. This work evolved slowly and gained many political and social overtones. Many of these places had mysteries or treasure stories applied to them later to both entice and confuse the seeker. Along the way many aspects of folklore and mythology were applied in such a way as to suggest coded information or reveal truth via interpretation.

The end result of this tradition was a series of octagonal structures based on the Tower of the Winds in Athens that actually used their plan and orientation to "point to" other places of value on the earth. In this way royal entities began to establish their domains in a way that could be compared with other claims leading to the legal definition of property.

People like Fulcanelli, Swedenborg, and Sir Francis Bacon were likely aware of all of these concepts leading to this tradition coming to North America and having an impact on the development of the colonies and United States of America. Here we will view how this tradition was valued in the eighteenth and nineteenth century leading us to the mysteries of Shugborough Hall, Rennes le Chateau, and The Shepherds of Arcadia. While this information does not solve either mystery it may expose the true nature of these mysteries that fascinate us so.

Amazingly the truth of all of this mythology and lore including places like Oak Islands seems to have been known of and written about by many literary figures. Just as artists like Leonardo may have included real historical secrets in his work writers from Dante to Edgar Allan Poe seemed to have also used their craft to tell a true story based in allegory and metaphor. Through many previous eras of history the written word was used to convey meaning and understanding on many different levels. The era of Dante may have marked a period when literature developed into its modern form while escaping the control of those that wished to dictate not only what was printed but who may have been trained to even read it.

All of the structures discussed here are actually used as prime meridians that were used to measure and relate these sites to other important sites using the Arcadian theme. For instance, the octagonal form of the Kings Knot at Stirling can be used to create eight azimuths or arcs on the globe using its octagonal form. This is similar to using that point on earth as the center of a map projection and using that point from which to measure its relation to other points on the globe. While Google Earth is more accurate than the means used to do this in the recent past to antiquity we may utilize that tool to see the relationships between these places today. Given that all of these places not only "point to" each other on the globe but seem to have all been created by a related family group and philosophy.

Note that some significant points are repeated in each chapter in order to convey understanding of how all of these places are related to each other.

Thank you. –Cort Lindahl

"Visita Interiora Terrae Rectificando Invenies Occultum Lapidem Veram Medicinam"
Visit the interior of the Earth; by rectification thou shalt find the hidden stone.
   – Christian Rosenkreuz (according to some sources)

Chapter 1: The True Story of Oak Island and Arcadia.

What if the story of Oak Island is essentially a fictional story that had been told long before anyone supposed the presence of treasure there? Is it possible that this story had been applied to the island for reason's other than inspiring the reader to look for treasure? The truth may reveal that the entire saga was meant to inform one of the true nature of the name Acadia (Arcadia) while also displaying the contentious history of what would eventually come to be known as Nova Scotia. As the story unfolds it is clear that both the French and English factions of Nova Scotia and the other maritime provinces had a distinct value of the Arcadian concept that had come from the same Greek mythology.

A value of Arcadia also involve a value of navigation with regard to the Pole Star also known as Stella Maris. The name Arcadia derives from the Greek mythological character Arcas. Ultimately Arcas and his mother are cast into the sky with Arcas as Ursa Minor and his mother as Ursa Major. The Pole Star is located at the tip of the tail of Ursa Minor making this an important constellation to both Pilgrims and Pilots. This somewhat hidden navigational theme is of course valued throughout the entire tale of "Arcadia" and the real people surrounding the Oak Island mystery. The theme of Arcadia is also one of a pastoral utopia where life is good and simple.

It is clear that both the French and English factions of Acadia valued this mythology and its pastoral themes. Though the Academy of Arcadia of the Vatican was not formed until the mid seventeenth century these themes are especially evident in the application of the name Larcadia to this region by Italian cartographer Bolongnini Zaltieri in 1566. It is likely that Bolongnini had used this name in response to explorer Verrazano's naming of what would become Delaware "Archadia" during his 1525 voyage. Originally these regions were claimed by France yet soon disputed by England. When the French first settled the area of what would become Port Royal Nova Scotia in 1605 they became known of as "Acadians." The use of this name comes from an era of history during which the image of Greek Arcadia as a pastoral utopia was appreciated and began to manifest itself in visual and literary arts.

With this in mind it is no surprise that Verrazano and Bolongnini chose to use this name for previously unnamed regions during their voyages. Given this it is easy to see why later artists and writers would value and revere this concept via their literary guild of Arcadia. Strangely the use of literary guilds in this manner may reveal a great deal about the Mystery of Oak Island and many other questions that seem to have been placed in the minds of the public at large. One literary figure in particular may in fact hide the secret of the Oak Island Treasure! The Academy of Arcadia of the Vatican was not established until the mid seventeenth century and likely included among its members Nicolas Poussin famous for his renderings of "The Shepherds of

Arcadia" known in the mysteries of Shugborough Hall and Rennes le Chateau. As it may be discerned there is yet another somewhat earlier literary guild who seemed to value the Arcadian theme in England.

Sir Philip Sidney was a writer and courtier during the Elizabethan era. Both he and his sister Mary Sidney Herbert Countess of Pembroke were favorites at court during that time. Both Philip and Mary were talented writers who were part of Mary's writer's guild known as the Wilton's Writers Circle. Many people speculate as to this guild's involvement in the production of the works of Shakespeare as well as involvement with Sir Francis Bacon and Edward de Vere the 17th Earl of Oxford. Mary Sidney Countess of Pembroke also once penned a book about Enochian Geomancy or the reading and interpretation of lines on the earth.

In about 1570 Philip dedicated an extensive work to is sister simply titled "Arcadia." This tome refers to the idyllic land of Greek Arcadia and as we will see provided a few moments of crucial history to the world of mystery and intrigue. Some of the details of the story include the book opening with a maritime battle that includes Pirates and the destruction of the two protagonists ship leaving them stranded in Arcadia.

The sons of Mary Sidney Herbert Countess of Pembroke both married the daughters of the 17th Earl of Oxford Edward de Vere. The Herbert son's were great patrons of the arts and funded the publication of the famous First Folio of Shakespeare as evidenced by the books dedication to them by famous author Ben Jonson. The First Folio is an interesting publication of Shakespeare and is thought by many to contain codes and ciphers. The First Folio and indeed all of the works of Shakespeare postdate the authorship of "Arcadia" by Philip Sydney but did occur in the era during which William Alexander edited the work. If these code crakcers are correct then these ciphers were placed in the First Folio in response to what Philip Sydney had written in "Arcadia" that had first been written whcn Bacon was about twelve years old. Again this may indicate that the suggestion of treasure at Oak Island had come from and had been a copy of the story included in Sidney's work. The First Folio was published in 1621. Sidney wrote "Arcadia" in the 1570's and it was finished by 1580. Both his sister Mary Sidney Herbert Countess of Pembroke and later William Alexander 1st Earl of Stirling amended and edited the work. It is clear that Sir Francis Bacon had nothing to do with the production of "Arcadia" nor to the ciphers in the first folio actually refer to his work. They refer to something Philip Sidney had written or done. Not Sir Francis Bacon.

King Charles I last words were from a portion of Sidney's "Arcadia" known as "Pamela's Prayer." This in turn leads us to the imagery of "Et in Arcadia Ego" on the Shepherd's Monument of Shugborough Hall and will unravel the mystery of Oak Island as well as point to solutions to other mysteries such as the Bruton Parish Church Vault of Jamestown and Williamsburg and the Beale Treasure of Virginia. Throughout all these mysteries the Arcadian theme or use of the Pole Star to navigate from clue to clue to find treasure is central. This includes Oak Island, Rennes le Chateau and Shugborough mysteries. This information proves that the Shepherds Monument was intended as a memento mori for the beheaded Charles I. In addition as this tale unravels we will see direct connections to a series of popular mysteries.

Amazingly artwork and architecture present at Admiral Anson's other estate Moor Park unravels the entire mystery. Philip Sidney also owned Moor Park at one point that is only a few miles from Sir Francis Bacon's Gorhambury Estate.

What will be revealed will also connect the octagonal Kings Knot of Stirling Castle originally built by Charles I to the Tower of the Winds of Shugborough Hall and the strange star in the landscape of Rennes le Chateau as defined by brilliant author Henry Lincoln. The octagonal Kings Knot "points to" both the Tower of the Winds of Shugborough and the star in the landscape of Rennes le Chateau as defined by Henry Lincoln. The star at Rennes in turn "points back" thus defining a single arc on the globe that includes the Shugborough Tower of the Winds between the two. It will soon become clear why and how all these places and themes are related together including Oak Island. The Arcadian mysteries are all linked via a geographic scheme indicated by monuments present at each location.

What if in addition to all of these revelations Philip Sidney's "Arcadia" also revealed the original story of how the Money Pit on Oak Island was found? In fact "Arcadia" contains the exact story that reflects the origins of the modern Oak Island myth as it is read today. What if there was a direct connection between Charles I and the Arcadian theme that would rationalize why all the monuments and associated mysteries at Stirling, Shugborough, and Rennes le Chateau even exist in the first place? What if the entire scheme also included Oak Island Nova Scotia?!

The original folklore of Oak Island tells of how three young men sighted strange lights on the Island and went to investigate. Upon a search of the Island a strange depression was found with a ships tackle hanging from the branch of an Oak Tree above. The young men decide to excavate the pit hoping that local tales of Pirate's hoards could be true. First the surface of the depression was covered with flagstones. As they excavated strange platforms of oaken logs were encountered until finally at about ninety feet a strange stone was encountered that included an enigmatic inscription that some interpret as saying treasure is located in a vault below. The true story is similar yet with the young men living and owning property on the island. It may be that the men who found the treasure had once been part of Montagu's "Carolina Corps" during the revolutionary war with some of them being from Virginia and North Carolina originally.

Here below in a excerpt from Philip Sidney's "Arcadia" published in 1580 we see almost the exact story being told. "Arcadia" had been published over two hundred years prior to the first revelation of any hint of treasure at Oak Island as exposed in the original tale. Here now read the truth of the Oak Island Money Pit:

"Master," answered Dorus, " you have so satisfied me with promising me the utmost of my desired' bliss, that if my duty
bound me not, I were in it sufficiently rewarded. To you therefore shall my good hap be converted, and the fruit of my labour
dedicated. Therewith he told him, how under an ancient oak (the place he made him easily understand by sufficient marks he gave to him) he had found digging but a little depth, scattering lying a great number of rich medals, and that, piercing farther into

the ground he had met with a great stone, which, by the hollow sound it yielded, seemed to be the cover of some greater vault, and upon it a box of cypress, with the name of the valiant Aristomenes, graven upon it : and that within the box he found certain verses which signified that some depth again under that all his treasures lay hidden, what time for the discord fell out in Arcadia, he lived banished. Therewith he gave Dametas certain medals of gold he had long kept about him, and asked him, because it was a thing much to be kept secret, and a matter one man in twenty hours might easily perform, whether he would have him go and seek the bottom of it, which he refrained to do till he knew his mind promising he would faithfully bring him what he found, or else that he himself would do it, and be the first beholder of that comfortable spectacle ; no man need doubt which part Dametas would choose, whose fancy had already devoured all this great riches, and even now began to grudge at a partner, before he saw his own share. Therefore taking a strong jade, laden with spades and mattocks, which he meant to bring back otherwise laden he went in all speed thitherward, taking leave of nobody, only desiring Dorus he would look well to the princess Pamela, promising him mountains of his own labour, which nevertheless he little meant to perform, like a fool, not considering, that no man is to be moved with part, that neglects the whole.

Thus away went Dametas having already made an image in his fancy, what palaces he would build, how sumptuously he would fare, and among all other things imagined what money to employ in making coffers to keep his money ; his ten miles seemed twice so many leagues, and yet contrary to the nature of it, though it seemed long, it was not wearisome. Many times he cursed his horse's want of consideration, that in so important a matter would make no greater speed : many times he wished himself the back of an ass to help to carry away the new sought riches (an unfortunate wisher, for if he had as well wished the head, it had been granted him). At length being come to the tree, which he hoped should bear so golden acorns, down went all his instruments, and forthwith to the renting up of the hurtless earth, where by and by he was caught with the lime of a few promised medals, which was so perfect a pawn unto him of his farther expectation that he deemed a great number of hours well employed in groping farther into it, which with logs and great stones was made as cumbersome as might be, till at length, with sweaty brow, he came to the great stone. A stone, God knows, full unlike to the cover of a monument, but yet there was the cypress box with Aristomenes graven upon it, and these verses written in it,

A banish'd man, long barr'd from his desire
By inward lets, of them his state possessed,

Hid here his hopes, by which he might aspire.

To have his harms with wisdom's help redressed.

Seek then and see what man esteemeth best,
All is but this, this is our labour's hire :

Of this we live, in this we find our rest ;

Who holds this fast no greater wealth require,

Look farther then, so shalt thou find at least,

A bait most fit for hungry minded guest.

He opened the box, and to his great comfort read them, and with fresh courage went about to lift up that stone. But in the meantime, e'er Dametas was half-a-mile gone to the treasure-ward, Dorus came to Miso......

Later in the story:

THE almighty wisdom evermore delighting to show the world that by unlikeliest means greatest matters may come to conclusion ; that human reason may be the more humbled, and more willingly give place to divine providence; as at the first it brought in Dametas to play a part in this royal pageant, so having continued him still an actor, now that all things were grown ripe for an end, made his folly the instrument of revealing that which far greater cunning had sought to conceal. For so it fell out that Dametas having spent the whole day in breaking up the cumbersome work of the pastor Dorus, and feeling in all his labour no pain so much as that his hungry hopes received any stay, having with the price of much sweat and weariness gotten up the huge stone, which he thought should have such a golden lining, the good man in the great bed that stone had made, found nothing but these two verses written upon a broad piece of vellum.

Who hath his hire, hath well his labour plac'd ;
Earth thou didst seek, and store of Earth thou hast.

The above narrative from "Arcadia" seems to be the original source of the tale still told today in relation to Oak Island. Of course the alternate name of Nova Scotia is Acadia which is also French or short for Arcadia. The fictional work does reveal the solution to a missing "treasure" that has not yet happened at Oak Island. This literary work takes place in the original Arcadia of Greece and does not at first glance have anything to do with Nova Scotia. Or does it? Given all the similarities in this story to the original tale of Oak Island there is absolutely no way this story in Nova Scotia did not derive from Philip Sidney's "Arcadia." If this fictional tale is the original source of the Money Pit story then this does not bode well if the real Money Pit serves the same purpose as the one in the story. "Arcadia" is indeed a story about Acadia.

This story seems to describe a hidden or lost stash of treasure that someone had already dug for and had found some of the loot. He then sends an additional person in search of what remains at the same site. This would leave a depression in the ground just as described in the original story. The inclusion of Aristomenes' box also fits the Money Pit story as does the inclusion of a graven stone reminiscent of the "ninety foot" stone said to have been found at the Money Pit. The papers in the box indicate a great treasure hidden below possibly in a vault where the box and stone were found. The description of "logs and stones" being removed also resembles the layers of oaken logs said to have been encountered in the Money Pit story. The story of Sir Francis Bacon's papers being present is suggested at both Jamestown/Williamsburg and Oak Island by some. Something similar is also told in this excerpt of "Arcadia." The plot of "Arcadia" reveals that the treasure story is simply an elaborate ruse to confound Dametas while Dorus escapes with the object of his desire. There are other aspects of "Arcadia" that do mention pirates and looted treasures but not in relation to the treasure story discussed here.

Sir William Alexander 1st Earl of Stirling was an admirer of Philip Sidney's work and was a favorite at the court of James I. William had even been educated with the future king Charles I in Scotland as a young man. His association with Charles may indeed link us back to Shugborough Hall and the notion that the Shepherds Monument is a memento more for Charles. The Shepherds Monument may indeed display a strange small casket or reliquary that may represent the Oak Island treasure. Eventually Sir William would be given Nova Scotia in one of the early English possessions of the Maritime region. His intention was to establish a Scottish Colony and he is credited with naming the region Nova Scotia. Sir Alexander is the origin of the Baronetcies of Nova Scotia and the Nova Scotia flag. The history of this region has it passing back and forth from English to French hands several times in a contentious manner that was not really solved until after the invasion of General George Lawrence in the early eighteenth century. Strangely William Alexander 1st Earl of Stirling also has a very direct and unmistakable link to the Arcadian concept that had already been applied to the region by French influences.

William Alexander wrote an addendum to Philip Sidney's "Arcadia" in 1621 that does not include this strange tale resembling the later Legend of the Money Pit at Oak Island. The first governor of Acadia had written part of "Arcadia." This means Philip Sidney is the source of the story that would later seemingly be copied at Oak Island in Arcadia. Still Alexander's addendum was about one hundred and seventy-four years prior to the revelation of the story we all know and love at Oak Island. This amazing fact coupled with the presence of the Oak Island story so long prior to its use later near the turn of the nineteenth century have now be examined in a different light. In fact this information may also reveal that that entire later manifestation of the Legend of the Money pit was contrived and that no treasure is located at Oak Island. The first Baron or Governor of Arcadia wrote part of "Arcadia!"

Of course this story may also be interpreted as having been the template for the deposition of valuable items as described in both the Legend of the Money Pit and Sidney's "Arcadia." The fact that this fictional tale was composed so long before the Money Pit was discovered may indicate the falsehood of the entire later history that has them simply copying a tale germane to the history and identity of Acadia or Nova Scotia. An alternate scenario suggested by this story would mean that if true the treasure had already been found. The fact that the Money Pit story had obviously been crafted from "Arcadia" may also indicate the folly of the original story. Or had men later replicated the entire story at Oak Island to hide a real treasure? Though that would have been difficult it does not make sense unless someone was intentionally conjuring images from Sidney's "Arcadia." Though this tale in Arcadia does not mention the Oak in question being located on an Island could he have known of a treasure there as early as 1570?

One important factor that may point to the existence of real treasure at Oak Island is Philip Sidney's close friendship with Sir Francis Drake. Drake is included in a long list of people who potentially created the Money Pit and the chronology of his voyages do indicate that Sidney could have included his "Arcadian" treasure tale in response to something Drake had told him. Still even if Drake was involved there is no record of him coming to Nova Scotia though his position in the English naval hierarchy would have exposed him to a great deal of information from other sailors and sea captains.

In the end the repetition of theme and identical elements of the story point to the fact that the later Money Pit mystery was crafted to intentionally match the story from Sidney and Alexander's "Arcadia." That is almost without question at this point. There may be many real and verifiable reasons that this is true within the scope of intelligence services and use of literature and art as weaponized constructs. Again the entire cast of characters on both the French and English sides of the story have direct relations to the intelligence networks of the monarchies of both France and England. Thrown into the mix is the defacto intelligence network of the Society of Jesus also known as the Jesuits.

Many elements of the progression and editing of "Arcadia" later resemble the way the famous work "Amadis de Gaula" progressed with one addendum even being the earliest source of the name "California." Works such as these may have contained hidden metaphors or even codes that would only be appreciated by an initiate or one intimately associated with the history surrounding them. Evidence of this comes in the form of a communication from Sindey's close friend Fulke Greville to Sir Francis Walsingham. Sir Francis was also Philip Sidney's father in law. Walsingham was of course considered to be one of the "spymasters" of Queen Elizabeth and holds close relations to many people in this tale. Greville's concern seems to stem from the fact that portions of Sidney's "Arcadia" are too revealing to be published:

"Sir this day one Ponsonby a bookbinder in Paul's Churchyard, came to me, and told me that there was one in hand to print, Sir Philip Sidney's old Arcadia asking me if it were done with your honour's con[sent] or any other of his friends/I told him to my knowledge no, then he advised me to give warning of it, either to the Archbishop or Doctor Cosen, who have as he says a copy of it to peruse to that end/Sir I am loath to renew his memory unto you, but yet in this I must presume, for I have sent my Lady your daughter at her request, a correction of that old one done 4 or 5 years since which he left in trust with me whereof there is no more copies, and fitter to be printed than that first which is so common, notwithstanding even that to be amended by a direction set down under his own hand how and why, so as in many respects especially the care of printing it is to be done with more deliberation,.....".

Why would the publishing of this story be of concern to those included in the intelligence circle of Elizabeth? Were there specific points of the story private to this family or did they have knowledge of a treasure left by Sir Fracis Drake? Here again is more fuel to the fire to the notion that the entire Money Pit legend was in turn contrived. Still we have reasonable evidence that a shaft was excavated at Oak Island that included layers of logs as in the Sidney and Alexander story of "Arcadia." Could this entire treasure hunt have been contrived to resemble Arcadia to stash another more real treasure or had this been done to confound one's enemies that were known to be in search of specific religious relics or treasures such as the fabled Temple Treasure of Jerusalem? Alternately Walsingham as Sidney's father in law may have seen "Arcadia" as meant to be for immediate family only. "Arcadia" was originally written for Mary Sidney Herbert Philip's sister and was only read by those of the Wilton Writer's Circle.

It is clear that the stories match down to the description of layers of logs and the strange "ninety foot" stone. The Money Pit mystery is frustrating due to the absence of the ninety foot stone which has not been seen since the period of its discovery. No photos of the original stone exist only drawings. What is amazing is that this work is associated with William Alexander who personally edited and added to the work in 1613-18 only a few years before he was awarded control of Nova Scotia by James I. It appears as if Alexander viewed this work in a metaphorical manner that could be applied to "Arcadia" in Nova Scotia thus adding a Scottish identity beyond the name of the colony. What does this mean with regard to goings on at Oak Island and the Money Pit? Did Alexander know of or have something placed there to resemble this story intentionally? Or was he privy to a real treasure hidden in this manner there? It is clear from Scottish wills and land deeds that the central portion of Scotland was referred to as Arcadia as early as the twelfth century. This in turn leads us to the true meaning of "Sancto Claro" that strangely also applies to the family heritage of William Alexander Earl of Stirling.

Is it possible that Sidney and later Alexander were privy to a treasure hidden in the money pit or had the later story been contrived as simply a heritage lesson for the English and Scottish inhabitants of Nova Scotia? Is "Arcadia" telling us a story about a treasure that is located somewhere other than Oak Island? It is clear that both Sidney and Alexander were included in a circle of people of influence that have been suspects in literary intrigue including the disputed authorship of the works of Shakespeare. This same dynamic would dictate their association with people that were essentially spies who would tailor stories and mythology that may be used against their enemies in this case the French and Spanish. The poem or lines of verse at the end of the above quote from Sidney's "Arcadia" also seems to indicate that a search for treasure is a folly that should not be taken lightly. Is this a warning or indication that there is no real treasure? The Beale Ciphers original pamphlet also contains such a warning. In fact this line of verse seems to indicate that what will be found is simply an indication of further lost treasures at additional locations:

"Look farther then, so shalt thou find at least, A bait most fit for hungry minded guest."

The story surrounding this new information may indicate the presence of a series of mysteries meant to confound and frustrate the searcher who may in fact be finding a treasure of neglected historical information as the search progresses. This is the basis for a real "National Treasure" quest. Some have speculated in the past that the "Oak Island Treasure" is a metaphor for Masonic concepts. This version of the story would match the veiled warning present by suggesting the "treasure" is information for an initiate. Amazingly all of this includes the use of Sidney's literary work and not Shakespeare or Sir Francis Bacon. Even Sidney's nephew's involvement in the first folio seems to point one to Arcadia which is a reference to their Uncle and not the works of Shakespeare.

Not to be forgotten in this tale is the French side of the story. None other than the d'Abbadie family had a great influence in the establishment of the Acadian or Arcadian name and historical theme to the maritime region including Maine. The d'Abbadie's are well known to mystery lovers via the work of researchers Jay Weidner and Vincent Bridges via their views of the Great Cyclic Cross of Hendaye. Jean Vincent d'Abbadie St. Castin and his two sons had a lasting impact on the development of this region and their family legacy may have also lent itself to the development of treasure legends and mythology similar to what we see at Oak Island. It is possible that Sidney is telling us of an even more unknown French relation to the entire mystery at large.

In addition lurking in the wings of this saga is the famous Pirate Peter Easton who also had many of the same connections to influential people that Sidney and Alexander possessed. Easton is one of the only Pirate's to have left North American waters with a verified treasure worth a great deal. Is it possible Easton had used this story of Sidney to actually find something? Or had he used it to fool later seekers of a fictional hoard? As a coincidence Easton was said to have left Maritime waters with "2 million English Pounds" worth of loot. This is the exact amount that many suggest was beneath the ninety foot stone as suggested in the code on the stone. There are many things about the subsequent activities and family relations of Peter Easton that may suggest this is true. Among these factors is the presence of the Mortimer (Mortuo Mari i.e. "Dead Mary" or "Dead Sea") family in the genealogy of the Sidney family.

Of interest in the French story of Oak Island and Acadia is the Louvre Museum in Paris. The Louvre may represent a clue in the entire Frankish view of Oak Island and Nova Scotia. Many speculate the presence of biblical relics at Oak Island. Here we may have a case of representative artwork combined with imagery from a popular movie that may give us a clue to the truth of Oak Island. Strangely this array of involved architecture also may help to verify elements of Sidney's Arcadia and why the treasure story in his literary muses is important.

The modern linear orientation of the I.M. Pei Pyramid and Inverted Pyramid of the Louvre Museum in Paris may be used to form an arc on the globe. This array of architecture was included in the famous movie "The Da Vinci Code" as being the hidden site of the crypt of Mary Magdalene. The arc on the globe created by this linear array of two pyramids "points to" Migdal Israel to the east and Oak Island Nova Scotia to the West. Migdal is of course the birthplace of Mary Magdalene. The French version of the Oak Island saga may indeed include the imagery of Mary Magdalene also repeating the theme of the possibility that biblical relics or "treasure" is stashed at Oak Island. Again all of this could be a metaphor to incite one to learn about the French point of view in relation to Arcadia and religious concepts. Again the date of the publication of Sidney's "Arcadia" long predates any French settlement of the Maritime Region including Nova Scotia.

Poussin's painting of "The Shepherds of Arcadia" that is central to the themes of Rennes le Chateau and the Shepherd's monument is displayed in the portion of the Louvre Museum that is situated on the famous Paris Meridian. Here again is the specter of Arcas and Pole Star and how it is used in these landscape mysteries. Poussin was a member of the Academy degli Arcadia of the Vatican. Overlain over the entire cast of characters we see here is the Latin Church and its interest in such mysteries. Some of these stories indicate the presence of biblical relics that the church would naturally have an interest in. The French were mostly Catholic during this early era of colonial development and many English and Scottish people kept their faith hidden during this period of persecution in England and her holdings.

Famous American author Edgar Allan Poe penned a work entitled "The Gold Bug" that refers to this entire mystery as well and is replete with the imagery of the Oak Tree and Skull of Mary Magdalene and other figures. The story also infers the involvement of Thomas Jefferson and even has many undeniable references to Rennes le Chateau. Poe is telling us of his knowledge of this entire scheme that may have come to him via his involvement with the Society of the Cincinnati and other American literary figures. In fact the revolutionary war era of Nova Scotia reveals the involvement of many "American" people in the post revolutionary war saga of Oak Island including members of the Society of the Cincinnati as well as former soldiers from the "Carolina Corps" of Montagu.

Many elements of Sidney's Arcadia including what is apparently a description of the Money Pit resemble later stories in Virginia such as the Legend of Bacon's Vault in Jamestown and Williamsburg and later elements of the Beale Treasure legend. These legends in turn relate us back in time to Emperor Constantine and Holy Roman Emperor Charlemagne and their "Man in the Mountain" myths. It is clear that this template was later used to infer hidden vaults and lost biblical relics and treasure. The use of the imagery of Arcadia in this manner will now in turn lead us to Shugborough Hall, its famous Shepherd's Monument, and finally the legendary Rennes le Chateau mystery. At each of these places the theme of Arcadia and "Et in Arcadia Ego" is inferred as central to the mysteries there.

Along the way this incredible story will include Dante, Sir Francis Bacon, the de Vere family, Edgar Allan Poe, The Pre-Raphaelite Brotherhood, Joaquin Miller, Henry Wadsworth Longfellow (wrote "Evangeline" about Arcadia and had family there), Samuel Morse, James Fenimore Cooper, Thomas Jefferson, Ben Franklin, George Washington (and descendants), Franklin D. Roosevelt and too many more to list. It is clear that organizations such as the Wilton Writer's Circle and the Academy of Arcadia had communicated themes used in these mysteries in architecture, art, and literary forms. Does it mean there is no treasure anywhere? Absolutely not. But this information may change the way people view places like Oak Island, Rennes le Chateau and the region where the Beale Treasure is located. The treasure begins with the monumental literary works, architecture, and art that was created by these people.

Drake's Oak Island Treasure?

Philip Sidney was close friends with Sir Francis Drake the first Englishman to Circumnavigate. This is interesting when we consider that Admiral Anson was the third Englishman to Circumnavigate the globe. This may make two famous English Naval figures that also may have visited Oak Island though there is no record of this. Both men had been to the America's with Anson later being stationed at Charleston South Carolina in the early to mid 1730's. Both men seem to be involved in what may be termed the Arcadian Mysteries.

The Ansonborough neighborhood of Chaleston is named for Admiral Anson of Shugborough Hall who is said to have won it in a card game! Some theories do link the mysterious inscription on the Shepherds Monument on Anson's estate Shugborough Hall with the Oak Island treasure with one researcher claiming his decipherment matches the latitude and longitude coordinates of Oak Island.

If we view the Oak Island treasure legend from the perspective that states Sir Francis Drake left a treasure there then this would also make what Philip Sidney wrote in Arcadia seem more real. It is clear that Sir Francis Drake and Philip Sidney were close friends. Sidney had even attempted to accompany Drake on this later circumnavigation but was prevented from doing this by Queen Elizabeth herself. Some sources state that Sidney was intercepted at the dock ready to board the ship. This is after the time he had written "Arcadia." Is it possible the treasure story in "Arcadia" evolved from something Sidney knew as told to him by Sir Francis Drake himself? Let us examine both of these men's activities in as much detail as we can. It appears there could be a real rationale for why both of them may have known something was at Oak Island.

Drake's first voyages to the New World were undertaken in 1572. This was somewhat prior to his famous voyage of circumnavigation. This voyage culminated in him allying himself with famous French navigator and cartographer Guillaume Le Testu. A chance meeting by the two famous mariner's off the coast of Panama led to them pooling their resources to attack a Spanish treasure laden mule train that was crossing the isthmus of Panama with riches from Peru. Testu is considered one of if not the finest cartographers of this era. He had already published two important books that illustrated maps that were thought to be the most accurate of the day.

In the process of raiding the mule train in Panama Testu was said to have lost his life while Drake narrowly escaped with what was said to have only been a portion of the treasure. Testu's crew that survived later complained that they had not received their fair share with the English taking most of what had been captured.

The typical route to the New World by mariner's during the age in which Drake lived was to go southerly to near the Canary Islands where the prevailing currents and winds would lead them to the West Indies. The return trip then would follow the Gulf Stream along the East Coast of America thus also leading us to the region of Nova Scotia, Newfoundland, and Oak Island. Though there is no record of this it may be likely that Drake and his men stopped in more than one location along the east coast to find water and provisions. By this time there may have even been other places like Oak Island that were known of and recorded by mariners where ships could be beached and have their hulls cleaned of barnacles and other sea life. Oak Island may be such a place. It is a sheltered harbor whose presence is cloaked by other islands between it and the open sea. It was a kind of hidden harbor and a great deal of evidence and history suggests that it could have been possibly used as a safe haven for shipping on this route at various times by various nationalities.

Is Sidney's friendship with Drake the source of the Oak Island Treasure story? It is possible that Sidney included the imagery of Pirates and this treasure in his book "Arcadia" due to a real treasure that Sir Francis Drake had told him was there. Still in the book itself Sidney seems to be warning the reader of the folly of looking for something that when found may only lead to another location.

If true this story would involve Drake and the remnants of Testu's crew returning to Europe by sailing up the east coast. At some point, they may have stopped at Oak Island to resupply and clean the hulls of their ships. The process of maintaining their vessels would have given them some time to familiarize themselves with the local area and island if they had indeed gone there. It is also possible that Testu, even though he had perished in Panama had knowledge of Oak Island that had then been shared with Drake by his crew.

If Drake had created the Money Pit and deposited a treasure therein then this would also jive with the part of the saga that has the French crew of Testu complaining that they had been shortchanged by Drake. If we look back into the story of how Sidney's father in law "spymaster" Francis Walsingham had been distressed to find that "Arcadia" had been published this may also fit the fact that Sidney had originally written "Arcadia" for his sister and was meant to be seen only by members of the Wilton Writer's Circle. Unfortunately, this scenario also leaves the door open for the entire thing to have been created later based on the story that Sidney had written.

The discovery of a similar story to that of Oak Island in "Arcadia" may have been the result of a real treasure left by Sir Francis Drake. In this story with what we know there is nothing pointing to Oak Island beyond the fact that a story is told two hundred years later that a pit was found that contained a stone matching in many regards the one in Sidney's book. Over the years many locations up and down the east coast could have been a place where Drake deposited a treasure. There is a clear record of Drake having some sort of dispute with Queen Elizabeth over certain details of his voyage being altered and left out of the official narrative so this does add fuel to the fire of mystery.

An alternate view of this part of the mystery could have involved Drake seeing the Newport Tower if it had already been built. We see Drakes second voyage of circumnavigation coming at about the same time Star Castle on the Isles of Scilly was being built. Scilly was also a place where the legendary King Olaf of Norway had spent time as well thus also bringing us back to England's claim on New England which may have actually been based on the Norse Sagas.

The octagonal star shape of Star Castle on the Isles of Scilly does "point" an arc on the globe to the location of the Newport Tower. Along this arc is also the point at which Captains Archer and Gosnold may have claimed New England for England near what is today Provincetown Massachusetts. Later the Mayflower Compact would also be signed aboard a ship in Provincetown Harbor. Alternately had Drake had something to do with the construction of the Newport Tower? There is no evidence of this but he had passed that way on what seemed to be a long voyage home from Panama. There are few details about this voyage available and there may be a reason for that. Had Elizabeth used Star Castle as a datum or axis from which to claim the east coast of America?

Is the Shepherd's Monument at Shugborough telling us about Oak Island? As stated Anson spent about seven years in Charleston when he was a Captain in the English Navy. Charleston is an interesting early colonial town that maintains much of its charm today. Two of the most influential families in the development of Charleston includes the Montagu and Drayton families. The Drayton family is actually part of the de Vere family of which Edward de Vere is subject to theories that he authored the works of Shakespeare. The Drayton's take their name from one of their estates Drayton House in England. It was Edward de Vere's daughters that had married the two nephews of Philip Sidney who were also the subject of the dedication of the First Folio of the works of Shakespeare by Ben Jonson.

The Drayton's of Charleston South Carolina build Drayton Hall on what is the western margins of Charleston today. Interestingly the linear orientation of Drayton Hall creates an arc on the globe that "points to" Oak Island Nova Scotia. Coincidence? Perhaps, yet another octagonal structure in downtown Charleston also points the way to Oak Island in the same manner. Washington Square in downtown Charleston is actually an octagonal plaza which may suggest an arc on the globe pointing the way to Oak Island. George Washington had a direct lineal link to General Lawrence who invaded and took Nova Scotia for the English in 1710. The name Lawrence Washington derived from their family association to General Lawrence's Family. This may in turn link us to Louis Lawrence who once owned the land where the "Pontil's Tomb" was once located near Rennes le Chateau in France.

The Montagu family also has an interesting connection to Halifax Nova Scotia if not the entire province of Nova Scotia. Charles Greville Montagu was the last acting governor of South Carolina and was from Charleston. One wonders whether his name "Greville" is a family connection to the Fulke Greville, Philip Sidney's friend. He is also directly related to the 2cnd Lord Halifax who Halifax Nova Scotia is named for. During the revolution Montagu approached captured rebels from the colonies and conscripted them after promising them they would fight only against French forces. Many of these men fought admirably and were taken to the Halifax area of Nova Scotia after the war with many being awarded grants of land near what is termed Oak Island today. In fact some records indicate that Daniel Mc Ginnis (Mac Innis) one of the original discoverers of the Money Pit had been a member of the Carolina Corps. After the war Charles Montagu had also relocated to Halifax Nova Scotia for a time. Later we will also see the name Montagu directly involved in the saga of the Frenchman's Tower in Palo Alto, California.

The introduction of former members of the Carolina Corps into Nova Scotia at that time may have had some interesting results. Many people in Nova Scotia had remained loyalists and now the Carolina Corps men had fought for the English during the Revolutionary War. Nova Scotia was also comprised of some families that had fought for the colonies during the war yet were allowed to retain their land in Nova Scotia after the war. This included elements of the family of famous poet H.W. Longfellow, relatives of the Roosevelt family, and even distant relatives of poet and author Edgar Allan Poe.

This dynamic may lead us to a rationale that leads one to the assumption that the Money Pit had been put there by these American loyalists in order to befuddle or punish what they may have considered to be traitors. Either way it is interesting that men likely associated with the Carolina Corps had been given property on Oak Island as part of their reward for helping the English during the war. In fact it will become obvious later that a direct relative of the Longfellow family named Prescott had been the person who had awarded these men their specific property on Oak Island as he was the tax collector and assessor for that region during the post war period.

Had the entire Money Pit story been concocted by American interests as part of a psychological ploy against their enemy? The end of the Revolution did not mark the end of hostilities or intelligence gathering on both sides of that conflict. It is also clear that the American descendants of Sir William Alexander of Stirling also had a great interest in Nova Scotia as part of their family legacy. (next chapter!)

The entire story in this book continually refers to people who include the name Montagu in their titles and names. Given this it is interesting that Lord Halifax the namesake of Halifax Nova Scotia was also a Montagu. It is also interesting to note that Charles Montagu has the middle name Greville. Fulk Greville had been the friend of Sir Walsingham and Philip Sidney who had warned them that "Arcadia" was being published thus raising concern on the part of Walsingham. Fulk Greville had also been among the people in a circle of Walsinghams who may have served as intelligence operatives.

So in 1734 we have a young Captain Anson stationed in Charleston South Carolina long before the revolution and the Carolina Corps. If the Shepherds Monument does refer somehow to Oak Island then Captain Anson could have also visited the Halifax or Oak Island area on his travels back to England. Anson also held a title and position within the English Navy to have been aware of any stories of lost treasure that had descended from Sir Francis Drake. He was also an educated man who had likely read the work of Philip Sidney and many others.
While in Charleston he also patrolled the East Coast and West Indies and likely had contact at all of these places with members of families that had been sent by investors of the Virginia Company long ago. Anson certainly would later follow the legacy of Sir Francis Drake in his circumnavigation.

So we have two grand mariners who could have known of Oak Island yet there is no evidence at all to suggest this in any of their writings or memoirs beyond what some interpret from the Shepherds Monument. Here a later chapter will explain a great deal as to how Admiral Anson was aware of the Arcadian mysteries and that he was likely aware of whatever secrets were being hidden in the pages of Philip Sidney's "Arcadia."

One of the things that Sidney's "Arcadia" may expose is the involvement of Sir Francis Drake in whatever Oak Island truly represents.

The Sidney Oak

"Caption for Penshurst, The Park, The Sidney Oak 1891: Covering 350 acres, Penshurst Park has many fine oaks; a chancel screen in St John the Baptistís church is made of Penshurst oak. Born at Penshurst Place in 1554, Philip Sidney is known to have planted oaks in the park. One oak is thought to have been here during his time, and is called the Philip Sidney oak. Philip Sidney was a poet and soldier. He entered Parliament in 1581, and was knighted in 1583. In 1585 he was made Governor of Flushing in the Netherlands, and died fighting the Spaniards at Zutphen in 1586."

As this story unfolds we may note a distinct value of the oak tree. Often an oak would be named for a specific person of note or to mark a significant historical event. This tradition may extend back to the time of the Druids and Celts. Three examples may be important to understanding the mysteries here as well as the use of the imagery of the oak tree at Oak Island Nova Scotia. Other oak trees that may have been used as clues or imagery in the American mysteries may include the Charter Oak of Connecticut and the Hooker Oak of Chico California. Later in our examination of Chico we will see how the Hooker Oak was inspired by the concept of the Charter Oak and even refers to Reverend Hooker who is credited with establishing Hartford Connecticut where Chico founder John Bidwell's family also been among the first families of Hartford.

One such talismanic oak tree is known as the Sidney Oak located at the family's Penhurst estate in England. This oak was named for Philip Sidney and may have some importance with regard to the Oak Island Legend and others given what we have learned about the importance of Sidney's "Arcadia" to this whole story. Interestingly the Sidney Oak is also referred to as "The Bear Oak" thus adding some distinctly Arcadian imagery to this particular tree. There are some hints that the Sidney Oak is important and valued by the cast of families that we see involved at Oak Island and Washington D.C. This tradition was likely known of by the Alexander family and many other colonists and first families. Both the Sidney Oak and Hooker Oak of Chico are considered to be "millennial oaks" of over a thousand years in age. Both the Hooker Oak and Sidney oak are now dead but still remembered.

The Sidney Oak recently fell but prior to that many of the acorns from the tree were collected and planted at various locations around the world. It is very hard to find the location of the said progeny of this tree as it has not been published anywhere. Is it possible that seeds from this oak were planted on Oak Island or other important places? Is the value of the oak in these mysteries linked to Philip Sidney and his named oak?

If true this would fit the whole scheme of how Sidney's "Arcadia" tells the Oak Island Legend long before it was exposed to the public. This would also explain why what are described as "non-native oaks" on Oak Island at one time. Unfortunately, none of the oaks from the Island survive today. Continuing the theme is the nine layers of oaken logs said to have been located in the original money pit there.

All of this may add up to the presence of an oak tree being a sort of clue that tells the initiate that there is something more afoot at a given location. This is true in both the story of the Charter Oak and Hooker Oak so why not the Sidney Oak and oaks of Oak Island as well?

If one were to project a scheme involving the Sidney Oak of Penhurst then what may be buried beneath the remains of said oak tree today? Is it possible that clues had been left by Sidney on his estate in England? Maybe he stashed a clue there or indeed the entire treasure that is the subject of so many hopes and dreams at Oak Island. The entire scheme of these mysteries and what we see at Oak Island may dictate that something of importance is located on the Penhurst estate that may inform us of Oak Island.

Unfortunately, the location of the Sidney Oak is disputed with many insisting the one that is marked today with a small plaque was the original tree of value. The Sidney Oak is a true mystery and undoubtedly is part of the entire mystery of Nova Scotia and Oak Island. Someday it is possible that some hint, clue, or even treasure will be recovered there that will tell us the truth. Next we will see the mighty oak of Washington D.C. rise out of the swamps of the Potomac River guided by the hand of the Alexander family and others.

A recent photo of what remains of the Sidney Oak today.

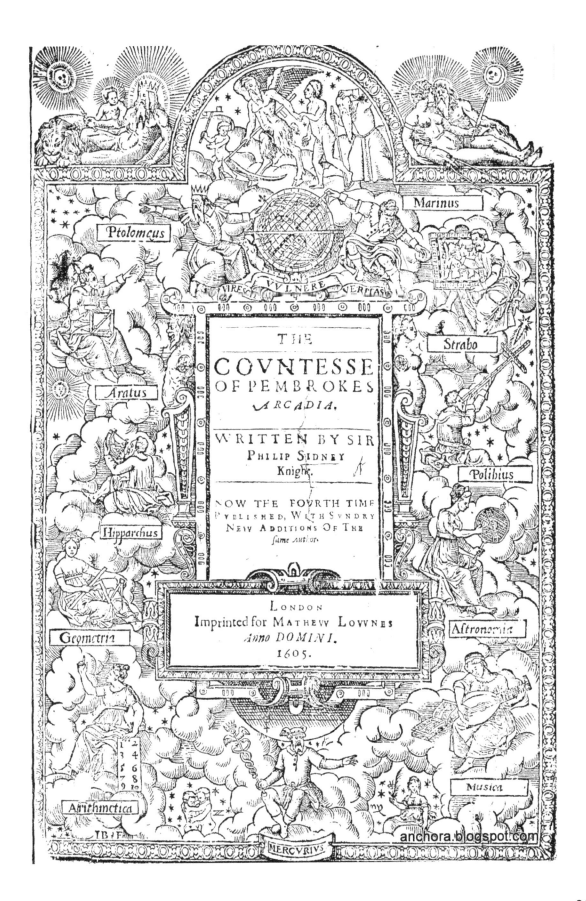

Chapter 2: Oak Island, Washington D.C., and the American Mysteries.

William Alexander 1st Earl of Stirling's involvement in the fictional story of "Arcadia" by Philip Sidney does appear to be the source of the original Oak Island Treasure story. Why would this story be applied to this mystery? What further evidence is there to support this notion? Any examination will compel us to consider one of two possible scenarios as to how this happened. Either the treasure at Oak Island was contrived to fit the fiction of Arcadia or the fictional story is referring to a real treasure that they knew was buried in the Money Pit at Oak Island. What may become obvious is the distinct hand of the United States in these matters.

There are many factors which may compel one to take either side of this argument. There are no references beyond the name of the work "Arcadia" and its relation to "Acadia" or Nova Scotia in the text of the work. The entire fictional story takes place in the province of Arcadia in Greece. So this metaphor may be interpreted as meaning Nova Scotia though this is not stated outright. The fact that Alexander had a hand in editing it later may serve to fuel the idea he did this intentionally to lead one to the similarities in the description of the treasure and that deposited in the Money Pit. Alternately this story may have been copied in any intentional ploy or ruse that involved making others believe there was a treasure on Oak Island.

It would be somewhat easier to suppose that the Money Pit was there and somehow Sidney, his sister Mary Herbert Countess of Pembroke, and then William Alexander had added this information somewhere along the line as a kind of hidden message within this literary work. Again this could be used to infer a real or contrived treasure story. It does appear that Alexander had edited "Arcadia" at around the time he was also awarded the Baronetcies of Nova Scotia in 1621. It is also clear that his son William Alexander "the younger" had actually gone to what is Port Royal (Annapolis Royal) Nova Scotia today and created a settlement known at the Habitation left by the French there. After a period of about ten years the Scottish colonists were forced to leave as the region had been officially come under French domain.

Given this there is some speculation that members of the Alexander family had stayed in Nova Scotia at this time and were allowed to retain their lands. This is indeed possible given the scheme of real history of the time. William Alexander 1st Earl of Stirling and his family were forever closely tied to the fortunes of Charles I and II. William had served as tutor for both of James I son's Henry and Charles the future king. Charles was eventually beheaded for his lack of cooperation with the Parliamentarian government and in part because of his Catholic faith. Charles I last words were also said by some to be "Pamela's Prayer" from the text of Philip Sidney's "Arcadia" thus further highlighting the importance of this work in the eyes of powerful interests in Scotland and England.

The date range of these happenings in Nova Scotia and Charles' beheading are at close to the same time. Charles' Catholicism and descent from Mary Queen of Scots would have also given him a close association with the French Monarchy at that time who were in effect his distant cousins. This would of course be the same French regime that had taken Acadia back and may have found reason to value the former close allies of Charles I. These facts may contribute to the reasons the following information is true.

Through time in the later Jacobite cause we do see the exiled Scottish nobles James II, III, and Bonnie Prince Charlie spending their exile for a time at the summer palace of Louis XV at St. Germaine en Laye near Paris. This palace was also managed by the d'Abbadie St. Germain family who were related to important early French Acadia military figure Jean Vincent d'Abbadie St. Castin. The fact that the French allied themselves with the American's in the Revolution also jives with the fact that the Jacobites (adherents to the exiled kings) had played a significant hidden role in the creation of the United States.

During the time of French control of Acadia after the expulsion of the Scottish Colony at Port Royal there are records of members of the Alexander family remaining in Nova Scotia on what is described as one of their estates there. Amazingly there are records of an Alexander Alexander living in New Ross Nova Scotia in 1654. Though some question these records we will consider them here. Through the history of the Alexander family there were many members named Alexander Alexander.

This is an amazing association that also fits directly into the mythology or truth of Oak Island. New Ross is a site that has been pointed to as including "Sinclair's Castle." The site appears today as some dry laid stone foundations and other various associated features. This site near New Ross is speculated as having been built by Henry Sinclair the Earl of Orkney who many suspect of having made an early off the record voyage to the Maritime region. What we are seeing here with genealogical proof is the fact that the Alexander family may be the people who built the site many attribute to Henry Sinclair. This property according to this source was part of the Alexander's domain in Nova Scotia and the French had allowed them to maintain ownership and occupancy. This would not mark the first time that members of the Sinclair family were given credit for or "blamed" for things members of the Alexander family had actually done. It is possible the whole story of New Ross and its legacy are connected to William Alexander's influence on Sidney's "Arcadia."

This is indeed possible and if the Alexander's really did live at New Ross it may explain why the story of the Money Pit was included in "Arcadia" later. In past works this author has speculated as to the involvement of interests of the United States in the Money Pit legend. When England regained Acadia from the French by General Lawrence in about 1710 many colonists from Maine and New England were offered land in Nova Scotia. When the American Revolution occurred many of these men returned to the colonies to fight for the American cause. Amazingly after the war these people were allowed to retain their property in Nova Scotia.

This included many well known families whose members had fought as officers in the Revolutionary War. This would include members of the Allan (Edgar Allan Poe's relative), Longfellow, and Delano (Roosevelt) families. These men were also members of the Society of the Cincinnati comprised of former military officers that had fought for the United States including colonial, French, and German men. This organization would go on to back many democratic movements during this period of history including the French Revolution. It also appears as if they were scheming to make Nova Scotia and the other Maritime provinces part of the United States. As this story progresses we will see none other than the influence of the Alexander family of the United States having a large effect on not only the Oak Island question but other similar mysteries there.

All of the subsequent members of the Alexander family discussed here descended from William Alexander 1st Earl of Stirling or one of his brothers. Many of them emigrated to the United States during the seventeenth century including John and Philip II Alexander who were given land grants that include what is today Alexandria Virginia and most of the portion of land that would become the old District of Columbia south of the Potomac River. One is left to wonder if Philip was indeed named for Philip Sidney. Here again we see the Alexander's intimately involved in the creation of a City that would also supply us many mysteries and a strange street plan that also suggests many metaphors and classic myths. Given what we are learning here we see how the Arcadian mythos is included in the imagery of Washington District of Columbia.

Is it somehow possible that whatever treasure was recovered at Oak Island funded in part the creation of Washington D.C. or possibly the American Revolution?

The City of Alexandria Virginia is named for these two men. This area was part of what was termed the Truro Parish named for Truro Cornwall that also included many illustrious Northern Virginia families such as the Lee's, Mason's, Moncure's, and others. During this time the Alexander's were closely associated with members of the Washington family with one female descendant marrying into portion of the Lewis family making George Washington's sister her mother in law. It is of some interest that Truro Parish shares the same name as one of the major organizations that later would be formed to recover the Oak Island Treasure.

In past works I had speculated that the Lee family was aware of Oak Island via my interpretation of the hexagonal Ft. Carrol built by Robert E. Lee while he was a Colonel in the U.S. Army (ca. 1849-50). There are many strange connections between the American colonies and Nova Scotia and at this point this was simply speculation on my part. Subsequent evidence may suggest this is true. It does appear that there were plans for Nova Scotia to become part of the United States of America after the Revolutionary War and the entire saga of Oak Island may have been part of that plan. Subsequent chapters here will display these connections in more detail.

Amazingly another hexagonal axis Portus of Rome also "points to" Oak Island and Ft. Carroll in a single azimuth on the globe. The Port of Portus was built by Emperor Trajan and this port was where both the Heliopolitan Obelisk of St. Peter's Square and the much-vaunted Temple Treasure arrived in Rome. Portus had just been rediscovered at about the same time Ft. Carroll was built and may have even inspired its hexagonal design. Ft. Carroll "points to" the Lee's Arlington Estate to the southwest and to the northeast the opposite direction the same arc or azimuth transects the globe to reach the Dome of the Rock on the Temple mount in Jerusalem which was of course the original location of the Temple Treasure. (Word Search "General Lee Oak Island" and see what pops up).

Included in the American descendants of the Alexander's of Scotland is another man named William Alexander. William had branched off from his Virginia relatives and was living in Basking Ridge New Jersey at the time of the Revolutionary War. William was directly related to John and Philip Alexander as well as Alexander of New Ross Nova Scotia mentioned earlier. William Alexander became a General in the American Army during the Revolutionary War and worked for a short span under the command of General Charles Lee. He took part in the first defense of New York and continued throughout the war to have an exemplary record in combat. He was of course a distant relative of George Washington via the Lewis family and the two men may have been aware of their relation in this manner.

Interestingly prior the war General Alexander returned to England and attempted to regain the title of Earl of Stirling that he felt was due him as part of his family legacy. There are other cases of Americans retaining their titles after the Revolution. Of course, if Alexander could regain this title it would also give him defacto "ownership" of Nova Scotia as well as huge tracts of Long Island. General Alexander was awarded his title by the Scottish Peerage at that time but the English House of Lords denied his application to retain and use this title. Despite this Alexander refused to accept their decision and continued to use the title "Lord Stirling." The entire scheme involving Nova Scotia and the Alexander family may indicate that General Alexander's attempts to regain Nova Scotia prior to the war was part of a plan to make that region part of the United States later.

Alexander's attempt to regain his title would also have an impact on theories that an effort to subsume Nova Scotia on the part of the United States continued after the war as well. Here we have a continued rationale as to why there was an effort involving the Society of the Cincinnati after the war to take Nova Scotia and make it part of the United States. General Alexander had attempted to make a case that he was due compensation or control of these regions which could easily lead to them being considered American territory eventually. Here again we see the specter of William Alexander, Philip Sidney, and the story of the Oak Island Money pit included in the text of the literary work "Arcadia." This era of General Alexander is also the time during which the entire Money Pit mystery was first exposed to the public. Could General Alexander have been behind the entire mystery? To General Alexander and other American's of Scots descent Nova Scotia was a treasure in and of itself. The Alexander family of America may have felt that they held title to Nova Scotia legally.

The story of how Alexander attempted to regain his title illustrates the fact that he was likely privy to the truth of Oak Island and the Money pit possibly via a family legacy or fraternity. His ancestor of the same name had amended the work. Had he shared this information with any of his other early American relatives like the Washington's and Lewis' extending to close friends like the Lee's? Also note here the Lewis' close relation to Thomas Jefferson and the Beale family. It may be that Alexander's Society of the Cincinnati compatriots including those in Nova Scotia had helped to arrange what we know of as the Money Pit today. The Society of the Cincinnati was composed of former Revolutionary War officers and one of their descendants. This included some French and a few Polish and German officers as well who were admitted.

The fact that Alexander had attempted to regain his title along with the presence of so many people in Nova Scotia who had fought for the American's in the war does seem to call into question the legitimacy of there being any actual treasure at the Money Pit at Oak Island. At least at first this may be discerned. What is possible is that the 1634 occupants named Alexander at New Ross had somehow constructed the Money Pit, installed a treasure in a vault below it, and left the layers of logs and 90 ft. stone to be found later.

This may also fit in with the real original story of people who had been awarded lots on the Island having actually found the Money Pit instead of the original folklore of three young men seeing lights on the island one night and subsequently finding the Money Pit. It is possible that these early Nova Scotian Alexander's of New Ross had also recovered riches from the free gold deposits of the Gold River which is adjacent to New Ross. Or had this same family later left a psy-op meant to befuddle former members of the Carolina Corps?

The fact remains that no one really knows the truth as to what this all means. This is however a great deal of additional info that we must digest and game out to see the possibilities. The fact that the Alexander's and American cause was so closely associated with the French during this era also adds another layer of possible misunderstandings. Given all of this it is starting to look more and more as if one of three possibilities had already happened.

If something was at the Money Pit it had been recovered by the earlier Alexander's of New Ross who were likely aware of the treasure story in "Arcadia." Alternately they had crafted the entire legend of the Money Pit as a Masonic initiation quest of some kind or had done it to confound the new English rulers of Nova Scotia. They may have been crafting a folklore that informed one of the true ownership and heritage of Nova Scotia. It is clear that groups like the Wilton Writer's Circle of Mary Sidney, the Academy of Arcadia of the Vatican, and Society of the Cincinnati had involved themselves in producing representational art and literature that supported their philosophies and values. In some way we may be looking at a grand joke played by those loyal to the United States on their Carolina Corps neighbors who they may have viewed as traitors.

The settlement of New Ross and Oak Island are also in a region that saw a gold rush at about the same time this was happening in California (mid nineteenth century). The headwaters of the Gold River itself begin near New Ross and the River empties into the Atlantic Ocean just a few miles north of Oak Island. It may also be possible that the early Alexander's of Nova Scotia had been aware of this gold deposit and had been taking advantage of it for many years leading us to the Oak Island Money Pit that was created to either stash their loot or to cover up the fact that they were recovering gold there in the first place. The original William Alexander of Stirling was also highly involved in mining in Scotland so he and his family would have had knowledge of different kinds of mineral deposits.

The recovery of gold to be used by the American's in the Revolution is also a distinct possibility and may serve as further rationale as to why there is no remaining treasure at Oak Island. Though Presbyterian the Alexander's had always been staunch supporters of the beheaded and exiled

Catholic Stewart Kings of Scotland and England so it would be no surprise that any gold deposit in Nova Scotia would have gone to support the Jacobite and Cavalier causes that also seemed to have shaped this period of history in Virginia and New England. This scenario by also fit the theory of Louis Buff Parry that a treasure had been hidden at Oak Island that may have been used or searched for by Jacobite interests.

This information supplies a strong rationale with no "smoking gun" saying there is nothing at Oak Island. It does reveal a strong value by American interests in both the mystery of the Money Pit and the land of Nova Scotia itself.

The influence of Philip Sidney and William Alexander in this story also has a direct tie to the Menteith Earls and the concept of "Sancto Claro." Though Alexander has a very direct connection to the development of the Stewart family and Robert the Bruce from a genealogical perspective Sidney possesses a link to Walter Fitzalan from the time he spent in Wales with the Count of Pembroke prior to his exile in Brittany.

Many have speculated as to the involvement of coded portions of the First Folio of Shakespeare that had been funded by Philip Sidney's nephews the sons of Mary Sidney Countess of Pembroke. As it turns out the mythology of the Money Pit is also closely related to a Scottish author and poet William Alexander 1st Earl of Stirling who had edited a work that both Mary Countess of Pembroke and their uncle Philip Sidney had both had a hand in creating.

Later it truly does appear that "Arcadia" had been edited by William subsequently gaining its associations to the Money Pit. A resounding "why" does not fully answer the riddle of the Money Pit but does infer a high degree of skullduggery in whatever its true purpose was. There are too many coincidences along the way for us to assume that the entire thing was not either a misinterpreted Masonic quest or had been covering up the recovery of Gold or some other enterprise or industry at Oak Island. In the end we are now forced to consider the fact that the literary inspiration for the Money Pit was not Sir Francis Bacon but Philip Sidney who died when Bacon was but twelve years old.

Other Alexander Connections to Washington D.C.

Over time the Alexander family gained many family ties that would also seem to point to them as having a personal desire to develop Washington D.C. in ways that would tell the true story of its history. By the time of the Civil War many of them seemed to have sided with the Union cause but there were members of the family that also fought for and supported the ideals of the Confederacy. Surprisingly many of the Alexander's who fought for the South in the Civil War were also related to George Washington the 1st President of the Republic of the United States of America.

It is in this way that the Confederacy may have been privy to the secrets of places like Oak Island and the Newport Tower. Many mystery school overtones are seen in the Knights of the Golden Circle which was a secretive Confederate group that carried out intelligence operations during the war and worked to preserve the Confederate point of view after the war much in the same way the Society of the Cincinnati worked to establish and American identity via the arts and literature. Mystery school techniques have always been employed by persecuted groups of people throughout history and may have contributed to many of the enigmatic questions examined throughout this book. From the lost and angry race of fallen kings to the defeated ideals of the Confederacy all of this contributed to aspects of the Civil War that happened after hostilities had ceased. This is especially apparent in the assassination of President Lincoln and the many legends of lost confederate gold.

Among those Confederate Alexanders was a man named Dr. William Fontaine Alexander.

"Born at Walnut Farm, the son of Charles and Mary Bowles Armistead Alexander. Wed to Anna Maria Washington. Father of Charles A. Alexander. He was a druggist that enlisted with the Second Regiment of Virginia Infantry in June of 1861 at Bolivar Heights. He served as a steward at hospitals in Charlottesville and Lynchburg before being permanently assigned as druggist at Chimborazo Hospital in Richmond."

(https://www.findagrave.com/cgibin/fg.cgi?page=gr&GSln=alexander&GScid=684861&GRid= 6045750&)

Fontaine Alexander's wife was Anna Maria Thomasina Blackburn Washington a direct descendant of Augustine Washington and sister of John Augustine Washington the last family owner of Mt. Vernon. John Augustine Washington also fought for the Confederacy during the Civil War. John Washington served as an aide de camp to Robert E. Lee himself thus no surprise as they were related via the Custis family. Arlington National Cemetery was once the estate of Robert E. Lee via his wife's Custis family who were the original owners. This is the family of Martha Washington George Washington's wife.

John A. Washington:

Confederate States Army Officer. Great grandnephew of George Washington and the last Washington to own "Mount Vernon". In 1840, he graduated from the University of Virginia. Three years later he married Eleanor Love Seldon. He purchased a farm in Fauquier County, Virginia called "Waveland" where he made his home. His wife died in 1860 from childbirth. When Virginia seceded from the Union John volunteered to defend Virginia in the oncoming conflict. He served as aide-de-camp on the staff of General Robert E. Lee in the campaign of western Virginia. He was commissioned Lieutenant Colonel on this campaign. While reconnoitering in the Cheat Mountains of now West Virginia he was shot by a bushwhacker and killed. In a letter written on September 6th, 1861 to his brother-in-law, Dr. W. Fountain Alexander from the "Camp of Valley Mountain" John expresses his concerns of his own survival. "...I don't know when I shall leave this region, or indeed whether I ever shall do so, as of course my chances are the same as those of other men, and I know some of us will never get away..."signed, "Most Affectionately yours, John A. Washington". He died one week later.

(https://www.findagrave.com/cgi-bin/fg.cgi?page=gr&GRid=6045745)

Alexander's that fought for the Union side included Colonel Charles Madison Alexander. Charles served with distinction in the defense of Washington D.C. throughout his army career in the Civil War. Charles Madison Alexander's name alone denotes the family relation to James Madison 4th President of the United States of America. Charles Madison Alexander was the brother of Thomson Hankey Alexander a Union officer who married Sarah Jane Kennedy the sister of the founder of Chico California John Bidwell's wife Annie Ellicott Bidwell (Kennedy). The Kennedy family from which Mrs. Bidwell descended is directly related to Andrew Ellicott a principle designer of the street plan and boundaries of the original City of Washington District of Columbia. (More on that in the chapters about Chico later! Chico is a "miniature Washington D.C." in plan due to this relationship).

Colonel Charles Alexander:

Son of Charles Alexander and Martha M. Madison (grandniece of President Madison).

(from) The Lewis Family of the Seventeenth Century
Charles Alexander graduated at Marietta College, Marietta, Ohio and located in Washington City, D.C. in 1856. During the Civil War he served as a private for three months in the Army after which he acted as Colonel of the 2nd District of Columbia Regiment. During President Johnson's administration, he acted as Postmaster in Washington City. He was an eminent lawyer and a man of sterling integrity.
(https://www.findagrave.com/cgi-bin/fg.cgi?page=gr&GRid=37206197)

It is interesting that the word "Sterling" is used to describe Charles. He is descendant of William Alexander 1st Earl of Stirling in Scotland. It is possible that all of these Alexander's were aware of the truth of what Oak Island represents spanning time all the way back to Philip Sidney's "Arcadia." In a very real way the stories surrounding the founding of Washington D.C. are part of the rich tapestry of the Arcadian Mysteries.

It appears that from the time of the Revolutionary War that the Alexander family had a long and extensive military tradition. In turn, they also showed a concern for the development of the nation's capital and had contributed many of their efforts in assuring that the new country would survive. Along the way they had intermarried with some of the most important and influential families including the French de La Porte family, The Washington family, The Madison family, and even the family of Annie Ellicott Bidwell (Kennedy). Annie Bidwell may indeed be distantly related to the famous Kennedy family of President John F. Kennedy.

As this story progresses we will see their influence in many pieces of architecture that tell a representative story of the United States. Many of these works of art, architecture, and literature would have been appreciated by them as telling what was at the time a uniquely American point of view. It is unfortunate that members of their family as well as the Washington family had sided with the Confederacy in the Civil War.

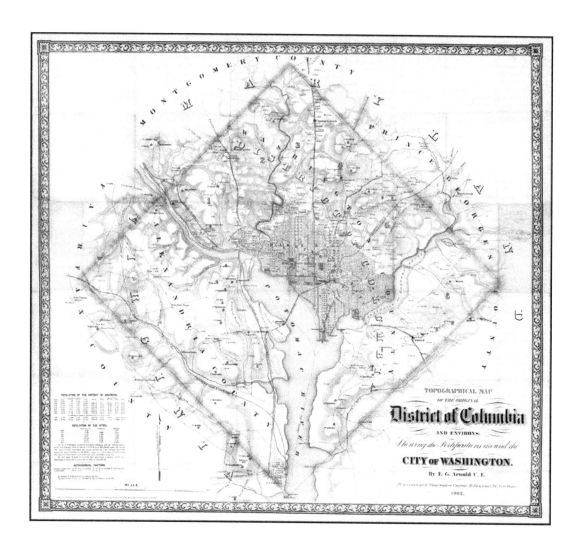

Chapter 3: Arcadia in Scotland and "Sancto Claro"

It is interesting to ponder the reasons why and how events in early Scotland had influenced not only the creation of what may be termed the Arcadian Mysteries but also the development of the United States with an emphasis on Washington D.C. itself. A great point of pride in the Alexander family must have included the heritage of Sir William Alexander of Stirling and his family relations to many important characters in the saga of Nova Scotia if not the Oak Island Legend itself. It is likely all of this family had read Philip Sidney's "Arcadia" which had been amended by Sir William himself.

These American's truly valued their Scottish heritage with all its French associations thus leading us to the Revolutionary War in the Colonies. The Alexander family even gives a rationale as to why Robert E. Lee and his family may have been aware of Oak Island as speculated via the geographic relationships of the hexagonal Ft. Carroll in Baltimore harbor that had been designed and constructed by a younger Robert E. Lee. The legacy of the Lee family may also extend to the Earls of Lichfield in Staffordshire England home of Shugborough Hall and its Arcadian imagery.

From the conclusions drawn from the involvement of Sidney and "Arcadia" we see a distinct connection between this concept and Scotland long before the time of artist Nicolas Poussin whose "The Shepherds of Arcadia" has been central to the Arcadian themed mysteries examined here. The Academy degli de Arcadia of the Latin Church was not officially formed until the mid-seventeenth century though an appreciation of the Arcadian theme may have become more of a popular notion during the era the Latin Kingdom ruled the real Arcadia of Greece during the fourteenth century. In past works I have also compared the appreciation of the Arcadian theme to a value of St. Andrew who is also central to the symbols of Scotland and indeed the Order of the Thistle.

Many of the cast of characters in the saga of Arcadia have a direct relation to a group of families from the region around Stirling Castle. This would include both the family legacies of Sir William Alexander and Philip Sidney. It may be that the concept of "Sancto Claro" is distinctly different and separate from that of the Sinclair family. In the last chapter we saw how the Alexander family became an important factor in freemasonry yet only after the time speculative freemason's were allowed to be initiated into the craft. Prior to the Sinclair family had been the benefactors of operative stonemason's who had practiced the same systems and values prior to this time. As this story unfolds we will also see how the cultural character of Nova Scotia was shaped by the Earl's of Menteith and subsequently the Stewarts who held that legacy after a time. Is it possible all the metaphor and symbolism we see in the Oak Island Legend is due to their involvement and not that of the Sinclair's?

In recent times we have seen a great interest in the Sinclair or St. Clair family of Scotland. Many people speculate as to the truth of Legends that suggest Sir Henry Sinclair the Earl of Orkney came to North America during the fourteenth Century. Indeed this story is embraced and communicated as being true by many people. Several have even written books that supply us with some evidence that this is true. The possible exploits of Henry Sinclair or others in Nova Scotia do lend themselves to the Arcadian theme of one name of this region. As it turns out the naming of what would later be Nova Scotia as "Acadia" or Arcadia stems from the influence of Philip Sidney who penned a work entitled "Arcadia" during Elizabethan times. This work is important in this mystery as its links to Scotland include the fact that Charles I (HRM) last words prior to his beheading were from a psalm or portion of Sidney's "Arcadia." As it turns out Sidney was likely referencing a much older name for a region of Scotland that had been in place since at least the thirteenth century. Both Charles I value of Arcadia and the fact that a similar treasure story exists in the text of "Arcadia" may communicate a different story than has been told before.

With some patience and attention to history and genealogy we may be able to discern a pathway of initiation and instruction that leads us from place to place in a similar fashion to what is seen in the popular movie "National Treasure." That film portrayed a uniquely American view of an initiatory quest meant to inspire and inform one of the American philosophy and culture. We see a similar dynamic at play in the book "The Da Vinci Code" where Langdon is sent on a quest of discovery by the deceased Jacques Saunière. In so doing a great many historical truths are exposed that have been overlooked in the past as insignificant or having no meaning at all. It is clear that a trial of clues including architecture, literature, and artwork that expresses these themes as well as suggesting other sites of interest to the seek. Other similar quests or mysteries were arranged in league with religious organizations, fraternal organization, as well as Masonic groups. Many different nationalities have adapted this type of representative art to communicate essential beliefs that also display the rich history of these lands. It may be in this manner that the streets of Washington D.C. have gained a somewhat legendary status and is interpreted many different ways by a variety of authors. It may be no coincidence that the Alexander family of Scotland is involved in both the history of Nova Scotia and Washington D.C.

Nothing exposed here says that Henry Sinclair didn't come to North America. What will be exposed may show an alternate rationale as to why a myth or legend like this would have been developed for political reasons. Part of this dynamic involves the fact that French and Scottish/English interests have been fighting over the maritime region of what is today Canada also known of as Acadia since the very first settlers came there in the early seventeenth century. In the process both of these cultural groups would have strong ties to both the concept of Arcadia and Sancto Claro. It is likely that their similar value of these concepts stems from their Norman backgrounds in places like Normandy, Italy, Sicily, England, Hungary, and Scotland. Characters such as Stephen of Hungary, Prince Rupert of the Rhine, The Earls of Orkney, St. Clare herself, and many others have a direct impact on how these images were later applied to cultural and landscape mysteries that referenced these terms and concepts. A closer examination may reveal how specific families maintained their dominion over Nova Scotia no matter who ruled it.

Amazingly this story will lead us to other strange and mysterious events in history such as Rennes le Chateau and Oak Island. These two mysteries have also been suspected by others as being linked. Here exposed may also be the truth of that potential reality. Both of these famous conundrums also involve the concept of "Arcadia." Along the way a story of intrigue based on the ancient mystery schools will be laid bare in order to see the truth. Rennes le Chateau and Shugborough Hall may include the imagery of Poussin's "The Shepherds of Arcadia" associated with the true meaning of "Sancto Claro" in relation to both the Scottish, French, and Italian families involved in this story. As we will see even the Arcadia region of Greece was once ruled by the Angevin or Anjou dynasty that is associated with the legacy of Mary Magdalene and the concept of the "ancient regime" leading us to the pastoral utopian concepts seen not only in France and Italy but also Scotland via the Earls of Menteith or "Sancto Claro."

One of the factors involved in unraveling this mystery may have to do with our understanding of different terms as they are expressed in different languages. In past works I have examined the similarities in the names "Shakespeare", "Alighieri," and "Edgar" (Poe). Each of these famous literary names infer the term or concept of the "Noble Spear." In fact the similarities of these names may have been valued or even designed by later literary guilds and societies such as the Academy of Arcadia of the Vatican which may have included Nicolas Poussin among its members. Members of the Academy of Arcadia referred to themselves as "The Shepherds of Arcadia." It would not be beyond the scope of these kind of groups to know the difference and similarity between St. Clair and Sancto Claro.

Using this path of reasoning what secrets may the name "Sinclair" reveal? Sinclair is a Scottish name that developed from de St. Clair in its Norman form. It is suspected that this family's name came from the French Norman village of St. Clair sur Epte and spread throughout Norman England and Scotland via that source. Indeed one of the earliest St. Clair's recorded as coming to Scotland was "William Sancto Claro" who may have landed with Queen (St.) Margaret of Scotland in about 1068. That story also includes the origins of the Drummond family of Scotland who some feel originated in descent from the man who was captain of the ship that brought Margaret from England. If the St. Clair name had spread from Normandy to Scotland via Norman influences could not have it also transferred to Italy, Sicily, and Eastern Europe via other Norman influences? Is the French or Latin form of "Sancto Claro" being suggested?

Some of this confusion may become apparent via an examination of the saga of Margaret of Scotland. St. Margaret was the last of the line of Anglo Saxon Kings and was attempting to escape England and return to her native Hungary when fate intervened and brought her to Scotland . Her father Edgar Aetheling had escaped as the last legitimate king just prior to the Norman invasion of England by William the Conqueror in 1066. As a result Margaret had been born in Hungary and her mother according to some sources had been Hungarian nobility. As Margaret was attempting to escape back to the continent from England a storm wrecked her ship on the Firth of Forth bringing her to Scotland. This will supply us with a family link to Prince Rupert of the Rhine later in this saga in addition to their Stewart relations that had not been born yet during the era of Margaret. Margaret would later marry King of Scotland Malcom III thus becoming part of the genetic lineage of all subsequent Scottish and English Kings and Queens.

If this William Sancto Claro was the same one who came with William the Conqueror in 1066 why as the story goes was he with Queen Margaret when her ship landed in Scotland supposedly

33

on the way back to Hungary via France? Why would he help her escape if he was a Norman invader of England? It is one thing to let the nobility of one's enemy escape it is quite another to have someone accompany her on such a voyage. Was the story of St. Margaret of Scotland changed to make it look as if her arrival was an accident as the standard story goes? It may be that this William Sancto Claro was of Hungarian origins which would make him later more closely related to the Anjou's and Stewarts than the would have been to the St. Clair family.

It is quite an honor for the Sinclair family to have been associated with this important historical event involving the future Queen. A man referred to as "Sancto Claro" came to Scotland with Margaret though there is very little information available about this individual. The name of William "Sancto Claro" is said to be a French form of this name though it appears to have been drawn from Latin words often used by chroniclers or scribes of this era that were often monks or ecclesiastical figures. If we view "Sancto Claro" as Latin and not French some startling observations are made. People from Hungary likely would not use a French form of Latin.

Using the standard Latin to English translator available on the internet "Sancto Claro" spelled using capital letters for the two words reveals the name "Sinclair" as being the meaning of "Sancto Claro" even though Sancto is not a word used to describe a saint. Amazingly if one enters the words "sancto claro" with lower case letters only this term is interpreted as meaning "menteith." Amazingly the name Menteith has some startling associations with many concepts that are commonly associated with the Sinclair or St. Clair family of Scotland. Alternately if one uses the English to Latin translation of "saint clair" this interprets to "seyncler" in Latin. Seyncler is the Latin form of the name St. Clair.

The title of Menteith was never used by the Sinclair family though it is associated with a much more powerful line of Scots rulers leading us to the English and Scots Royalty of the current era. In many ways this line of the Menteith's and later Stewart's would all have a strong and loyal association with the Latin Church of Rome. In fact many of the Earls of Menteith would oppose the Norwegian cultural influences in Scotland that the Sinclair family had sprung from and were more identified with at times. The Menteith or Stewarts also in part sprang from a source in Brittany France thus providing us with a very early allegiance with interests of that country through history. Scotland and France have always maintained some very strong connections via their royal heritage and more.

In reality all Scots nobles named James are named for Santiago including Douglas' uncle James Stewart who he was named for. It is clear that both Sidney and Alexander's references to the Black Knight in "Arcadia" are indeed referring to Sir James Douglas. Douglas is most known for losing his life at the Battle of Teba in Spain fighting the Moors while wearing the Heart of Robert the Bruce in a small enameled casket around his neck. There are many suggestions in the story of Douglas and the other lost Knights of Teba that hint the story is but a fairy tale meant to cover up clandestine activities taken on by Douglas under the guise of his death. In past works I have speculated that James and his crew of lost Knights had at least made an attempt to come to North America. Douglas' character being included in Sidney and Alexander's "Arcadia" may be a sign that there is some truth to this notion and that Douglas and the lost Knights had gone to

34

Nova Scotia. This would again fit the imagery suggested by later authors such as Poe and Longfellow.

True all of this seems coincidental and may be a quirk of the way Latin is translated from "Sancto Claro" to "Menteith." Conversely this theme seems to match a great deal of history associated with the Earls of Menteith as well as Frederick the Great of Norman Italy and Sicily as well as other Balkan states that may have retained a more Greek or Eastern view of Christianity at large. These views of Christianity would be important later in English history during the reformation and subsequent persecution of Catholics during that era and beyond. We do see the influence of Frederick II HRE later in the story in the form of his descendant Prince Rupert of the Rhine who was also a Stuart via his mother Elizabeth of Bohemia. Rupert would also go on to be the first governor of the Hudson's Bay Company.

Is it possible there is some confusion on the part of historical writers of the meaning of "Sancto Claro" as actually representing the ancestors of the Earls of Menteith and not the Sinclair family? An examination of some of the events and mysteries associated with the Sinclair family may infer this word game confusion has caused history to ascribe many things to the Sinclair family that were done by the Earls of Menteith and their associated families. Of course, all of this would rely on this misinterpretation inferring one thing while actually meaning another. In the course of the use of this term it may be that this confusion was left as a kind of smoke screen making it more difficult to distinguish between Sancto Claro, St. Clair, de Clare, Seyncler, and Sinclair. It may be that especially earlier references to Sancto Claro were in reference to the future Earls of Menteith and not the Sinclair's.

Perhaps the Seyncler's were involved in the legacy of Sancto Claro in Norman Italy and Eastern Europe as well. It is clear that both Frederick II Holy Roman Emperor and his successor Charles I both had mothers that came from the Hauteville family of Normandy. The Scots form of the name Hauteville is Wishart. These men were both Kings of Naples and Sicily and Frederick was also a Holy Roman Emperor and King of Germany. In some instances both these men had relations to Stephen of Hungary and their Norman cousins in England and Scotland. Frederick would marry Eleanor of England and the Anjou's of Charles would contribute lasting imagery to the legacy of Mary Magdalene and likely the concept of the "ancient regime" that mirrors the concept of Arcadia valued by later prominent figures such as Antoine d'Abbadie in France. All of this occurring in the early to mid thirteenth century during which the land of Arcadia is referenced in Scots land titles and wills. The d'Abbadie family was also instrumental in the development of French Acadia.

In many ways the Earls of Menteith seem to be the root of the Stewart family of Scotland with links to the most powerful families of England and the rest of Europe. The inclusion of St. Margaret in their family also brought with it the overtones of the last anglo saxon kinf of England prior to Norman domination. This blood was now part of Scots heritage!

In fact the lands of Strathearn and Menteith in Scotland likely represent the true home of Arcadia as referred to in the Rennes le Chateau mystery, The Shepherds of Arcadia of Poussin, The

35

Shepherds Monument at Shugborough Hall, and the namesake of Nova Scotia as "Acadia." It is even possible that the origins of both the Arcadian theme and the term "sancto claro" have their roots in this same saga stemming all the way back to the Hungarian origins of St. Margaret of Scotland and the Hungarian men "Sancto Claro" and Drummond that had accompanied her on her initial if somewhat accidental voyage to Scotland. It is important to note that many people have considered William Sancto Claro the Norman as later being a St. Clair of Scotland without really being sure. In some cases we may be looking at a reference to an entirely different legacy.

Many 13th century wills and land titles refer to the country around Stirling Castle as "Arcadia." Of course these documents are also written in Latin during that period. The use of this term is an early reference to what would later be included in historical questions that may have been presented to specific individuals as part of a family fraternity or initiation. Later these clues and concepts may have been exposed to the public and taken on the overtones of "Holy Blood, Holy Grail," the Rennes le Chateau Mystery, Oak Island and others. The region which said land titles and wills refer to includes the domain of the Menteith Earl's who controlled that region of what is today Strathearn and Menteith.

Later the Earl's of Menteith would also include both Walter Stewart the basis of the Stewart royalty of many countries and later the Earldom of Pembroke which would include some characters aligned with the legacy of Shakespeare, Sir Francis Bacon, and the 17th Earl of Oxford Edward de Vere. This will include an interesting man named Philip Sidney that wrote a literary work entitled "Arcadia" for his sister Mary Sidney Herbert Countess of Pembroke. It appears that these thirteenth century Scottish people had an abiding value of the mythology of Arcadia as it refers to Arcas and the Pole Star. Their appreciation of Arcas many have also led to Stirling Castle which sits at the nadir of Scottish Arcadia being the home to other initiatory mysteries that even span the globe to Williamsburg Virginia and similar legends.

This value may have also led Charles I to construct the grand octagonal earthworks at Stirling known as the Kings Knot. Some legends state that the Kings Knot was the original site of the round table of King Arthur. This would be fitting given the theme of Arcturus in the legends of Arthur. In addition we may see this imagery being responsible for why the bear of Ursa Minor is a symbol for the Plantagenet dynasty of France and England. Strangely the star and bear are also present on the California flat with Sir Francis Drake having once claimed that region.

In previous work I linked the octagonal Kings Knot of Stirling Castle to the famous Star in the landscape of Rennes le Chateau as actually "pointing to" each other on the globe. The octagon of the Kings Knot points the way to and matches the orientation of the star at Rennes le Chateau and crosses the Tower of the Winds at Shugborugh Hall on this azimuth's transect. Of course Shugborough is home to the famous Shepherds Monument that illustrates Poussin's "The Shepherds of Arcadia" in mirror image bas relief with the addition of a small, strange casket atop the tomb from the original painting. (This is covered in greater detail here in the Stirlilng Castle Chapter).

This association between what we know now are three locations of Arcadian imagery are very compelling evidence or clues that lead us to Stirling Castle and the Scottish region of Arcadia. Clues in the artwork of Admiral Anson's estate Moor Park near London also supply us with many other useful clues via the imagery of Greek Mythology including Arcas and Argus the All Seeing that also link to Philip Sidney who also once owned Moor Park. While Anson was the owner of Moor Park he also constructed another Tower of the Winds on that estate.

It does appear as if Philip Sidney son of the Earl of Pembroke who penned the work entitled Arcadia may have some distinctly Scots relations that eventually led to what we today call Nova Scotia being referred to as "Acadia" (Arcadia) over time. In turn Sidney was likely referring to the older us of the term "Arcadia" in Scotland. Sidney is also descendant of the Mortimer of Mortuo Mari family that descended from Alfred the Great of England. This family includes the real and Shakespearean fictional character of Roger Mortimer. In fact some of the works of Shakespeare seem to contain hidden references to the fallen Kings of Wales which the Sidney's and Herbert's are also direct relations of.

Philip Sidney was the brother of the Countess of Pembroke Mary Herbert (Sidney) whose son Philip Herbert would be the 4th Earl of Pembroke. The Earls of Pembroke were closely related to via intermarriage to the title of the Earl of Menteith as referred to clandestinely in the meaning of Sancto Claro. Countess Mary and her brother were part of the Wilton's Writers Circle that had in many ways been created by the Countess. The Wilton Writer's Circle included many of the more prominent literary figures of the Elizabethan and James I eras. This included people like Inigo Jones and Ben Jonson two people that are many times also associated with Sir Francis Bacon, the Society of Jesus (Jesuits), and Freemasonry.

The name Arcadia would also apply to large portions of what is the States of Maine and Massachusetts today. This legacy would later in history lead us to still another artists and writers organization based on the Academy of Arcadia of the Vatican. It is even possible that the Wilton's Writers Circle had a direct impact on the concept of the Academy of Arcadia which was established about thirty years later. The Academy of Arcadia may have in reality been inspired by Jesuit connections and the loyalty displayed to the Church on the part of many Scottish Kings, Queens, nobility, and citizens.

Given this it may be that all of the speculation as to the origins of the works of Shakespeare may have come from a kind of brain trust or organization that may have even been centered on the Wilton's Writers Circle of Countess of Pembroke Mary Herbert. The Countess even penned a book about Enochian Geomancy at one point. There are some amazing connections to Sir Francis Bacon in the sons of Mary Countess of Pembroke William and Philip. Both men marred the daughters of the 17th Earl of Oxford Edward de Vere who many also include on a list of people who potentially produced the plays of Shakespeare. Bridget and Susan de Vere's Grandfather was Earl Cecil. Their grandmother was the aunt of the Sir Francis Bacon via his mother (Cooke). This would have made Sir Francis Bacon Grand Uncle to both the de Vere women and the sons of Mary Sidney Herbert Countess of Pembroke. Philip Sidney the author of Arcadia would have been the nephew of Sir Francis Bacon. Philip and William Herbert are the subject of the dedication by Ben Jonson of the famous First Folio of Shakespeare and in fact they are said to have financed its printing. It may be that out of all this Elizabethan secrecy and literary intrigue that the theme of Arcadia was applied to what we know call Nova Scotia today.

As discussed earlier it appears that Philip Sidney's nephews could have had a hand in placing any hidden information in the First Folio of Shakespeare that may lead us to the mysteries. This is how and why this hidden information secreted in the works of Shakespeare are actually referring to Philip Sidney's "Arcadia" thus begging the question as to how much Sir Francis Bacon was even involved in arranging all this in the Folios.

"And in Shakespearean, the Boy/Male name Menteith means The Tragedy of Macbeth' A nobleman of Scotland." (http://thenamesdictionary.com/name-meanings/181353/name-meaning-of-menteith) A Menteith is actually a minor character in "Macbeth" that is described as Scots nobility.

The attempted colonization of Port Royal or Annapolis Nova Scotia under the auspices of William Alexander would also begin the rivalry between French and English influences that felt they had a right to that region. In the process both factions had distinct Norman backgrounds that may have also led them in turn to a value of Arcadia as defined by Philip Sidney and later inferred at Rennes le Chateau via the more modern association of Poussin's work "The Shepherds of Arcadia." In some ways this concept may have been used in a kind of psychological warfare in a mysterious silent war or game. Later this concept may have been used by American interests of the Society of the Cincinnati in the nineteenth century. Evidence suggests that a mystery may have been left at Stirling by Alexander and his Scots Royal forebears that served as a template for other quests or initiations later in history. Is it possible the story of the Oak Island treasure adds up to mere royal intrigue and not a real treasure?

It is clear that there are many similarities between the questions surrounding the Bruton Parish Church vault, The Service Stone of Stirling, and two separate books of symbols produced by Wither's and Quarles the same year of 1634/5. Some even theorize that these books of symbols were created by a Bacon or a group similar to the Wilton's Writer's Circle. In addition it is interesting that wife of prominent mystic and Masonic author Manly P. Hall, Marie Bauer Hall, had been the one to note the mystery at Williamsburg while never mentioning the Service Stone which had been created at about the same time North America was being settled.

The fact that Ms. Bauer-Hall's theory about the Bruton Parish Church also matches elements of gravestones at Stirling Castle obviously indicates that this activity was present at Stirling Castle at about the same time the headstones in Williamsburg were being produced for deceased colonists. No had noted this similar activity that resembled what Ms. Bauer-Hall had said prior to the publication of my book "The Sacred Towers of the Axis Mundi." Please see that book for a detailed story about the Service Stone and how it relates to the legend of the Bruton Parish Church Vault in Williamsburg.

Note also that William Alexander 1st Earl of Stirling came from the same line of Earls of

Menteith and Stathearn that valued referring to their lands as "Arcadia" about four hundred years prior. Both the family of Philip Sidney and William Alexander had direct links to the title of the Earl of Menteith which in a strange way may also be termed the Earl of Sancto Claro. How is it possible that a value of this concept had been alive in Scotland for so long before it became apparent to modern ears via the works of famous artists such as Poussin and others later? A distinct value of this concept seems to have been later valued by the more Catholic or Royal oriented factions of Mary Queen of Scots, Charles I, Charles II, James II and III, Bonnie Prince Charlie, and those who valued the Jacobite and Cavalier causes later in history.

It is clear that all of this does not have an impact on the legacy of the St. Clair or Sinclair family and their exploits through history. It is simply interesting that a similar term may have been mistaken as being associated with such a well known family name. In turn the Sinclair's and their history are closely intertwined with that of the Earls of Menteith and the history of Norway, Scotland, England, and the rest of the world. It is also possible that they are related by other Norman means or via the de Clare family of England. As stated before it is also possible that any forms of these names may have been present in other parts of the sphere of Norman influence in the world at that time. As this story unfolds we will see the real and very impressive extent of the involvement of the Sinclair family in these sagas.

What are the connections between both Sancto Claro and Arcadia in places like Italy, Hungary, Sicily, and France? There appears to be many links via family and royalty that may answer these questions. As it turns out the answer to that question does in reality lay within the bounds of what is considered Arcadia in the Principality of Achea, Greece. In many historical accounts the entire Peloponnesian Peninsula was referred to as Arcadia. In this way the mythology of Arcas and even St. Andrew may be referred to as Arcadian.

Much of the speculation surrounding the Sinclair family of Scotland centers on their involvement with the Knights Templar or The Poor Fellow Soldiers of Christ and the Temple of Solomon. Popular books and movies seem to infer that Rosslyn Chapel has many themes in its artwork that are associated with the Knights Templar. As it turns out the Earls of Menteith have a direct and historically documented association with the Knights Templar. The Sinclair family does not have a direct and historically documented association with the Knights Templar.

Here again we are compelled to consider the phrase "Sancto Claro" as meaning something other than an association with the Sinclair family and their possible association with the Knights Templar. What if this moniker is associated with another titled family group that has a documented association with that order to the point where they are described as being "patrons of the Knights Templar in Scotland" from the earliest days of the Order's inception. This storied family would later become Earl's of Menteith and rulers of both England and Scotland. It is possible that the Menteith's involvement with the Knights Templar and their name meaning "Sancto Claro" led to this confusion with the St. Clair's or Sinclair's

Alain Fitzwalter, Second High Steward of Scotland was a great patron of the Knights Templar in Scotland. Later his son Walter Bailloch would go on to participate in the 7th Crusade of Louis IX also known as St. Louis. The 7th Crusade (1248-1256) was an invasion of Egypt that failed though the Crusaders held the port of Dammaitia for a time. There are records of Knights Templar losing an engagement there where Count Robert Artois was also said to have lost his life. It may be possible that Walter Bailloch even knew Robert Artois and both may have been associated with the Knights Templar. Either way this association illustrates two links that will be important in understanding the connections between Santo Claro, The Earl's of Menteith, and the Knights Templar. Subsequently the Order of St. Louis of French nobility would be named for Louis IX. There are many family links between the Artois and Stewarts that would have a large impact on the Jacobite era of Scotland and later the French Revolution.

Robert Artois was from the famous family of the King of France and his other ancestors including Charles I and II Kings of Naples and Sicily. Part of Robert's grand lineage included Charles I Artois and Frederick II Holy Roman Emperor both sharing mothers that came from the Hauteville family of Normandy. The Norman influence in Italy, Sicily, and even Greece was strong at different points in history and had direct links to the same Norman families that had a great impact on the history of England and Scotland. Given this it may be that some Norman St. Clair's had come to Italy, Sicily and other surrounding regions. This may have also resulted in not only those of St. Clair blood but other Norman families also occupying Greece during the phase of the Latin Kingdoms. The Artois dynasty controlled what is referred to as The Principality of Achea during this and some of their noble class did occupy this region.

Interestingly there is a piece of specific architecture in Naples, Italy that demonstrates the bond between the Artois' and Menteith or Sancto Claro of Scotland. The St. Chiara (St. Clare) Cathedral of Naples Italy was built by family descendant of Count Robert Artois who lost his life on the 7th Crusade in Egypt. St. Chiara was built in the mid fourteenth Century by Sancta of Majorca wife of King of Naples a later Robert Artois. Though they lived about one hundred years apart both men even had the same first name and shared the same relations to the Kings of France, the Mentieth's and many other noble families of Europe.

If one creates an arc on the globe that corresponds with the orientation of St. Chiara Cathedral on the globe it transacts in a northwesterly course to Inchmahome Priory on an island in the Lake of Menteith Scotland. Inchmahome Priory also includes effigies of Walter Bailloch who fought with Count Robert Artois in the 7th Crusade. Is this a coincidence or a planned homage from the Artois to this in Scotland they felt related to and allied with? The fact that Walter had gone on a Crusade led by St. Louis (Louis IX) illustrates the historical links between Scotland and France that many ignore. This talismanic geographic relationship is also displayed through time in a Scottish and French mingling of religion and family that may have contributed to many of the Arcadian mysteries being linked to each other in theme and meaning.

The effigies at Inchmahome Priory also includes another effigy of Walter's Wife Mary I daughter of Muireadhach II, Moramaer of Menteith. It was in this fashion that the Earldom of Menteith passed to what we now term the Stewart family of Scottish and English Kings later in history. The image of these effigies lends some credence to the thought this is all associated with the Knights Templar. Other places associated with the Knights Templar including the Temple

40

Church and Rosslyn Chapel also include effigies of Knights that seem to lend a air of authenticity to these stories. Here at Inchmahome Priory we may have the effigy that is being suggested by all this imagery and it is not of a member of the Sinclair family. This effigy depicts a man whose family were said to have been the patron's of the Knights Templar in Scotland. These relations may also explain why the later Order of the Garter includes similar imagery to that of the Knights Templar.

Incredibly this little told tale also involves the Artois family being the Prince's of the real region of Arcadia in Greece for a short time during the Latin Kingdom. The establishment of the Principalities of Achea (1205) and Athens was the result of the 4th Crusade. This Crusade is interesting in that in pitted the forces of Latin Rome against the Eastern remnants of the Byzantine Empire that also included the Eastern Church. At this time the Latin forces occupied the entire territory of their enemy and established new fiefdoms and administrative units based on the Latin Church. As a result the region was under the Frankish control of the Villarhedron family and their allies.

This is important to our Scottish story because two potent symbols of Scotland are represented in Greece. This may include the traditional land of Arcadia and the story of St. Andrew which took place in this region now controlled by western Europeans who had their own views of these subjects. As we may see as this saga unfolds it is no coincidence that both native Greek and Scottish people wear kilts and play bagpipes! These beliefs may have ultimately contributed to why the Shepherds Monument at Shugborough Hall was constructed or even portions of what is considered the Mystery of Rennes le Chateau. It is important to note here that the Order of the Thistle's symbols include the "X" Shaped cross of St. Andrew combined with the Auspice of Maria or "AVM" symbol among others.

As part of the division of regions in these conquered lands portions were given to cooperative local lords, Church interests, with additional portions being given to the Knights Templar, Hospitalier, and Tuetonic. In 1266 the Principality became the domain of Charles of Anjou who did not cooperate with the Latin Church as well as the former inhabitants. Though Charles was never known to have visited Achea it is still an interesting link to the concept of Arcadia. Charles' son Charles II would go on to play a central role in the legends of Mary Magdalene in southern France. Still later Rene' of Anjou would be a central figure in the story of Joan of Arc which does seem to include elements of the Sacred Feminine and saga of Mary Magdalene.

What is important to note about the Anjou's is how they are related to the same Merovingian and Plantagenet families that nobility in Scotland and England are from as well. The link between these two groups has always been a strong Norman heritage that seems to express itself at times beyond any national differences or borders. Though this faction of families were identified as being Catholic or even Holy Roman Emperors it is clear that they had an independent spirit that did not adhere strictly to Church doctrine and beliefs. Some elements of Eastern Christianity and even Gnosticism seem to have been appreciated by the Artois and others associated with them.

At about the same time that Alain Fitzwalter was patronizing the early Knights Templar the development of another order would display the concept of Sancto Claro though at a much later date than St. Margaret's landing in Scotland with William Sancto Claro. The Order of Poor Clares sometimes known of as The Order of St. Clare was founded by St. Clare of Assissi in about 1212. The Poor Clares as they are known of were comprised of Nuns. The order was founded in 1212 by Clare of Assisi who was a devotee of St. Francis of Assisi. This is an interesting link to a value of the name Francis in later history. The inclusion of the word "poor" in their name also harkens to the original name of the Knights Templar as well.

The order eventually grew to include monasteries all over Europe including one near Paris. The Poor Clares of Paris later would educate both Marie of Guise and her daughter Mary Queen of Scots. This also included their instruction in the art of weaving and needlepoint which is a tradition of nuns going all the way back to Empress Theodora of the Byzantine Empire. Theodora was an independently minded woman who had created orders of nuns trained in the art of weaving as Theodora herself had once been. This factor may even have Coptic Christian overtones that may include a belief in the Gnostic Gospels and other concepts like Mary Magdalene associated with Theodora's religious instruction in Alexandria Egypt. It may be that these orders of nuns have kept alive many popular notions with regard to Mary Magdalene and women's roles in faith.

The Order was founded about 144 years later than St. Margaret's arrival in Scotland with William Sancto Claro. It is entirely possible that this phrase was valued at the time of St. Margaret extending to the later eras where we see its alternate meaning being applied to an Order of nuns. Then in succession we may observe a value of this order of nuns by the descendant family of Alain Fitzwalter and his Crusader son Walter Bellioloch. Margaret of Scotland had come from Hungary as well. Hungary would also later have a strong connection to the Poor Clare Order. The Poor Clares became similar to the Knights Templar in that many well healed and wealthy young women chose to become members of the order. This included potential brides of Frederick II Holy Roman Emperor and Robert II Anjou both also mentioned earlier in association. Both men were to be betrothed to women who chose to become Poor Clare nuns instead. Is it possible that the Hungarian background of Margaret of Scotland had brought the concept of Sancto Claro with her along with possible future family members related to Alain FitzWalter and his son Bailloch?

Mary Queen of Scots and Marie of Guise were educated at the St. Marcel (Order of St. Clare) monastery near Paris founded by Queen Margaret of France wife of Louis IX who had also led the 7th Crusade that included Robert Artois and Walter Bailloch. The connection and name of Queen Margaret may have also been an inspiration to Mary Queen of Scots. Of course this likely would have represented a strong link to earlier Scottish history and its Queen Margaret. Mary Queen of Scots was known to have had a strong fascination with St. Margaret or Queen Margaret of Scotland whose story is discussed above.

Mary Queen of Scots valued St. Margaret of Scotland so much that she was even known to have kept the head of the Saint as a talisman during her pregnancy and childbirth including that of her son the future King James I. It is entirely possible that the true meaning of Sancto Claro was known of by this entire cast of characters and may have even resulted in the naming of the Order of St. Clare. It is also possible that the heads of both St. Margaret and Mary Queen of Scots are part of the mystery of Shugborough Hall in England.

Given the association of Robert Beale and Mary Queen of Scots prior to her beheading an interesting theory may be espoused. Beale was the liaison between Mary Queen of Scots and Queen Elizabeth I when she was being held captive by the later. At this time Beale was said to have become close to Mary Queen of Scots and that she even gifted him a jeweled necklace. One of the mysteries surrounding the death of Mary Queen of Scots is the disappearance of a strange casket that may resemble the one atop the tomb in the Poussin rendering seen at Shugborough Hall in Staffordshire.

This casket is rumored to hold the personal belongings and writings of Mary Queen of Scots. This missing item has been legendary since the death of Mary Queen of Scots and Robert Beale may have been one of the last people to have actually seen this item. As part of a theory developed in my book "The Geographic Mystery of Sir Francis Bacon" it may be that this casket and its contents comprise what is known of as the "Beale Treasure" today in the modern world. In turn the Beale Treasure legend of Virginia would develop in response to an older mystery that included a vault of Sir Francis Bacon's papers that had been stashed in a vault somewhere in Jamestown or Williamsburg. This is of course an educated guess on the part of this author as there is no solid proof to back up these assumptions. Still lost objects seem to be a major part of this story.

Chapter 4: The Real Roseline of Rosslyn Chapel and the Prime Meridian of Orphir Round Kirk.

Is Rosslyn Chapel home to an "Arcadian" mystery? If we examine Rosslyn as marking a prime meridian on the globe some surprising associations become apparent that may lead us to reason's Norse culture was valued in the history of America during the time of poets Longfellow and Poe who both may have family connections to this entire mystery saga.

In recent years a great controversy has resurfaced as to the true origins of the Newport Tower in Rhode Island. Some ascribe its origins to the Norse who they insist came to what is New England today long ago. Through time we have seen how people like Eben Horsford and Henry Wadsworth Longfellow may have promoted the idea of the Norse discovery of North America for reasons of their own. Unfolding is the story of how Longfellow's "The Saga of Olaf" may contain many hidden clues as to the reality of this entire tale. To understand Olaf we will now examine the Earls of Orkney who were his contemporaries and in many ways continued to promote his Christian faith leading us to the much vaunted Round Churches of Scandinavia that are based on the Church of the Holy Sepulcher in Jerusalem.

If we examine the motivations for these men's belief in the early Norse in America theory many political overtones are revealed that link to an English right to "own" New England vs. a Spanish ownership or claim. These national differences also reflect the differences between English monarchs and the Latin Church during many periods of English history. It may be that English factions saw reasons why they would have a more legitimate claim via an earlier discovery of this region by Norse interests that over time became part of the domain of England via Scotland. The use of this heritage as a rationale for claim may not have been undertaken until the time of Elizabeth I or subsequent King James I.

In the Norse sagas it is speculated that one portion of this tale may describe the Viking settlement of L'Anse Aux Meadows in Newfoundland. Beyond that much of the evidence for Norse incursions or claim to North America have been claimed and disputed. People like Horsford lobbied for the Norse theory using faulty evidence in the mid nineteenth century as examined earlier.

In response an entire mythology was supported and created by the works of people like Longfellow and Edgar Allan Poe who also seemed to be aware of the truths and falsehoods of this movement in American politics. As part of this story it may be that proponents of the Norse theory had planted relics and stone inscriptions that were meant to suggest that either Vikings or Knights had come to North America long before Columbus set foot in the West Indies. It was in this spirit that Horsford and others of a group known as the Boston Brahmins erected a statue of Leif Erikson in Boston amidst this controversy. Later we will discuss another important statue of Leif Erikson in Washington D.C.

Near the end of this era is when the famous Kensington Rune Stone was discovered by farmer Olaf Ohman in Minnesota. Still later a group produced a replica of a Viking Ship that was

44

moored near the Chicago Exposition that honored Christopher Columbus. It may be that all of these facts and events have clouded the waters to a point where the truth of Norse exploration in North America will never be known through this fog of political and property disputes. It is clear that at the time of Horsford and the other Norse proponents of New England that no knowledge of L' Anse Aux Meadows was known of. At that point it may have been somewhat wishful thinking for these people to believe that a Norse city known as Norumbega had once existed where Boston now stands. It is now clear that no evidence of this actually being true has ever been identified.

What we are left with is the fact that Norsemen came at least as far south as L' Anse Aux Meadows and possibly ventured further south using that location as a base to spend the winter somewhere near date +/- 1000 A.D. It may be that a trail of truth was left via these incursions into virgin territory and who may have become privy to it later via cultural ties to Scandinavian royalty. Coupled with this are the very same people who may have seen this discovery by Erikson and others to be representative of their right to own and rule New England or the Eastern Seaboard in later times during which Spain felt they had already claimed it.

All of this does suggest that some Norsemen or other entity from later history did visit the eastern seaboard prior to Columbus' "discovery" of North America from an island in the West Indies. That is not what is in question. What is being examined here is that there are no records or evidence of such explorations and that it is possible that false historical clues were left to support a much later political point of view. This may have begun in Elizabethan times and extended through later eras for many different reasons. Among these reasons may have been the distinct lack of any material or physical evidence of the Norse having come leading us to the tale of the Newport Tower, Westford Knight and much more.

Many also relate the construction of the famous Newport Tower to interests associated with Henry Sinclair the Earl of Orkney during the late fourteenth Century. Our examination here may display how this legend was propagated due to his relation to the people that had actually came to North America long ago and had established L' Anse Aux Meadows. It appears that Henry Sinclair had both a political and genetic link to to the Norse Sagas that describes what may have been L' Anse Aux Meadows long ago. Evidence provided here will show how this secret chain of information was transferred via the title of the Earl of Orkney in its many forms and used later as a rationale for an English claim to North America. Through all the national and political changes the earldom has survived and retained a kind of ownership of this legacy that would ultimately help to solidify England's claim to New England and Virginia. Note also that the life and saga of King Olaf coincides with the dates matching the founding of L'Anse Aux Meadows.

This story will also illustrate how the Newport Tower was built in Elizabethan times in an attempt to make it appear as if people had claimed New England for Scandinavian rulers whose mantle of power would later fall to the Scottish and ultimately the English monarchy. The entire story of the Lord High Admiral of Scotland Henry Sinclair coming to America may have been meant to bolster the theory that his forebears had been the ones that had established a Norse foothold in North America in an era prior to the discovery of L' Anse Aux Meadows. Given

Sinclair's title of Lord High Admiral of Scotland it is unlikely that he would desert the homeland to explore unknown lands when his duty lay with his country's navy at that time. The Newport Tower is often pointed to as proof these stories are true and that a Norseman had constructed the tower at an early date thus establishing their claim. These same rights of claim may have also been propagated by French interests and their Norman culture as well.

No matter the truth of the Newport Tower why is it that there is no record of its existence by settlers of the region prior to its mention by Benedict Arnold Sr. as his "stone built windmill?" No Plymouth colonists or other early settlers made their way to what is Newport today at that time? Apparently, someone has gone through any documented recordation of this structure and eliminated it from the historical record? As stated earlier there is no mention of the Tower by earlier English explorers such as Captains Archer and Gosnold who spent an extended period within sight of the Newport Tower and yet did not record its existence in any way. How and why if this tower is ancient would it have been kept a secret or covered up? If the tower bolsters their claim to New England then why keep it a secret?

Most of the evidence that there was ever a tower at Newport at an earlier date is tied to unreliable maps that have been in many ways misinterpreted and repeated by subsequent cartographers that never even visited the region themselves. The "Zeno Map" often touted as evidence of the Newport Tower's antiquity records a "Normanville" with a map symbol for a settlement that includes a tower for example. Note also that Normanville is a town name and not an indication of anything more or less.

It may also be considered that this faction considered the establishment of L' Anse Aux Meadows as representative of their claim to the entire continent. Is it possible that this strange tower in Newport located on Mill street was only a windmill that had later been spun into a story of Norse construction by those that wished to support the notion of Norumbega or English claim to the region? Is the Newport Tower representative of a Norse Round Kirk or a form of architecture commonly seen as a windmill in England and Europe? Or had the tower been built to resemble a Norse structure intentionally? As this story unfolds it may also become obvious that the mysteries of Rosslyn Chapel may also reference Leif Erikson's voyages to North America and not any possible trip by later people. None of these assumptions alter the notion that the tower was built by Elizabethan factions in order to establish their claim to New England using Star Castle on the Isles of Scilly as a datum or place from which to measure thus also establishing a prime meridian at both places.

These ideas may have been followed by the misguided notion that later Crusader era Knighthoods or Chivalric orders may have also later came at a date prior to the voyages of Columbus thus furthering the English claim to North America. Is it also possible that later suggestions of medieval exploration of North America had also been placed by this same group of wishful thinkers? In truth we will see how Knighthoods such as the Orders of the Garter, Bath, and Thistle had more influence on these dynamics at a much later date thus creating the entire seed of what people like Horsford and Longfellow would later come to believe. This imagery may also contribute to the notion that Knights Templar under Lord High Admiral of Scotland

46

Henry Sinclair had made their way to North America at an early date.

In order to understand this entire scheme or plan an examination of the rich and varied history of the title of the Earl of Orkney is required. In turn this study will include the use of an amazing prime meridian centered on the famous Rosslyn Chapel. In this way Rosslyn may actually live up to what many consider a misnomer as representative of the "Rosslyn," Roseline, or Prime Meridian similar to what we see in the famous Paris Meridian. This meridian may have been originally established by the construction of the Oriphir Round Kirk (Church) in Orkney in a circular form based on the Holy Sepulcher in Jerusalem.

The Orphir Round Church and Rosslyn Chapel are due north and south of each other 180/0 degrees true north. An examination of the family and titles involved in the construction of both chapels some undeniable truths are exposed. Rosslyn Chapel may be showing us what happened in the Norse sagas that include the exploits of Leif Erikson and others and not a trip to North America by Henry Sinclair or any other member of that family prior to what is recorded in common history.

The story of both Rosslyn Chapel and the Orphir Round Kirk expose some interesting factors in any story of Norse exploration of North America. This trail of evidence also leads us to some bizarre references similar to those noted in France at Rennes le Chateau! These events take place only about one hundred years after the settlement of L' Anse Aux Meadows, King Olaf, and their possible mention in associated Sagas. The entire legacy of Orkney in this story may in turn link us directly to the true nature of the Newport Tower, Powder Magazine in Colonial Williamsburg, The International Peace Garden, as well as the Kensington Rune.

During the earliest historical times of Orkney is was part of the Kingdom of Norway and the Earls of Orkney were of Scandinavian blood. This would be true until the time of Earl William Sinclair who built Rosslyn Chapel. The Orphir Round Church was built by Earl Hakon (Haakon) Paulsson in about 1124 A.D. Haakon built the church as part of his penance for murdering the joint Earl of Orkney at that time named Magnus Erlandsson.

In a foreshadowing of the same religious and political dispute that would create the United States Haakon and Magnus were separated by matters of faith and politics. Magnus was more oriented with the Catholic church while Haakon seemed to have still valued elements of the former Norse Pagan culture. The slaying of Magnus by Haakon in a church also strangely resembles the story of Robert the Bruce slaying his rival on the altar of a church.

As penance for the slaying of Magnus Haakon went on pilgrimage to Jerusalem and returned to build the Orphir Round Kirk in the form of the Church of the Holy Sepulcher in Jerusalem. The Kirk is also known as the St. Nicholas Chapel thus named by the Earl himself. The Orphir Round Church is circular in form and includes and apse that extended from its southeast side. The apse is all that remains of the structure today as it was inexplicably demolished in the eighteenth century. The Round Kirk is surrounded by an extensive graveyard. Adjacent to the Church was the "Bu" or hall of the Earl.

47

Since Magnus had been more associated with the Latin Church and had been slain by Earl Haakon he was eventually given sainthood status and a grand cathedral in Kirkwall was built in his name. Both of these structures and their history would be intertwined with that of all the Earls of Orkney, Royalty of Norway and Denmark, Scottish royalty and of course English monarchs and gentry. Even the story of Mary Queen of Scots, St. Magnus Cathedral, and the Earl of Orkney are related. The history of the Chapel of St. Nicholas or Orphir Round Kirk may also have a direct bearing on why the Newport Tower was later presented to the public at large as a manifestation of Norse culture and not the English culture that had produced it.

The succession of the title of the Earl of Orkney always included members that had a direct blood line to the original Norwegian Earl of Orkney and this includes some amazing people whose families would later have a major impact on the development of Newport Rhode Island and any value of the Newport Tower in their family tradition. Here we have an early Earl of Orkney building a Round Kirk design that many would later relate to the form of the Newport Tower. Starting with the Norwegian Earls of Orkney the title then goes to the Scottish Earls under the Norwegian crown.

Eventually Orkney was gained by Scotland via James III marriage to Margaret of Denmark as part of her dowry. When her father Christian I of Denmark did not pay the specified dowry the Orkney Islands were ceded to him as part of the agreement. Here displayed is yet one example of the strong ties between Scottish and Danish nobility through time. Later we would even see the son of Mary Queen of Scots James I marry Anne of Denmark. Many speculate that Queen Anne of Denmark had a large and somewhat overlooked role in the kind of Baconian mysteries of the day.

When the Orkney's were given to James III the Earl of Orkney was William Sinclair who is famous as the builder of Rosslyn Chapel. This entire incident involving the dowry of Margaret may be the real reason Rosslyn was ever built where it was. As a result of this change from Norwegian to Scottish influence William Sinclair was made the Earl of Caithness and given the lands in southern Scotland as compensation. These parts of the story now solidly link the further association of the Sinclair family with that of Scotland while still holding very strong connections to Scandinavia via their family and Queen of Scotland Margaret of Denmark.

There are many associations between the Sinclair family and the Orkney Islands through time even prior to the era of William Sinclair. Later the story of Bishop Honeyman of St. Magnus Kirkwall in the seventeenth century is tied to the legacy of the Stewart and Sinclair families via his marriage to Mary Stewart. In turn we will see a Rev. Honeyman of Newport Rhode Island playing a role later in this saga.

Again we must consider the fact that what is being exposed here is the original "Rosslyne" or Rose Line. The familial and cultural connections between Haakon Paulsson and William Sinclair are very strong and include a legacy of the tradition of building family chapels. These chapels always include representative art and motif that display the allegiances and beliefs of the churches benefactor. This is the case at Rosslyn Chapel done in grand style.

The Orphir Chapel of St. Nicholas is due north of Rosslyn Chapel and was also said to have included representative artwork. These two structures create a "Rosslyn" due to their spatial relationship arranged along a line of latitude on the globe with regard to the polar axis of the earth. The Earl of Sinclair William had paid his respects to a forebear by aligning his structure with an early chapel that also served as a marker for a prime meridian. It is entirely possible that the site for the construction of Rosslyn Chapel was dictated by its geographic relationship along the "Rosslyn" in relation to the Orphir Round Kirk of Orkney. If this is true then the Orphir Kirk had been designated an Axis Mundi marking a prime meridian that defined the domain of the Earls of Orkney. Here again is yet another reason that the Newport Tower in Rhode Island is also valued in a similar way regardless of its date of construction.

This is not to say there were no intermarriage or family ties between the Stewarts and Sinclair's. Those ties did exist but may have also included different priorities or values.

This is also the story being related at places like the Newport Tower and Powder Magazine of Colonial Williamsburg that both also have strong ties to subsequent earls of Orkney that even held title during the periods in which the common history tells us these structures were created. Both of these structures have been discussed in depth in my last book "The Geographic Mysteries of Sir Francis Bacon."

During the eras in which places like the Orphir Round Kirk and Rosslyn Chapel were being built family ties and an appreciation of one's heritage would be displayed at a family chapel or church. If a member of a specific family was successful enough then they may have chosen to express their dedication to Christian spirituality in this manner. This may also be the case in other cultures and religions. Often these churches were funded by specific individuals that also may have dictated the themes of artwork and salutary included. Rosslyn Chapel was also originally built to have been a collegiate church mean to educate members of the clergy and prominent citizens.

Though many speculate as to the involvement of Freemason's or Chivalric Orders such as the Knights Templar at Rosslyn a closer examination may reveal that William Sinclair was telling us about his family's history at Rosslyn and not an over reaching symbolism such as many modern interpretations imply. Given this it is not out of the question that he had somehow obtained the location where Rosslyn would be built because he knew it was associated with Orphir in a north to south meridian.

This may also suggest that William Sinclair held a belief that Earl Haakon had also held knowledge of the use of a prime meridian and had built his church to illustrate this notion. The early 12th century construction date (1124 estimated) is 124 years after one of the commonly accepted dates for the advent of the magnetic compass in 1000 A.D. This date also matches the establishment of L'Anse Aux Meadows in Newfoundland. Given this it is not out of the question that learned men could arrange buildings along a fixed line of longitude using astronomical calculations coupled with the compass and sighting the pole star even somewhat prior to that date. Yet that is not in question here as even the Round Kirk was built after 1000 A.D.

The Orphir Round Kirk of Orkney and Rosslyn Chapel may form a Prime Meridian.

Rosslyn Chapel seems to point an arc on the globe to the Orphir Round Kirk.

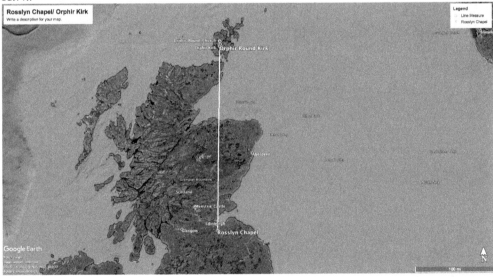

The arc created by the orientation of Rosslyn Chapel extends northward to The Orphir Round Kirk. Both Structures were built by Earls of Orkney who had strong Norwegian cultural ties.

The arc from Rosslyn Reaches the Orphir Kirk on Orkney.

Chapter 5: Et in Orcadia Ego. The true story of Templars in Scotland.

If the Sinclair's had been the source of a claim of North America by the English later then what other factors may be at play here? Many modern narratives suggest the involvement of the famous Knights Templar in historical events that happened long after their dissolution by Papal Bull in 1307. Why is this a persistent theme in this history. It appears there is a rationale for these stories yet there are many dynamics of the saga that suggest there is more at play than the activities of the Knights Templar.

In recent years much has been made of the possibility of pre-Columbian incursions into North and South America by a cast of characters that includes Phoenicians, Norse Vikings, Knights Templar, and Romans among others. Each ancient culture seems to provide the possibility that people came at different times and attempted to claim or settle these regions. It is not beyond the scope of possibility that ancient peoples happened upon a new land that they did not previously know existed. What is really in question is who came to these new lands and established a lasting presence to back up their claim.

To date no evidence of extensive settlement by any parties prior to the establishment of L' Anse Aux Meadows Norse site in northern Newfoundland has been exposed. Evidence of any earlier settlements or visits by ancient people have elements involved that are questionable yet it still is possible that Romans or Phoenicians visited the new lands though no verifiable evidence has yet come to light. In addition the historical record suggests that later people also for lack of a better term faked artifacts and sites that they believed would prove the existence of these earlier cultures.

Due to these factors, here we will examine all of this in the context that includes L' Anse Aux Meadows having actually been one of the sites that had been described as Vinland in the original Norse Sagas of this era. This line of inquiry will also suggest the involvement of a individuals who held the title of the Earl of Orkney in its different incarnations. As it turns out all of the men who held this title may have also held direct genealogical relationships to the earliest of the Norwegian Earls of Orkney.

As in all the Arcadian mysteries the value of Arcas and the Pole Star is present. Part of an expression of this value is illustrated in the creation of a Prime Meridian or north to south axis from which additional geographic measurements may be taken. We see this concept being applied in places such as the White House Meridian in Washington D.C., and the famous Paris Meridian associated with the Rennes le Chateau mystery supplying us with yet more Arcadian imagery related to the suggestion of a pentagram in the landscape and the artwork of Nicolas Poussin's "Shepherds of Arcadia." In association with each of these stories is an individual that was well versed in land surveying, navigation, astronomy, and cartography.

The spatial relationship of the Orphir Round Kirk (1124) and Rosslyn Chapel (1456) includes them both being related via the same longitude designation on the globe. This association could have been executed long before the advent of the modern form of latitude and longitude using this meridian as the "0" line in their own scheme of measurement similar to what we see at Greenwich England today and as illustrated in the famous Paris Meridian. If true we then see the influence of early Earl of Orkney Haakon Paulsson and the axis mundi he had created using the site of the Orphir Round Church. It may be far beyond a coincidence that two Earls of Orkney, family related, had both constructed emblematic structures in this tradition stemming back to Constantine, The Tower of the Winds of Athens, and more ancient cultures.

What is more amazing is what these family and architectural clues may mean to the history of North and South America later more precisely the history of the United States of America. The legacy of the Orphir Round Kirk and Rosslyn Chapel may expose how later the Newport Tower in Rhode Island was used to suggest imperial ownership of New England in order to degrade a Spanish and French claim to the region and later possibly to even dispute the control of the Hanoverian faction of the Stuart family that had gained the English throne thus alienating the Stewart's of Scotland who many feel are the rightful heirs to that crown.

In the end the establishment of L' Anse Aux Meadows may have provided a rationale as to why the original Stewart Kings had a more legal claim to what would become New England later. This concept would be displayed later in history and portions of the truth of this saga are brought to light in examining the legends of Oak Island, The Newport Tower, The Stafford Hill Memorial, The Kensington Rune Stone, The Beale Treasure, and "Bacon's Vault" of Williamsburg. As the United States grew westward additional "mysteries" would be planned and clues would be left that may or may not lead to a real treasure but would reveal true hidden aspects of the history of North America.

Later it is possible these claims had been argued over and disputed by Norwegian, Scottish, and English factions coupled with religious differences between Catholics, Protestants, and those with more secular views in the United States. The Norwegians may have felt they had a claim to parts of North America. Their progeny that would later be considered Scottish such as the Earls of Orkney may have also seen this claim to North America as part of their cultural legacy that developed independently of Norway. This right of claim even extended to Sir William Alexander Earl of Stirling and his attempt to colonize Nova Scotia in the seventeenth century. Still further as the Scottish Kings became the English monarchs others were led to believe this claim would now extend to the crown of England. All three of these separate views may have also depended on disproving or devaluing the accomplishments of Cristobal Colon a.k.a. Christopher Columbus.

In part what we may reveal here is a legacy spanning centuries that involves the influence of the Earls of Orkney in their many different forms. Over time the Earls of Orkney would display a distinct allegiance to both their Scandinavian and Scottish roots. What we may be looking at here in terms that mystery lovers will appreciate is a case of "Et in Orcadia Ego" as opposed to "Et in Arcadia Ego" which upon closer examination does involve many of the same characters. Evidence presented here will also link distinctly Orcadian Norse symbols to other points of mystery in North America including the Newport Tower, Kensington Rune, The Archer

Reliquary of Jamestown, Runes present in Orkney, and finally the symbology of the Order of the Thistle of Scotland.

Many myths that seem to include treasure legends may be part of this phenomenon. Later this same Orkney influence would extend to the mysteries of the Newport, Rhode Island in which some do suggest a Norse origin. A clear path from the Earls of Orkney and the Honeyman family of England and Scotland leads us to the Newport Tower, Orphir Round Kirk, The Kensington Rune, and the real reasons many associate the imagery of North America with Rosslyn Chapel and the supposed exploits of Henry Sinclair in the new land.

This amazing story also includes some of the most revered and fascinating stories of their respective eras. Though an examination of the Honyman (Honeyman) family a saga is exposed that may show us the political and cultural truths hidden by the Newport Tower and other structures like the Orphir Round Kirk and Rosslyn Chapel. The Honeyman's have had significant interface with Mary Queen of Scots, Her husband an Earl of Orkney, as well as other members of the Stewart and Sinclair families over time. One of the earliest and most interesting was Robert Honeyman (Ioniman) of Magdalen College Oxford:

Rev. Robert Honyman, of Staffordshire, England:

"There was a Rev Robert Honyman of Staffordshire, England, of a generation earlier than Bishop Andrew Honeyman of Orkney of whose family I can give but the briefest sketch. Without a doubt he belonged to the same later Scottish family of the same name. He is one of the earliest persons bearing the name to which my researches bound light. He matriculated at Magdalen College Oxford, Nov. 17, 1581 at the age of twenty-seven. He must have been therefore born about 1554. He graduated from that College with the degree of B.S. and received an M.A. in 1587. He was noted as a clerk at Magdalen College in the 1570's. He held this position until his death at the age of seventy-one and was buried in the College Chapel. He had been licensed to preach at the chapel there and was also entered on the books as a "college chaplain." His name spelled on records as Ioniman. I suspect that from these records he was related to Bishop Honyman of the Orkneys. There is no proof of him being married."

This Robert Honeyman is interesting for many reasons. His association with Magdalen College is notable as well as his relation to the later Bishop Andrew Honeyman of Orkney. Also of note is the appearance that this man came from Staffordshire and will later be associated with the same Stafford family of Newport Rhode Island as well as a later Rev. Honeyman who established the first Episcopal Church in Newport in about 1700. Later still during the Revolutionary War another member of the Honeyman family would be known as "Washington's Spy." In the end we may even see some amazing connections to the first and only English Pope Nicolas Breakespeare who in turn may link us to the very famous Sir Francis Bacon and his concept of the "New Atlantis." In fact it is possible that Breakespeare had an impact on how and why the Orphir Kirk and other round churches on Bornholm Island in the Baltic Sea were even constructed in the first place. The Honeyman family relations will show intimate knowledge of the Orphir Round Kirk as well as associations with the Stewart family royalty of Scotland and the Earls of Orkney in turn leading us to Newport Rhode Island. The seemingly latin spelling of Honeyman or Ioniman may be suggestive of deeper connections. The Isle of Iona in Scotland is associated with St. Columba. These images would later become part of the symbols of the United States.

In order to put this amazing story in its proper context we must travel back in time to the era of the Norman Conquest of England and the First Crusades in the Holy Land. The era of the development of L' Anse Aux Meadows, The Norman Conquest, and the mystery of the Orphir Round Church all took place between the mid eleventh century (1000 A.D.) to the mid twelfth century (1100 A.D). These three events were to have a major impact on these stories over time extending even to the current era of the early twenty-first century. This of course is also the era of the first Crusades and the Latin Kingdoms of the Levant, what is today Turkey, also including Greece and Macedonia.

The amazing story of King Sigurd of Norway and the Norwegian Crusade to the Holy Land holds many hints and clues as to the value of the Orphir Round Kirk and Rosslyn Chapel later. Both the Norman Conquest and the Norwegian Crusade all took place within one hundred years of when we are told L' Anse Aux Meadows was established in Newfoundland. This was a great time of development for the Scandinavian culture as they emerged from their pagan Viking roots to take a seat in the grand monarchies of Europe. Coincidentally this same period marks what most agree to be the advent of the magnetic compass. The history of Northern Scotland and especially the Orkney Islands is reflective of these events and many clues may have been left for us to ponder in discerning the truth of this era. Note here that the entire saga of the Norwegian Crusade took place just prior to the establishment of the Knights Templar. That order did not even exist so as to have any impact upon the following story. In fact much of this history will display a complete lack of the involvement of the Knights Templar and may instead point to the influence of Scandinavian and German knighthoods that were never associated in any way with the famous Knights Templar.

King Sigurd and his men made the long journey by sea to Jerusalem but took a leisurely course that first led them to Santiago de Compostela and the rest of Galicia. It is likely that Sigurd and his men made port at A Coruna. Santiago de Compostela is an important place to both the Scottish and Scandinavian people including Denmark, Sweden, and Norway. During the eras in which these kingdoms were aligned with the Catholic faith Santiago de Compostela served as a major pilgrim's destination. Part of this value may involve the legend of the namesake of Scotland Queen Scota who once made the Galician Port of A Coruna her home. Santiago de Compostela represents a kind of hidden link that reveals many aspects of the values of our Norwegian and Scottish nobility. During periods of history that Jerusalem was inaccessible Santiago de Compostela served as a kind of New Jerusalem that stood proxy for the original in the hearts and minds of European pilgrims of those eras. This is interesting in that even the Orphir Round Kirk of St. Nicholas seemed to have been built to reference the concept of a New Jerusalem or the creation of a holy place that referenced the original.

A Coruña is the site from which according to legend Scota's husband sighted Ireland from atop the famous Torre de Hercules lighthouse (6th Century) there. Some speculate that the original form of this lighthouse extended from Phoenician times thus matching any association with the Queen Scota Legend.

In some ways Scottish people may have viewed this region as a homeland that took on added significance in relation to the cult of St. James and its associated Pilgrimage. Scottish and Scandinavian pilgrims would also arrive at A Coruña and follow a different pilgrimage route from there to Santiago de Compostela in comparison to their European cohorts. Galicia had also been long ruled by the Suebi tribe who hailed originally from the Swabian region of what is today Germany. During the era of Sigurd this Swabian link may have also represented a common culture linking the Normans and the French culture of the day which included southern Germany. This is all occurring at the era just after the reign of Charlemagne as well.

Some researchers speculate that even the Danish red cross flag was inspired by the Cross of Santiago. The Cross of Santiago appears as a red cross that infers the shape of a knife or sword. This is also the primary symbol of the Knights of Santiago. The story of Sigurd and the Scotsmen coming to Santiago de Compostela may also infer an association between these men and the Order of Santiago over time.

In past works we have discussed the membership of Sir James Douglas and William Sinclair builder of Rosslyn Chapel as possibly being members of this order. As we see this tradition may go all the way back to King Sigurd and his army's time in Santiago de Compostela. Much of the confusion in others associating the Sinclair's with the Knights Templar may come from their actual association with the Order of Santiago and a value of the Camino de Santiago. There are many mysteries associated with Santiago including speculation that the sepulcher there actually contains the remains of James the brother of Christ in addition to those of Santiago or James the Apostle of Christ. The story of Sir James Douglas even includes him taking the heart of Robert the Bruce to Santiago de Compostela prior to him being slain in the battle of Teba in which he bore the heart into battle in a locket around his neck. Note also that Robert the Bruce also descended from the same genetic stock as King Sigurd and all of the subsequent Earls of Orkney.

An interesting geographic twist may lend credence to the notion that some Scots nobles were Knights of Santiago. The octagonal baptistery of the Cathedral of Santiago de Compostela may be used to form an arc on the globe that extends to Rosslyn Chapel. This octagon "points to" Rosslyn Chapel which was built by a Knight of Santiago. It is also showing regard to a prime meridian that was created by William Sincliar.

Parts of the saga of James Douglas also infers that the heart of the Bruce may have later been interred at Santiago de Compostela though the common history tells us it is located at Melrose Abbey not far from Rosslyn Chapel. Interestingly Sir James Douglas was named for Santiago via being named for his uncle James Stewart who in turn was known to value Santiago de Compostela and the entire culture of St. James. Yet another strong piece of evidence that supports the notion that all the Templar confusion in association with Henry Sinclair and Rosslyn Chapel is a mistaken value of Santiago and the lore of Scota in Galicia. Beyond the similarity of their icons and symbols there may exist political reasons as to why this version of the story was not told later in history.

Sigurd's exploits in the Holy Land were what one would think a band of fighting men from Scandinavia could accomplish during this post Viking era of the Norman Conquest of England. They served King Baldwin in many military capacities with great success and after a period of three years Sigurd departed the Levant and travelled to Constantinople under the protection of one of the last Byzantine rulers. This episode of the travels of King Sigurd supplies us with the amazing story of the Viking Varangian Guards of the Byzantine Emperor. As part of his bargain with the Emperor Sigurd left a division of his elite troops to serve as bodyguards for the Byzantine Emperor. Runic graffiti in Hagia Sophia in Istanbul verifies this historical footnote.

The establishment of the Varangian Guards also seems to have continued the use of Scottish and Scandinavian bodyguards that was also practiced by none other than Charlemagne himself in the 8th century. The tradition and influence of personal bodyguards to monarchs would also later extend to the Cavalier culture of Virginia and the presence of Wilhelm Bruce bodyguard of Napoleon later in Gold Rush era California. Again note that the entire saga of Sigurd's journeys in the Holy Land took place several years before the establishment of the Knights Templar.

It is within this framework of history that Haakon Paulsson would visit the Holy Land in penance for murdering Magnusson on the altar of a Church in Orkney. As further penance Haakon would build the Orphir Round Kirk. Haakon's trip to the Holy Land and his construction of the Orphir Round Church of St. Nicholas was also prior to the establishment of the vaunted Knights Templar. It appears that all of the history and imagery that is recorded in the meridian of the Orphir Round Kirk and later repeated at Rosslyn Chapel is not a result of any involvement with the Knights Templar.

Other odd coincidences associated with the Orphir Round Kirk include the presence of two rune stones. One of them includes a portion of the Lord's Prayer. The other stone may supply us with an interesting link to a theme seen at the famous Rennes le Chateau mystery.

The second stone includes an inscription in runes that is interpreted "This is a bad Church." This is strangely similar to the inclusion of "This Place is Terrible" over the entrance to the Chapel at Rennes le Chateau. It is possible that both inscriptions are referring to the story of Jacob's Ladder. Upon his return to earth Jacob was known to have said that "This place is terrible" in comparison to heaven. This theme is often misinterpreted as meaning something else. Haakon Paulson's association with his pilgrimage to Jerusalem may supply us with a rationale as to why this rune is included at the Orphir Church of St. Nicolas on Orkney. Is this a coincidence or are the two places connected via the Arcadian theme so early in history?

The Orphir Round Kirk does resemble the plan of the Temple Church in London as both structures were inspired by the Church of the Holy Sepulcher in Jerusalem at different times for different reasons. Given this history it is clear that if any Knighthood is associated with these exploits it is the personal bodyguard of King Sigurd and their descendants or more obviously the

58

imagery and symbols of the Knights of Santiago that is repeated on the Danish flag today. The symbols and imagery of the Knights of the Garter values St. George and more closely resembles the heraldry of the Knights Templar. These simple factors and a total ignorance of the historical background of the Earls of Orkney may have contributed to the views of many that the Knights Templar are associated with not only the Sinclair family but the Battle of Bannockburn.

If there were Knights at Bannockburn displaying "Templar Crosses" then this would also point to Scandinavian help and not necessarily that of the Knights Templar. Robert the Bruce was of the same Norwegian descent as the Earls of Orkney. King Sigurd included a Greek "Templar Cross" on coinage commemorating his Crusade prior to the establishment of the Knights Templar. A later rejection of the tenets of the Latin Church in England and Scotland may have also contributed to this muddying of the historical waters in favor of a more desirable story.

These factors may have also contributed later to much of the speculation that the Newport Tower is of Norse origin when in fact it was built by Benedict Arnold or the Easton's who the common history states as its creator. Given this it appears that a coincidence in the form of the Newport Tower resembling a Round Kirk may have later been used as an argument bolstering the assumption that Norse interests had built it long ago thus supporting England's claim to that region. All of this may boil down to a rejection of the Catholic Church by specific factions in early America thus linking us to a rejection of the accomplishments of Columbus. This may be easy to understand when the true story includes the many heroic exploits of men who fought in the Holy Land for the glory of Church of Rome and the Latin Kingdom. As this story unfolds it may become obvious that the notion of the Newport Tower being a round kirk did not evolve until after 1700.

The Knights Templar may serve as a potent symbol of a rejection of the tenets of the Church thus the reason they may have had many things attributed to them after the date they supposedly no longer existed. Many of these false notions have made them alternately scape goats and heroes. This may also be why an attempt to portray a man like Henry Sinclair as a Knights Templar after the time they had been persecuted has been adapted by many people. It is in this manner that history is distorted and changed to match the political and religious views of a given era.

Henry Sinclair was likely a Knight of the Tomb (Santiago) and not a Knights Templar. The term "Knight of the Tomb" is also featured in Philip Sidney's work "Arcadia" in the section that had been written by William Alexander 1st Earl of Stirling! Alexander used this term in association with the "Dark Knight" that is reminiscent of the figure of Sir James Douglas mentioned earlier.

His heritage and association with Scotland in addition to his Norwegian Royal blood at a time Scotland was not governed by England may also attest to this truth. Many sources point to a lack of involvement on the part of the Knights Templar in Scandinavia during their entire existence and the history of the Sinclair family and the Earls of Orkney would not reflect any involvement with this Order as a result of that view. Rosslyn Chapel is telling you the story of the sagas and their association with North America.

The portion of the book "Arcadia" amended by William Alexander of Stirling refers to a "Dark Knight" and "Black Knight" thus giving us an image associated with Sir James "The Black" Douglas. Alexander also refers to this character in the book as being a member of the "Order of the Tomb." Given his knowledge of this it may be that even Alexander himself was a Knight of Santiago. Later we will see a woman who is said to be related to him named Maria de Salazar having a surprising impact on the legacy of the Oak Island Treasure and Nova Scotia history at large.

Is it possible that a chance resemblance between the Newport Tower and the Orphir Round Kirk inspired later people to promote this structure as being part of an earlier period of history? Who could have come up with such an idea in the early history of Newport Rhode Island? Though it is possible the Newport Tower is of an older origin there are many things about the history of Newport Rhode Island that suggest that these legends had been applied to the Tower later.

The Reverend Robert Honeyman of Scotland was the very first Episcopal minister in Newport Rhode Island. Rev. Honeyman came from the same storied line of ecclesiastical figures that had produced our Robert Honeyman of Magdalen College, and the Bishop of Orkney Andrew Honeyman. Quite a coincidence in any possible legacy connecting the Newport Tower to the real Rose Line of the Orphir Round Kirk. Though there are no records of Rev. Honeyman influencing views of the Newport Tower it is within the realm of possibility that given his heritage he would have recognized this form of architecture as being similar to the famous Round Kirk of Orkney. Here in the person of Reverend Honeyman we have a direct link to this family and its Orcadian legacy including Rosslyn Chapel, the Orphir Round Kirk and much more.

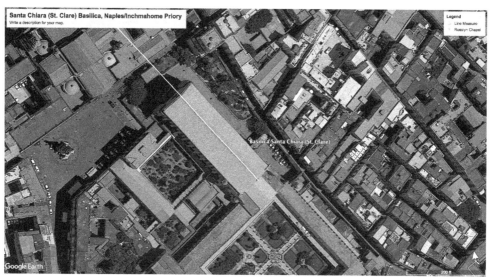

The orientation of Basilica Santa Chiara in Naples "points to" Inchmahome Priory in Scotland. There are direct connections between the families of St. Chiara And Inchmahome.

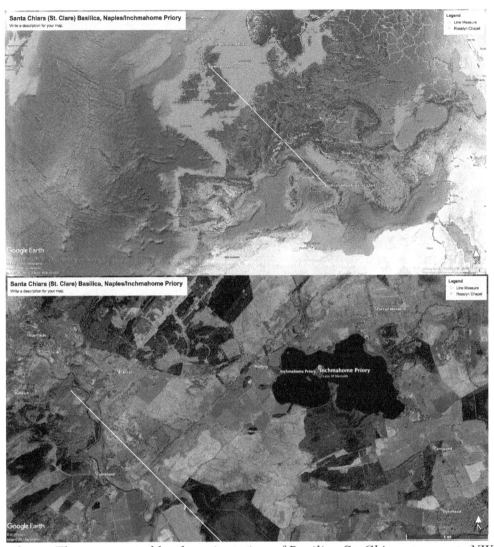

Above: The arc created by the orientation of Basilica St. Chiara transects NW to reach near Inchamahome priory. The history of Robert Artois and the Ninth Crusade may apply here.

A coin minted by King Sigurd the Crusader showing a "Templar Cross" from before the time the Knights Templar existed. Both Sigurd and Haakon Paulsson Earl of Orkney visited the Holy Land prior to the establishment of the Knights Templar.

Chapter 6: Shugborough Hall and its follies: The Tower of the Winds and Shepherd's Monument

As history progressed from the time of William Sincliar and others it may be possible to see the development of the use of a prime meridian in the same way it connects Rosslyn and Orphir. Eventually this practice seemed to have become the provenance of wealthy and landed individuals who expressed these values by building homes and architectural follies that harkened back to the Tower of the Winds of Athens and other temporally sensitive structures from antiquity. In short what William Sinclair had done in building Rosslyn became a kind of fad among the gentry of Europe. Those who took part in the Grand Tour of the continent seemed to have been taught these concepts as part of their education.

It seems that the theme of Arcadia is involved in many different mysteries that may be designed to teach the seeker the truth of hidden or forgotten history. Two of the more popular conundrums using the Arcadian theme are Rennes le Chateau and Shugbrough Hall and its Shepherds Monument. Many have speculated a connection between Rennes le Chateau and Shugborough Hall while others have even speculated associations between both of these mysteries and Oak Island.

Here we will examine Shugborough and its architectural follies which may have been left to help us solve any attached mysteries. The legacies of many powerful early American families may be connected to a value of these concepts as we have seen in the form of the Stafford's, Alexanders, Lee's, Washington's, Jefferson, Adams, Madison, and others. It seems that these people may have known of and valued the secrets of Arcadia and its utopian ideals. In fact Sir Francis Bacon's "New Atlantis" has many overtones of the Arcadian ideal. Did they in fact leave us a trail of breadcrumbs that lead us to historical truths or do these questions lead us to hidden treasure of some sort?

History says that it would not have been possible for Constantine and Charlemagne to align structures with the accuracy displayed in the spatial relationships of buildings they constructed or valued. Later in the eighteenth century the use of the sextant, octant, and nautical clock made it possible for anyone trained in the art of navigation to execute these associations. It is no surprise that they used this new technology to set up axis and templum as they seemed to believe the ancients had done. In fact many aspects of this study reveal that they not only suspected this was true but actually had proof that it was true.

Admiral George Anson is one of the most unsung heroes of England. Anson was the third Englishman to circumnavigate the Globe. In so doing he captured a treasure Galleon of Spain near the Philippines and returned to England incredibly wealthy and well known. Anson was granted both a Lordship and was made Lord of the Admiralty as well. His exploits may have inspired the Horatio Hornblower saga of 'Master and Commander.' Many parts of the book and subsequent movie seem to reference Anson and his cat and mouse game with a French sea captain all the way through the Atlantic and on to the Pacific coast of South America. Anson lost four ships and nearly seven hundred men but still emerged to circumnavigate and bring home a fabulous prize.

Even though Anson was a hero and fabulously wealthy he already had been the Earl of Litchfield and had inherited his estate Shugborough Hall from his father. George's brother Thomas was also an incredibly well educated and resourceful individual as well who had a large appreciation of history and the classics. Shugborough served as Thomas' residence even though Admiral Anson paid for improvements to the estate. George Anson would later obtain an estate closer to London not far from Sir Francis Dashwood and Sir Francis Bacon's estates. Moor Park would serve as the Admiral's home and possesses some interesting aspects similar to Shugborough Hall. Both Shugborough Hall and Moor Park would feature reproductions of the Tower of the Winds in Athens.

The title of the Earl of Lichfield had a grand heritage including forebears of Confederate General Robert E. Lee and members of the Stewart line of English and Scottish kings. In fact relatives of future United States president's John Adams and John Quincy Adams would marry into the Anson line and assume the title Earl of Litchfield shortly after Admiral Anson's death in 1767. This is curious in light of the Adam's "accidental" pilgrimage on the Camino de Santiago as Secretary of State to France. As we may see this family or title included a reverence for Santiago de Compostela and the Way of St. James and other places of interest here.

The title of the Earl of Lichfield also included an association with Staffordshire where Shugborough is located. The Anson family had intermarried with the Earls of Stafford thus connecting them to the Stafford's of Newport Rhode Island and the Tower there. This family association may indicate that the Anson's also had knowledge of the truth of the Newport Tower. As we may see the Anson's may have been aware of the secrets of many places like Newport, Charleston, Shugborough, Stirling Castle, Rennes le Chateau and Santiago de Compostela. Both of their Tower of the Winds replicas may have been situated to "point to" many of these places on the globe. Here we may see how the Tower of the Winds at Shugborogh and West Wycombe served the same symbolic and practical function as the Newport Tower.

The octagonal form of the towers they constructed were emblematic of an octagonal scheme that may have indicated associated places on the globe. In cartography this kind of plan would use the tower as the center of the map somewhat similar to what can be viewed in map using a polar projection that displays the entire world. An earlier concept in cartography known as a cosmography also serves a similar purpose. Both of these kind of maps shows the rest of the world in relation to a center point. In this case the center is the location of the Tower of the Winds replicas that seemed to fulfill the same purpose as the original octagonal Tower of the Winds in Athens.

Lady Anson was also said to have been quite an appreciator of art and somewhat of an artist herself. The interior of the house contained many features with classical mythological and esoteric themes. Anson had the main house of Shugborough Hall redesigned to resemble what some say is the Temple of Jupiter at Baalbek. This would echo his friend Sir Francis Dashwood's appreciation of that place in the construction of his West Wycombe Estate as well.

In fact both men would create an array of architectural follies on their estates that would have classical themes. Thomas Jefferson would later appreciate the same Palladian style of architecture as the Anson's and Dashwood in the form of his estates Monticello and Poplar Forest. During this age men of means expressed their beliefs in the form of architectural follies with esoteric themes. This tradition did make its way to many influential people in United States history as well.

One of the follies that Anson had built on both Shugborough and Moor Park estates was a large-scale reproduction of the Tower of the Winds in Athens with some Greek revival English style thrown in. First we will examine the Tower of the Winds at Shugborough Hall.

Amazingly Anson's Tower of the Winds does function as an axis just as the Tower of the Winds in Athens and points to two of the most famous ancient sites in England if not the entire world. Admiral Anson was said to have entertained his friends while playing cards in the Tower at Shugborough. Anson was quite the gambler and even the borough of Ansonborough in Charleston South Carolina was named for him after he won it in a card game. Anson was stationed in Charleston as a young naval officer. Interestingly Charleston would later be the birthplace of the Scottish Rite of Freemasonry. There are also some amazing associations between Charleston, the Drayton or de Vere family, and Oak Island Nova Scotia.

Anson the navigator may have had a unique appreciation of the true function of the Tower of the Winds. As we shall see some of his friends and associates had direct knowledge of the Tower of the Winds and its ancient function. His axis also seems to define many places pertinent to the study of the Holy Grail or Mary Magdalene. Other azimuths from the Shugborough Tower of the Winds point to the Hill of Tara (Lia Fail), Lincoln Cathedral, Burrow Mump, Willersly Castle, and Ponferrada Fortress along the Way of St. James in Spain. The other follies on the estate also seem to possess significant directional information.

When one creates an azimuth or line on the globe using the Anson's Shugborough Tower of the Winds southerly orientation it transects the middle of Avebury Circle and the center of Stonehenge! Anson is pointing to Avebury and Stonehenge using his axis! TwoTower of the Winds that point to Avebury including the original in Athens! This suggests that not only did Anson have the skills and knowledge to execute this association but also knew of the association between Avebury and the Tower of the Winds in Athens! This line of reasoning would have also led to the conclusion that the Tower of the Winds is indeed descendent of the true function of Avebury Circle.

The Anson's are telling us in their secret language: "Look what I am showing you. I am doing what the builders of The Tower of the Winds, Stonehenge and Avebury were doing!" "I realized one straight line from Shugborough to Stonehenge would cross Avebury so I built a structure to display this relationship!" or "I knew the Cistercian monks of England or the previous occupants of Lichfield had arranged this and I built the Tower of the Winds to display it."
"Wait until you see where the other follies I built point!"

What would compel Admiral Anson and his brother Thomas to build a series of structures on his property that have hidden meanings? The Anson family is said to have been Knights Hospitaller of St. John for generations and members of many other secret societies and men's clubs from which a value of ancient architecture would have come. Thomas Anson inherited Shugborough after Admiral Anson passed and was known to have been a member of the Dillettante Society, which had connections, and members in common with the famous Hellfire Club, which he may have also been a member of. Both of these organizations may have been associated with Brooke's a well known gentlemen's club in London. Moor Park the Admiral's home near London is but a short distance from West Wycombe.

The Tower of the Winds at the Shugborough Estate.

The Anson's chose architect James "Athenian" Stuart to design many of the follies that are located at Shugborough. Beginning in 1750 Stuart created The Tower of the Winds, The Chinese House (pagoda); a triumphal arch based on Hadrian's, a Doric Temple, and the cats monument. It stands to reason that Stuart would have been aware of the secrets contained in the monuments he was building. Stuart was almost single handedly responsible for the Greek Revival movement popular in mid eighteenth century England if not all of Europe. He had actually travelled to Athens and other ancient sites and precisely recorded much of the architecture and art there. He published his results in his book "The antiquities of Athens" which would influence the world of art and culture for the next two hundred years. His value of classic art and architecture may have created the impetus for the creation of groups like the Pre-Raphaelite Brotherhood in the nineteenth century.

It is appropriate for a man named Stuart to take part in this activity at Shugborough. This is the European form of the well known Scottish name Stewart. Many of the structures discussed in this book are the result of this family's effort and it is no coincidence that earlier Earls of Lichfield were Stewarts. James Stuart is one in a long line of inter related family that traveled the world to unlock the secrets of antiquity. It was almost as if this activity was part of their destiny and the origin myths of Scotland's Celtic and Egyptian heritage would seem to support this idea. Traveling scholars and mystics like Michael Scot and James Bruce may have inspired Stuart and others like Dashwood and the Anson's. There is no proven family legacy between James "Athenian" Stuart and the Stewarts of Scotland and Lichfield but his involvement here may indicate some truth to this relation as well. As this story unfolds further we may see that the "Arcadia" being referred to at Shugborogh Hall is a veiled reference to Scotland.

The southerly line points an azimuth from the Anson's Tower of the Winds that transects through the center of Avebury and Stonehenge.
8

What of the additional monuments of Shugborough Hall? One in particular has gained notice as a possible clue or coded information source to the object that many consider the Holy Grail. In turn other mysteries are associated. In fact the mystery of Anson's follies may include or be part

67

of other conundrums such as The Kensington Rune Stone, Rennes le Chateau, Lincoln Cathedral, The Lia Fail, and Santiago de Compostela. At the least we may see the same tradition being carried out by associated people over a long span of time.

One of the most enduring myths of western civilization is that of the Holy Grail in its many different interpretations. Opinions on what the Holy Grail is vary from the cup of Christ to technical knowledge sown on the earth by aliens meant to be deciphered by the human race someday. Fascination with this concept has also spawned phenomena involving the definition and search for what the Holy Grail actually is. Some groups may have valued this Quest to such a degree that it was used as a right of initiation. The entire concept may have originated from ancient techniques involving navigation, astronomy and the legal definition of property. Through time men like Constantine the Great and Charlemagne may have helped to define it in its modern context. Others would choose to portray this technical craft as being 'magic' in a cargo cult fashion.

The tradition of the Tower of the Winds both in Athens and Shugborough infers a grand tradition at work. In the Roman world this would have involved establishing a temple or Axis Mundi that marked the center of a Templum or sphere of influence of those that created it. The use or knowledge of the templum would have taken skills that the public at large does not possess or intentionally would not be taught. This secret alone may explain many of the so called "Catch 22's" or inexplicable events in history. This tradition may have in turn led the entire activity to being the exclusive pursuit of the elite and powerful personages of history. Massive amounts of effort and planning have gone into how and why this activity is planned and executed. In turn many wondrous and terrible truths may be exposed.

The initiatory rite of what may be termed the Quest may have been part of the process of becoming a member of a strictly secret order in which only the most influential or skilled people in the world would be inducted. Eventually this activity may have become so revered that members built structures or monuments that may have had hidden or secret

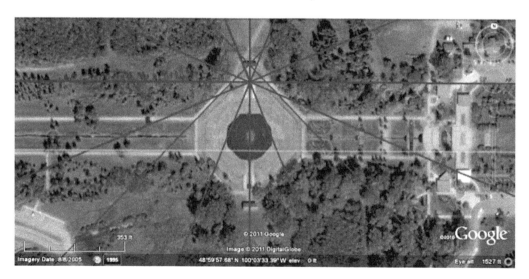

The Axis of the International Peace Garden on the Border of the United States of America and Canada.

attributes that could only be recognized by other members. By examining the architecture and occult meaning of arrays of monuments that were built in response to this activity many interesting and sensational differences are inferred when compared to the standard history of a given region or culture. It is possible that over time several different groups of people became aware of this tradition and practiced it over time. Could this be Fulcanelli's 'Brotherhood of Heliopolis?'

Some of the most enduring myths of England, Scotland, North America and France may all have an intertwined thread of occult evidence that would suggest relics and talismans were hidden in even spatial association with each Axis Mundi that was created. Places like Rennes Le Chateau France, Oak Island Nova Scotia, Washington D.C., Williamsburg Virginia, Newport Rhode Island, Kensington Minnesota, Stonehenge, Avebury Circle, Rosslyn Chapel, and as we see here Shugborough Hall England, may all have an intertwined theme or message that tells a story of truth and religion. In many cases they even may physically point the way to one of the other sites or clues involved in the tale.

This amazing story is linked together through a series of men and women who all seemed to have shared the same values and philosophy. The structures they created contained directional information hidden in aspects of their construction that lead the way to further clues somewhat like a map in a Pirate movie or novel.

If one examines the value placed on a single point on the earth that seems to have been valued by a wide array of luminaries and secret societies a true history of North America and the secret philosophy of those who created it may become apparent. The site of the modern day International Peace Garden on the border of the United States of America and Canada may hold the key to understanding the true history of those two countries.
Patience.

The Shugborough link is coming.

Here situated neatly between Manitoba and North Dakota on the 49th parallel is a park dedicated to peace and friendship between the two nations. The actual reason this point is valued on the globe is a secret and amazing phenomenon. In the process we may see a lineage spanning the gulf of time back to Dr. John Dee, Charlemagne, Frederick II, and Constantine the Great all associated with the International Peace Garden.

This point on the earth marked by an octagonal fountain at the International Peace Garden (IPG) may represent the earliest axis mundi or place from which to map in North America. A variety of talismans and monuments may have been left at even 45 degree true north increments as measured from the octagon of the IPG. The legacy and heritage of those that created this monument will expose many details of history that have been overlooked or ignored. In addition

69

one very early colonial octagon in the United States is intimately linked to the International Peace Garden.

The famous Kensington Rune Stone lies at very close to this angular orientation with regard to the IPG axis at 135 degrees true north from the IPG's fountain. The octagon of the IPG points the way to the Kensington Stone. Author Scott Wolter (The Hooked X) speculates that this stone was left by Scandinavian explorers in 1362 as evidenced by that date being inscribed on the stone and his professional analysis of the weathering patterns present. The stone was found within three miles of an azimuth or line on the globe created using the IPG axis as a datum or point of measurement. Close enough to consider that those using star sightings to navigate would be able to calculate given a margin of error also involving location and logistical concerns such as individual user error, geographic features and topography. The Kensington Rune stone may have been left here to mark the extent of a claim that these early explorers were making with regard to the future location of the IPG.

The octagon of The Dome of the Rock also points an evenly divided azimuth to a point about seven miles south of the said discovery site of the Kensington Rune stone. This same azimuth transects or crosses Alexandria, Minnesota where the Kensington Rune Stone Museum and hence the stone are stored today. Is it possible that the people who left the Kensington Rune stone were attempting to place it at the intersection azimuths or rays emanating from the Axes of the International Peace Garden and the Dome of the Rock?

Remember the IPG may represent an axis left by earlier explorers that the Kensington Rune may have been placed to mark as well. Some evidence also suggests that early Portuguese and Spanish pilots would reference the landfalls were land was claimed with regard to the location of the Dome of the Rock.

They would claim property at points transected or crossed by one of the sixteen evenly divided octagonal divisions of the Dome of the Rock. The claiming and discovery of Mexico and the Philippines seem to bear this theory some relevance. The Solomon Islands are likely named such for this reason.

Other theories espouse a solstice event at the Newport Tower in Rhode Island pointing the way to the Kensington Stone. In fact the octagonal orientation of the structure can also be used to create an azimuth or arc on the globe that extends from Newport to the stone. A modern octagonal plaza around the Newport Tower also echoes this association. The octagonal form of the Newport Tower points to the Kensington Rune every day of the year all day. Not just on the Solstices.

There is also a sandstone pillar or so called "Hoodoo" located on the Milk River in Alberta that serves the same function of boundary marker as the Kensington Stone. This sandstone pillar lays less than six miles from the 49th parallel and the U.S./Canada border. This is the same latitude as the IPG and may suggest this pillar was carved there and was meant to be associated with the axis left by earlier explorers. Again using celestial navigation techniques may produce a small margin of error. Those who left the stone in this arrangement may have been aware of the axis and used it to hide this valuable item. It may be that the sandstone pillars along the river were close enough and representative of a monument for them to use it as such.

It is also possible that both the Kensington Stone and the sandstone pillar were left as boundary markers for the Hudson's Bay Company as the boundaries of this company's claim match the location of both the Kensington Stone and the sandstone pillar. Alternately the Hudson's Bay Company knew of their existence and used them to define their domain. Prince Rupert the creator of the H.B.C. was both nobility of England and Germany. Prince Rupert does have a lineage that includes members of the Stewarts and Douglas' of Scotland. He certainly would have had the pedigree to have been made aware of such hidden information including the existence of both the sandstone pillar and Kensington stone.

The works of two early botanists and Linnean Society of London members Pehr Kalm and Alexander Von Humboldt wrote of the La Verendrye party's recovery of the stone. The narrative collected from La Verendrye states that the senior La Verendrye then gave the stone to Jesuit priests who took it to Montreal. From there it was put aboard a ship bound for France.
After this point the stone disappears from history. There is absolutely no evidence this stone was seen again my Admiral Anson or anyone else. At this point this stone disappears from history though theories exist of it being hidden somewhere in England and other places. Amazingly at the end of the saga Admiral Anson was the person said to have had possession of the stone. If true did the Anson's leave any clues as to the truth of this tale? If the Anson's were secretly Jacobite sympathizers is it possible they knew the stone was on this ship prior to capturing it? English Naval records indicate that Anson himself did not intercept the incoming fleet from Canada. The time frame during which the stone is said to have been captured only included one of Anson's Captains capturing two ships bound for France for repair. To some historians this incident may translate to Anson capturing the stone since he was in command ultimately. Perhaps one of these vessels carried the stone and it was given to Anson?

The incident which may have started this legend did include a battle between Admiral Anson and Admiral Jonquierre of France. This battle was during the French fleets return voyage to Canada via the West Indies and not arriving in France. This battle is known as the Battle of Cape Finesterre. Several of the accounts of the battle include much of the French fleet being destroyed or captured. Anson himself captured one of the French Captains identified as the Marquis de St. George.

These accounts go on to say that these men later became life long friends and that St. George stayed with the Anson's at Shugborough Hall for an extended period. Perhaps M. St. George possessed the stone and surrendered it to Anson? There is absolutely no record of this beyond theory. Were Anson and St. George members of the same order or society? It is easy to speculate that this man's or the stone's capture may have been planned. Perhaps the appearance of St. George fueled the many myths and legends that the Anson's were friends with and frequently entertained St. Germain himself. If it is true that the more important battle was the French leaving France then something is wrong with the notion that the stone was captured inbound. If it was captured outbound then it may appear to more of a 'set up.' Either way it makes sense that no clear indications of the stone are revealed in the common history. At this point it appears that this strange missing stone may have only once been a boundary marker for the Rupert's Land and Hudson's Bay border and thus of interest to the Comte de Maurepas and others. This may especially apply if the La Verendrye's had taken the stone left by the HBC and moved it further west to expand the claim they now controlled. Many things do not add up in the entire history of this missing stone in relation to the border of Louisiana and Rupert's Land.

Many of the standard histories of La Verendrye and sons state that they also may have found the "Verendrye Rune stone" near what is today Minot, North Dakota. Minot lies at an even 225 degree true north heading from the octagon of the IPG. What is terribly interesting about this tale is the fact that on the opposite or 45 degree true north heading lays Preston England one of the last places where history records the Stone of Destiny being in Jacobite hands some of whom were said to be ancestors of Admiral Anson. "Preston" is also the Hebrew word inscribed on the sandstone pillar once thought to hold the stone.

This is a spectacular coincidence. It may be that this is the only reason the La Verendrye's included the Hebrew inscription when they moved the boundaries of the claim far to the west thus gaining a huge amount of land in one fail swoop that could not be disputed. There are many reasons why during this era the Jacobite Hudson's Bay Company would have made the French privy to all of this in an attempt to gain a larger legal claim that the original stone in Minot marked. The Jacobites naturally during this era were allied with French interests that even extended to the alliance between the fledgling colonies and France during the revolution. Later this same kind of skullduggery displayed in the use of these stones to inspire legend and folklore in the minds of the public was manipulated by the Society of the Cincinnati that existed in both France and the United States. This is but a theory.

Is it possible that the entire story of the "Verendrye Rune stone" in Minot was developed simply to lead one to this association? If not this may represent an amazing coincidence. The subsequent interviews of La Verendrye by Pehr Kalm that establish he recovered the stone in the vicinity of the sandstone pillar do not mention any additional rune found by that family near Minot or anywhere else. Another curious clue that may be interpreted many ways. The same interview also does not clearly establish the location that the stone was found at all. Anywhere. This story combines to include one missing stone; one missing sandstone pillar in Minot; One known sandstone pillar on the Milk River in Alberta which also includes Ogham script, and a great deal of mythology and folklore associated with what may have been a boundary claim marker. There is not a great deal of evidence beyond gross speculation and misinterpretation of the historical record that anyone ever saw this stone again after it was given to the Jesuit Priests as the La Verendrye's stated.

Anson and the Marquis de St. George were known to frequently play the violin together and St. George was indeed well known for his musical skills. His family is rumored to have been part of the Knights Templar for many generations. It is likely that this Marquis de St. George was not the famous African American musician and military figure from the French Revolution and early Napoleaonic era though his description has many things in common with the Marquis. Many myths and legends have sprung up through the years that the Stone of Destiny may be located somewhere on Anson's Shugborough Estate in central England. The famous book "Holy Blood, Holy Grail" by Baingent, Leigh, and Lincoln identified the estate as one possible location of the Stone today. Some of the secrets of Shugborough are undoubtedly locked up in interpretive analysis of the follies on the estate.

To many this entire story may boil down to the secret encoded in one of the Anson's follies. The folly known as The Shepherd's Monument is pointed to as being related to this mystery and also possibly the mystery of Rennes le Chateau. The lore surrounding this monument states that "it may lead one to the Holy Grail." The monument displays a stone relief of Poussin's famous painting "Et in Arcadia Ego" (in arcadia I am) or "The Shepherds of Arcadia" that was featured prominently in the Rennes Le Chateau mystery and also featured in "Holy Blood, Holy Grail." Other evidence reveals that this statue may be also associated with the International Peace Garden.

The Shepherds Monument is a relatively small memorial that includes a mirror image bas relief copy of Poussin's "The Shepherds of Arcadia" painting. The rendering on the Shepherds Monument also includes a strange small casket or reliquary atop the tomb from the original painting. The bas relief of "Shepherds" is surrounded on both sides by what appear to be sandstone pillars that may harken to the ones seen in the saga of the La Verendrye's and the missing stone. Still these sandstone pillars also resemble those seen at Montserrat in Catalonia. This monastery is one of the places said to be the resting place of the Holy Grail itself. Interestingly the linear array of the Paris Observatory points an arc on the globe directly to the monastery that is surrounded by sandstone pillars very similar to those depicted on the Shepherds Monument of Shugborough.

Our investigation here will center on similarities in the theme and style of the Poussin work to those seen in other properties that were owned by Admiral Anson. There may be a story being told in metaphor and artwork by the Anson's that has been overlooked due to the media and public preoccupation with the mystery of the coded portion of the Shepherds Monument. Other elements of art owned by Admiral Anson may shed a great deal of light on this story later. If one measures the orientation of the Shepherds Monument itself using Google Earth digital globe a startling association becomes apparent. From plan view the statue appears as a small rectangle that is large enough to measure.

Reminder: If a heading is plotted using the statue's northwest orientation the resulting line or azimuth on the globe transects the north Atlantic and Canada directly to the center of the octagonal fountain at the International Peace Garden on the Border of the United States and Canada! In a previous expedition the La Verendrye's had navigated to Minot after having first gone to Turtle Mountain the future site of the Peace Garden. This plan mimics the angular association of the two places today which is 225 deg. true north an even octagonal designation.

Now we have the Kensington and Verendrye Stone, The Newport Tower, Powder Magazine, and Poplar Forest all related to the IPG as well as the Shepherds Monument. Given the tale of the Stone of Destiny and Admiral Anson it is likely that this association is intentional. To put this in context the Powder Magazine in Colonial Williamsburg that also points to the IPG was built long before any of the follies at Shugborough Hall. Likewise the Newport Tower is older than both places. It is possible that there are earlier older axes in Europe that point to the IPG as well.

The Shepherds Monument from plan view. Line points or leads to the International Peace Garden Axis.

The same azimuth from the above picture (yellow line) on its way to the IPG.

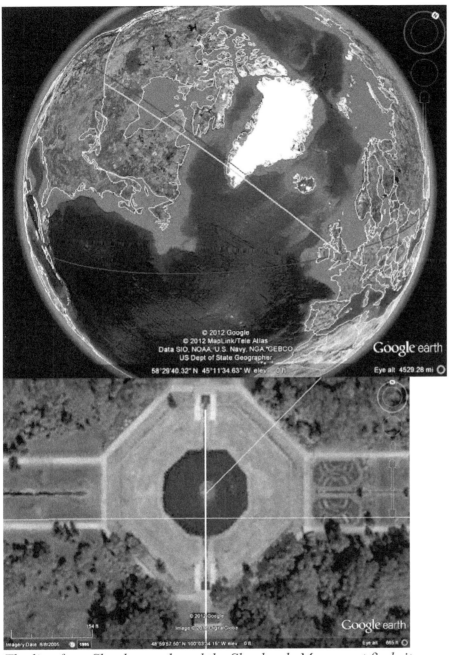

The line from Shugborough and the Shepherds Monument finds its way to the IPG.

There is something very special about the current location of the IPG. We have seen previously how the octagonal Newport Tower points the way to the Kensington stone and how the IPG does the same. Colonial Governor of Virginia Spotswood also seems to have oriented the octagonal Powder Magazine in Williamsburg (once used as an octagonal church in a Byzantine and Templar tradition) to point to the International Peace Garden. The more modern builders of the Peace Garden built a Masonic compass and Square shaped building there that is oriented to point an azimuth to the Powder Magazine in Williamsburg. The Powder Magazine points to this

75

building and it points back! (More will be revealed about the International Peace Garden and this relationship in subsequent chapters). Of course all wrapped up in this is the fact that Thomas Jefferson may have been taught or initiated into this tradition by the example of the Powder Magazine.

It seems all of these men that were possibly members of various orders of Knighthood knew of the significance of the International Peace Garden's future location. They must have been aware of its use as an axis by explorers that claimed North America over 130 years before the voyages of Columbus. Is it possible that the same explorers had left something in addition to the axis it seems they had created? Or had it all been set up later to resemble something that was much older?

The International Peace Garden is in fact a kind of copy of the array of Temple of Peace of Rome. The Temple of Peace of Rome is part of a linear array of fora including those of Julius Caesar, Trajan, and Augustus. This array of architecture may be the inspiration for later linear parks and malls like that of Williamsburg and Washington D.C. Amazingly the linear orientation of the Temple of Peace of Rome and the fora of the Emperors points an arc on the globe that leads directly to the International Peace Garden. Even part of the landscaping of the International Peace Garden resembles the original plan view of the Temple of Peace of Rome. The Temple of Peace of Rome once housed the Temple Treasure from Jerusalem that had been captured by Titus in about 70A.D. This treasure may be the basis for many of the myths being examined in this book and other written by this author. So. It is interesting that the Shepherds Monument seems to point the way to the International Peace Garden and its possible associations.

Three additional monuments located at Shugborough seem to point the way to important places in this mystery. The Doric Temple styled after that type of Greek structure seems to have a north to south orientation that points an azimuth on the Globe directly to the Cathedral of Santiago de Compostela and the Sepulcher of St James. This may be related to a value of the concept of St. James whose sepulcher or place of burial is at the Cathedral there. St. James' Sepulcher is the subject of the pilgrimage to Santiago de Compostela that has been going on for over one thousand years.

Santiago de Compostela may represent an extremely secret and important influence on the Jacobite movement throughout its existence and later the creation of the United States. Given what may be concerning St. James and the Camino in both historical and alchemical terms it seems obvious that the Anson's were also paying homage to the concepts and history involved with the saga of Santiago. All of this coded and metaphorical secrecy infers that they may have believed an alternate truth to what lies in the Sepulcher of St. James in Santiago de Compostela. Also supporting this tradition of respect for the Way of St. James is the fact that one of the azimuths directed from the Tower of the Winds at Shugborough Hall points the way to Ponferrada Fortress along the Camino de Santiago. This was thought to be a 'Templar' stronghold throughout the age of the Moorish invasion of Iberia.

Many alternate researchers and grail theorists believe that the Sepulcher of St. James in Santiago de Compostela actually holds the remains of the brother of Christ James. The symbol of Santiago is also the scallop shell which many interpret as a symbol of Venus, Neptune, and Mary Magdalene. One of the most famous representations of this symbol may be in Botticelli's 'The Birth of Venus.' The presence of relics associated with the family of Christ may even extend to the remains of Mary Magdalene or others of her children at Santiago de Compostela as well.

Others relate the mysteries of Santiago to James the brother of Christ as well. Some sources do indicate that the Plantagenet family groups did value St. James as one of their forebears thus also fitting the "Blood of Christ" theories.

So just as Flamel and Fulcanelli would later understand we see a possible veneration on the part of the Anson's for the pilgrimage and its hidden meanings. The Anson's veneration of significant points in Galicia also echoes the very same value in the hexagon of Jacques Coeur and hinted at in Fulcanelli's "Mystery of the Cathedrals." Also not to be ignored is the association of the orders of Spanish Knights including Santiago, Calatrava, and Alcantara that existed in concept and form prior to the so called Knights Templar that the Anson's may have been associated with. The Moors never fully captured northern Spain and these men were the main reason.

The Knights of Calatrava were drawn from the ranks of Cistercian Monks and were known to sleep in their armor. They had been battling the Moors long before the beginning of the Crusades of the Kingdom of Jerusalem, or the creation of the Knights Templar. Many Knights of Calatrava lived a monastic existence for four days a week and were allowed to have wives and families. St. James in Latin is referred to as "Jacobus." The German and French forms also indicate a pronunciation like this. Interesting that the English version comes out James. One would assume that Jacob would be named thus in other languages. This 'Jacobite' culture and philosophy may have also been applied to those who supported James II in the so called Jacobite cause in England. Many speculate that the Jacobites after having been defeated in England fled to the Colonies and helped to begin the United States since they had a common enemy. Others speculate further that the Untied States was a Jacobite plan the entire time.

Not to be forgotten is this name's association with the biblical story of Jacob and 'Jacobs Ladder.' A tale that seems to have great relevance not only to modern Mason's but the story of the lost stone that Mr. Perry seeks. Mr. Parry believes the lost stone from the pillar in Canada may be hidden on the grounds of Shugborough possibly in the contrived ruins there.

Many clues seem to also point to Santiago de Compostela as the nadir of this mystery. Anson's ancestors were said to be Jacobites and many researchers claim that the Anson's and Dashwood were all Jacobites. Let's not forget that Anson 'captured the stone' during the battle of Cape Finesterre which is adjacent to Santiago de Compostela. The later name 'Jacobin' was associated with those who favored the French Revolution though many scholars say there is no connection between the 'Jacobites' and the 'Jacobins.' Many associate the Jacobite cause as being exclusively Catholic in nature. The record states that only twenty percent of 'Jacobites' were of the Catholic Faith and that many different social and political views were considered.

It is interesting that the Jacobites assumed the cultural identity and symbolism of the Camino de Santiago as part of their cause as well. In many ways English ties to Norman France and occupations of Northern Spain may have been part of the Jacobite culture all along. Some of the most ancient invaders around the region of Santiago include the Celts and later the Britons. Later even Germanic tribes would inhabit northern Spain.

The Roman port just south of Santiago was once named Irea Flavia for its Irish population. Subsequently the Britons invaded this part of Spain as well. The kilt and bagpipes are also part of the Galician culture as in Scotland and Greece. The creation myths of Scotland and Ireland involving Queen Scota dictate her presence in northern Spain for several generations before moving to the isles. In addition James II and Bonnie Prince Charlie center of the Jacobite cause were exiled in France.

In many ways France values the Camino de Santiago or Way of St. James as much as the Spanish do. The Patron Saint of France is St. James. In many ways the Camino de Santiago is truly an international place of importance. It is possible that the history and metaphors of the Camino became a secret type of language to these men and women.

The Triumphal Arch at Shugborough has long been an enigma of itself. It is easy to see why Admiral Anson would value or deserve such a monument given his exploits as sea. Its design is said to be based on the arch of Hadrian. Elements of the monument comprise a kind of personal pastiche of what are likely familiar symbols to Anson.

78

As his other follies do the Triumphal Arch seems to also have a hidden use as a directional device. This monument is oriented such that its longer axis may be used to create an arc on the globe that points to the octagon of the Cathedral in Girona, Spain. As we will see shortly this octagon in Girona is known as Charlemagne's Tower and also points to the International Peace Garden just as the Shepherd's Monument does. This monument also may hold some similar metaphorical secrets such as those included on the Shepherd's Monument. The Triumphal Arch may also be displayed in an enigmatic painting known as the 'altar painting' located in the Chapel of Rennes le Chateau. This relationship is displayed in the spatial relationship of Stirling Castle, Shugborough, and Rennes Le Chateau.

Some of the elements of the Triumphal Arch also seem to be clues or metaphors for the true philosophy of the Anson's. Two large roundel's or medallions are present on the arch just below the pediment portion of the monument. The left medallion is about 4 feet in diameter. It includes what appears to be a rendering of the Quinotaur or similar creature. This rendering differs from the standard in that what appears to be an image of Athena accompanied by an owl is riding the beast. Some sources state that the Quinotaur actually represented a hornless goat's head instead of a bull's head. The reason the goat is hornless comprises part of this version of the story. The rendering at Shugborough may also be interpreted as a lion's head. In any case more research will be needed to ascertain the meaning of this symbol to the Anson's. If it is indeed the Quinotaur then an association or value of the concept of Merovingian lineage is possible.

The roundel on the right is more easily interpreted. This medallion seems to have all of the elements of what may be termed a Jupiter Pole. These poles were once common in German territories that had been conquered by the Romans. In this case the Romans may have even been referencing the native value of the Irminsul pole. In any case a rendering of Hercules and Hermes were commonly displayed as part of four gods on each side of the base of a Jupiter Pole.

This is the case in this two-dimensional representation at Shugborough as well. This theme is also echoed in the central statue included in the pediment of the monument. This statue is comprised of a headless armored figure with his helmeted head at his feet. Propped against the figure's knee is a shield with the head of Medusa illustrated. The motif of this statue echoes the rendering of the Jupiter Pole with wing like elements extending laterally from the central area of the statue just as on the medallion's rendering of the pole itself. These images are repeated in other artwork owned by Anson that may reveal the truth about the Shepherds Monument and what it means.

To the left and right of the central figure are stone reliquaries with statues of Lord and Lady Anson atop them. This use of an architectural folly as a funerary symbol is also present at the West Wycombe Estate of Sir Francis Dashwood in the form of his hexagonal mausoleum. Most importantly a reliquary similar to these is one of the elements added to the rendering of 'Et in Arcadia Ego" included on the Shepherd's Monument. The reliquary seen atop the tomb in the piece does resemble those included on the Triumphal Arch.

The Chinese Pagoda at Shugborough Hall may in part be meant to commemorate Admiral

Anson's capture of the Manila Treasure Galleon during his circumnavigation. In a more clandestine manner it may display the Anson's value of Galicia, its Celtic influence in general and the ancient art of navigation more specifically. Shortly before his capture of the Galleon Anson spent an extended period in Macau China. This may have inspired him to later create a folly on his estate in this form. Though the theme of the architecture is Chinese the hidden aspect of this monument is much different. If an azimuth is extended on the globe at the northwest to southeast long axis orientation of this structure it extends directly to the Torre de Hercules ancient lighthouse in A Coruña Spain.

The Torre de Hercules originally known as Farum Brigantium is said to be the oldest continually operating lighthouse in the world. The Farum is a nod to the Pharos or Lighthouse of Alexandria. It was built in the second century likely by Trajan and many feel there may have been a Phoenician structure here prior to that. It is possible that Trajan's architect Apollodorus of Damascus had a hand in the design of this lighthouse. Apollodorus designed the hexagonal port of Portus near Rome, Trajan's Column, and Trajan's Forum. Many architectural historians feel he is responsible for the hexagonal forecourt present in the ruins of Baalbek Lebanon. The lighthouse is located in a region known to the Romans as Finestaria or 'lands end.' Even though the lighthouse is not located at the furthest point east the entire region was once known by this name. The octagonal plan of the Torre de Hercules also functions as a directional device just as the Anson's follies do. The Newport Tower's octagon points to the Torre de Hercules.

"........we examined the fuci and the mollusca which the north-west winds had cast with great profusion at the foot of the steep rock, on which the lighthouse of the Tower of Hercules is built. This edifice, called also the Iron Tower, was repaired in 1788. It is ninety-two feet high, its walls are four feet and a half thick, and its construction clearly proves that it was built by the Romans. An inscription discovered near its foundation, a copy of which M. Laborde obligingly gave me, informs us, that this pharos was constructed by Caius Sevius Lupus, architect of the city of Aqua Flavia (Chaves), and that it was dedicated to Mars. Why is the Iron Tower called in the country by the name of Hercules? Was it built by the Romans on the ruins of a Greek or Phoenician edifice? Strabo, indeed, affirms that Galicia, the country of the Callaeci, had been peopled by Greek colonies. According to an extract from the geography of Spain, by Asclepiades the Myrlaean, an ancient tradition stated that the companions of Hercules had settled in these countries." –Alexander Von Humboldt-'Cordilleras.'

Again Anson is referencing an important part of Celtic and Scottish history. Legend states that Queen Scota resided in A Coruña for several generations before they invaded Ireland and later moved on to Scotland as well. Part of this legend goes on to tell the story of how Scota's king sighted Ireland one day from a tower in A Coruña. It is entirely possible that the Torre de Hercules was build to commemorate this event. Alternately Trajan later simply rebuilt or constructed a tower at that location which was subsequently rebuilt in the eighteenth century.

There is also a clear Celtic veneer to the entire story of Santiago landing at the port of Irea Flavia near what would become Santiago de Compostela. It seems undeniable that the follies of Shugborough Hall are telling us to explore the mysteries of the Camino, St. James Field of Stars and the Holy Grail. The bay in which the Torre de Hercules is situated would also prohibit a view of England at this point. Only points west would have been visible from the Tower. One of the greatest accomplishments of Admiral Anson is his defeat of French Admiral Jonquierre in the Battle of Cape Finesterre. Anson's Chinese Pagoda points to the Torre de Hercules in the region of Roman 'Finesteria.' Later we see Anson is in a maritime battle named for this region. This is the confrontation discussed earlier in which Anson captured the Marquis de St. George and also some say a mysterious stone that may have later rested temporarily in a sandstone pillar near what would become the border of the United States and Canada. Here we have distant reference to Queen Scota and what is known to be the 'real' Stone of Destiny. This incident and stone would later involve many people that are germane to the story of occult architecture in this light. Figures like Salvador Dali, Jean Cocteau, and Nicolas Roerich all had a role to play in the saga of this stone and its associated quest. It is obvious that Admiral Anson was privy to the network of these structures and how they related to each other on the face of the globe. Given his service in the Colonies earlier in his career he was likely also possessed knowledge of the Newport Tower and its secrets as well.

Anson's service in the Colonies included extended stays in Charleston South Carolina. This city today has an extensive array of occult and Masonic architecture. Charleston is the Birthplace of the Scottish Rite of Freemasonry. This beautiful city is and was a place of great importance to interests related to this mystery. It is interesting to think of Anson socializing with the De Vere Drayton's and Montagu's in early Charleston. Charleston and its octagonal plaza share an even spatial relationship to a Cistercian Monastery just as in Chico California and its City Plaza. Author John Kale writes extensively of Charleston and its starmap architecture in his book "*The Starmap of Charleston*." Earlier we examined how Drayton Hall and the octagonal Washington Square in Charleston both point to Oak Island Nova Scotia.

Is it possible that four of the Shugborough follies are oriented to point to places that are central to this mystery and that this occurrence is a fluke or uncalculated coincidence? Not likely. The Tower of the Winds, Triumphal Arch, Shepherds Monument, Doric Temple and Chinese Pagoda all seem to have themes and directions inferred that are important to both Admiral and Thomas Anson. It has to be more than simple folly that they point to other significant and very similar places. The hidden aspects of The Torre de Hercules would likely have been an important part of Admiral Anson's life for many different reasons.

It is easy to see why Thomas and George Anson would choose to leave clues in this manner. These types of arrangements of monuments had been around for centuries prior and he had knowledge of this activity as exemplified by the association of the Shugborough's Tower of the Winds with Avebury and Stonehenge.

Somehow Shugborough was aligned with these two ancient sites. This situation would adhere to the many theories that state the order values geodesy and the spatial arrangement of monuments. Others obviously knew that the location of this estate possessed these associations and valued them. Anson's training in the navigational arts also lent to his ability to envision and execute this unique scheme of symbolism and architecture. Anson had been trained in the tradition of Dr.

John Dee who earlier had taught navigation to the Royal Navy.

If the Anson's had been Knights of St. John then this tradition had a rich lineage including people like Byzantine emperors Justinian I and II, Charlemagne, All the Holy Roman Emperors, The Vatican, The Greeks, The Egyptians, and more. This practice may have extended to the west via Charles Martel's Byzantine operative stonemasons. The Anson's and James "Athenian" Stuart had arranged to have the Shepherds monument oriented to point an azimuth to the future site of the IPG just as Thomas Jefferson, Governor Spotswood, and Governor Arnold had done or had knowledge of prior. This could mean all of these men were Knights Templar or other order who have a distinct value of the point on the earth at which the IPG is now located. It is rumored and indicated in the "Book of the Holy Grail" by J.R. Ploughman that both Jefferson and the founder of the Mormon faith Joseph Smith were considered members of the Knights Templar Strict Observance. It is well documented that Alexander Von Humboldt was a member of a Strict Observance lodge thus making it possible that he too was a KTSO.

What is at the International Peace Garden that is so important to these men? The possibility exists that no treasure, stone or grail is hidden at the IPG. It is possible that simply coming to the realization of what it represents is the treasure that many seek. In order to solve this mystery one must learn and divine the true nature of history and the philosophies of the powerful men and women that created it. It may compel one to develop a faith of his own based on what he has learned. In turn the International Peace Garden seems to point to places that were created to have significance in this plan. Because of the International Peace Garden this author has leaned a great deal of alternate views of faith and history.

This search from monument to monument teaches many valuable skills such as navigation, map reading and drawing, geometry, and history. It compels one to contemplate the true nature of humankind and how those who rule society may go about it. It exposes many historical truths by inferring an alternate reality that only those who have studied may understand. If this is true then there would be others who had been initiated just as the Anson's had and many before them. One must learn to understand 'the language of the birds' or possess what many today interpret as 'the eyes to see.'

The Shepherds of Arcadia Revealed. Admiral Anson's Moor Park.

Within the jargon associated with globes and maps the word "arc" also has a unique interpretation in the language of the birds as applied to this mystery of the navigators. It may also relate to the origins of the name "Arcadia" that is central in our studies of Shugborough, Rennes le Chateau, and other places. The story of how Arcadia got its name may have many interpretive applications in other aspects of these mysteries as well as relating directly to how people were to make geographic associations from place to place. Ultimately Arcadia is named for Arcas the son of Callisto consort of Zeus.

As this story progresses we will see the consorts of Zeus and their offspring having a role in many stories in a similar way to how Shakespeare applied real families and real history that

82

seemed to have a bearing on the development of North America later. The story of Arcas and Callisto involves Zeus and her becoming lovers. Eventually Calisto becomes pregnant. Hera Zeus' wife becomes jealous and turns Callisto into a Bear still holding the human child. The child is born and is named Arcas. Zeus hides Arcas in the mountains in a region that will come to be known as Arcadia via this myth. Arcas becomes a great warrior and hunter.

Eventually Arcas is involved in a part of this myth that may reveal a great deal as to why the concept of Arcadia is valued by a bloodline later. These connections raise many mysterious and interesting questions.

At one point Arcas serves a kind of morbid player in a grotesque scene perpetrated by Callisto's father Lycaeon. In an attempt to test the all seeing eye of Zeus Lycaeon attempts to cook Arcas on a grill to serve the parts to Zeus to see if he "knows" this without seeing what had been done. Inevitably Zeus sees what is going on and saves and reanimates Arcas while condemning Lycaeon to be a Wolf. This is the origin story that may serve as a great symbol or metaphor as to why a kind of predator class of people may have been lured to a value of our studies here through history. Later we even see the active involvement of the Biddulph family of Staffordshire. Biddulph literally means "War Wolf." This metaphor may be part of what is being valued in this saga leading us to Poussin, The Anson's, Rennes le Chateau and Shugborough Hall. The All Seeing Eye of God or Zeus in this case is also a recurring theme in a value of Arcadia on the part of the cast of characters studied here.

As the story of Arcas and Callisto continues many other pertinent metaphors are exposed. One day while hunting Arcas encounters his mother the bear in a sacred district of forest and begins to take aim to kill the bear. Zeus seeing this places Calisto and Arcas in the heavens in the form of the Constellations Ursa Major and Ursa Minor. Arcadia is named for Arcas who is identified with he and his mother as a Bear in the heavens placed there by Zeus. The constellation Bootes is known as the "Bear Driver" but most important to our discussion also known as "The Shepherd." Arcas is the Shepherd of Arcadia using this line of reasoning.

Most important to our studies here is the association with this entire mythology with the Pole Star also known as Ursae Minoris. The Pole Star was of course used by ancient and modern navigators to figure True or Polar North. The tail of the constellation Ursa Minor is the Pole Star. This is why it is named for Ursa Minor. The most important star to navigation and indeed the use of the navigational techniques discussed in association with a prime meridian or axis mundi is referenced in the story of Zeus, Callisto, and Arcas the namesake of Arcadia. This imagery is urging one to be a navigator. This is exactly the terms used by Flamel and Fulicanelli to describe a kind of initiation that involves interpreting art and architecture.

This is applicable to the reasons the Poussin painting is associated with the Paris Meridian via the imagery of the Pontil's Tomb near the village of Arques. It is obvious that this small town was named after Arcas. An alternate pronunciation or language of the birds interpretation of Arques would include even a similar pronunciation to that of the name Arcas. In other versions of this myth Arcas is associated with Ursa Minor thus also relating him to a value of the Pole

83

Star it self. Either way it is amzing that the Poussin work and the paintings at Moor Park suggest a classic theme that involves the ancient art of navigation. The imagery of Arcadia is leading us to a group of people who seem to value navigation and the association of specific temples in a topology or scheme that is told of and recorded at each place in metaphor and the orientation of the structure or temple itself.

One of the major clues linking Shugborough Hall and Rennes le Chateau is the presence of a rendering of Poussin's "The Shepherds of Arcadia" in bas relief mirror image on the famous Shepherds Monument there. We saw how this monument's orientation actually points an arc to the International Peace Garden. This painting has been associated in many stories and theories concerning Rennes le Chateau as well. The mysteries of Rennes le Chateau and Shugborough may be linked via the imagery of Poussin but some interesting links also exist with architecture and themes at Stirling Castle. The octagonal Kings Knot at Stirling creates an arc that passes over the Shugborough Tower of the Winds extending to Rennes le Chateau matching the portion of Lincoln's Star in the landscape there that was suggested on a since destroyed headstone there. The star of Rennes le Chateau points back to Shugborough and the Kings Knot. Its seems all the navigational metaphors of the Pole Star and story of Arcas are also being told to us via the imagery of the Shepherds Monument. The monument in this manner is a clue in an over all scheme that includes geographic information that will lead you to other places of mystery that include similar imagery.

The imagery of Poussin is repeated in the landscape near Rennes le Chateau in the form of the "Pontil's Tomb" located very near the Paris Meridian. We also see the Poussin painting displayed in the Louvre precisely on the Paris Meridian within the Museum. The imagery of the Shepherds in the painting is important to consider when comparing these themes to artwork that is prominent at Anson's Moor Park. The themes of Moor Park match the themes we see at Shugborough and Dashwood's West Wycombe Estate. All of these values may link directly to the myth of Callisto and Arcas. The village of Arques near Rennes le Chateau may have even been named in reverence for this connection and may be more pertinent to the Pontil's Tomb imagery than anyone suspects.

The Ballroom or main room of Moor Park is lavishly decorated with reproductions of several classic paintings that display characters that appear similar to the same characters in Poussin's paintings. The art at Moor Park references a fairly obscure myth and legend that may change the scope of or interpretation of the Poussin piece in relation to Rennes le Chateau and what it may mean by being included in the Shepherd's Monument. Much of this artwork also contains Arcadia references that may apply to the concept of navigation. It appears that the people who valued the Poussin painting valued Pole Star. In fact many forms of mythology include references to the constellations in the sky. To even measure any of these relationships the Pole Star was referenced as a baseline for measurements on the ground. This is why and how Prime Meridians were developed for practical use in part by having these mythical and spiritual overtones.

The main room of the Estate House at Moor Park is also reflective of a value of the Tower of the

Winds in Athens. Even though Anson's Tower of the Winds had been demolished the remaining artwork of the house indicates a value of this concept. Included in each corner of the main room is a rendering of the Greek god of the Wind of that direction just as displayed at the real Tower of the Winds. The Von Humboldt Estate in Potsdam also repeats this theme with each corner of the structure being decorated with a similar bas-relief to that seen on the original tower in Athens. The house itself still serves as a clue as to a directional value suggested by the orientation of the building that also matched the once present Tower of the Winds there. The ceilings of the great room include representations of Goddess Aurora of the Dawn and a "fake" two dimensional representation of the interior of the dome of St. Peter's Basilica. This may serve as a Catholic reference.

Present with in the main great room of the mansion is a series of paintings that display the story of Io the mortal woman and her relationship with Zeus. These paintings are all copies of classic works reproduced by Thornhill. Strangely this story has many overtones of the later story of Europa the nymph that inspired the name of the continent. Hidden in this value of Greek mythology may also been some strong hints that the mythic genealogy of Zeus and Io was somehow valued in metaphor or reality by the same later cast of characters that valued the concept of Arcadia and the Tower of the Winds. Given this we may see how these concepts were being communicated in Fulcanelli's work "Mystery of the Cathedrals." This concept appears to have been expressed on may estates in Europe during this era in the form of architectural follies or structures that actually served as a prime meridian or place from which to measure. During this era the navigational skills needed to interpret such a secret would have been limited to those in the Navy, astronomers, architects, and landscape designers. It may also be noted that surveying and astronomy seemed to be a pursuit of the wealthy landed class many of whom were proficient in the use of astrolabes and later sextants.

Other artwork seen at Moor Park may also display a value of navigational concepts while also revealing the political views of the patron of each piece. The paintings that tell the story of Io, Zeus, Hermes, and Hera at Moor Park will help us to further understand the true nature of "Et in Arcadia Ego."

In a story very similar to that of Callisto and Arcas Zeus was smitten with Io who was a beautiful mortal maiden. Hera noted that Zeus was gone and went looking for him. Zeus saw Hera coming and quickly turned Io into a White Cow. Hera immediately recognized this cow as Io and demanded that Zeus give her the Cow. Zeus reluctantly agrees planning on returning Io to a woman as soon as he can.

To prevent Zeus from seeing Io Hera arranges for Argus Panoptes (all seeing) to guard the white cow. Argus is also representative of a Shepherd thus repeating the theme of the Poussin painting "The Shepherds of Arcadia." Argus had one hundred eyes so could still rest with some of them closed making him a superior guard for Io. Zeus seeing this employed Hermes (Apollo) to steal the cow away from the guard Argus. At this point Hermes also disguises himself as a Shepherd. Ultimately Hermes is forced to slay Argus by beheading him and is compelled to present the head to Hera who then took Argus' eyes and placed them in the tail feathers of the Peacock thus explaining that in myth.

This myth has some fascinating parallels with the concept of the All Seeing Eye that was referred to in the myth of Arcas and Callisto. Argos Panoptes means Argos "all seeing" in one translation. It may be that this myth and the character of Argos is a metaphor for the concept of the All Seeing Eyes of God and the Egyptian parallel of the same concept using a single eye. Freemasons and other secret societies would later value this concept. The All Seeing Eye is also prominently featured on the Great Seal of the United States an may also reference this mythology. Could this be the "Argotique" that Fulcanelli describes?

It appears that the Peacock may serve as a metaphor for the All Seeing eye as interpreted in this myth of Io and Argos. Note the similarity in the sound of the words "Argos" and "Arcas." According to Fulcanelli's "Mystery of the Cathedrals" the concept of Argos and Jason and the Argonauts is also central to interpreting many aspects of several different mysteries that appear to have been intentionally placed into the public realm. In turn the tale of Jason and the Argonauts also resemble the Apocryphal Gospels of St. Andrew. Each of these conundrums will teach you many concepts needed to understand what has been left to follow. In the process many historical truths are revealed. Many of the metaphors in "Mystery of the Cathedrals" also point to the navigational concepts and a value of the Pole Star as discussed above.

Upon being freed from captivity Io is left to wander the world. Hera seeing this sends a "gadfly" to continually torment the white cow. In an attempt to escape the gadfly Io swims the Bosporus in what would be Constantinople thus inspiring the name of that waterway. Bosporus literally translates to "Ox Crossing" or "Cattle Crossing." Eventually Io makes it to Egypt where Zeus manages to turn her back into a beautiful woman. There she eventually marries a Pharaoh and has many children and grandchildren. Among these progeny is Europa the namesake of Europe. Europa is the great great granddaughter of Io herself. Io is in fact the root of all the human and god hybrids that are documented in Greek Mythology. The entire story references a bloodline of humans that intermingled with the gods. The parallels to the story of Christ and his family as viewed from a Gnostic perspective are obvious.

In a story very similar to that of Io Zeus later kidnaps Europa in the guise of a White Bull. This is interesting symbology in relation to the earlier story of Io being turned into a white cow. Now her descendant also involved with Zeus in kidnapped by the White Bull and taken to Crete thus inspiring the name of Europe. The blood of Io and Zeus is now returning to Europe. This is similar to the story of Mary Magdalene, The Three Mary's, and Merovingian mythos all rolled into one. This saga also has overtones that may point the way to Queen Scota as well. In a strange way this may also reflect the concept espoused by people like Michael Tsarion who say the Celts expanded throughout the western world spreading druidic ideas and that they eventually boomeranged their way back to Ireland and Scotland via Queen Scota.

This is likely the reason that these themes are valued and are present in the Rennes le Chateau, Shugborough, and now Moor Park mysteries. These images have been presented to you with clues that infer Arcadia and Mary Magdalene via the mythology of Io. Here is the reason why.

This is the same message being shown to you at the Shepherd's monument at Shugborough with out the addition of the paintings from Moor Park to clue one into the true identities of the characters in the Poussin painting which may in metaphor include Europa/Mary Magdalene, Hermes, and Argos. Et in Arcadia Ego. It may be that the Shepherd's monument can't be interpreted correctly without the additional information about Io included in the paintings at Moor Park.

All of the messages of these places also infer an organized group of people used the art of navigation as a way to lead one to other places that were important in the tradition of the Axis Mundi. These people had created geographic schemes of art and architecture laid out with regard to each other that told a story. It makes sense that someone like Admiral Anson would appreciate such a plan, as he was the third Englishman to circumnavigate the globe. Anson himself was undoubtedly a highly skilled navigator who may have even been trained in the tradition of Dr. John Dee who taught navigation to the English Navy during the eras of Elizabeth and James I.

Both of these stories are strangely related and include what may be interpreted as Merovingian imagery. The story of Io has her coming from Europe to the Levant and Egypt. Then later her descendant is taken by Zeus back to Europe even inspiring the name of the continent on the back of a white bull echoing the story of how Io came to Egypt. Combined this tale also resembles the story of the how the Merovingian's came to Europe on the back of the sea beast Quinotaur. The Merovingian origin story and the story of Io, Europa, and Zeus have many parallels and this may be the reason this story is displayed so prominently at Moor Park as valued by Admiral Anson and others. This saga is noteworthy also because it displays a distinct value of severed heads and mythology that fits the values of the people that owned and sponsored the artwork in question. The story of Lycaeon, Arcas, and Zeus may also imply that a race of wolves were known to exist.

It is strange that such a story is related to the Arcadia mythos. Many people may have identified with the concepts suggested by the story of Lycaeon in relation to Vampires and Werewolves. The themes suggest by the story of Lycaeon have many later myths and legends attached that continue into the modern world in the form of theories involving shape shifting beings and "reptilians." It does possibly also expose a Saturnalian view of these myths and legends as used to control the temporal fabric.

All of the paintings at Moore Park are in the same style and seem to depict similar characters to those seen in Nicolas Poussin's "Shepherd's of Arcadia." Indeed Io was originally from an area of Greece that may be considered Arcadia or Achaea. The Romans referred to the entire Peloponnese region as Arcadia and a city named Arcadia exists in the Peloponnese as well. It appears as if the political divisions shown on maps of the region today do not reflect what may be considered "Arcadia."

The symbolic representation of Hermes presenting the head of Argus to Hera may also have many overtones valued by the Knights of St. John and Knights Templar in reference to John the Baptist. Hermes is representative of the many magi present in occult traditions of this era. The

Anson's were said to be associated with the Knights of St John. Some sources also state that Argos was once the King of Arcadia. If true then the entire tale of Io would take on different overtones with regard to the head of the King in relation to many of the stories of Royal skullduggery in the works of Shakespeare. The symbol of the head may also be suggestive of the Green Man as seen at many stops in this saga. The sacrifice of Arcas by Lycaeon subsequently saved by Zeus may also apply to the fallen kings of later history.

This entire series of images and myth may serve as a metaphor for the story of Queen Scota and how she came to Spain then Ireland and Scotland. It may also serve as a metaphor for how the Merovingian mythos began as well as the arrival of the Three Mary's at Saintes Maries de La Mer. In addition this maritime tale of people arriving from points east to Europe may also apply to the story of St. James also associated with the land of Scota in Galicia and Santiago de Compostela (pointed to by the Moor Park Tower of the Winds). In short this is an extravaganza of hidden Jacobite beliefs and mythology. Why and how did Anson know about the Kensington Rune, Stone of Destiny, and site of the International Peace Garden? Why is he referencing the Ark of the Covenant connection to Lalibela?

Here again at Moor Park is another impressive array of art and architecture that suggests there is a belief that they are related to the blood of not only Jesus Christ but Queen Scota. All of this is reflective of a true value of their Egyptian and Scythian heritage as stated in the Declaration of Arbroath. It appears that a specific cast of families and individuals had identified with the stories of Io and Europa as a metaphor for themselves. Their way of telling us may include specific architecture, metaphorical interpretation of different myths and legends from many different cultures, and intentionally contrived "quests" that may teach one the truth about what they believe and value. Over the centuries many may have mistaken these families values of myths and legends as an indication of their pagan beliefs when in fact many of these symbols and metaphors conceal a distinctly Christian message. They were using mystery school techniques learned from the early Christians of Rome to conceal their true philosophical and spiritual beliefs which were at various times illegal in England and elsewhere.

All of the references to Io and Europa could also easily apply to Mary Mother of Christ just as well as Mary Magdalene. In fact it may make more sense in the long run that much of these stories of Mary could have just as easily applied to Our Lady. Upon her death Mary also rose after tree days just as Christ had. This also leaves the door open for the possibility that she also escaped to Europe with other members of her family in the same fashion the legends of Mary Magdalene suggest. If true this process would have resulted in the same hidden tradition of the blood of Christ we associated with Mary Magdalene in other views. In short the Auspice of Maria AVM symbol seen through this entire string of mysteries may actually be referring to Ave Maria. All of this possible hidden truth may also apply to James brother of Jesus and the mysteries of Santiago de Compostela that seem to have a great appeal to many different factions of alternate Christian belief in addition to the standard Catholic beliefs applied to Iago. Either way via Mother Mary, James, or Mary Magdalene there was a belief among certain quarters that they had descended from the blood of Jesus.

In tandem with what is known about St. Andrew and Arcadia is it possible that this reference to Io is also associated with that region and the Poussin Painting? Is it Argus the Shepherd in the tomb in Poussin's version of the story? Are Arcas and Callisto represented as well? Note phonetic similarity between the names Argus and Arcas. Given our interpretation here it is also easy to see why the figure of Europa may be representative of the figure of Mary Magdalene or the bloodline of Jesus that included his brother James. It is possible that the Shepherds of Arcadia are somehow referencing Argus and his missing head? The image of a "missing head" may be interpreted many different ways.

In Williamsburg the story of how Blackbeard's head was fashioned into a punchbowl (w/ silver ladle apurtant) echoes of this value. Ultimately is "what is in Arcadia" a reference to Io who is also associated with the Moon by some descriptions? It is possible that Poussin was commenting on the original paintings that the ones at Moor Park are copies of. He was at least painting in the same style with a similar theme. He is steering us to the same set of myths that suggest Io and Europa leading us to a metaphor for Mary Magdalene or the Three Mary's and Sara the Egyptian girl of Saintes Maries de La Mer. Sara may be representative of Io nee Scota the Egyptian Queen. The story of a man's beheading in association with a Queen or royal figure cannot help but remind one of the stories of Salome and John the Baptist.

In this realm it may be enlightening to examine the person who owned Moor Park prior to Anson obtaining the property.

James Scott 1st Duke of Monmouth, 1st Duke of Buccleuch (1649-1685) was the original owner of Moor Park. James was the Bastard son of Charles II. After his father's death James attempted to take the crown by force from his first cousin James II. After having failed Scott was beheaded. This is also ironic with regard to the theme of one of the series of paintings ending in Hermes

presenting the head of Argus to Hera.

Also noteworthy is Scott's relation via his wife to those that would later play a large role in not only the development of the Untied States but the symbols that are valued by the country. Scotts would be involved in the creation of the Great Seal of the Untied states and other representative artwork such as the famous Washington campaign buttons that are highly collectible today. The name Scott, Scot, or Scotus has also been associated with many "magi" or intellectual scholars in the alchemical tradition. The name Scot or Scotus somehow became associated with the magi of both Charlemagne and Frederick II Holy Roman Emperor. It appears that during the age of Charlemagne any Scottish intellectual "Magi" may have been known of as "Scotus" regardless of their given name. Here an association with such an array of artwork may be considered to have hidden overtones especially when related to a Scott i.e. Stewart that would be king. There is no doubt that the addition of this specific artwork and a reproduction of the Tower of the Winds at Moor Park on the part of Anson was a nod of respect for the estates former tenant. Later more evidence will show the involvement of this family with French factions in the possible knowledge or creation of myths like Rennes le Chateau and Shugborough Hall.

It is true that James Scott had opposed what would later become a Jacobite symbol in the form of King James II. Note that he is named for Santiago just like many other Scottish and English noble of the Stewart line. Scott was protestant and James II was Catholic. It appears that Scott had opposed the forces that would come to create a country out of the colonies in North America. The entire tale of Scott's beheading in relation to the series of paintings displaying the beheading of Argus and the story of Io may be a way of Anson valuing Scott in a deaths head cult kind of way. If Anson was a Knight of St. John it is also known that they valued the story of John the Baptist thus making the severed head a symbol of interpretive importance to this organization. This type of value may be viewed as a kind of grotesque but legitimate form of respect as well. The Duke of Monmouth was a Stewart who had attempted to regain his title in an armed insurrection. This would have also possibly been a source of inspiration to the Jacobite cause even though he was not Catholic. The severed head theme is repeated on the Triumphal Arch at Shugborough Hall.

Lost among all of this imagery of the severed head and Charles I is a direct connection to the imagery of Arcadia. The character of Philip Sydney the brother of Mary Sidney Countess of Pembroke wrote a work dedicated to his sister entitled "Arcadia." The last words of King Charles I prior to his beheading was a passage from Arcadia known as "Pamela's Prayer." This prayer contains imagery directly referencing Argo and his and Zeus' all seeing eyes in addition to many secular themes that are surprising given the Kings Catholic faith.

The prayer seems to be an admonishment of the view that Charles was intolerant of other faiths. The fact that Charles chose this passage from a work entitled Arcadia may be directly related to the theme of the paintings at Moor Park and the imagery of Poussin we see on the Shepherd's Monument at Shugborough Hall. This may be the message that Anson is telling us. The Shepherd's Monument and other artwork valued by the Anson's is an admission of their Jacobite sympathies to the lost Kings of the Stewart line of rulers. Though other sources say this prayer was only included in Charles' Prayer Book many also say he recited it prior to his beheading. This entire part of the story is also amazing given what we have seen relating Sidney's "Arcadia" to the development of Nova Scotia and the Oak Island Legend. (Shakespeare and History, Orgel and Keiland, Stanford University, Garland Publishing Group, New York and London, 1999: P. 29)

"All-Seeing Light, and eternal Life of all things, to whom nothing is either so great that it may resist, or so small that it is contemned: look upon my misery with thine eye of mercy, and let thine infinite power vouchsafe to limit out some proportion of deliverance unto me, as to thee shall seem most convenient. Let not injury, O Lord, triumph over me, and let my faults by thy hand be corrected, and make not mine enemy the minister of thy justice. But yet, O God, if, in thy wisdom, this be the aptest chastisement for my inexcusable folly; if this low bondage be fittest for my over-high desires; if the pride of my not enough humble heart be thus to be broken, O Lord, I yield unto thy will, and joyfully embrace what sorrow thou wilt have me to suffer. Only thus much let me crave of thee, ,—let my craving, O Lord, be accepted of thee, since even that proceeds from thee,—let me crave (even by the noblest title which in my great affliction I may

give myself, that I am thy creature; and by thy goodness, which is thyself) that thou wilt suffer some beam of thy Majesty to shine into my mind, that it may still depend confidently on thee. Let calamity be the exercise, but not the overthrow of my virtue: let their power prevail, but prevail not to destruction. Let my greatness be their prey; let my pain be the sweetness of their revenge; let them (if so seem good unto thee) vex me with more and more punishment. But, O Lord, let never their wickedness have such a hand, but that I may carry a pure mind in a pure body!"
-Pamela's Prayer from Arcadia by Philip Sydney

There are few characters in this era of English History that are more connected to the works of Shakespeare than Philip Sidney and his nephews, Mary Sidney Herbert Countess of Pembroke's sons, Philip Herbert and brother William Herbert. As discussed William and Philip were the subject of the dedication in Shakespeare's First Folio written by Sir Francis Bacon's friend and associate Ben Jonson. These associations may show why it is important that Charles I chose a passage from Sidney's "Arcadia" and what this may tell us about the Wilton Circle of authors and artists associated with Mary Sidney Countess of Pembroke. The Wilton Circle and those associated with Sir Francis Bacon have overlap in people, themes, and Philosophy. Mary Sidney appears to have been the intellectual and artistic equal of Sir Bacon. It may well be that Lord Bacon was well aware of the concept of The Shepherds of Arcadia and its hidden meanings to these people and himself.

Sidney was also an important character in the political and social scene of the day. He was a close friend with Giordano Bruno who was later burned at the stake for his heliocentric model of the solar system. Bruno was a Dominican Friar and dedicated two of his books to Philip Sydney. It seems this family has many books and literary works dedicated to them. They seem to be involved in the production of literary material, artwork, and architecture.

Philip Sidney extensively traveled the courts of Europe. He was married to Frances Walsingham the daughter of Elizabethan "spymaster" Francis Walsingham. It appears that Sidney was closely associated with many people who may have been part of the intelligence gathering apparatus of that era. Philip Sidney and Robert Beale were present with Sir Francis Walsingham at a riot in Paris that saw many Huguenot's massacred. Robert Beale may be associated with the Beale Treasure Legend of Virginia.

These associations would have put Sidney in association with many of the characters families who seemed to propagate different "mysteries" in colonial America as well. Each of these families in turn comprised many of the rebel characters from the works of Shakespeare. Walter Montagu also served as "spymaster" for James I and his family was involved in the development of Halifax Nova Scotia, Charleston, and Williamsburg Virginia. Philip Sidney was also close friends with Sir Francis Drake.

Illustrative of how Mary Sidney and her sons are connected to the Bacon family is the fact that the Gorhambury Estate features a full length painting of Philip Herbert from the era of Sir Francis Bacon. Philip Herbert had also married Susan de Vere the daughter of the 17th Earl of Oxford who some consider to be a secret author of the works of Shakespeare. It may be important that Moor Park is so close to the site of the St. Alban's and Lord Bacon's original Gorhambury House. It appears many of the families of others suspected as being involved in the works of Shakespeare are Bacon and descendant family associates.

Many people have even deciphered codes present in the dedication passage of the volume in the Herbert brother's honor. The entire scope of his influence in this realm may be viewed with regard to the influence of their mother and the Wilton Circle of artists and writers that were part of this group including Ben Jonson who wrote the dedication in the first folio. The fact that Charles I would choose a passage from this particular work of Sydney is interesting and applicable to the mysteries we see Anson displaying at Shugborough and Moor Park. This combined with what we already discovered about Sidney's "Arcadia" and the Oak Island Legend is simply amazing.

Here again an additional Arcadia connection from another mystery we have examined here may come to bear. The Wither's "Book of Emblems" that is theorized to have been used on headstones at the Bruton Parish Church is thought by some to have been produced by the brain trust of Bacon as well. Interestingly Wither's was the author of poem's in additional works using "Arcadia" in the theme of the work. Both the Wither's book and another similar book that applies to headstones at Stirling Castle entitled Quarles "Book of Emblemes" were both printed in 1634 during the reign of Charles I. Poussin's Shepherds was completed in 1637-38 also during this era.

Quarles also wrote about the theme of Arcadia, which he copied directly from the work of the same name by Sidney. It seems both authors of the "Books of Emblems" involved at mysteries at Stirling and Williamsburg were familiar with the theme of Arcadia in relation to Charles I. The association of the design on the Service Stone taken from the Quarles book is amazing given the directional qualities of the Kings Knot that includes other places of mystery such as Rennes le Chateau and Shugborough in its templum as discussed earlier. Via this same theme we can also see the concept of Arcadia coming to Virginia via the philosophy and influence of Sir Francis Bacon.

This chronology raises the possibility that The Shepherd's of Arcadia is also referring to Mary Queen of Scots and the story of her beheading as well. It seems many Stewarts met their end this way in this era of history. Many art historian interpretations of the Poussin painting state that the overall theme is that of a Memento Mori. It appears they are correct yet this context addresses this themes association with Shugborough Hall and Rennes le Chateau. Many of those valued with this Arcadian imager include those close to or admired by George Anson, Sir Francis Bacon, The Wilton Circle, the Stewarts and beyond. The de Vere family and its association with the Wolf or Werewolf theme also may place them in a special position to value the image of Arcadia and its mythology.

With this in mind it is of note to mention that William Herbert 3$^{rd.}$ Earl of Pembroke once owned the Moor Park property prior to James Scott. William Herbert married the sister of his brother's wife Bridget de Vere. Another de Vere cross over into what is becoming a culture of artists and authors in the vein of Shakespeare. William is of course another subject of the first folio dedication directly involved with a property that George Anson would later build a Tower of the Winds replica on just as he had at Shugborough. Even the Shepherd's Monument was later arranged by a later Earl of Lichfield into the Shepherd's Monument as a display of Anson's knowledge of the meaning of this entire scheme of imagery and symbolism related to the Poussin painting in tandem with the artwork seen at Moor Park.

William was undoubtedly aware of the symbolism of his uncle's work "Arcadia" and why Pamela's Prayer was an important symbol in relation to the Shepherds of Arcadia. William was also a great patron of Shakespeare as was Philip. If there were any two men in the know with regard to the secrets of Sir Francis Bacon and William Shakespeare these two would seem to be among the best candidates to have used and applied this information in many different ways. It is possible that these intelligent writers and minds of the Wilton Circle were involved in a form of intelligence gathering coupled with Enochian and other occult imagery in the tradition of Dr. John Dee. We may see a later version of this same culture nearby Moor Park at Sir Francis Dashwood's West Wycombe Estate and its famous "Hellfire Club."

It is also entirely possible given all of this intrigue that figures like Mary Sidney and her sons Philip and William may have even been involved in arranging all or parts of these mysteries in association with Sir Francis Walsingham and Sir Bacon. Admiral Anson and other subsequent owners of the property would have all added to the mystery and displayed their knowledge of it by adding additional artwork and talismans to the property as time went on. In this way they displayed their knowledge to others in the know. All of this may help to form a window into the philosophy and values of those that may have used the works of Shakespeare in a mystery school or intelligence service way to represent their ideals and goals. Apparently their codes and ciphers extended beyond the arrangement of words and letters in books to include a metaphorical quest that may be interpreted by the artwork, architecture, folklore, and places they valued. As we may see as this all unfold a distinct Scottish overlay and appreciation of Arcadia is viewed.

All of this is suggestive of a closed network using hidden symbols and metaphors for their own purposes. Where does this leave us with the "alchemical" misspelling of the names "Breakspeare" and "Shakespeare?" We know Nicolas Breakspeare also known as Pope Adrian IV was also from nearby St. Alban's Monastery. Is it a coincidence the famous bard in question in relation to Bacon and others has a name so similar to that of the only English Pope? Much of this mystery and intrigue certainly seems to center around a group of hidden Catholics that surrounded Sir Francis Bacon and even seemed to value the "Rosicrucian" overtones of his thought and Philosophy. It is looking more and more as if Mary Sidney, her brother Philip, and two sons Philip and William may have had intimate knowledge of the truth of this theory. It is entirely possible that the creation of the works of Shakespeare where metaphorically linked to Pope Adrian IV a.k.a. Nicolas Breakspeare. Breakspeare is also representative of another line of people named Nicolas who seemed to have had a great impact on these mysteries as seen as the St. Nicolas Church in Monaco.

We also see the hidden hand of the Wilton Writer's Circle of Sidney and the Countess of

Pembroke in all of this mystery and intrigue.

Supporting this thought is the fact that the property of Moor Park was originally owned by the nearby St. Alban's Monastery only about six miles to the northeast of the estate. Another significant family that once owned the property has been a subject of interest in this story. John de Vere the 13th Earl of Oxford was once lord of the manor there. De Vere was obviously the progenitor of the 17th Earl of Oxford Edward de Vere who many suspect of having involvement in the works of Shakespeare. Willam and Philip Herbert again married the daughters of Edward de Vere. In addition, they are the subject of the dedication of the famous First Folio of Shakespeare's works.

Some also associate the family name of de Vere with the legend of the Werewolf referenced in the mythology of Arcadia and its namesake Arcas. The German version of Vere is Weir. Again this is reminiscent of the meaning of the Biddulph/Bidwell name interpretation of "War Wolf" phonetically similar to "Werewolf." The de Vere family in a very real way may value this story if they somehow believed they had descended from real Greek Arcadian nobility of myth and legend.

This may also relate them to others who may apply the lineage of Troy to their family values and beliefs. If true all of this may also explain a value of the Tower of the Winds, Constantine, the Merovingian dynasty, Mother Mary, Mary Magdalene and Christ. Given the fact that Pope Adrian IV was originally from St. Alban's also brings us to the coincidence of the similarity of his name when compared to that of the bard Shakespeare. Pope Adrian's original given name was Nicholas Breakspeare. It is possible that Breakspeare trod the grounds of Moor Park at the time it was part of St. Alban's Abbey. Is it really possible that even the name of Shakespeare is related to the name of Breakspeare in this mythology?

Later the property was owned by Robert and Lady Anne Franklyn after Admiral Anson. It may be the Franklyn's are related to Benjamin Franklin of the United States. This property has been owned by a cast of characters that are related to the circles of Sir Francis Bacon and what would later be considered Cavalier and Jacobite ideals. The Franklyn family also have an association with the Beale family via their memorials in All Saints Maidstone that seem to have been replicated in the Bruton Parish Church in Williamsburg. James Franklin, Benjamin's brother, actually produced a celestial almanac he published at Newport Rhode Island as well. This would be an activity that has been theorized here as being associated with the reason the Tower was even constructed in the first place.

Almost every connection to this property has a role in other aspects of the history discussed in this book to this point. All the families are there. All of the theories of their involvement in the works of Shakespeare are inferred in a mystery of this type. Many of these families and characters seem to have been referenced in the works of Shakespeare and later literature and artwork. The fact that Philip Sydney meant "Arcadia" to be for his mother and close circle of friends attests to how they may have expressed themselves in metaphor and meaning that only the other well read authors and intellectuals of his circle could understand. This group also obviously included people as influential as King Charles I himself.

It is also important to note that one of the more prominent figures impeached just prior to Charles I was his supporter the 1st Earl of Stafford. Part of the struggle of Charles I was his problems negotiating his rights with Parliament. His largest supporter as a Member of Parliament was Thomas Wentworth Earl of Stafford (1593-1641). Eventually relations between Parliament and Charles deteriorated to the point that they were demanding the head of the Earl of Stafford for crimes he had committed in the process of supporting the King in the legislature. Eventually Parliament forced the King into a corner from which he was forced to consider losing his monarchy or executing his loyal friend Wentworth. In the end Charles had to sign the warrant for Stafford thus making him another martyr in the Jacobite cause.

This relation between Anson and the Earl of Stafford may also be one of the major reasons that the imagery of The Shepherd's of Arcadia and its associated mystery were valued by Admiral Anson and his brother Thomas who may have even been named for a Stafford. Stafford represents another beheaded individual in reference to the tale of Argus Panoptes All Seeing. This is also referenced in the Poussin painting featured on the Shepherds Monument at Shugborough and works present at Moor Park. Of course other Stafford's were likely involved in the construction of the mysterious Newport Tower that is essentially another Tower of the Winds for us to find. It seems that Towers of the Winds such as those of Shugborough and Moor Park were meant as symbols that fulfilled a very practical function in the mysteries left behind by these people. Many have visited both the Newport Tower and Shugborough Hall and missed this connection.

Many have also suspected the Anson's and Dashwood as well as other tower builders of being Jacobites who supported the exiled Kings of Scotland and England regardless of the variety of Christianity they practiced. The Stewarts had gained a loyal following of people from many different backgrounds that had benefitted during their reign and were subsequently not included in the plans of the new Hanoverian Parliamentary government. This may be why many Jacobite artists and architects seem to reference the "Ancient Regime" or lost era of Royal society and world domination. The Jacobites quietly set about plotting a new country in North America that would reflect their values in the form of a Republic which they would form and help to dictate in many obvious and secret ways. With the Jacobites came acceptance by citizens of the Untied States of the influence of the Catholic Church as part of the new country. The theme of the "Ancien Regime" is also repeated in the works and architecture of the d'Abbadie family of Hendaye who were also governors of French Arcadia and Louisiana. All of the symbology of Et in Arcadia Ego would later be applied to Rennes le Chateau using the same Poussin imagery that is seen at the mystery of Shugborough and Moor Park.

How are these representations of Io and Argo or Argus applicable to the Poussin painting "The Shepherds of Arcadia" beyond the resemblance of some of the subjects and characters in the paintings at Moor Park? Argus in myth also has a significant connection the region of Arcadia where St. Andrew met his end as well. In addition to the myth of Io and how he was beheaded by Hermes Argus had also been involved in helping the Arcadians avoid a crisis. The lands of

Arcadia (Achaea) were being ravaged by a bull that Argo slew thus saving the people and crops. After this he is also said to have killed the Echidna or half serpent half woman creature that guarded the entrance to Hell. The Echidna was the daughter of the Typhon who disassembled Zeus only to have Pan and Hermes put him back together. Some accounts of Argo also have him actually being an Arcadian himself. The Shepherds of Arcadia are Argo and Hermes. In Greek Mythology Arcadia was frequently the domain of Pan. Coincidentally the top band of designs on the Shepherds Monument of Shugborough includes a sculpture of the head of Pan.

This entire association is very curious given the similarity in especially the yellow clad characters representative of Hermes in the Moor Park paintings compared to the Poussin painting which displays a very similar character in relation to a female figure many speculate represents Mary Magdalene. If this analysis rang true then Mary Magdalene is also playing the role of Europa in the Greek theme that serves as what many people believe to be a metaphor for Mary or the Merovingian bloodline. This is what is being told to us in the stories of Io and her progeny Europa both consorts of Zeus. Mother Mary is of course defacto part of the real bloodline. Somehow many forget this.

So what may this have to do with the Pontil's Tomb that has been presented to us as part of the Rennes le Chateau mystery as being associated with the Poussin painting? "Et in Arcadia Ego" or "In Arcadia I am?" Does this famous phrase refer to Argos (Argus)? Is this part of what Fulcanelli is referring to in his work "The Mystery of the Cathedrals?" He refers to "Argotique" as being a metaphor for gothic art. He also stresses the tale of Jason and the Argonauts in which three characters named Argus or Argos are present. The name of the ship in the myth is also the Argo. Ancient mariners or navigators value the constellation Argo Navis as well. Noted before are the similarities to the story of Jason and the Argonauts and the stories of St. Andrew. The Argonauts and St. Andrew traveled to many of the same places encountering many miraculous things along the way. Of course the Jason story ends with him obtaining the Golden Fleece yet ultimately becoming a destitute failure at the very end of the story. Later we may see members of the Order of the Golden Fleece applying the imagery of the Argonauts to many mysteries as suggested by Fulcanelli.

All of this combines to lead one to the conclusion that the Poussin painting, The Shepherds Monument of Shugborough Hall, and artwork of Moor Park are telling us about these people's belief in the Holy Bloodline coming to Europe via the stories of Io and Europa. Both stories have references or imagery that is very similar to the myth of the Quinotaur bringing Merovich to the shores of Europe. This entire tale in turn is obviously derivative of the story of Europa and Io. Even the myth suggests a bred bloodline including the paternal input of Zeus himself consorting with human women that is in a very real way similar to the story of Mother Mary and Jesus. This does not address the modern version of the Rennes le Chateau mystery yet may provide a rationale as to why the Poussin imagery was applied to the Pontil's Tomb and other aspects of the area.

The stories of Rennes le Chateau, Shugborough and the Shepherd's monument, the Kings Knot at Stirling, Oak Island, and the mysteries of Bacon's Vault in the colonies all harken to this

96

mythology. This is the reason the imagery of Poussin was injected into the entire story at more than one place. In turn we do see this imagery associated with the Louvre that served as home and birthplace to many French Kings. The Shepherds of Arcadia painting is located on the Paris Meridian within the Louvre Museum. This entire phenomenon may also be related to the "Man in the Mountain Myths" of Charlemagne and other Holy Roman Emperors including Frederick Barbarossa and Frederick II. The Kings Knot, Shugborough Hall, and Rennes le Chateau were all aligned using clues to tell you this at each place including the Poussin imagery and octagonal architecture and artwork. In the past I have speculated here that the altar painting of Rennes le Chateau displays the Tower of the Winds at Shugborough Hall. This may be more likely now given this new evidence.

To repeat from our Mary Magdalene chapter earlier. The Louvre I.M. Pei Pyramid and inverted pyramid create an alignment that forms an arc on the globe that transects to Migdal or Magdala Israel the birthplace of Mary Magdalene. In the opposite direction this arc on the globe extends to Oak Island Nova Scotia. Is it possible that some remains or relics of Mary Magdalene or her followers were left in the Money Pit or somewhere else on Oak Island. This remains to be seen. This story is wrapped up in the imagery of the Plantagents of France, Scotland, England, and Ireland as well as other groups such as the House of Hapsburg. It is clear that reliquaries and impressive artifacts are being recovered in Jamestown while nothing has been found at Oak Island. Something of this sort is at least being suggested in association with the array of architecture present in Halifax and Lunenburg Nova Scotia.

They are telling you they believe they are related to Mary Magdalene.

The entire mystery may have been formed to lead one to this conclusion. This belief took on many mystery school overtones under the Jacobites who created the United States in tandem and contrast to many of their Catholic beliefs. It appears that to many of this elite class that is was indeed acceptable to be an acolyte of Mary Magdalene and a good member of the Latin Church at the same time. This also lent the Catholic faction something in common with those of alternate or Gnostic Christian belief including Protestants, Rosicrucians, and Pagans. All of these views were maintained via a mystery school belief and the desire to establish freedom of religion in the colonies. This is why the image of Mary Magdalene is associated with Rennes le Chateau. None of this new information means the mystery there has been solved yet some light may have been shed on why there is even a mystery there in the first place.

The answer to a question involving why this imagery would be present in both England and France may involve a similar series of events that were played out in France during the French Revolution. The beheading of Louis XVI and Marie Antoinette were among only a few of hundred in a purge of the ruling class of France during this era. It is entirely possible that the imagery of the Poussin painting was valued in metaphor by the gentry class that survived the revolution by viewing this work in the same mystery school manner the Anson's had. The same concepts of the lost kings, beheadings, and the longing for a more ancient pastoral idyllic life that many of the elite imagined under the "Ancient Regime" of the lost kings of Scotland, France, and England. Later we see many others such as Antoine d'Abbadie openly lamenting past eras that of course were more beneficial to the lifestyle they saw disappearing in the Republics of France and United States as well as the Parliamentary Monarchy in British Isles. Even Philip Sidney in his work "Arcadia" lamented and longed for a more peaceful lifestyle of days gone by in chivalric England. To them Arcadia undoubtedly is also referring to its use in Greek mythology as a kind of utopian land where life was uncluttered and simple. Hidden within this mythos is the story of the werewolf and the cold hearted nature of man. In contrast to this are many similar views on the part of people like Sir Francis Bacon and his circle that seemed to favor a more open and fair society geared towards the needs and goals of the common man. It may be that in this spirit that these gentry concepts were later turned against the Royal class in a kind of psychological warfare in which one's knowledge of the other sides secrets was valued in a very real and sometimes talismanic way.

This conclusion does support some of the notions and factors injected into the Rennes le Chateau mystery by Pierre Plantard. Some of his claims seemed to indicate that he felt that if he solved the mystery there it would lead him to the evidence he would need to prove his royal legacy. This is a theory. If true this activity on his part may have been informed by some older legend of the remains of his forebears being hidden somewhere near Rennes le Chateau. This mystery would have adhered to similar parameters set forth in the mysteries left behind by Charlemagne that may have also included the theme of right to rule if the mystery was solved. This may also account for much of the additional landscape geometry discovered by Henry Lincoln in that region.

It may be that many of the mysteries associated with Sir Francis Bacon are based on a similar template. Charles I and the Earl of Stafford lived during the age of Bacon. It is also likely that some of the same families mentioned in this chapter would have an impact on the use of intentionally contrived mysteries to both initiate on one hand while confusing and confounding additional parties on the other. As time progressed it may be that later people viewed these sacred landscapes and prime meridians as a way to encode the location of hidden objects. Just as likely is an associated belief that involves an individual viewing a geographic association with an Axis Mundi as being favorable for their business and personal ventures. This in turn may have led to military applications such as the location of major battles and confrontations. The application and use of time measurement may have also led to a belief in time based vortexes in association with certain points on the earth that had been marked by temples of many different eras including megalithic structures such as stone circles and dolmens. Meanwhile these places are put into the psyche of the public as many visit these places blissfully unaware of their hidden meanings.

"Et in Arcadia Ego" is leading us to stories of Argo, Europa, St. Andrew and the legacy of the Kingdom of Aragon and Anjou family in the later Latin Kingdom of Constantinople and Greece via their control of these regions. Even the name Aragon infers "Argo" or the "Argotique" as in Fulcanelli. These families had a distinct value of St. Andrew, St. James, Mary Magdalene, Constantine, and of course Jesus Christ XP. Charles I and other English and Scottish monarchs may have gained a value of such concepts from France. It may also be that Bacon was inspired in many similar ways during his studies there. It may be that this entire directional tradition had

98

been built into all the gothic cathedrals whose operative stonemason's were aware of. Architects like Capability Brown, Inigo Jones, Issac de Caus, and John Webb seemed to be aware of these concepts and had built them into the structures of many powerful people.

This concept had its different continental and family meanings. In this realm we may also see a rationale as to why Christopher Columbus sometimes signed his name in Greek characters. He likely did that in association with his relation to the Paliaologos family who were Princes of Arcadia in Greece during the era of the Republic of Genoa. The Paliaologos family monogram is very similar that of Justinian I and Theodora as well. More on Columbus in upcoming work. Henry the Navigator was also obviously privy to this information as well and had Scottish family connections.

It is easy to see how the Anjou's being Princes of Achaea could come to adapt the imagery of Io, Europa, St. Andrew, and Argo into their mystery school interpretation of the Mary Magdalene history they valued and loved. The may have also valued a Trojan bloodline via their association with this region. The Merovingian dynasty had already applied this imagery in their origin mythology including many of the same metaphorical references. They also valued the Chi Rho including the Alpha and Omega symbol which may actually represent the original Rosy Cross XP (CR Christian).

Outsider attempts to decipher or interpret these values have led to a wide variety of misinterpretations and distortions of reality. Often concepts more based on mythology and whimsy is applied to any such concepts. There remains a practical and rational use of any array of monuments that represent a fixed point on the earth. The modern day equivalent may be an Astronomical observatory such as Greenwich and Paris Observatories. The Naval Observatory in Washington D.C. serves this purpose in the United States and also displays many of the traditional talismanic overtones of the Greenwich and Paris Meridians.

Note the similarities in the monogram of Justinian I Byzantine Emperor and the logo of the Paleologos family of Greece.

The great room of Moor Park showing the reproductions of classic works including far left: Zeus seducing Ios; Center Left; Argus being entertained by and lulled to sleep by Hermes; Right center; Argus asleep about to be beheaded by Hermes; right; Hermes presenting the head of Argus to Hera who places his 100 eyes into the tail feathers of the Peacock.

Poussin's "The Shepherds of Arcadia." Note similarity in theme and characters to the paintings present at Moor Park.

Hermes about to behead Argus while the White Cow Io and Zeus from above looks on.

102

Hermes presenting the head of Argus (Argos) to Hera as part of the myth.

If the Anson's and James Stuart were aware of this ancient practice there were likely others who were aware as well. Both men had blood association with a tradition that includes exploration and the legal definition of property in both the physical and alchemical sense. In fact they may have learned of this tradition from one of the most notorious elite gentleman of this era.
There are four additional English estates that have reproductions of the Tower of the Winds in Athens built on them in the form of follies or whimsical pieces of architecture. West Wycombe, Summerhill, Mt. Stewart, Shugborough, and Moor Park. Oxford Universities Radcliffe Observatory is also a reproduction of the Tower of the Winds. Additional information supporting the notion that the Tower of the Winds on Shugborough Estate was meant to function as an axis would also include another famous Estate a little further south closer to London. Moor Park

would serve as Admiral Anson's home near London and place of retirement.

Moor Park and its associated Tower of the Winds and artwork may hold many clues germane to the Rennes le Chateau mystery and other mysteries discussed to this point in North America. First an examination of how the Tower of the Winds at Moor Park works will help to illustrate the similar themes as displayed by the Tower of the Winds at Shugborough. Shugborough, West Wycombe, and Moor Park were all constructed in the Palladian style of architecture that Thomas Jefferson would also later value and use in his structures.

The Moor Park Tower of the Winds was demolished but writing about the house suggests it was oriented the same way as the main building of Moor Park about 13 degrees east of True North. This additional Tower of the Winds was said to have been situated in the middle of a small pond. Though it has been demolished the foundation is still partially visible. The Tower of the Winds at Moor Park may have been meant as a sighting device pointed at places on the globe valued by Admiral Anson. Each facet of the octagon may be used to infer an arc or azimuth on the globe. Using this orientation the Tower of the Winds at Moor Park points an azimuth on the globe directly to the Kensington Rune Stone in Minnesota. This is an amazing correlation that now has Anson associated with both the missing Stone of Destiny from the sandstone pillar on the Milk River in Alberta and the Rune stone that seems to keep popping up in many instances of this tradition including the fact that the Dome of the Rock, Newport Tower, and Ames Pyramid all point to the Kensington Rune. There are indisputable family links between all of these monuments.

This association may indicate that Anson was aware of the International Peace Garden that the Shepherd's Monument points to, and the Kensington Stone that the Peace Garden points to on the globe. Note also that the sandstone pillar where the Stone of Destiny may have once rested is associated with the Peace Garden by being situated nearly exactly on the same latitude or 49th parallel. This indicates that Anson was also aware of the hidden significance of the site of the International Peace Garden. His friend Dashwood was part of the family group that would later establish Dunseith North Dakota and the International Peace Garden. It is also likely that Anson had true knowledge of the Newport Tower not only via his Admiralty connections but via his family relation to the Earls of Stafford.

Anson's Moor Park Tower of the Winds also displays another "Kensington" connection. The octagonal form of the tower creates an azimuth or arc on the globe that points directly to Kensington Palace in London. This azimuth represents the opposite direction that points to the Kensington Rune in Minnesota. Indeed part of the landscaping of the park to the east of the Mansion house itself seems to match this azimuth coming from Moor Park Tower of the Winds. This connection is bizarre. Two Kensington's pointed to by the same Tower of the Winds both situated on a single arc on the globe suggested by Anson's Moor Park Tower of the Winds. Is it possible that Anson is telling us he knows why the stone in Minnesota is named for Kensington? Is it a coincidence that the location of the Stone is named for the same place pointed to in England Kensington Palace? Earlier we examined the influence of the Hill, Eaton, and Ames family in the region near where the Kensington Rune is located. This may also include the influence of the Douglas family. It appears that the builders of the Newport Tower, possibly the Stafford's, were aware of this. This makes sense in that the Stafford's had intermarried with the Anson family in the past. Staffordshire and its nobles seem to be a kind of center for this tradition.

Amazingly the azimuth on the globe that points to Kensington Palace from Moor Park continues across the globe in a southeasterly track finally intersecting with Basilica San Vitale in Ravenna Italy. This is amazing. The octagon of San Vitale also points back along the same arc on the globe to Moor Park. The structures point the way to each other. An additional azimuth suggested by the octagon of San Vitale also points to the Mausoleum of Theodoric just a few miles to the northeast. Ravenna may be the place where the early origins of an appreciation of Arcadia came from (See my book "The Prophecy of Dante and the New Jerusalem of Ravenna).

Theodoric's Mausoleum is also an octagon from plan view. The roof or lid to Theodoric's crypt is one of the largest cut stones ever produced by man in history. The octagon of Theodoric's Mausoleum points an azimuth or arc on the globe directly to the Church of St. George in Lalibela, Ethiopia. The rock hewn churches of Lalibela are famous for possibly once housing the Ark of the Covenant. The array of obelisk and windrose at the Vatican point the way to Lalibela. Discussed already is the relationship of follies in Halifax Nova Scotia and how they may relate to the travels of James Bruce in Ethiopia.

The example here at Moor Park displays a value and knowledge of what Lalibela truly means on the part of Admiral Anson before Bruce's trip to Ethiopia. Lalibela also fits into some of the notions of Sir Francis Bacon's "New Atlantis" and "New Jerusalem" concepts and may have even helped him to develop this concept. Mescal Lalibela originally built the array of churches there as a "New Jerusalem" or place for pilgrims to visit after the Muslims gained control of Jerusalem and associated Holy sites. Later we see many of the landscaped arrays in Williamsburg, the International Peace Garden, and Washington D.C. representing the "New Atlantis" concept.

This array of Moor Park, San Vitale, Mausoleum of Theodoric, and Lalibela echoes the layout of talismans we examined earlier in Halifax Nova Scotia and even repeats the association to Lalibela. The fact that Anson's Moor Park Tower of the Winds points to San Vitale is also significant in light of what we learned about Empress Theodora and Mary Magdalene from the mosaics present at the basilica. It is amazing that many of the new axes or directional structures built by this family group continue to reference many of the same places that are valued by others in the know. The Moor Park Tower of the Winds is no exception. The alignment of the Rennes le Chateau Chapel, Chateau Hautepol, Chateau Blanchefort and the Village of Arques point an arc on the globe to Basilica San Vitale as well. The Star of Henry Lincoln points to Basilica San Vitale. Note also that the word "arc" is also associated with the story of "Arcadia" via its namesake Arcas. In turn Arcas is associated with the constellation of his mother Calisto known as Ursa Major that was placed in the sky by her lover Zeus. It appears that Arcas is associated with the Constellation Bootes though some variants of the myth identify him with

105

Ursa Minor.

A separate azimuth or arc suggested by Moor Park transects to the south directly to the Cathedral of Santiago de Compostela in the city of the same name. Here we see both of the estates that Anson was associated with including follies at Shugborough that point the way to Santiago de Compostela linking to all the mysteries of St. James and the land of Scota. If all of this is true then it may have been of significance to Anson that one of the most important victories The Battle of Cape Finesterre was fought right off of the coast of Galicia and the Torre de Hercules in A Coruna. The Torre de Hercules and A Coruna are both major symbols to Pilgrims traveling to Santiago de Compostela from England, Scotland, Wales, and Ireland. All of the Pilgrims from these regions landed in Galicia at A Coruna and made their pilgrimage on foot along the route between the two cities.

Another arc from Tower of the Winds Moor Park reaches the Monastery of Montserrat in Spain. The Paris Observatory grounds also generate an arc on the globe that points the way to the Monastery. Montserrat is one of the locations that many authors and researches suspect as being the place where the Cup of Christ or archetypical Holy Grail was once located.
An arc also extends to the fortress of Gisors and all its associated "Cutting of the Elm" history that is so important to both the French and English lines of Norman families we see valuing the spatial arrangement of architecture on the face of the globe in a talismanic or mystery school manner. Gisors also possesses an extensive history involving the Normans, Knights Templar, and mythical Priory of Sion.

The Tower of the Winds at Shugborough Hall.

Chapter 7: Sir Francis Dashwood and his West Wycombe Estate.
Add info from masters thesis about Dillitante that confirms every word here.

Sir Francis Dashwood is representative of many families and philosophical movements that are involved in this tale of talismanic architecture. He was among those that seemed to have rediscovered the use of the Axis Mundi and how the Greeks, Romans, and Egyptians had applied this concept. As we may see his legacy includes him being a descendant of the de Vere family as his grandmother's maiden name was Mary de Vere daughter of Horace de Vere of Tilbury.

Horace was a first cousin of the 17th Earl of Oxford de Vere who many suspect having actually penned the works of Shakespeare. Other Dashwood's would also be included in the Baronetcies of Nova Scotia. The Drayton de Vere family would also establish Charleston South Carolina where Admiral Anson spent time as a Captain.

We will see here how one of the architectural follies on Dashwood's estate does indeed point the way to Oak Island Nova Scotia. It seems Dashwood had built his own Tower of the Winds at West Wycombe just as the Anson's would do at Shugborough and Moor Park. At Shugborough we examined the Anson's family connections to the Earls of Stafford who may have ultimately had some influence in the building of the Newport Tower. The Tower of the Winds at West Wycombe and Shugborough were built long after the Newport Tower and Powder Magazine in Williamsburg. This fact may go a long way towards deciphering what these men were trying to tell us via their value of these structures.

Most surprising is Dashwood's links to the families that created the international Peace Garden. Dashwood is directly related by blood to the Audley, Eaton, and Spencer families that seemed to be behind the creation of the International Peace Garden. As we have seen this also links him distantly to Sir Francis Bacon. Though it may be tempting to ascribe Francis Dashwood's first name to a veneration of Bacon it seems clear he was named for more than one person named Francis de Vere.

Dashwood was said to have been the primary force behind groups known as the Hell Fire Club and the Dilettante Society. Even American luminary Benjamin Franklin was said to have been a HFC member. This is interesting given the fact that Franklin's brother James lived in Newport Rhode Island and even produced celestial almanacs in Newport in a display of the tradition the tower is based on in the first place. Dashwood seemed to have constructed a series of follies on his property as well only a few years prior to the construction of similar features at Shugborough. Given this Dashwood may have inspired the Anson's to express themselves in this manner. In doing so Dashwood created one of the most impressive and meaningful arrays of architecture in this vein.

Dashwood's follies included an Arch of Apollo, Daphne House (referring to the Daphne of Constantine), Temple to Venus, a Temple of Music, and large hexagonal mausoleum. His manor house was constructed in the Palladian style that would later be used by Thomas Jefferson to build Monticello, Poplar Forest, Barboursville Mansion, and the Rotunda at the University of

108

Virginia. Interestingly the house was said to be inspired by the Temple of Jupiter at Baalbek, Lebanon. Dashwood's hexagonal mausoleum seems to be a reproduction of the hexagonal feature at Baalbek as well. In a possible Holy Grail reference Sir Dashwood also constructed the Church of St. Lawrence adjacent to the mausoleum. The church is noted for its large golden globe atop the spire. The globe is big enough to accommodate three people sitting and there are stories of Dashwood conducting experiments with mirrors to communicate with others situated at a distance. Also of note at the West Wycombe Estate are the famous "Hellfire Caves."

He even created a reproduction of the Tower of the Winds in Athens that functions just as the one at Shugborough and Athens operate! Amazingly Dashwood's Tower of the Winds is associated with one of the most famous Axis Mundi on the face of the earth and in history. A line created using the southeasterly orientation of the Tower of the Winds at West Wycombe transects the globe directly to the center of the hexagonal feature located in the ruins of Baalbek, Lebanon. Not only does this azimuth transect to Baalbek it matches the angle of its orientation! Both of these structures point the way to each other!

If one examines the layout of monuments on the Dashwood Estate the above spatial relationship is supported by the fact that at the NNE azimuth from his TOW Dashwood built a large hexagonal structure in the form of a Mausoleum. This mausoleum is also close to the same dimensions as the inner court of the hexagon at Baalbek! This entire structure seems to have been built as a copy of the hexagonal structure at Baalbek. Dashwood's value of this sacred geometrical scheme is evidenced by the fact that his wife's ashes are interred at the center of the hexagon! Dashwood's remains are also within the hexagon. He is symbolically being buried in relation to his axis. This is similar

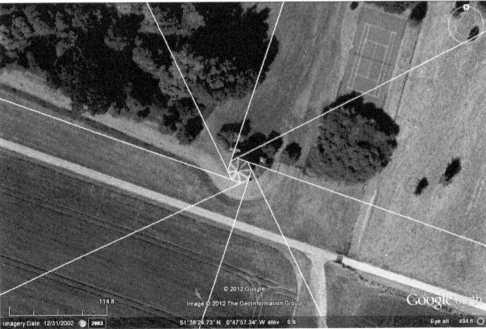

Dashwood's Templum of the Tower of the Winds West Wycombe.

109

to the situation of the Mausoleum of St. Helena, The Dome of the Rock, and the Vatican may represent as discussed earlier. This kind of tradition of funerary arrangement may suggest Constantine was actually interred beneath the Dome of the Rock on the Temple Mount in Jerusalem.

Continuing this amazing feat of architectural arrangement is the secret of Dashwood's hexagonal mausoleum. The southerly trending direction suggested by his hexagon transects the globe directly to the Tower of the Winds in Athens Greece! Dashwood oriented his Tower of the Winds to point to Baalbek while Baalbek points back. He then oriented his reproduction of Baalbek to point to the Tower of the Winds in Athens Greece. These associations may extend far beyond the realm of a chance occurrence. Here we have Dashwood valuing the Greeks, Romans, and Byzantines in a manner that displays his full understanding of this custom as defined by those who built the original structures.

Dashwood must have been aware of this spatial association even prior to James "Athenian" Stuart's trip to Greece to study architecture. This is the same azimuth extending from Baalbek that extends to Greenwich Naval Hospital (0 degree meridian, built by Anson), as well as Buckingham and Kensington Palaces all the way from Baalbek. The London Center Stone close by just to the northeast likely marks this association, as Baalbek seemed to have been valued by Roman and Byzantine Imperial rulers. The hexagon of Baalbek also functions as an Axis Mundi and points the way to many significant sites. This is the phenomenon that Dashwood and the Anson's were imitating. It is possible that London was developed at this location due to this special relationship.

The southerly orientation of the Dashwood Tower of the Winds transects to Nimes, Languedoc, France. This is the location of the Maison Careé Roman Temple that Thomas Jefferson would copy in the form of the first Virginia State Capitol. This azimuth then extends to Marseilles near where the Mary's and Joseph of Arimathea were said to have landed on their sojourn from the Holy Land.

The northeasterly azimuth from Wycombe Tower of the Winds points to Bornholm Island in the Baltic Sea. Researchers Henry Lincoln (Rennes Le Chateau Mystery) and Ehrling Haagensen have identified patterned arrays of Knights Templar Churches on Bornholm that are very precise. They speculate that the Cistercian monks associated with the Templars there were adept at geodesy or the accurate measurement of the globe. An azimuth created on the globe at the angle of Rosslyn Chapel's orientation also leads to just south of Bornholm Island. Bornholm Island may represent a point of equal importance to that of the International Peace Garden. Both the Rennes le Chateau Chapel and Rosslyn Chapel contain strange octagonal sculptures that may indicate their use as axis or mapping datum.

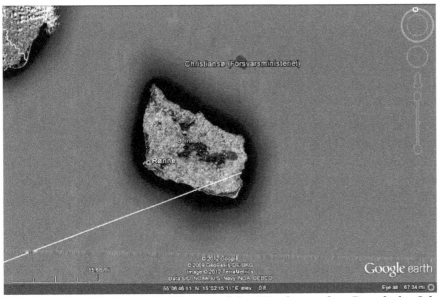
The line from Dashwood's Tower of the Winds reaches Bornholm Island.

The famous Michael Line that is generated from hexagon Avebury also 'points' to or transects the globe to Bornholm Island. The Michael Line may be generated from a hexagonal axis that Avebury was built to represent. Interesting that Anson pointed his Tower of the Winds towards Avebury and Stonehenge in this context. He obviously viewed these ancient sites as datums used in the tradition of the Axis Mundi.

When examining the scheme of what these men were doing using the spatial arrangements of architecture one curious fact emerges. In all of the value of the Tower of the Winds in Athens in a more modern era the earliest copy of this form in this mystery was located in Williamsburg, Virginia! In 1714 what is now known as the Powder Magazine in Williamsburg was constructed. This octagonal structure resembles the ones on the Dashwood and Shugborough estates but was built at least 26 years prior to the one located at Wycombe! The powder magazine as discussed earlier functions in the same manner as the Tower of the Winds (all) and seems to point an azimuth to the International Peace Garden and its octagonal fountain. Is this where Anson found out about the Axis of the future IPG? Earlier in his Naval career Anson spent extended periods of time in the colonies mostly in Charleston South Carolina. He may have visited Williamsburg during this time.

Sir Francis Dashwood's Tower of the Winds points to Oak Island Nova Scotia. Though many would attempt to ascribe this to a chance association in relation to the other places his Tower of the Winds points it is possible this was also an intentional association. This may indicate that Dashwood was aware of the truth of Oak Island. His family ties and associations as discussed earlier would have put him in a family circle that may have even perpetrated all of these myths at different places in colonial America that were being developed by his extended family. The indication of Oak Island by his Tower of the

Winds also continues a tradition of "Man in the Mountain" treasure myths. Is it possible that Dashwood knew about what ever was at Oak Island? To this point this is speculation but it is clear that now we are seeing more and more evidence linking the creation of the Oak Island myth to the same people that built the Newport Tower, Williamsburg, Charleston South Carolina and also exhibited a kind of hidden hand in the development of Halifax, Nova Scotia. It may also be considered that this rash of building follies on the estates of people like the Anson's and Dashwood was reflective of a value of the concepts of Sir Francis Bacon, Inigo Jones, the de Caus' and other architects and landscape designers. This tradition continued to give us the architecture of Thomas Jefferson and the famous street plan of Washington District of Columbia. If the above facts weren't enough to convince the reader that there is a special significance to the Tower of the Winds at West Wycombe and Shugborough may the presence of a third reproduction of that monument on another estate be sufficient?

Amazingly a third Tower of the Winds reproduction is present at the Mt. Stewart Estate just to the southeast of Belfast Ireland. The 1st Marquis of Londonderry built this reproduction later. This tower of the Winds is amazing in that it points an azimuth to the Tower of the Winds at Shugborough and the Tower of the Winds at Shugborough points back. Both structures are oriented to point the way to each other! This arrangement was undoubtedly intentional and may suggest that the Marquis searched out this particular piece of property to attain this alignment. This is the same Stewart or Stuart family in Scotland who are the 'stewards' of the famous Stone of Scone upon which all English and Scottish Royalty have been crowned. Indeed this region of Ireland has many links to Scotland and the tale of St. Columba bringing the Stone of Scone to Scotland and later Templar settlements in western Scotland as discussed by Baingent and Leigh in their book 'The Temple and the Lodge'

It is entirely possible that the use of these types of arrangements or arrays of architecture and art were rediscovered in their ancient context by Dr. John Dee. Dr. Dee was a Trinity College trained navigator and taught that art to the Royal Navy during the Elizabethan era. Dr. Dee was Queen Elizabeth I astrologer as well. His code name to the Queen was "007" as this may have inspired the use of that name by fictional character James Bond. Spotswood's (Williamsburg Powder Magazine), Dashwood (Tower of the Winds West Wycombe), Anson's (Shugborough Tower of the Winds), and Thomas Jefferson's (Poplar Forest) value of this form of architecture evolved from the Tower of the Winds in Athens and the navigational skills of Dr. John Dee and Sir Francis Bacon who was a student and associate of Dee's. Dee's skills may have had an influence on the construction of Star Castle in 1582.

Is it possible that these men's value of the this form were a function of their appreciation of ancient art or was there more at play? Some speculate that Dr. Dee had a hand in the construction of the famous Newport Tower as well. In turn Bacon was an investor in both the Jamestown Colony and the Cupids Newfoundland Colony. This is entirely possible given the facts exposed here and by other researchers.

Dee was an early cartographer who actually studied under Gerhardus Mercator the developer of one of the first modern truly functional map projections that displayed the entire globe. Ancient

112

forms of this knowledge likely did exist but was cloistered or secret information that was kept from the public at large. It is obvious that the Romans and subsequently the Church may have been aware of these arrangements as early as the

Tower of the Winds Mt. Stewart estate.

The Tower of the Winds at Shugborough points to the Tower of the Winds at Mt. Stewart!

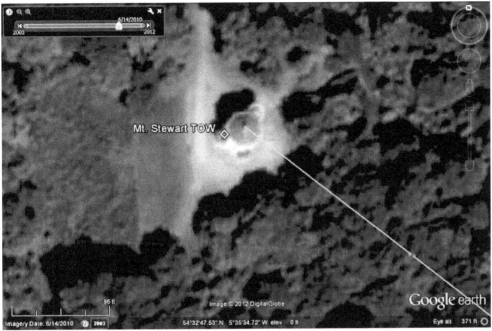

The Tower of the Winds at Mt. Stewart points back to Shugborough TOW! These two structures were intentionally built to point the way to each other.

erection of the Egyptian Obelisk at the Circus of Rome in 40 A.D. by Emperor Caligula. Both St. Peter's Square and the Dome of the Rock function the same was as these men's towers. This may be one of the secrets that were discerned or recovered by the Knights Templar in Jerusalem during their stay there. It is just as likely that they arrived in the Holy Land already being privy to this information given St. Bernard's former association with the Carthusian order and a possible tradition of geodesy among his Cistercian Order. This may have been one of the real reasons they were sent to Jerusalem in the first place. The Knights Templar likely already knew of the directional aspects of the Dome of the Rock.

It is likely that the Knights Templar solved the puzzle of what the octagonal buildings were via their appreciation and veneration of the Dome of the Rock. Alternately this information was more likely handed down via the priesthood of Augurs and the Legio de Christi of Emperor Constantine and subsequently spread through Europe by the operative stonemason's and cloistered monks who lived there after the fall of the empire as well. It is also possible that all of this is the result of the labors of an unknown mystery school or order whose purpose is to keep the Byzantine Empire alive despite its lack of real estate. These influences could have been involved with a variety of historical events from the Nazi regime to the creation of the United States of America.

We have discussed before the history of the Dome of the Rock and how it may have been built by Constantine or manipulated into being by Byzantine Emperor Justinian II. This tradition began during Constantine's reign and continued when Justinian I built Basilica San Vitale in Ravenna Italy. All of these men's appreciation and understanding of geodesy may have come from their knowledge of the Tower of the Winds in Athens,

Greece, the hexagon of Baalbek and possibly the Great Pyramid itself. The possibility that Dashwood, the Anson's, Spotswood, Governor Arnold, The 1st Marquis of Londonderry, and Jefferson were all Knights Templar (Strict Observance) may be considered when examining this evidence. (*Continued below*).

Dashwood's Tower of the Winds at the West Wycombe Estate.

The Powder Magazine in Colonial Williamsburg, Virginia circa. 1714.

Thomas Jefferson's country estate Poplar Forest. It functions as an axis just as the other men's octagons do.

A common thread with many of the characters that seemed to be involved in this activity would include the fact that they spent time in France. During their time there they may have been made aware of the mysteries surrounding arranged arrays of architecture

specifically the value of the octagonal shape and the directional attributes of ancient monuments. The Cultures of France and England are forever intertwined via the legacy of the Norman's, The Knights Templar, The Knights of Malta, The Roman Church, and the Royal interests of both nations.

Charlemagne via the legacy of Charles Martel displayed a value of this philosophy. During the Elizabethan era figures like Dr. John Dee and Sir Francis Bacon would develop and keep this tradition alive. Later Gold Rush era Californian's John Bidwell, Leland Stanford, Joaquin Miller, Jean Baptiste Paulin Caperon, and William Randolph Hearst would seem to fit this mold as well. More modern manifestations of this tradition would include the Georgia Guidestones, The Hoover Dam Star Chart, and the International Peace Garden.

At times what is today England controlled vast portions of modern France. The French and English share a rich Norman heritage. During this era there were undoubtedly periods where a common culture were shared and relations were relatively good. At such times a common mythology and symbolism may have developed with regard to sacred values such as the possibility that a bloodline of Christ actually exists. It may have been at these times a mystery was created that included significant sites on both sides of the English Channel. All of this may have changed in association with the famous "Cutting of the Elm" episode at Gisors that saw the two groups permanently split in a division that may have included French and English Knights Templar going their separate ways yet still having a value of each other. After this parting of the ways references and new clues were added to the mystery independent of what may have been occurring in the separate camp. In both England and France we do see influential people orienting their structures to display hints of their philosophy over a wide period of time.

Ultimately the clues may lead to a point on the earth valued by interests in the United States of America, England, and France. The International Peace Garden and its octagonal "Sunken Garden" fountain may represent these men and women's values and philosophy. The region in which it is located is rich in the culture, history, and lore of all three cultures. It is entirely possible that these men believe North America is the "New Atlantis" of Sir Francis Bacon. Evidence may suggest that the mysteries of Girona and Rennes le Chateau in their modern form were propagated by the same group at different periods of history.

The pyramids of Merowe resemble the pyramid on the Great Seal of the United States. ("Sudan Meroe Pyramids 2001" by Photographer: B N Chagny - taken from en.wikipedia.org, there under CC 1.0, with descripton: Aerial view of the Nubian pyramids at Meroe Image owner: Francis Geius - Mission SFDAS 2001. Licensed under CC BY-SA 1.0 via Wikimedia)

The West Wycombe Estate Tower of the Winds built by Sir Francis Dashwood.

Chapter 8: Stirling Castle and the mystery of the Kings Knot. The Stewart Family and the Mysteries of Rennes le Chateau.

Stirling Castle is best known as the Royal seat of Scotland and home to its monarchs. Most notably the line of Stewart (Stuart) Kings and Queens ruled from Stirling. Some historians go as far as to link the legends of King Arthur and the Knights of the Roundtable to this fortress. The Castle has a long history of occupation beginning in the ninth century and includes all the elements of art and landscaping that one would expect from such a grand symbolic location. As such this structure has been witness to many great historical events including many clandestine and secret happenings.

In the scope of the geographic mysteries that we are pursuing this place seems to have been the nexus of many of the architectural and geographic mysteries of the Western World. The tradition of the Magdala or sacred tower is displayed through the history and architecture related to this place. As we will see one particular landscape feature of Stirling may have been meant to echo the spatial relationship of Amiens Cathedral to the Dome of the Rock, Battle of Teba, and the saga of Robert the Bruce's heart. Via this study the concept of 'vortexes' or 'whirlpools' of energy that these people believed in may become apparent. It is possible that Stirling Castle and the Kings Knot specifically were designed to define and be the root of many mysteries including Rennes le Chateau, Sion (Switzerland), Perillos, The Great Cyclic Cross of Hendaye, Shugborough Hall, Girona, Santiago de Compostela, The Newport Tower, The Powder Magazine, and International Peace Garden to name a few.

Stirling has always been a place of power and intrigue and has gone through several phases of destruction and renovation. Most of what is seen today was built during the heyday of the castle in the period between 1490 and 1600. The castle even once included a large talus or defensive structure that was pyramidal in form. Illustrations from this period seem to depict a pyramid in front of Stirling Castle. In reality the talus was comprised of half of a pyramid abutted against the wall of the Castle to prevent tunneling beneath the structure. This was a common defensive measure developed during the Crusades.

The Stewarts of Stirling Castle came to appreciate and value architecture, land surveying, and navigation as expressed via the clues they have left us via the legacy of the structures they created. The genealogy of this family includes the earlier Norman influences of Henry II including the Plantagenet and Merovingian dynasties mingling with the ancient Egyptian Scythian lines coming from Ireland and Spain as stated in the Declaration of Arbroath. Whether this is genetically true or not may not matter in this examination as the signators of this document likely went about their business as if this were true regardless. Their heritage links this family to many mysteries present all over Europe. Further we may see how all of these architectural mysteries are associated with claiming a spiritual as well as physical domain for those that created them. Many modern or New Age concepts such as vortexes, time warps, and remote viewing may be an interpretive part of their beliefs.

The Stewarts seem to have been involved in the construction of a series of towers and

120

architectural follies scattered over the face of the earth that are all interconnected via their shape and orientation on the globe. They created buildings that pointed to each other on the globe using the shape of the octagon and hexagon. In an age old custom best exemplified by the Greeks and Romans several of these structures may have been built in association or as part of the Templum or sphere of influence of more ancient axes such as hexagonal port of Portus near Rome. Part of this heritage may include the design and construction of many of the gothic cathedrals of Europe including Amiens and its octagonal labyrinth.

This may infer that points on the earth where these associations could be made were especially valuable. For example if one of an octagon's sides or facets points at 225 deg. True North then might not a position along this azimuth be valued? An additional monument may be added and oriented at the correct angle to point back and make each association. This would have been possible by applying astronomical concepts and using ephemeris or star charts that had been collected at the main axis or temple. The collection of ephemeris would have also been important in astrological forecasting and divination. It does seem as if the Stewarts and associated branches of their family did value this art and the use of an octagonal form as a template.

The Stewarts and their near relations have indeed created octagonal and hexagonal structures such as the Powder Magazine in Colonial Williamsburg, The Moorish Tower of Druid Hill Park Baltimore, Ft. Carroll, Thomas Jefferson's Monticello and Poplar Forest, and a series of reproductions of the Tower of the Winds situated on estates in England including one at Oxford University, West Wycombe, Shugborough Hall, Mt. Stewart, and Summerhill estates. We will examine how the Tower of the Winds at Shugborough and Summerhill both have unique spatial relationships with Stirling Castle and other more well known mysteries on the continent.

The value of the octagon is nowhere more obvious than in the shape and form of what is known of as the Kings Knot at Stirling. The Kings Knot is a large octagonal earthwork garden created especially for a visit from Charles I in the late 1620's. Charles I seems to have been the first Stewart to use the octagonal form in this manner though he may have been aware that this tradition spanned back to the Byzantines, Greeks and Egyptians. Later during Victorian times the Kings Knot would be restored. Some accounts of this restoration have the orientation of the octagonal shape changed somehow. This is unclear and only mentioned from questionable sources but we may examine the influence of Queen Victoria in some of these mysteries many of which came to light during her reign. As noted before Charles I has a unique link to the concept of "Arcadia' related to him quoting the book as his last words prior to his beheading.

Here at Stirling which was also in a real way the domain of William Alexander 1st Earl of Stirling it is no surprise that the Arcadian theme is valued. This is also evident in old land deeds and wills that term the region around Stirling "Arcadia." A value of this name and concept on both the part of the English and French concerns may have led to the French name for Nova Scotia as Acadia which in turn would also be appreciated by what seemed to be a French and Scottish Coalition that controlled that region no matter who "owned" it.

The creation of the Kings Knot during the reign of Charles I is notable in association with the imagery of Arcadia we have examined in relation to the King to this point. Here again we may see an octagonal structure in conjunction with other architecture that may have been assembled in a form of landscape mystery. As we may see this array at Stirling is intimately related to the landscape mysteries present at Shugborough Hall and Rennes le Chateau both of which incorporate the imagery of Poussin and The Shepherds of Arcadia.

Earlier in history Charlemagne had built his octagon in the form of Aachen Cathedral. As with many of the other structures discussed here the octagon of Stirling Castle does function as a directional device on the globe that indicates many places likely important to the history of the family and mystery lovers at large. Charles and Queen Victoria later would have likely also been privy to the secrets of the Tower of the Winds in Athens, the Dome of the Rock, Basilica San Vitale and the octagonal Daphne of Constantine the Great.

The later builders of the Tower of the Winds reproductions in England may have also been inspired by the Kings Knot. As discussed Constantine also may have built an octagonal structure in the same location we now see the Dome of the Rock and an additional one in Antioch named in honor of Nero's Domus Aurea. All of these structures would have been seen and appreciated by the forebears of Charles I. This among many other historical facts makes it seem odd that the Muslims would willingly build such a structure (the Dome of the Rock) in a form popularized by Constantine himself. In this scheme of architectural history this simply does not make any sense at all.

More specifically this octagon indicates a south/southeasterly azimuth that includes the site of the battle of Bannockburn, and two of the Tower of the Winds reproductions in England while extending further to include one of the most famous landscape mysteries on the face of the earth. First this SSE azimuth passes over an octagonal Tower of the Winds once located on the Summerhill estate in Northwestern England. This tower is now in ruins but its octagonal foundation is still visible and measurable. This line from Stirling passes less than a hundred meters west of the tower. At this scale that is a direct hit. The Summerhill tower was likely built to achieve this association.

Next the arc or azimuth suggested by the octagon of the Kings Knot continues its transect and extends directly over the Tower of the Winds at Shugborough Hall. The Anson family of Shugborough is lineal descendants of the Stewarts fitting the value of the octagon by this Bloodline. One of their friends and architects also the designer of many of the follies at Shugborough was named James "Athenian" Stuart. The Kings Knot is pointing to one of the important places in our understanding of the concept of "Arcadia" in both the Rennes le Chateau and Shugborough mysteries. The entire mythology of Shugborough links it via directional clues to many other mysteries such as the stone of destiny, Stonehenge, Avebury, Lincoln Cathedral, and the Lia Fail among others. The Shugborough Hall Tower of the Winds points to both Avebury and Stonehenge in a single arc on the globe.

The Shepherd's Monument rendering of Poussin's 'Et in Arcadia Ego' seems to symbolically link Shugborough to Rennes le Chateau. These people are telling you to pay attention to the

122

Tower of the Winds in Athens and other structures that are descendant of it. As it turns out these images are one hundred percent appropriate given the next target of this azimuth or arc on the globe.

Next the very same azimuth continues its course across the English Channel and western France to 'the environs' (Haywood) of Rennes Le Chateau. Indeed this azimuth closely matches the position and orientation of the star identified in the landscape of Rennes Le Chateau by writer Henry Lincoln. This means that Lincoln's star and the Kings Knot point the way to each other while also indicating the Tower of the Winds at Shugborough and Summerhill. In addition to all of the other associations noted at Shugborough this would indeed make the estate a kind of talismanic crossroads in this belief system. Once more we may be seeing French influenced Jacobites venerating and taking part in this ancient tradition. He we see a real physical link via directions suggested at the Kings Knot and Rennes le Chateau that Shugborough is indeed linked philosophically to both places. At each site the theme of Arcadia is suggested.

This is a direct result of the family relations of the Stewart family that also link to each place where this theme is present. This will be presented in more detail as the story progresses. One may be surprised to see their influence later in Gold Rush era California at a date prior to the follies at Rennes le Chateau being constructed.

This amazing association solidly again links the imagery of Arcadia to Charles I. In a very real way he built the Kings Knot. In addition the Kings Knot was constructed during the life of William Alexander as well. As Earl of Stirling he may well have been the driving impetus behind the construction of the Kings Knot. Later Jacobite influences such as the Anson's repeated this imagery while adding to the mystery of the Kings Knot. Given this scheme it is beginning to appear as if there were an English or more apropos a Scottish influence in the mysteries of Rennes le Chateau. It is true that Charles I was related to the Kings of France including later exiled King Henri V who many associate with the building of the architectural follies at Rennes le Chateau that include the Tour Magdala, Villa Bethania, and the renovated Chapel there. It well may be that the concept of Arcadia is referring to these fallen kings and the concept of the "Ancient Regime" which they viewed as representative of a simple more pastoral society that they of course ruled. Life was so much simpler then in their eyes.

Here we have the Anson brothers and their architects arranging and adding to a talismanic array that had been built one hundred and fifty years prior at Stirling and possibly much further back at Rennes le Chateau. Alternately given this scheme it is possible that the more modern version of the Rennes le Chateau mystery was arranged in context with Stirling and Shugborough by Henry Artois (Henri V) whose wife by coincidence was an individual that was touted as being heir to the exiled throne of the Stewarts. She had descended via the daughter of Charles I Henrietta of England.

This information and the surprising geographic relationship is defined by architecture at all three sites and adds weight to the many notions that Shugborough and Rennes le Chateau are somehow related. This may be why forms of the Poussin painting are featured in both mysteries.

Here is also a situation that may have included the influence of the d'Abbadie's. We have already noted the direct involvement of d'Abbadie Saint-Germain in assisting James II at Saint-Germain-en-Laye. It is possible that the d'Abbadie's were in part helping to finance the Jacobite cause. There may be a metaphorical or real association between the theme of the Poussin's 'Et in Arcadia Ego' and the d'Abbadie governor of French Arcadia. This theory may also seem more legitimate given that we have learned that Bonnie Prince Charlie and even the Marquis de Lafayette were intimately involved in the genealogy of the de La Tour d'Auvergne group of families in France. This of course links us to the first governor of French Arcadia Charles de La Tour and how his mother was said to have been a lady in waiting to Queen Henrietta Marie and a direct family relation of William Alexander of Stirling. Charles father Claude de La Tour of course holds the same associations as husband of the former Ms. Salazar his wife. Both the de La Tours in the French Acadia story were also Barons of Nova Scotia so that is very telling as well.

Even if Poussin was a Jesuit agent of some kind his association with Jacobites or those that would become Jacobites may be telling. James II and Bonnie Prince Charlie were both Roman Catholics who were even interred in a crypt inside St. Peter's Basilica of the Vatican. Jesuit sympathies or cooperation would be no surprise in association with the Jacobites or the exiled Kings. The fact that the Poussin painting has become an intricate part of the mystery at Rennes le Chateau leaves the door open for some Jacobite involvement in the development of the mystery at Rennes le Chateau during the seventeenth and eighteenth centuries. The Kings Knot directly relates both places that include mysteries associated with Poussin's painting.

The village of Arques, the Blanchefort Tombstone, and the star in the landscape of Rennes le Chateau and Rennes le Bains all harken to the Arcadian mysteries. Each of these mysteries had had a mania attached to it that has them included in many popular books and television shows. Each of these places has a cult like following that developed theories wide ranging in their speculation. None of them have documented what is revealed here.

Via the authors interpretation the famous altar painting at Rennes le Chateau seems to depict the Triumphal Arch at Shugborough further adding to the similarities and hidden clues. The perspective of the painting may include the fact that the Shugborough Tower of the Winds is depicted just to the left of the arch in the altar painting. In addition the basic three points of the pentagram in the landscape of Rennes le Chateau first noted by Lincoln were said to have been created by the Blanchefort family that had direct relations to the de La Tours and Marquis de Lafayette. This along with possible familial ties may further link goings on at Rennes le Chateau to Stirling Castle. Subsequent more modern events at Rennes le Chateau such as president's daughter Elizabeth Van Buren living in the area and creating somewhat of a mystery herself may be a result of a value of these concepts. This inclusion of Van Buren, Jefferson, and Lafayette in whatever is going on at Rennes le Chateau is also explained by the same family group's direct relation to Bonnie Prince Charlie and James I.

Another possible link between the concepts involved in the Great Cyclic Cross of Hendaye and Rennes le Chateau would include an alignment of significant monuments that point from Rennes le Chateau to The Arian Baptistery in Ravenna, Italy. This alignment does not include any structures that 'point to' San Vitale. These places align to create an arc that extends to the Arian Baptistery in Ravenna built by Theodoric the Great. It includes the Rennes le Chateau Chapel, Chateau Hautepoul, Chateau Blanchefort, and the octagonal Arian Baptistery. This alignment also matches the northern east to west trending part of the star in the landscape of Rennes le Chateau as espoused by Henry Lincoln. This alignment may relate directly to the influence of Empresses Theodora and Sophia in the propagation of the truth, myths, and legends of Mary Magdalene that we may see interwoven into the mysteries at all of these places. Again all of this imagery could more easily be interpreted as being associated with Our Lady or Mary Mother of Christ.

In addition the Arian Baptistery of Ravenna built by Theodoric's octagonal form not only points to the Rennes le Chateau Chapel but also matches the cross-piece of the pentagonal star in the landscape suggested by the pentagonal star again relating to the Poussin painting. Ravenna is likely the home seat of all this Arcadian imagery related to Emperor's Arcadius and Honorius and also Bishop Ursiana (the bear of Arcadia). The image of the bear of Ursa Minor relates to the symbols of Arcas and in turn a value of the pole star and navigation. The story of Emperor Justinian I wife Augusta Theodora may have also been the basis for the Cult of Mary Magdalene that emerges later. (*See my book "The Prophecy of Dante and the New Jerusalem of Ravenna" for the origins of the Arcadian mythos in Europe*).

The Star identified by Henry Lincoln "points to" the Arian Baptistery. The Arian Baptistery "points" back. The Arian Baptistery is a copy of the original Holy Sepulcher in Rome and does resemble the Orphir Round Kirk of Orkney that was also inspired by the same structure in Jerusalem. In fact we may discern that a "copy" of Jerusalem had been constructed in Ravenna prior to the time this was planned in Jerusalem. This scheme of architecture in Ravenna predate's the array of architecture in Jerusalem and may have even been the inspiration for what we see there today in many ways. This includes the octagonal form of the Dome of the Rock which was built over one hundred years after Basilica San Vitale in Ravenna which it does resemble very much.

Given what we have seen with regard to Basilica San Vitale of Ravenna as written of by Jacob Abbadie in his tome on the Book of Revelations it may not be out of the question that a millennial monument similar to the Great Cross of Hendaye would be included in any talismanic association with Rennes le Chateau. If not for these factors this could be written off as a chance or freak coincidence. It now may be viewed as being well within the realm of possibility that this was part of the intent of the alignments of Rennes le Chateau from the beginning. It is also no coincidence that there is a cross near the Rennes le Chateau Chapel similar to the Great Cross that even includes a similar "O Crux Ave" inscription. More and more it appears that many of the mysteries that seem to have been placed in the mind of the public through history may all be related to one another via a similar philosophy and family line.

This type of association may indicate that the Rennes Le Chateau mystery was perpetrated or planned at least in part by factions related to the Stewarts or Stuarts, as they are known in France. There are familial ties between the Stuarts and the Anjou family of France via the Plantagenet

125

and Merovingian lines. These connections include Henry Artois or exiled King of France Henry V.

Many people speculate that Artois was indeed the man or family that had funded the construction of the follies of the Tour Magdala and Villa Bethania at Rennes le Chateau. The associations with Navarre, The Stuarts, and Bourbons run throughout both the mystery of Rennes le Chateau and the Great Cyclic Cross of Hendaye. In fact it is clear that the Anjou's played a role in other mysteries such as those surrounding Joan of Arc, Mary Magdalene's remains at St. Maximim, and Saintes Maries de La Mer. This may also lead us to a rationale as to why the Kensington Rune is valued even though it may have been left by French concerns. During many periods of colonial history and development the Scottish were more allied with the French thus opposing the English.

Rene' of Anjou was a companion and some say lover of Joan of Arc who played a large role in the events associated with her. Some even speculate that he planned it all as a matter of inspirational history. Anjou's Order of the Crescent may also have had a value of these architectural arrangements.

So. The Kings Knot points to Rennes le Chateau. Via the Summerhill and Shugborough Tower of the Winds. From Scotland to France with similar mysteries at both ends of the array involving the same Bloodlines. When viewed on the globe the azimuth extending from Stirling Castle seems to define what this family may have seen as their domain including both their Scottish, English, and Norman heritage. After all the Stuarts and St. Clair lines possess a lineage that includes Rollo the Viking who first settled in Rouen France to establish the Norman culture in France.

The Kings Knot also indicates some other places of talismanic value to those that created this interesting array. The additional stellations or arcs emanating from the Kings Knot also indicate additional important places. The Kings Knot even points to the Star Pyramid a.k.a. the 'Salem Stone on the grounds of Stirling Castle via an azimuth extending from its Northeast orientation. In 1863 a man named James Drummond built what is known of as the 'Salem Stone' or the Star Pyramid at Stirling. The Drummond family is a direct relation of the Stewarts as well. As we have seen Mr. Drummond filled the mold of family explorer or adventurer just as his relations, James Bruce, and Sir William Drummond had done before him. James Drummond fits the mold of the creator of many pieces of talismanic architecture in that he was a professional land surveyor just as John Dee, Thomas Jefferson and Alexander Von Humboldt were. This man was a professional at the arts or craft if you will required to make these geographic associations.

The 'Salem (Jeru'Salem) Stone also features a kind of time capsule that includes a copy of the bible and other unknown objects. The fact that this monument was originally named the Salem Stone is telling you basically that it is a "Jerusalem Stone." Isn't this entire mystery about lost stones and the quest to find them? Perhaps the Holy Grail itself is in the hidden chamber of the Star Pyramid? Not likely but this monument does inspire one to contemplate its origins. Given the monuments shape and heritage this would be an appropriate place to hide something in plain sight. In fact they are telling you something is within the pyramid to begin with. Why would a pyramid be called the 'Salem Stone?'

In this context it is interesting that the Kings Knot also points to the Dome of the Rock on the Temple Mount in Jerusalem. William Drummond may have been aware of this association when he added Star Pyramid to the grounds of Stirling.

There is one pyramid in Jerusalem known as the Tomb of Zechariah that is similar in size to the one at Stirling. The Jerusalem Stone also resembles smaller steeper sided Nubian pyramids located in the modern country of Sudan in what was once considered Upper Egypt that Drummond may have seen in his travels to Africa. This pyramid at Stirling is very similar to those seen on the U.S. dollar bill and other imagery associated with that country.

Later in history members of the same lineage were involved in the reasons why this type of pyramid is rendered on currency and is included in The Great Seal of the United States of America. The same bloodline seemed to have been fascinated with the art of engraving and metallurgy to the same degree they studied astronomy and cartography. Their relations especially those of the Scott family had a huge yet little told impact on U.S. history (Gianotti 2014).

Much of the heritage of Scotland involves interwoven tales of the orders of Knights, Robert the Bruce, William Wallace, Masonry and later the Jacobite and loyalist causes. During the era of the Latin Kingdom of Jerusalem (Salem) the Knights of the Temple included many men from different branches of and related to the Stewarts or Stuarts as it is spelled in France. These people occupied the Temple Mount in Jerusalem and valued the architecture there very much.

As discussed previously the Templars likely had a clandestine value of the architecture there including the Dome of the Rock and the Al Aqsa Mosque that involved them having actually been built by Constantine and Justinian I. Charles Martel (the Hammer) and his grandson Charlemagne had perpetuated this value prior to the Templars. Elements of Charlemagne's Aachen cathedral resemble the Dome of the Rock in what he meant as a tribute to Byzantine architecture.

This information may well comprise what many consider the secrets of the Templars. They were aware of the real scheme of history and kept specific details about what these temples were for and who had actually constructed them in the past. It may be that many aspects of past history have been altered to hide the existence of this network. It is possible that this information was handed down to them long before the crusades or the Latin Kingdom of Jerusalem had been formed. Indeed the Knights Templar came to the Temple Mount with a pre ordained purpose that included finding Constantine's remains and deciphering that directional qualities of the structure. This info may have made it to them via Charlemagne.

The Templars came with their templates to the Temple Mount and Temple of the Dome of the Rock to study the Templum that Constantine had created to establish temporal control. They wanted to find out which way the Dome of the Rock pointed on the globe. It is possible that the Knights quested along the arcs of the templum of the Dome of the Rock searching for more information. This could be the genesis of the concept of the Grail Quest. One of these quests may have led them to Lalibela, Ethiopia.

Subsequent history and structures that were built seem to bear this out. They knew what it was before they came. Somehow this information had been rediscovered or found by the Cistercian monks who actually created the order. Part of the reason for the Crusades to the Holy Land may have even been to retake the Dome of the Rock and pursue a study of its Templum. From a strategic point of view it does not make sense for them to have invaded the Holy Land while the Moors were occupying most of Spain. There may have been a reason beyond the normally given rationales as to why this region was so important. The Temple Mount is already one of the most contentious pieces of real estate on the planet. It is not hard to imagine there would be some hidden truths as to why it is so important.

Members of the Stewarts, St. Clair's and other branches of their family were among the earliest rulers of the Latin Kingdom of Jerusalem. These are people who would have had a deep and abiding appreciation of the Temple Mount and the secrets they were aware of. Later this story will involve the famous Knights Templar Grand Commander Godefroy de Bouillon.

This inside information may have also raised many questions and mysteries that they felt needed to be solved. Many of these beliefs and secret concepts may have sprung from Byzantine royalty's value of Egyptian Coptic Christian concepts. Knowledge of this way to legally define property was also made part of a mystery school apparatus that contributed to keeping all of this secret and veiled.

Supporting this notion is the fact that the East/Southeast trending azimuth suggested by the Kings Knot extends to the Dome of the Rock on the Temple Mount in Jerusalem just as the octagon of Amiens does. The King's Knot points to the Dome of the Rock. The line or arc from Stirling does not match a facet of the Dome of the Rock but the fact that this array points to the Dome of the Rock may be interpreted as a value of the Dome of the Rock as it applies to the Stewarts who created the King's Knot. As we observed earlier the octagon of the Dome of the Rock points to St. Peter's Square at the Vatican and the array there points back. Just like the arrangement here between Stirling and Rennes le Chateau.

Is this the reason that the star in the landscape of Rennes le Chateau was 'created' in the first place? Is it possible that Scottish interests are responsible for the entire mystery of Rennes le Chateau? Not likely. There is a great deal of evidence indicating Henry V exiled King of France as being responsible for the follies at Rennes le Chateau. Henry was a descendant and member of the House of Bourbon and was indeed related to the Stuarts, Anjou, and Habsburgs. As we will see Henry V may have also been responsible for the construction of the Frenchman's Tower of Palo Alto, California during the Gold Rush era.

In addition it may be that the octagon of Amiens Cathedral inspired this entire arrangement and how it was valued by past members of many of the Kings of Scotland's family or court. As we have learned Charlemagne employed two Scottish magi named Scot or Scotus. It is not out of the question that these men had played a hand or helped to inspire Charlemagne's construction of

Aachen Cathedral. The Battle of Teba and its imagery may be one of the things that the Kings Knot was built to venerate. Both the octagon of Amiens and the Kings Knot point the way to Jerusalem and the Dome of the Rock. Octagon to octagon. Note that the tomb of Zechariah a pyramid similar to Star Pyramid at Stirling is very near to the Dome of the Rock just to the southeast of the Temple Mount. A New Jerusalem array of architecture had been created at Stirling Castle.

The Templars had possibly obtained or logged ephemeris or star charts from the Dome of the Rock that would allow them to make these associations from anywhere on the globe. These people were legally describing their claims to property in an ancient way. It is possible that this was the method used to place the Kensington Rune Stone, which is 'pointed to' by the Dome of the Rock, Newport Tower, Ames Pyramid, and International Peace Garden. The stone may be a talismanic marker that actually denotes some type of ownership only shared among the initiated parties. This ownership may also translate to the public at large via alternate explanations.

Research is ongoing into the history of Scotland and how some of the additional azimuths emanating from the Kings Knot may be appreciated elsewhere. Since other structures had been identified as being built in this tradition it is important to note if any of them point the way to the octagon at Stirling. Many times structures will be built that point to the main axis if they are not located on one of the primary octagonal divisions in this scheme or plan. In this way people who are allied or additional family members may display their knowledge of this tradition and respect for the mother axis in a talismanic way without being directly aligned with the existing topology. Thomas Jefferson built two structures one with an octagonal element at Monticello and the other an octagon in plan at Poplar Forest. Many architectural historians compare Poplar Forest to the Dome of the Rock yet evidence suggests he may have been valuing the Daphne's of Constantine and Justinian and not the Muslims.

In an amazing and revealing association the octagon of Thomas Jefferson's Poplar Forest suggests an arc on the globe that points the way directly to the Kings Knot at Stirling Castle. This same azimuth passes just 400 yds to the west of Jefferson's main estate Monticello and transects part of Charlottesville. This azimuth then passes just west of James Madison's estate Montpelier. Interestingly the orientation of Montpelier points the back to Monitcello.

The octagonal portion of Jefferson's other home Monticello in Charlottesville creates an azimuth on the globe that leads the way to Rosslyn Chapel and then continues on to the Sans Souci estate of Frederick the Great of Prussia. These associations may be considered intentional. Jefferson valued Scotland and the Stewarts or he may have never cared to make this association. These associations also point to places where two of the me that were considered to be 'King of America' were Scottish (Bonnie Prince Charlie) and Prussian (Frederick Henry Louis Prince of Prussia) nobility.

Amazingly the back azimuth or opposite direction from Monticello to Sans Souci via Rosslyn leads to just six miles south of the famous Georgia Guidestones. It is entirely possible that in the modern era the Guidestones were placed in relation to this array. In the modern world this may have been the closest and most desirable location to place an additional monument and does fall with the tolerances of accuracy that was used to orient Monticello and Poplar Forest originally. It is interesting to note here that Poplar Forest is also included in the templum of The Great Cyclic Cross of Hendaye, which he may have learned of from Alexander Von Humboldt.

Hendaye's templum points to Poplar Forest raising the possibility that these associations are why he placed his house there to begin with. He wanted his house to point to the King's Knot and be pointed to by the templum of Hendaye. Jefferson's knowledge of these dynamics has to mean that he had been initiated into these mysteries and would have been aware of concepts that included the relationships between places like Rosslyn Chapel, Amiens Cathedral, The Great Cross of Hendaye, Ronda and the Battle of Teba.

Here in a symbolic way he had come full circle from Hendaye and its similar angry sun motif, to the Sunstone being featured on the Capitol rotunda, and on to the Kings knot and his other octagons of Barboursville and Monticello. He had linked it all together in a scheme that included these places all pointing to each other. Even Madison had 'aimed' his home at Monticello. Jefferson was privy to the truth of history and could have led his life using this information. He expressed this knowledge in the shape and orientation with regard to true north of both of his personal properties and also possibly the Barboursville Mansion, which he also designed with an octagonal element.

The southerly arc extending from the Kings Knot reaches just two miles to the west of Ronda Spain to the small village of La Indiana. In effect the Kings Knot also points to Ronda and its mysteries just as the Great Cross of Hendaye does. This may also be interpreted that Jefferson was also aware of these Native American associations and thus his and Von Humboldt's interest in the Aztec Sunstone and its later rendering on the United States Capitol rotunda. The porch of Palacio Salvatierra featuring the Incan figures and the Native American Green Man along with Palacio Monctezuma were both built in their present forms in 1798 just five years before Von Humboldt examined the Aztec Sunstone. The village of La Indiana is a suburb of Ronda and is basically part of that town. At this scale it is safe to consider the possibility that Ronda is being pointed to by the Kings Knot. The name of La Indiana itself is also intriguing in light of the Native American themes present in Ronda.

It is possible that this association between the Kings Knot and Ronda was meant to inform us of the information available at both Palacio de Salvatierra and Palacio Monctezuma. It seems that this area of Spain does hold a great deal of significance in the mystery including being close to the site of the Battle of Teba and the disappearance of several members of Scots nobility. As an aside in this vein it is interesting to note that Ronda Spain is home to the final resting place of actor and writer Orson Welles.

What hidden values or associations may we infer from this geographic scheme? The fact that Jefferson built two octagonal structures that value the same places in turn may mean that he was a blood relative of the Stewarts. Many of the other people who created structures similar to this were related blood. Was he an ally or relative of Fredrick the Great? We do know that

Jefferson's friend and fellow Linnean Society member Alexander Von Humboldt was the Prussian royal court geographer and minister of mines during this period so there is one connection.

Monticello's octagon points to both Rosslyn Chapel and Fredrick the Great's palace in one arc on the globe. The Von Humboldt estate which is festooned with bas-relief copies of the gods of the Tower of the Winds in Athens is very near Sans Souci. If Jefferson did not have some value of these people or places is this simply a geographic fluke? There is too much here to suggest that this was not arranged intentionally by Jefferson long after the Kings Knot had been built. Some researchers do suggest a genealogical link between Jefferson and the Stewarts. Possibly this link is present in Prussia as there are many ties between the Royal houses of Europe. The fact that the Von Humboldt estate of Alexander's brother Wilhelm includes imagery of the Tower of the Winds in Athens is also very suggestive that all of this is indeed true.

The Kings Knot displays the tradition of the use of the octagonal form as a point from which to observe the stars and plot ones location on the globe. The Stewarts were also setting a prime meridian similar to that at Greenwich and Paris. Along the way through the march of history many powerful people had upheld this tradition as a way of establishing a domain or templum. A sphere of influence so to speak in which they could understand the location of each place of importance in an octagonal scheme in relation to a center point.

This practice would later translate to the concept of a map projection. The Romans used this tradition to establish colony cities in this manner as well as the location of temples and even important events such as military battles. We do see the battle of Bannockburn taking place on the same azimuth leading to Rennes le Chateau from the Kings Knot. It is possible that in the recent past this practice was still being utilized by Masonic factions in the United States. If this association with Rennes le Chateau is legitimate than what does this mean about the mysteries there? It may infer that the saga of father Saunière and the architectural follies are somehow part of the entire scheme or value of this strange topology of places linked on the globe.

It fits the pattern of what has come before too closely not to be part of the same tradition. Perhaps elements of the Anjou family related to the Stuarts had planned this as a connection between the two like family groups from different countries. A kind of talismanic family link that comprises a huge mystery to the casual observer but is obvious to them. Given this no one fits the bill as the 'creator' of the Rennes le Chateau mystery better than Henry V (Artois) exiled King of France.

Many speculate that Habsburg factions were responsible for the follies that have been built at Rennes le Chateau in the form of the Tor Magdala and Villa Bethania. The Anjou's and Stewarts both of course have blood ties to the Habsburg's including Henry V. It is also obvious that other royal factions valued and practiced this tradition in ways separate from the Stewart faction. In a way we may see that both views are true and legitimate.

Alternately this may mean that a greater and more ancient mystery is lurking in the environs of Rennes le Chateau that would involve earlier royal entities that began these traditions long ago. It could be possible that later groups of people chose the area to establish a more modern mystery in a place that had a long tradition of this through history. There is already a preponderance of Knights Templar lore infused into the mystery at Rennes le Chateau so that era as well as the earlier era of the Goths and Byzantines may be included in the hidden attributes of that mystery. A distant association with Basilica San Vitale may be present in this vein.

Ultimately it is possible that the blood of Constantine and Justinian I and II are part of the family heritage of the Stewarts and Charlemagne. The value of the octagon is present in the histories of Constantine, both Justinian I and II, Charlemagne, the Anjou's, Amiens and the Great Cross, The Church, and now as we see the Stewarts of Stirling Castle. It is clear that if nothing else these family groups have a strong admiration and appreciation of the Roman and Byzantine way of doing things.

Stirling Castle showing unique pyramidal defensive structure known as a 'talus.' ("Stirling Castle John Slezer" by John Slezer - This image is available from the National Library of ScotlandFrom John Slezer's THeatrum Scotiae [1]. Licensed under Public Domain via Wikimedia).

The Graveyard at Stirling may have been the inspiration for a similar mystery at the Bruton Parish Church in Williamsburg. ("StirlingCastle1900". Licensed under Public Domain via Wikimedia).

The Service Stone of Stirling Castle and the page from Quarles Book of Emblems that the artwork was copied from. This stone and Book of Emblems was produced at about the same time a similar mystery was being created in Williamsburg Virginia.

133

Chapter 9: Edgar Allan Poe, Henry Wadsworth Longfellow, The Westford Knight, Oak Island, and Newport Tower.

There is no overt proof that Edgar Allan Poe knew the truth of the Newport Tower. Some of the places that the Poe visited during his life along with some of his works may indicate not only knowledge of the Newport Tower and what it represents but also an understanding of all the mysteries we have examined here and many more. What possible proof is there that Poe may have known about even the Newport Tower? There are no records of him commenting on this mystery though we see him at least mentioned in association with the famous cipher on the "90 foot stone of Oak Island." Why and how would Edgar Allan Poe have known of these phenomena even in some cases they mysteries were not known to the public until after his death?

Earlier we examined Poe's legacy with the Society of the Cincinnati that may have contributed to his exploits and investigations. An examination of the lineage of Poe's Mother Elizabeth may reveal some startling associations that may have manifested themselves in what Poe viewed as a family legacy. Elizabeth Poe's maiden or given last name was Arnold. When Poe was a student at West Point he was known to have bragged that Benedict Arnold was his grandfather. An examination of his genealogy shows that Poe was not the grandson of Benedict Arnold. What is not commonly discussed is the fact that Poe's mother was directly related to and descended from the same source as Benedict Arnold Jr. and Sr. Benedict Arnold is a member of the 9th generation extending from Richard I Arnold of England. Elizabeth Poe/Arnold is a member of the 11th generation of Richard I Arnold. A theory involving the application of long-range family goals in association with other relations would support the notion that Poe may have been initiate of these mysteries in a similar manner to which Thomas Jefferson had been introduced.

Benedict Arnold Sr. is the man who common history tells us built the Newport Tower. It appears highly possible that Benedict Arnold jr. the famous traitor of the Revolutionary war may have been the Grand Uncle of Elizabeth Poe. It is possible that this information was exposed to Poe as part of a family legacy he held. This is a startling connection between Poe and the mystery of the Newport Tower with all its possible connections to President Jefferson via his relation to the famous Easton family of Newport Rhode Island. Benedict Arnold was also present in London at the time of Elizabeth Arnold's birth in 1787. Benedict Arnold returned to England to live for the rest of his life in 1791.

All of this may indicate some sort of knowledge on the part of Edgar Allan Poe with regard to the truth of the Newport Tower. Our examination here does suggest that the deductive talents of Poe would have also led him to investigate all the associations with other places that the Newport Tower holds including the Kensington Rune. The roots of the Kensington mystery may even lay in Virginia where both Jefferson and Poe have family connections to those that may have had knowledge of or even had arranged these mysteries as part of an intelligence gathering and manipulation operation.

That is only one of the possibilities suggested by Poe's involvement in these mysteries even if only hinted at. Taken in total this all suggests that he not only knew of but used these concepts in

134

his writing. Poe's inclusion in the Society of the Cincinnati and his lineage including links to the Arnold family put him in a class of people that included Thomas Jefferson. Poe would go on to become a sort of American Sir Francis Bacon. Given all of this information in total it is easy to imagine Poe being a acolyte of Bacon's who did a great deal during his life to propagate the philosophies and plans of Sir Francis. Poe was of an intellect and aptitude comparable to Bacon's. Poe's work with cryptography and ciphers along with his deductive abilities place him squarely in this class of scholars.

In Poe's work entitled "Eureka" he even discusses Bacon's deductive reasoning in comparison to the method employed by Aristotle. In this text Poe refers to Bacon as "Hog" and Aristotle as Mr. Aris Tuttle. Eureka is interesting in that it even briefly discusses the existence of time based vortexes in association with specific points on the earth. This is an amazing correlation to late nineteenth century and early twentieth century views of the attributes of certain places on the globe that may be marked by temples. Poe's speculation in this realm also matches many of the things the Cassini and d'Abbadie families of France were interested in. The notion of these type of vortexes may have also been part of what was valued at Rennes le Chateau thus bolstering the notion that Poe had knowledge of that phenomena as well as others that fell into the same category.

Poe's family relation is interesting but what other hints may there be that Poe knew of the Newport Tower and what it represents?

One of the most famous sites pointed to by researchers who believe that elements of Henry Sinclair's navy had come to North America in the fourteenth century is located in Westford, Massachusetts. Westford is the site of the famous "Westford Knight" stone carving. This rock art illustrates what resembles a Knights Templar burial slab from Scotland. It depicts the figure of a Knight who may have been of the Gunn family. This carving is also recently discovered to include the famous X letter or font with the extension on the upper part of the X as seen on the Kensington Rune. Many researchers have linked this rock art in Westford to those that they feel had constructed the Newport Tower.

The inclusion of this strange X symbol on the Westford Knight may also support the notion that Poe was aware of it and all the meanings it held with regard to his Virginia heritage. This symbol is present on the Archer Reliquary of Jamestown, The logo of the College of William and Mary, The Kensington Rune, and the burial slabs of the Royalty of Monaco at the St. Nicholas Cathedral there. There is an established familial connection between Thomas Jefferson and Peter Easton a.ka. The Marquis of Savoy in Monaco. Jefferson visited Monaco during his trip to France and Italy as Secretary of State. We have examined in other work how the octagon of the St. Nicholas cathedral points an arc on the globe to the Newport Tower and Poplar Forest (Jefferson's octagon) in Virginia. Given our studies of Poe here this is an amazing geographic correlation that likely extends far beyond a chance association.

Edgar Allan Poe visited Westford Massachusetts several times to meet "Annie" the subject of some of his poetry and a love interest developed by him after the death of his wife Virginia.

Annie lived in Westford and Poe visited the town several times and was even noted as "exploring the local area thoroughly." Today there is a monument to Edgar Allan Poe in front of what was once Annie's house. It is possible that part of Poe's fascination with Westford was yet another more ancient monument. Poe's presence in Westford may indicate this is true. If nothing else Poe had a talent for showing up in places that are associated with this occult activity and associated overtones. There is a huge amount of metaphorical and anecdotal information that suggests Poe had not only been schooled in the skills needed to understand all of this but to add to it and interpret it in ways many had never thought of. Here in the personage of E.A. Poe we have an individual eminently capable of deciphering any mystery that was left behind by Sir Francis Bacon or his descendants.

Poe's love of Annie came near the end of his life during the period in which Poe wrote what he considered his Magnum Opus entitled "Eureka." Interestingly Poe dedicated "Eureka" to Alexander Von Humboldt. Von Humboldt surfaces at different places in this saga and he was associated with all the major players who seemed to value the concept of the Axis Mundi and Prime Meridian in a secret society if not talismanic manner. This again is another amazing coincidence tying Poe to the circle of people we have previously identified as having knowledge of and practicing this tradition. Edgar Allen Poe was educated for a time in England. This factor may have also contributed to his role in these mysteries.

Given this new information about Poe we may consider that he knew of and possibly used these concepts as part of an intelligence service. These tenets may have in turn been used against those that opposed a Republic in France as well as those that wished to undermine this concept in the United States. During this era a constant silent war between deposed monarchies and those that wished a Republic raged. Poe may have applied some of his knowledge of the traditional values of Royalty against them. These operations may have included other free thinkers and intellectuals such as Alexander Von Humboldt, Thomas Jefferson, Marquis de Lafayette, Alexandre Dumas, Dominique Cassini, Francois Arago, Antoine d' Abbadie, Samuel Morse, and James Fennimore Cooper. The Society of the Cincinnati played a clear role in supporting the notion of a Republic in both France and the United States. In many ways this group of intellectuals resembles description of the famous Priory of Sion or "Invisible College" of Sir Francis Bacon.

This poem entitled "Eldorado" was written by Poe during the last year of his life in the time frame in which he visited Westford Massachusetts. This poem both refers to the lost treasure of Eldorado and the passing of a Knight or chivalric figure as seen at the Westford Knight rock art. In addition the theme of the poem has a Knight dying in a quest for "Eldorado." The theme of Eldorado involves a distinctly North or South American connotation that would not have been applied to the "Old World." Poe may have intentionally applied this distinct American imagery to that of a Knight on a quest as part of what he may have known. We also this this theme during the same era being repeated by poet Henry Wadsworth Longfellow.

The saga whether true or false involving Henry Sinclair and his Knights coming to the Westford area and burying one of their own may be interpreted within this Poe work. The fact that he came to Westford at a time when the Westford Knight was considered to be Native American rock art is notable. Is it possible that Poe saw the Westford Knight and correctly interpreted it with his poem "Eldorado" serving as metaphorical proof or suggestion that this is true? Or had the representation of the Westford Knight as such was part of the "Norumbega" movement that espoused Norse settlement in New England prior to Columbus.

Eldorado by Edgar Allan Poe.

Gaily bedight,
A gallant Knight,
In sunshine and in shadow, Had journeyed long,
Singing a song,
In search of Eldorado.

But he grew old-
This Knight so bold-
And o'er his heart a shadow
Fell, as he found
No spot of ground
That looked like Eldorado.
And, as his strength
Failed him at length
He met a pilgrim shadow-
"Shadow" said he,
"Where can it be-
This land of Eldorado?"

"Over the Mountains
Of the Moon,
Down the Valley of the shadow,
Ride, boldly ride,"
The shade replied,-
"If you seek for Eldorado!"
-E.A. Poe 1849.

Henry Wadsworth Longfellow and the Newport Tower.

Henry Wadsworth Longfellow and Edgar Allan Poe were contemporary poets and authors. Both men gained a great deal of notoriety and had a great deal in common though Longfellow was from Maine and Poe was from Virginia. Longfellow and Poe are easily two of the most recognizable names from eighteenth century poetry. As we have seen Poe may have been privy to the secrets of the Newport Tower, Rennes le Chateau, Westford Knight and likely other similar historical oddities such as Oak Island.

An examination of the life of Longfellow may expose that he was both a literary and Society of the Cincinnati cohort of Edgar Allan Poe. It also appears that Longfellow could have easily been aware of the truth of Oak Island as well. It may be that Longfellow was one of the cadre of American literary and artistic figures that had decided or possibly been chosen to express American culture and political concepts in their work. In the process of this we see how Poe may have been a kind of spy who looked after the interests of the American Republic in the same way the Society of the Cincinnati was known to have done. There are some interesting things about Henry Wadsworth Longfellow that may show his loyalties with regard to the Society as well.

Longfellow's home in Cambridge Massachusetts once served as General Washington's headquarters during the siege of Boston of the Revolutionary War. Longfellow was apparently proud of this fact and even purchased two tea cups of the Society of the Cincinnati china that only members were allowed to have. There is a story of the Lee family demanding their Society of the Cincinnati china back after the Civil War so this tableware was of significant value to members. His mother, Zilpah (Wadsworth) Longfellow, was the daughter of General Peleg Wadsworth, who had served in the American Revolution. This would have made one male progeny of Peleg Wadsworth eligible for membership in the Society of the Cincinnati. Either way it is clear that he valued this house and its association with President Washington. The house had even been given to the Longfellow's upon intermarriage with the former owners during Washington's stay, the Craigie family.

These factors and many others all add up to suggest that Longfellow may have at least held the same patriotic sentiments as the Society and may have been part of an organized effort on their part to help establish and American identity in literature and art throughout the world. This may have been seen as a very important factor during the age of Poe and Longfellow prior to the advent of modern media. The tradition of using artists and writers as part of an intelligence service is nothing new. At this time Poe and Longfellow were opposed by a similar group in England that may have been associated with the Pre-Raphaelite Brotherhood. Joaquin (Cincinnatus) Miller of California may have also worked as a kind of literary spy for the Society of the Cincinnati.

As it turns out Longfellow also has a strong association with the Newport Tower and the concept of the Norse having come to America long ago. His poem "A Skeleton in Armor" was inspired by this belief and even refers to the Newport Tower. Longfellow was part of a group of elite Bostonians who even promoted the building of a statue of Leif Eriksson at one point there. Longfellow was a friend with Eben Norton Horsford. Horsford was a wealthy chemist who had invented a more efficient form of baking soda and became incredibly wealthy.

Horsford built what is known of as the "Norumbega" Tower on a site on the Charles River where he felt there had once stood a Viking settlement of the same name. Horsford was an amateur archaeologist who excavated some colonial stone foundations and insisted the period artifacts he had found were simply trash deposited atop the Vikings houses. Both Horsford and Longfellow also viewed the Newport Tower as having come from this Viking invasion. Horsford estimated that up to ten thousand Norwegians had come to New England and had established

"Norumbega." Some of Horsford's critics even suggest all of this as outright fraud though despite this he erected a plaque stating these foundations to be the first remnants of Norumbega to have been found.

The name Norumbega is likely of Native American derivation and is associated with both a place and another family that has been studied extensively in relation to their association with what is known as the Great Cyclic Cross of Hendaye. Governor of French Louisiana (Arcadia) Blaise d'Abbadie was governor at the time Thomas Jefferson was President and there is an extensive correspondence between the two. Blaise d'Abbadie was the governor at the time Louisiana was handed over to the Untied States thus possibly providing us with a link to even the Kensington Rune.

A prominent early military figue in French Acadia (Arcadia) was Bernard d'Abbadie St. Castin. Their capitol was known as Norumbega and was located in what is now Castine Maine named for the d'Abbadie family. Other d'Abbadie's included the d'Abbadie St. Germain family that maintained French Royal summer palace of St. Germain en Laye also home to the exiled Stewart Jacobite Kings at one time. Many things about the narrative presented here do indeed have intersections with other theories about several mysteries that seem to have captured the public imagination.

Antoine and Arnaud d'Abbadie were famous Ethiopian explorers in the tradition of James Bruce resulting in Antoine's construction of Chateau Abbadia considered the "Rosslyn Chapel" of France. This entire saga continually includes an intermarried web of direct relations. Even the son of Arnaud d'Abbadie Jean Pierre would marry a woman named Elena Bidwell whose family had branched out from the same Biddulph family as Chico founder John Bidwell. Since they were once governors of the province that includes Oak Island we should not discount their involvement in this complex story.

The son of Baron Bernard St. Castin d'Abbadie of Norumbega returned to France to claim his fathers title after the Maritime region came under British control. Bernard Ansleme d'Abbadie did regain his title and became known of as the Count of Norumbega. Eventually his daughter would marry a Bourbon of the Royal Family. This union would have possibly injected Mic Maq native blood into the Royal Family as this was the origins of his mother. This is also reminiscent of how members of the Monctezuma family were made Spanish nobility and intermarried with some of the noble houses whose families are involved in these studies.

The nineteenth century d'Abbadie's Arnaud and Antoine were part of a clique of astronomers and intellectuals including the Cassini family (Cassini Space Probe, Early map of France), Thomas Jefferson, Francois Arago (Arago brass medallions Paris Meridian, onetime director of the Paris Observatory), and Alexander Von Humboldt. To this group of men figuring out these geographic mysteries would be very easy. It would also not be beyond their understanding to have created similar legends of their own associated with American history and lore instead of the lore of the Old Country. Pierre L' Enfant may also fit into this category and he was indeed a member of the Society of the Cincinnati along w/ the Marquis of Lafayette and other French officers of the Revolution. The d'Abbadie family will be proven to be a central group in the associations we are seeing in the Arcadian Mysteries as this story progresses.

It is very interesting that both Poe and Longfellow seemed to be both associated with the Society of the Cincinnati and had written poems about Knights. Poe may have penned "Eldorado" based on the Westford Knight. In his work "Skeleton in Armor" Longfellow may have been inspired by the Newport and Norumbega Towers." Also amazing again is the familial connection that Poe had to Newport and Benedict Arnold Sr. the said builder of the Tower. It is possible that all of these coincidences add up to the fact that both of these men knew inside information about the truth or reality of both the Westford Knight and Newport Tower via their association with the Society and their family legacies.

It is clear that outwardly Longfellow believed that Norsemen had come to New England long before Columbus. There is no record of Poe knowing any of this beyond speculation based on his work and political associations.

Is it possible that this "Norumbega" movement was attempting to accomplish a goal of the Society of the Cincinnati? Horsford and his group of elite Boston residents who believed in the Norumbega concept may have also had a political agenda that included a kind of racist view of the development of North America. Part of their aim seemed to be to disprove that Columbus had discovered America. It also may be surmised that they went to great lengths to accomplish this goal.

During the early days of Nova Scotia a trading relationship had existed between the Acadian colonists and Boston. It may have been during this time that the relations of William Alexander of Stirling to the de La Tour family of Claude and Charles was known of. It may be that the trading partners of the French in Boston were known of by the Alexander family or their allies. This is an early hint of how some early American interests would have eyed Nova Scotia to take for themselves.

An examination of the "archaeology" done by Horsford reveals that none of the material he recovered was Norse in origin. Many people accused him of exaggerating to support a political and racially motivated agenda at this time. It may be for these reasons and the above associations with the Society of the Cincinnati that we may speculate that this was more of a socio-political play than a serious belief that was being manipulated. It is logical to assume Norse may have come to North America. What we may be forced to consider in relation to Poe and Longfellow's involvement here is that this belief also had a political agenda attached. L'Anse Aux Meadows Viking site in Newfoundland had not even been discovered during this era.

Later near the turn of the century we would see a Viking Ship being displayed at the Columbus World Exposition of Chicago. The symbolism of a Viking ship at the Columbus Exposition was not lost on many who wished to believe that Vikings had come first. What was it that made these people truly believe something like this with no proof? In addition as of publishing date no reliably confirmed "Norse" or "Viking" artifacts have been identified beyond L'Anse Aux Meadows, Labrador, and Greenland.

Alternately all of this may mean that these men were privy to whatever was being hidden by the existence of the Newport Tower and Westford Knight. Was this secret hiding how the English had claimed New England by using the site of the Newport Tower and later building it? Had "Norsemen" really built it and this was what was a secret for some reason? Is this why the Newport Tower "points to" the Kensington Rune? Involving the same Hill family with relatives in Kings County Nova Scotia? One of whom was the CEO of the Oak Island Eldorado Company also coincidentally the name of a poem by Arnold relative and Society of the Cincinnati agent Poe about the Westford Knight? Laugh out loud.

The Viking meme runs throughout the values and political views of this group of people especially in the mid to late nineteenth century. Coincidentally when the Kensington Rune was first deposited by the Hudson's Bay Company or interests of Lord Selkirk's Red River Colony. In a town primarily developed by the Hill family who were related to George Washington, Meriwether Lewis, and French explorer Jaques Marquette, known as Alexandria Minnesota where the Kensington Rune Stone Museum is now located. It all links together via an examination of the apparently fake Norse artifacts one of which is located in Mahone Bay Nova Scotia where Oak Island is as well. We have seen how even the word "Kensington" is related to William and Mary and the College of the same name.

Hill family member Gertrude Hill had moved the entire structure of the 15th century Chapel of St. Martin Seyssuel from her Long Island estate to Marquette University in the 1930's. The Chapel had originally been located in France and was first moved to Long Island. Eventually Ms. Hill (Gavin) donated it to the University and had it moved there and rebuilt. This displays their family relations to Jacques Marquette and continues a tradition seen in other American gentry families. The Hearst family of California has moved two medieval structures from Spain to Florida and California. So it the story of the church at Marquette University is interesting in the overall view of these mysteries.

It may be that there was knowledge that Scandinavian people had come before Columbus. Did some of these families have knowledge of this or was this point of view being presented for cultural reasons? We also may note that Columbus "discovered" North America by claiming the West Indies and not mainland North America. The big difference here is that Columbus came and used a predetermined method of legally claiming property that all other royal interests had agreed upon. This process may be one of the most practical functions of an Axis Mundi or establishment of a Prime Meridian. In addition the Spanish managed to possess and maintain their claims over time. Proving the Norse had "claimed" North America would involve proving that they had been here in significant numbers and had maintained a presence. This may have been one of the aims of the Norumbega group that included Horsford, Longfellow, and many other influential Bostonians.

Legal descriptions of Property require that the property in question be tied into a fixed point known to both parties with an angle and distance to the claimed land compared to the position of this point on earth. The Greek tradition of the Tower of the Winds displays this concept. Royal or elite factions would build a Temple that defined a Templum. Note the Temporal nature of both words. Time is relative to space via the spinning of the earth on its axis. Structures like those seen in Heliopolis, Baalbek, The Temple Mount, Ravenna, and the octagons of Thomas Jefferson were all built as kind of geodetic markers on the face of the earth that also among many other functions served to mark time. This helped to define the temporal power of the region being ruled. You were literally being told what time it was.

The Newport Tower is such a tower or Magdala. By plotting the position of the Newport Tower from Star Castle in England the claim of New England by Elizabeth could be legally described in terms that Spanish and Portuguese nobility could understand and agree upon. Many times a tower or monument is built at a point of claim where an ephemeris or star log was collected enabling comparison of this point to any other point where an ephemeris was collected. (This relationship between Newport Tower is discussed in depth in "The Geographic Mysteries of Sir Francis Bacon).

During their lives Poe criticized Longfellow and accused him of liberally borrowing the ideas of others. Poe was also known to criticize members of the opposing camp who seemed to have loyalties to England at this time. It is even possible that Poe was criticizing Longfellow as part of a ploy of some kind. It is clear that they were on the same side and both associated with one of the most patriotic societies in the United States.

What is known is that Longfellow seemed to value the concept of Norumbega and had written many works with Norse and Scandinavian overtones. In his own words:

[The following Ballad was suggested to me while riding on the seashore at Newport. A year or two previous a skeleton had been dug up at Fall River, clad in broken and corroded armor; and the idea occurred to me of connecting it with the Round Tower at Newport, generally known hitherto as the Old Wind-Mill, though now claimed by the Danes as a work of their early ancestors. Professor Rafn, in the Mémoires de la Socéité Royale des Antiquaires du Nord for 1838-1839, says:--

"There is no mistaking in this instance the style in which the more ancient stone edifices of the North were constructed, the style which belongs to the Roman or ante-Gothic architecture, and which, especially after the time of Charlemagne, diffused itself from Italy over the whole of the West and North of Europe, where it continued to predominate until the close of the 12th century; that style, which some authors have, from one of its most striking characteristics, called the round-arch style, the same which in England is denominated Saxon and sometimes Norman architecture.

"On the ancient structure in Newport there are no ornaments remaining, which might possibly have served to guide us in assigning the probable date of its erection. That no vestige whatever is

found of the pointed arch, nor any approximation to it, is indicative of an earlier rather than of a later period. From such characteristics as remain, however, we can scarcely form any other inference than one, in which I am persuaded that all, who are familiar with Old-Northern architecture, will concur, THAT THIS BUILDING WAS ERECTED AT A PERIOD DECIDEDLY NOT LATER THAN THE 12TH CENTURY. This remark applies, of course, to the original building only, and not to the alterations that it subsequently received, for there are several such alterations in the upper part of the building which cannot be mistaken, and which were most likely occasioned by its being adapted in modern times to various uses, for example as the substructure of a windmill, and latterly as a hay magazine. To the same times may be referred the windows, the fireplace, and the apertures made above the columns. That this building could not have been erected for a wind-mill is what an architect will easily discern."

I will not enter into a discussion of the point. It is sufficiently well established for the purposes of a ballad, though doubtless many an honest citizen of Newport, who has passed his days within sight of the Round Tower, will be ready to exclaim with Sancho, "God bless me! did I not warn you to have a care of what you were doing, for that it was nothing but a wind-mill; and nobody could mistake it, but one who had the like in his head."]-Henry Wadsworth Longfellow

The Skeleton in Armor.

By Henry Wadsworth Longfellow

"Speak! speak! thou fearful guest!
Who, with thy hollow breast
Still in rude armor drest,
    Comest to daunt me!
Wrapt not in Eastern balms,
But with thy fleshless palms
Stretched, as if asking alms,
    Why dost thou haunt me?"

Then, from those cavernous eyes
Pale flashes seemed to rise,
As when the Northern skies
    Gleam in December;
And, like the water's flow
Under December's snow,
Came a dull voice of woe
    From the heart's chamber.

"I was a Viking old!
My deeds, though manifold,
No Skald in song has told,
    No Saga taught thee!

Take heed, that in thy verse
Thou dost the tale rehearse,
Else dread a dead man's curse;
  For this I sought thee.

"Far in the Northern Land,
By the wild Baltic's strand,
I, with my childish hand,
  Tamed the gerfalcon;
And, with my skates fast-bound,
Skimmed the half-frozen Sound,
That the poor whimpering hound
  Trembled to walk on.

"Oft to his frozen lair
Tracked I the grisly bear,
While from my path the hare
  Fled like a shadow;
Oft through the forest dark
Followed the were-wolf's bark,
Until the soaring lark
  Sang from the meadow.

"But when I older grew,
Joining a corsair's crew,
O'er the dark sea I flew
  With the marauders.
Wild was the life we led;
Many the souls that sped,
Many the hearts that bled,
  By our stern orders.

"Many a wassail-bout
Wore the long Winter out;
Often our midnight shout
  Set the cocks crowing,
As we the Berserk's tale
Measured in cups of ale,
Draining the oaken pail,
  Filled to o'erflowing.

"Once as I told in glee
Tales of the stormy sea,
Soft eyes did gaze on me,

Burning yet tender;
And as the white stars shine
On the dark Norway pine,
On that dark heart of mine
    Fell their soft splendor.

"I wooed the blue-eyed maid,
Yielding, yet half afraid,
And in the forest's shade
    Our vows were plighted.
Under its loosened vest
Fluttered her little breast,
Like birds within their nest
    By the hawk frighted.

"Bright in her father's hall
Shields gleamed upon the wall,
Loud sang the minstrels all,
    Chanting his glory;
When of old Hildebrand
I asked his daughter's hand,
Mute did the minstrels stand
    To hear my story.

"While the brown ale he quaffed,
Loud then the champion laughed,
And as the wind-gusts waft
    The sea-foam brightly,
So the loud laugh of scorn,
Out of those lips unshorn,
From the deep drinking-horn
    Blew the foam lightly.

"She was a Prince's child,
I but a Viking wild,
And though she blushed and smiled,
    I was discarded!
Should not the dove so white
Follow the sea-mew's flight,
Why did they leave that night
    Her nest unguarded?

"Scarce had I put to sea,
Bearing the maid with me,

Fairest of all was she
　　Among the Norsemen!
When on the white sea-strand,
Waving his armed hand,
Saw we old Hildebrand,
　　With twenty horsemen.

"Then launched they to the blast,
Bent like a reed each mast,
Yet we were gaining fast,
　　When the wind failed us;
And with a sudden flaw
Came round the gusty Skaw,
So that our foe we saw
　　Laugh as he hailed us.

"And as to catch the gale
Round veered the flapping sail,
'Death!' was the helmsman's hail,
　　'Death without quarter!'
Mid-ships with iron keel
Struck we her ribs of steel;
Down her black hulk did reel
　　Through the black water!

"As with his wings aslant,
Sails the fierce cormorant,
Seeking some rocky haunt,
　　With his prey laden, —
So toward the open main,
Beating to sea again,
Through the wild hurricane,
　　Bore I the maiden.

"Three weeks we westward bore,
And when the storm was o'er,
Cloud-like we saw the shore
　　Stretching to leeward;
There for my lady's bower
Built I the lofty tower,
Which, to this very hour,
　　Stands looking seaward.

"There lived we many years;

Time dried the maiden's tears;
She had forgot her fears,
    She was a mother;
Death closed her mild blue eyes,
Under that tower she lies;
Ne'er shall the sun arise
    On such another!

"Still grew my bosom then,
Still as a stagnant fen!
Hateful to me were men,
    The sunlight hateful!
In the vast forest here,
Clad in my warlike gear,
Fell I upon my spear,
    Oh, death was grateful!

"Thus, seamed with many scars,
Bursting these prison bars,
Up to its native stars
    My soul ascended!
There from the flowing bowl
Deep drinks the warrior's soul,
Skoal! to the Northland! skoal!"
    Thus the tale ended.

Henry Wadsworth Longfellow had direct relatives in Nova Scotia in the Grand Pri area of Kings County. One of Longfellow's other most well known works illustrates this family relation. Strangely many people who write about his poem "Evangeline" insist that Longfellow gained his appreciation of "Arcadie" via his friendship with Nathaniel Hawthorne. During the era of Poe and Longfellow a kind of urban legend existed about two Arcadian lovers that were separated from each other when the English took over French Acadia and displaced the Arcadians ('Cajuns). It is interesting that Longfellow wrote such a poem about Acadia and Nova Scotia in relation to what we have learned about Philip Sidney's "Arcadia."

In fact Longfellow's appreciation of Nova Scotia and the Acadian story is because he direct family there of the Longfellow name.

"Jonathan I Longfellow (Nathan, William,) a first cousin once removed of the grandfather of Henry Wadsworth Longfellow, the poet, was born May 23, 1714, and Oct. 28, 1731, m. Mercy Clark, b. Oct. 28, 1731. In 1760 he removed from Nottingham, N. H., to Cornwallis, but in 1765 went to Machias, Me., where he spent the rest of his life, and died. Other Cornwallis men who went to Machias were, Jone Pineo, Archelaus Hammond, Jabez West, and Jonathan Woodruff. Before he left Cornwallis Mr. Longfellow sold his property to his son Nathan. Children:

i Stephen, b. July 19, 1733.

ii Mary, b. June 15, 1735.

iii Jacob, b. Nov. 6, 1737.

iv Sarah, b. Nov. 17, 1739.

v Elizabeth, b. July 17, 1741, m. to John Whidden.

vi Nathan, b. Dec. 30, 1744, m. Margaret, dau. of Isaac……"

(The History of Kings County Nova Scotia; Heart of the Acadian Land; Making a sketch of the French and their expulsion; And a history of the New England Planters who came in their Stead. With many genealogies. 1604-1910 by Arthur Wentworth Hamilton Eaton, M.A., D.C.L. – Priest of the Arch Diocese of New York; Corresponding member of the Nova Scotia Historical Society; Life member of the New England Genealogical Society; Member of the Boston Authors Club. Salem Mass. Salem Press Company 1910. P. 733)

The Longfellow's were an early family in Nova Scotia! Portions of this family then went to Machias Maine as stated above. H.W. Longfellow's family was also from Maine. There is little doubt that Longfellow would not have been aware of this Nova Scotia branch of his family in the region he studied so thoroughly in order to writhe "Evangeline." Many sources state that Longfellow was practically an expert on the history of French and English Arcadia by the time he finished his Poem. He was undoubtedly aware of the legacy of the Alexander's and de La Tours told in the story of Philip Sidney's "Arcadia." This is illustrated by the fact that Philip Sidney's birthdate is marked in Longfellow's "Book of Birthdays" so we know that he at least admired him enough to have made this entry. It is entirely likely that Longfellow had read "Arcadia" and was fully aware of the similarity of parts of that story to the Oak Island Legend.

What we are seeing here is a personal message from Longfellow about Arcadia. Longfellow is taking part is what is by now a long tradition of inferring the concepts of Arcadia in his literary works. This concept also may distantly suggest that he was aware of the interpretation of this theme as valued by the Cavalier and Jacobite sensibilities of many people during the Revolutionary War era. This also again suggests that he and Poe may have been aware of other instances where this imagery had been applied such as Shugborough Hall, Anson's Moor Park, Oak Island, and Rennes le Chateau.

In addition the above reference is applicable to studies of Oak Island and the other mysteries such as the Newport Tower that are being theorized here. The mention of Jone Pineo who is also a Wadsworth descendant just like Longfellow. There is another link with ties to the Society of the Cincinnati in Nova Scotia. The author of the book Arthur Wentworth Hamilton Eaton's name alone reveals two amazing families involved in this entire saga.

In the story of the International Peace Garden features the Eaton family in a prominent role. The Eaton's are members of the Stewart circle of families via Lord Audley. The arms of Eaton and Audley are identical using only different colors. Both sets of arms prominently display the AVM and X symbols germane to our studies in this book. The Eaton's established Dunseith North Dakota fifty years prior to the International Peace Garden and we all know "Dunseith" means "Fortress of Peace" in Scots Gaelic. It is all linking together via a web of inter-related families that may all identify with the Stewarts and their Plantagenet and Merovingian ancestry. The Longfellow's may now also be included in this group of true "Arcadians." There is more reality to the concept of Arcadia in Nova Scotia than anyone suspects. The inclusion of the Hamilton name also may provide a distant link to the story surrounding both the Powder Magazine in Colonial Williamsburg and the International Peace Garden with both of these places being in turn associated with the Kensington Rune.

Here once again the historical overtones propagated by the d'Abbadie family of French Arcadia may be displaying its more modern legacy at Oak Island and beyond. Via one interpretation of Longfellow's "Evangeline" we may be seeing traces of both his knowledge of the concepts of Arcadia but also of the hidden Catholic influences of the origins of the United States of America and Canada.

Poe, Longfellow, the Prescott family and Oak Island Nova Scotia!

In our studies here it is hard to ignore the associations of Poe and Longfellow with the Westford Knight and Newport Tower. Their involvement in the activities of the Society of the Cincinnati may be the reason they were privy to some of these mysteries. It seems Poe may have even known about Rennes le Chateau long before this mystery was developed in the mind of the public. Their knowledge of these phenomena may have been part of information they had gathered about their Royal class opponents in the U.S. and France. It is clear that Longfellow traveled the continent extensively and Poe is at least suspected of having gone as described in A. Dumas' letter.

Note also that Dumas may have written this letter in association with his time in Italy searching for the treasure of Alaric II the Merovingian King. Other legends state this treasure is located in Montaigne Alaric near Carcassonne France. This treasure legend in extreme southern Italy is said by some to include the Temple Treasure from Rome that had been originally taken from the Temple Mount by Titus under the auspices of Emperor Vespasian. This treasure in Italy was said to have been entombed in a river bed by Alaric II. This included the fact that the course of the river had been changed in order to deposit the tomb or chamber and then redirect the river back on its original course. Some feel that Alaric's treasuer featured items from the famous Temple Treasure of Jerusalem which he may have obtained from the Temple of Peace in the sacking of Rome by the Visigoths.

Jordanes on Alaric II's funeral:
His people mourned for him with the utmost affection. Then turning from its course the river Busentus near the city of Cosentia (Cosenza Italy)—for this stream flows with its wholesome

149

waters from the foot of a mountain near that city—the led a band of captives into the midst of its bed to dig out a place for his grave. In the depths of this pit they buried Alaric, together with many treasure, and then turned the waters backinto their channel. And that none might ever know the place, they put to death all the differs. They bestowed the kingdom of the Visigoths on Athavulf his kinsman, a man of imposing beauty and great spirit; for though not tall of sature, he was distinguished for beauty of face and form. (translated by Galus Mierow)

This story resembles aspects of how Sir Francis Bacon had also supposedly stashed a chamber full of documents in the River Wye in England using the same technique. It seems history repeats itself. This story also has much in common with the Legend of Bacon's Vault in Williamsburg, The Beale Treasure and many other stories. In fact this tale also has much in common with some of the theories we see being espoused at Oak Island today.

"Dr. Orville Owen, a physician of Detroit Michigan and one of the best known Baconians in the country, is holding public attention by his mining operations in the River Wye, England, though which he hopes to conclusively prove that Francis Bacon wrote not only the works of Shakespeare but also the works of Greene, Marlowe, Spencer, Peele, and Sir Philip Sydney, and was the son of Queen Elizabeth. Proofs of these statements were hidden in the River Wye at Chepstow by Bacon himself........" –Popular Mechanics Magazine June, 1911 p. 842.

Note that Sir Francis Bacon was only twelve years old when Sidney began writing "Arcadia."

Many speculate that a chamber is concealed on Oak Island and that the famous Money pit is the conduit that accesses this chamber. This story also in many ways resembles the mythology of Rosicrucian thought and the story of C. Rosenkreutz being entombed in a seven sided chamber in an unknown mountain location. Each of these treasure legends also revolves around a mystery possibly created by a specific family group for their own reasons. It may or may not have anything to do with a real tangible treasure. Is it possible that these treasure stories are designed more to teach you about alternate concepts of faith and spirituality while also weeding out those who are incapable of really understanding what they are addressing by hunting for treasure and relics? The story in Sidney's "Arcadia" may have also originally been meant to suggest these Rosicrucian themes.

It is not out of the question that our cast of characters including the de La Tour's, d'Abbadie's, and Stewarts had created an additional mystery in Nova Scotia using literature that they also saw as being part of their family legacy.

Given our links between Longfellow and Poe then it is no surprise that the family of Longfellow is directly related to those who had a major impact on the area of Chester Nova Scotia during the time the Oak Island Treasure was being developed in truth or mythology. In turn much of this indicates that if there is a treasure it is not on the Island but stashed in the Gold River that empties into Mahone Bay near Oak Island. Later during the mid nineteenth century there would be a gold rush in this part of Nova Scotia. Is this the real source of the name of the river?

What see unfolding in terms of the Oak Island treasure may hinge on knowledge of this gold deposit by specific individuals? It is possible that they were trying to conceal the presence of free natural gold in the region by concocting a story about Treasure on Oak Island. This may infer that gold was being recovered in a clandestine manner thus leading to the treasure legend as a kind of cover story. It is also possible as in other theories that Oak Island was a repository for this gold until it could be spent or converted into currency. All of this would have required the utmost in secrecy. Some of the this activity did happen around the time of the Revolutionary War leading to the suspicion that those that favored the American cause that lived in Nova Scotia may have been exploiting this resource both before and after the war. This would also link us to stories that a great treasure had been hidden there to be used by the Jacobite cause of Bonnie Prince Charlie. What influence if any had Alexander Alexander had on this entire plan or scheme?

After a time it was difficult to keep a secret like this and a corresponding gold rush occurred starting in about 1861. Though only an idea the presence of naturally occurring gold could explain the existence of the treasure legend. Now we also may consider the overtones of the Society of the Cincinnati who was involved in mysteries from Rennes le Chateau to Mt. Shasta California and everywhere in between. There mere mention of the fact this Society is involved goes a long way towards proving that the Oak Island Treasure may be something other than what it is being presented to us in media and lore.

The Longfellow and Prescott families of Nova Scotia have a long and proud history including close family in Halifax, coastal Maine, and Chester Nova Scotia. One prominent surgeon in Halifax Joseph Prescott was even a member of the Society of the Cincinnati. He had fought in the war but his fortunes had linked themselves to his Halifax Nova Scotia family. One of their relatives was named Samuel Prescott. Samuel actually took part in the same activity as Paul Revere in the famous midnight ride by warning the citizens of Concord that "The British are coming!" This may also explain one of Longfellow's most famous poems "Paul Revere's Ride." Note also Revere being related to the de Vere family associated with many strange occurrences and even possibly the production of the works of Shakespeare.

This branch of the Longfellow family would also intermarry with the Craigie family who owned what would become Washington's Headquarters and later Longfellow House near Boston. There is a direct family association with the Craigie's, Longfellow's, and Prescott's that all include close branches of their family in the area of Oak Island and Halifax Nova Scotia. These Nova Scotia families were also known to have been sympathizers with the American cause further possibly linking them to the interests of the Society of the Cincinnati. Part of the goal of the Society may have been to subvert or waylay any of these types of legends they saw being perpetrated by the Royal Class. They may have understood the importance of these legends and symbols of architecture in relation to an age-old tradition that could be manipulated.

These men may have also been working in concert with the family of American General William Alexander who had attempted to reclaim the tile of the Earl of Stirling. This factor alone possibly ties Oak Island in a representative league that includes the development of Washington D.C. and

Alexandria Virginia named for the same family. When one considers that a family like the American Alexander family may have been involved in whatever Oak Island represents then the overall plan at work may be viewed from a different perspective. The Alexander's would have almost definitely been aware of Philip Sidney and the original William Alexander's involvement in the writing of "Arcadia" and had most certainly read the book.

This may be in part why we see people like Franklin Delano Roosevelt interested in Oak Island later in history. It is also clear that Russian mystic Nicholas Roerich had manipulated F.D.R.'s second Vice President Henry Wallace to some degree using a kind of new age version of the similar myths and legends that lead us to Rennes le Chateau and Oak Island. The Roosevelt's are also related to Society of the Cincinnati members from Nova Scotia.

Is it possible that the story of Oak Island was a psychological ploy designed to subvert or fool people like Prince Edward later? Had this treasure legend been built as a psychological operation against the British in Nova Scotia? It seems unlikely that the interests of the Alexander's in Nova Scotia would not recognize the similarities between the original story of Oak Island and the story told in "Arcadia."

At this time Prince Edward actually lived in Nova Scotia and created a copy of the Temple Church in London known as the Halifax Round Church. This Church and other notable Halifax architecture display the royal value of these architectural schemes. It may be that Oak Island was a kind of false mystery designed on the part of the American sympathizers of the Oak Island area. It is also possible that the opposite was true and this legend was used against the American sympathizers. Either way it is clear that many things about the standard Oak Island story don't ring true with an examination of local history in its correct context. On the other hand Prince Edward was a Stewart as well and may have been just as aware as any other of the overtones of Sidney's work.

This may also account for many of the falsehoods and inaccuracies of the original story that have three young men finding and excavating the pit. It is clear that people were actually living on Oak Island at that time and some of them may have had American sympathies and knowledge of real gold in the rivers and streams of Nova Scotia. Even the family of Daniel McGiness' history may indicate he was a part of the "Carolina Corps" of Montagu from the American Revolution. It is possible that McGinnis had been an American soldier that had been captured by the English and asked to fight against Spain and France only and not his American countrymen. After the war it appears McGinnis came to Nova Scotia with Montagu who passed away and is interred in St. Peter's Halifax. One is left to wonder how well these Carolina Corpsmen got along with the members of the Society of the Cincinnati and their families that lived in Nova Scotia.

All of this subversion may have later been supplemented by the inclusion of any number of wild theories concerning Oak Island. It is even possible that people had falsely planted fake artifacts that suggested Romans or other earlier people had come there. The mythology of the island has also seemingly taken on a lot of the overtones of the activities and philosophies of Sir Francis Bacon. Our group of Longfellow's and Prescott's were likely as well versed as their Loyalist

152

English cohorts in the subtleties of how Bacon's ideas could be applied to these concepts. Bacon was a spymaster and these people were involved in a kind of intelligence war that included the Masonic and Rosicrucian ideals held on both sides of this silent war.

Is it possible that this is another one of our family groups of settlers that seemed to work together over long periods of time based on family ties? We have noted the Hill's, Lewis', Washington's, Lee's, Bidwell's, Spencer's, Jefferson's, and many others seemingly adhering to a tradition that included both contrived mysteries or treasure sagas combined with architecture designed to "clewe" one in to the true meanings of all of the intrigue. Along the way many uninitiated people are led to believe that a treasure or cache of relics is included. This may be a mechanism by which novices who are not part of the group are thrown off the scent of what is really going on in such instances.

It appears that the family group of Longfellow may be involved in the Oak Island saga. In addition their involvement provides a firm link to the "Norumbega" political movement and other mysteries that were intentionally contrived for purposes that may not include treasure but may hold meaning to specific families and their business ventures. Along the way these stories exposed the public to Masonic concepts that were being interpreted in an American and Canadian way for the first time. Stay tuned for more.

The Revolutionary War Machias Maine, The Longfellow's, and Edgar Allan Poe.

Authors Note: My good friend Ken Bauman has had a theory that the Oak Island Treasure or something like it is hidden on Machias Seal Island near Machias Maine. Ken was led to these assumptions based on a sword and coin that he inherited that were once owned by Ralph Waldo Emerson. Ken is related to Emerson. Emerson is yet another American literary figure who took part in this kind of silent war that Poe and Longfellow also took part in. The history of Machias Maine also exposes some links to author James Fennimore Cooper who is also suspected of being involved with the Society of the Cincinnati. It may be that Emerson and these other authors were on opposite sides of this silent war. Here we will examine some amazing evidence that both supplies more rationale for our theories to this point but will also support the findings of Mr. Bauman in his personal family quest. -Cort

In the notation above that shows Jonathan Longfellow's descendants it is noted that after settling in Grand Pri Nova Scotia he then moved to Machias Maine. Machias is a small port town near what is today the Canadian and United States Border. Jonathan set up a milling operation in Machias and was there when the Revolutionary War began. Longfellow fought on the American side in some amazing battles that pitted colonists on the shore with muskets firing on British Ships entering the narrow passage that leads to the town. These straights are near the modern town of Machiasport only a short distance from Machias itself.

The Revolutionary War engagements in Machias Maine were led by yet another man who would fight for the United States and live in Nova Scotia just as Joseph Prescott had. Colonel John Allan was a Scotsmen who was actually born in Edinburgh Castle during the 1745 Jacobite

153

uprising where his parents had taken refuge. The Allan family is a well known and respected family in Scotland. Like Prescott Allan was likely a member of the Society of the Cincinnati. Colonel John Allan would go on to serve in the Nova Scotia Assembly and also served as Clerk of the Supreme Court of Nova Scotia.

So. What is so important about John Allan?

So far we have seen how people like Edgar Allan Poe and Henry Wadsworth Longfellow were working at their craft in a way that both promoted their ideals of an American Republic but also may have acted as spies of a sort in league with the Society of the Cincinnati or U.S. Government. An important factor to consider in all of this intrigue is how all of these men had distant family relations to one another. Even though the Society of the Cincinnati had hereditary guidelines for membership these family groups and plans existed long before the Revolution. In fact in Machias we see some overlap of the Virginia, Hartford, Boston and Maine/ Maritime families all working together.

The presence of John Allan in Machias Maine also supplies us with a direct familial link to the family of Edgar Allan Poe thus leading us to the "Allan" part of his name. When Poe's parents passed when he was young he was taken in by a man named John Allan of Richmond Virginia. A cross checking of sources does show that both John Allan of Richmond and John Allan of Machias Maine and Nova Scotia had other Allan relatives in common. This is an amazing coincidence given the similarity of activity and themes presented by poets Poe and Longfellow. During the Revolutionary War Jonathan Longfellow was commanded by John Allan who was directly related via the same family to Edgar Allan Poe's stepfather John Allan.

In addition the same source listed here also tells how the Allan's and Poe's were intermarried and associated with each other over many generations in the Ayrshire region of Scotland. It appears the family legacy of the Poe's and Allan's may explain why John Allen took in the orphaned Edgar Allan Poe even though he was not that enthusiastic about it. It is also stated that Poe was sent to Irvine Scotland to be educated with this family group at that time. Many other sources seem to gloss this part of the Poe story over by simply stating he went to "England" during this time to go to school. He actually went to Scotland.

Could this somehow link to the story of Oak Island? Many people have theorized that Poe who was known for his cryptography abilities developed the cipher seen on the famous 90ft. stone. Could it be that one of his relatives had done this with his guidance or at the least been aware of such things via a family relation to Poe? At the least we are presented with a pathway via family relations that could have involved him or his ideas. The same could be said of the literary brain trust of all of these authors including Longfellow, Cooper, Poe, Joaquin Miller and others.

There is no easy answer to that question but what is starting to emerge is a trail of people associated with the Republican ideals of the Society of the Cincinnati. It is almost as if some factions in the Maritimes preferred to be part of the United States than under the Imperial domain of the British. This trail of intrigue and mystery does indeed include Oak Island. We are beginning to see real solid family links between the Newport Tower Williamsburg, the Kensington Rune and much more.

Even the Allan's have a link to the Hill Railroad baron that are part of the story of Jamestown, Williamsburg, and the Kensington Stone. Both Colonel Allan and John Allan Poe's stepfather are related to shipping magnate Sir Hugh Allan. The Allan shipping line would later merge with the Canadian Pacific Railroad of Kittson and Hill of Minnesota. We are coming full circle here via Maine to illustrate how these family ties expose that nearly all of these treasure sagas and mythology are associated with this group of people. This also explains why Poe and Longfellow likely had differences that were contrived so these associations were not generally known.

(Some Remarkable Relatives of that Remarkable Man John Galt): The Galt Papers PP. 67-71.http://www.irss.uoguelph.ca/article/viewFile/666/1106

Where does this leave us with the log standing theory that at least Poe's cipher was what was on the 90ft. stone? The stone was said to be seen in Halifax at times after its discovery. At this point it does appear as if Horace Hill of the Eldorado Company was of the same Hill family that lives in Minnesota and may have knowledge of the truth of the Kensington Rune. The Kensington Rune was also discovered during this era of the "Norumbega" political movement. What we may be looking at is a scheme perpetrated in order to make it appear as if North America had been claimed earlier. Whether people actually came before Columbus is not the point or what is at stake here. What is at stake is a cultural legacy and possibly the legal rights to resources of North America on a level not understood or known of by the public at large.

The Saga of King Olaf and Longfellow

It appears that Longfellow, Poe, and others were emulating the kind of literary intrigue we see in the application of the works of Philip Sidney to the Oak Island mystery. It is even remotely possible that these men were involved in how and why Sidney's "Arcadia" was applied to Oak Island. Even though that may appear to have been done just before they were popular in the mid nineteenth century they may have at least had knowledge of the truth of that legend via their family and Society connections.

With this in mind we may examine a portion of Longfellow's work known as the Saga of King Olaf which is part of his book "Tales of a Wayside Inn." In this portion of the book Longfellow is emulating a Norse saga and tells a relatively accurate historical tale of King Olaf who ruled Norway the mid to late tenth century. This tale is relative to our earlier examination of the Orphir Round Kirk of St. Nicolas and Rosslyn Chapel.

It seems that Longfellow may have been giving us hints about the Newport Tower, Norumbega, and even the Kensington Rune in this literary work. Longfellow was creating in a way his own "Arcadia" that applied to these myths and legends in New England and how they could be used to establish an American identity and culture. There are also hints that Longfellow was supplying us with real information as to how New England was originally claimed and why many

155

Americans desperately wanted to establish the fact that Norsemen had been the first to discover North America and not Columbus.

King Olaf was also the first Norwegian King to adapt Christianity and many of his conflicts with other Norse rulers revolved around this issue. Olaf's life was a complex tale of him being kidnapped as a young man and eventually becoming a powerful leader in Ireland in the tenth century prior to him returning to Norway to seize the crown. Amazingly part of the travels in his saga to him to the Isles of Scilly off of the southwest Cornish coast of England. The Isles of Scilly is of course the location of Star Castle built during Elizabethan times and later modified in the eighteenth century.

In previous works I have discussed the use of Star Castle on the Isles of Scilly as a datum from which it is theorized that Queen Elizabeth claimed New England. The fact that Olaf once resided here would fit into this theory nicely. Elizabeth's entire rationale as to why England owned this region and not Spain was linked to her control of the Earls of Orkney who held this legacy of discovery and heritage from King Olaf. Using Star Castle in this manner is similar to using that point on earth as the center of a map projection from which other points can be compared or plotted in association. Subsequently these points on earth can be found using the standard navigational and astronomical methods available during that era. Later the Newport Tower was built in this context, Gosnold and Archer may have placed a claim, and the Mayflower Compact was signed. All of these things may have been done intentionally in the geographic context of Star Castle "pointing" that direction.

All these associations are amazing if one examines the geographic qualities of Star Castle. Star Castle is an octagonal star shaped fort. The octagonal form of Star Castle can be used to suppose or create an arc on the globe that transects to the Newport Tower in Rhode Island while also crossing only about seven miles from Oak Island Nova Scotia. Star Castle built by Elizabeth in a location once visited by Olaf "points to" the Newport Tower. Not only does it point to the Newport Tower but the same arc or azimuth on the globe actually crosses Provincetown Harbor in Massachusetts. This is the place where Elizabethan Captains Archer and Gosnold may have claimed New England during their 1602 Voyage and where the later Mayflower Compact was signed. All of the activity associated with Star Castle and the Newport Tower from this perspective appears to be related to the legal description of property.

The association of Gosnold and Archer in this story will later link the entire phenomenon to Jamestown Virginia where both of their graves have recently been excavated. In fact vital symbolic information was recovered in the graves of Gosnold, Archer, and what is thought to be the final resting place of early Virginia Governor George Yeardely. Gosnolds grave yielded a pewter finial that may have been mounted on a staff thus signifying Gosnolds role as a standard bearer. Archers grave produced a strange small silver reliquary with markings that may later lead us to the Kensington Rune. Yeardely's grave was covered by what is known of as the Knights Tombstone which is still being analyzed. It is amazing that this large tombstone was brought from England at such an early date to Jamestwon. This was a a great effort to signify Yeardely's importance and the grave slab may yield more hidden information as time goes on.

156

With regard to Star Castle Elizabeth's claim may have relied on the fact that Norsemen had come there long before Columbus and now this claim fell under her dominion. From the Norse sagas the English and Scottish heirs of this information would have been aware that the Norse had been to at least L' Anse Aux Meadows. The date range of L' Anse Aux Meadows of 1000 A.D. also matches the time period of King Olaf who did have a relationship with Leif Ericsson and may have been aware of the existence of North America. Later in history these same claims would be promoted by Longfellow, Horsford, Poe, and others. Here in the form of King Olaf's Saga Longfellow is giving us another literary work like "Arcadia" that reveals many very real aspects of history.

So it is possible that the stories of Olaf, Star Castle, The Newport Tower, Oak Island, and Jamestown/Williamsburg are being told in the works of everyone from Longfellow to Philip Sidney. Somehow these literary works were meant to inform us of the truth. It seems that even Edgar Allan Poe was aware of this entire scheme going all the way back to how the works of Dante have been valued through time. In fact Dante may hold the key to understanding the origins of the entire "Arcadia" phenomenon.

Though it is only a theory of this author that Star Castle functions this way there are instances of other similar towers and architecture that seem to have been used in the tradition of the Tower of the Winds of Athens to mark an important map center and define a domain including other sites meant to align with the axial center. In fact this tradition is present in most of the mysteries discussed in this book.

Our first instinct may be to believe that the Newport Tower was built long before Star Castle and that Star Castle had been placed in a position they knew would "point to" the tower in Rhode Island. The story of King Olaf and his time on the Isles of Scilly in the late tenth century then the building of Star Castle in Elizabethan times may suggest that the Newport Tower had actually been built after the time that Star Castle had been placed. This also matches the date ranges of the theory of a man named Jim Eagan who operates the Newport Tower Museum in Newport Rhode Island. Mr. Eagan suggests a pre 1600 origin to the Newport Tower that may also work in relation to the 1582 construction date of the original Star Castle.

All of this information may leave the reader wondering if all of this means that there is a treasure at Oak Island and Rennes le Chateau as the standard stories suggest. It would be just as easy to develop a theory that these artists and writers were privy to the true stories and existence of real treasure. The only thing that may question this possibility is the fact that if so many people including these authors were aware of the existence of all these treasures and lost relics why have none of these things every been found? Were they hidden so well that even those that knew of them could not recover them. This is suggested in the Oak Island story and to some degree in the Rennes le Chateau saga. Still the fact that all these literary figures knew of these mysteries and wrote of them may suggest that most of these stories were fabricated for other reasons or that possibly these treasures and relics had been recovered long ago leaving us with nothing but these interesting tales.

Artwork from an early edition of Poe's "The Gold Bug." The imagery of this art resembles "A Magdalene Penitent" of Georges de La Tour and others. Jefferson owned a rendering of this theme by artist Rivera. This theme also resembles those of Oak Island and other treasure mysteries.

Chapter 10: Edgar Allan Poe and the Mysteries of Rennes le Chateau and Oak Island

It appears that all of these myths, legends, and geographic schemes have been carried out by a distinct bloodline that may also include a merger with the much written of Merovingian and Plantagenet families. This includes the Lee family and their associations with the Washington's and many other directly linked genetic relations. We may see the one of the furthest roots of this family line in the Hautepol family associated with Chateau Hautepol of Rennes Le Chateau. We have seen how this family is related to the de La Tours and Marquis de Lafayette. The Hautpol-Blanchefort's also have a Norman connection.

This is a form of the Hauteville name of Normandy, of which many powerful families sprang from including the Anjou's, Stewarts, and many other names involved in this saga. Both Frederick II and the Anjou's were directly descendant of the Hauteville family. Many of these family lines manifested themselves in all of Europe, Russia and beyond. They seemed to have a family legacy and tradition that helped to guarantee their success through time. They used generational plans designed to benefit each era while those in power laid the way for the future. One learning tool they used may have been these temples that established a prime meridian of their own. Over time secret societies and family fraternities may have applied their own mythology and interpretations to these places. Some of these geographic systems were used to hide family secrets, information, and possibly valuables. Being able to solve the mystery left by a forebear may have contributed to a person's legitimacy in any dispute between family members. This may have been one of many reasons these occult landscapes have been created. The Blanchefort's as we will see also have some very impressive relatives that will links us to both the Society of the Cincinnati, The Knights Templar, and the United States.

Edgar Allen Poe may have been aware of the Rennes le Chateau mystery 37 years prior to the mystery being exposed in the exploits of Bérenger Saunière. Again portions of Poe's book "The Gold Bug" including illustrations in an early edition of the book may give one pause to wonder if somehow Poe was aware of at least certain aspects of what would become the Rennes le Chateau conundrum. Many aspects of the book also infer the Oak Island Legend. The treasure is on an island and found beneath a tree with a skull hanging from a branch.

In his story Poe gives a clue that involves imagery present at a familiar site to those who are fascinated by Rennes le Chateau:

"A good glass in the bishop's hostel in the devil's seat twenty-one degrees and thirteen minutes northeast and by north main branch seventh limb east side shoot from the left eye of the death's-head a bee line from the tree through the shot fifty feet out."

One of the attractions in Rennes le Bains near Rennes le Chateau includes the "Devils seat." As far as any of the local people know the Devil's Seat has always been there since any of them can remember. Some note a well worn path from Rennes le Chateau to the Devil's Seat. Other sources have the Cassini family being responsible for the placement of the Devil's Seat in the eighteenth century.

159

The site the Devil's Seat is seen on the Famous Cassini Map of France as "Les Bains de Monferan le Cercle." There are no designations on this map entitled the "Devil's Seat" though this feature is part of the site marked on the map. Had Poe been inspired to use the concept of the Devil's Seat from some other source? At second glance it appears Poe was speaking of the very same Devil's Seat known of by those who study the mysteries of Rennes le Chateau.

The Cassini map depicted France with great accuracy and detail for the first time. Portions of this map overlain on Google Earth match the contours of the coast of France nearly perfectly. Still there are some minor imperfections when compared to modern methods but this map was an amazing feat of its era. This map was completed over four generations of the Cassini family with members actually surveying the countryside with instruments. This may be an example of family traditions in an activity that exposed them to all of the mythology and history of each place they worked including possibly Perillos, Rennes le Bains, Rennes le Chateau, and Hendaye.

Note that earlier we examined a letter to Ben Franklin asking that Dominique Cassini's son in law be admitted to the Society of the Cincinnati.

Their working map shows them having a point from which to measure very near Rennes le Chateau. They are known to have worked from Perillos, which includes a sort of mystery of its own that some speculate is associated with Rennes le Chateau. Undoubtedly during the course of their labors, the Cassini's worked in the vicinities of many strange local myths and historical facts. Land surveyors are many times fountainheads of unknown historical information.

In this way it is at least possible that the Cassini's became aware of some of the historical mysteries that still fascinate us today. It is possible that they turned this information into a sort of game or quest to identify other similar places around the world. A similar activity and philosophy was likely at work in the building of three Tower of the Winds replicas at Shugborough Hall, West Wycombe, and Mt. Stewart in England. Each of these Tower of the Winds possess amazing spatial relationships with other places of mystery and intrigue. These Tower of the Winds were produced in association with James "Athenian" Stuart who was a noted architectural historian credited with the popularity of the Greek revival movement in architecture.

It is even possible that the Cassini's and their cohorts created a few landscape mysteries of their own based on what they had learned. Alternately they were already aware of the significance of this tradition and were adept and finding and analyzing any new finds in this realm. These types of treasure myths and quests have many spiritual and alchemical overtones given the era in which they developed. One man's Christian interpretation of a given array of art and architecture may point to the apocalypse or even something more technical or rational to an initiate of a different school.

This use of the term "Devil's Seat" by Poe is very interesting and displays a specific connection between him and what would become the mystery of Rennes le Chateau. Interestingly the

160

Devil's Seat is very near the famous Paris Meridian (1 mile west) that was obviously valued by the Cassini's who had elected to include "Les Bains de Monferan le Cercle" on their famous map of France. This reference to a feature located in such an area near the 'Rose Line' is indeed fascinating. Is the Devil's Chair the only association between Poe, "The Goldbug," and Rennes le Chateau?

So far the use of the term "Devil's Seat" does not show a direct link that shows Poe knew the details of what would become the Rennes le Chateau phenomena. These links do suggest that all of the mystery of this area may ultimately be associated with the Cassini's and other's who held the skills to understand such a scheme.

Ultimately it may mean that the Cassini's had figured out what the Blanchefort's and Hautepol's had been saying by leaving clues as to the existence of a star shaped pattern in the landscape around Rennes le Chateau.

It may also be a point of speculation that members of the Cassini family may have been involved in the salon of Sophie de Grouchy that had also included Jefferson and the Marquis de Lafayette. Sophie's salon included many members of the French Academy of Arts and Sciences of which the Cassini family had always been members. This coupled with the letter to Ben Franklin asking for his son in laws membership in the Cincinnati may point us to this assumption.

What does this say about the involvement of the Cassini's in the development of the mythology and lore we see being expressed at Rennes le Chateau or Hendaye? The same distant associations between the Great Cyclic Cross of Hendaye and the Cassini's exists as that of their possible knowledge of and propagation of the mythology of both places. It seems to be a family tradition. Did they know about the Rennes le Chateau mystery or did they create the Rennes le Chateau mystery?

Many of the people involved in this tradition during this era are familiar with astronomy and cartography including Jefferson, the Cassini's, d'Abbadie's and others. In addition there are known correspondences between many of these people. Is there something about Rennes le Chateau that these people are trying to tell us beyond the metaphor of hidden treasure and lost riches? Something important happened here and someone is sending us on a quest to find out what it is the mystery hides. How did Edgar Allen Poe know about all of this? Is it possible someone left a path of evidence that tells us what all of this really means in the end? Or is the quest itself the lesson and value of this tradition?

Really what this infers is that Poe was somehow aware of the Devil's Seat and had included a similar concept in his story. But how had Poe come across this story? Had this information also been part of what had been told to Poe by his confident Zaccheus Lee? Then how had Lee known about it? It is clear that Lee's family was privy to this type of information. It may also make sense that other related First Families of Virginia would also be privy to these secrets. Specific members of the Lee family were also part of the Society of the Cincinnati as well. "Lighthorse"

161

Henry Lee had been a hero of the war. The Lee's and Alexander family of Alexandria Virginia were also historically closely related in the Truro Parish of early Virginia.

It is also interesting that this information may have been imparted to Poe while he was a student at the University of Virginia. The University of Virginia was created by Thomas Jefferson who also seemed to be initiate of these mysteries. It is likely that a copy of the Cassini map was even at the University of Virginia at that time that Poe would have had access to. Even so Poe would have had to have a more detailed story than simply looking at the map to inspire his story. The Devil's Seat is not even named on the Cassini map. There is a tantalizing six month overlap between the time of Poe's attendance at the University of Virginia on February, 14, 1826 and the death of Thomas Jefferson on July, 4, 1826 (The same day as President John Adams). Is it possible that this information was given to Poe by President Jefferson himself?

Jefferson was a contemporary of Jean-Dominique Cassini who completed the Cassini map. In fact Jefferson and Cassini corresponded with each other as to the correct method of using a timepiece to establish a meridian! (June, 13, 1787; July, 3, 1789). Had Poe somehow gleaned this story from Jefferson via his friendship with Z. Lee? Is there a version of this tale written by Jefferson lost somewhere in the dusty archives of the University of Virginia that Poe had found? It is possible that if Poe had access to the above two letters from Jefferson to Jean-Dominique Cassini then had his imagination filled in all the rest of the blanks? It seems he would have to be better informed than he was to have arranged all the commonalities between "The Gold Bug" and all of these other famous treasure stories. Again a possible meeting between Poe and Jefferson would explain all of this.

Could the Marquis de Lafayette or Pierre L'Enfant have instructed the President as to the mysteries in France? As discussed earlier Thomas Jefferson had once travelled within a few miles of Rennes le Chateau and Rennes le Bains and could have easily been aware of the story and mythology of the Devil's Chair. It could have easily been imparted to him at some point by one of his clique in Paris. If true does this mean that Jefferson had visited the Devil's Chair?

Jefferson could have easily heard of this in personal conversation or correspondence with Cassini himself or as part of Sophie de Grouchy's salon of free thinkers and intellectuals. Jefferson may have also acted as a kind of spy himself and learned this information via a network sympathetic to his cause. Still there is a great deal of suggestion that Lee's could have been exposed to some inside information in this sphere via their relation to the Washington family and other First Families.

Jefferson seemed to be part of a group of people that understood the geographic relationships of these sacred places. The source of this information ultimately had come from Constantine and made its way to the Holy Roman Emperors. Most of these men and women had been trained in the art of cartography, navigation, and astronomy. So there is some evidence that even if Jefferson did not visit Rennes le Chateau he may have heard of and noted the Devil's Chair in his journal. Given R.E. Lee's planning of Ft. Carroll and its associations it is clear that this family could have easily been aware of the truth of many of these types of questions including the truth of Oak Island. There is ample evidence that even George Washington was aware of this tradition. He had also been trained in land surveying. There is also a great deal of octagonal imagery associated with Washington and his estate of Mt. Vernon.

Jefferson's trip as Secretary of State was even a sort of clandestine trip. Jefferson does note being very near Rennes le Chateau and travelled to places adjacent to the Canal du Midi. If he had visited the environs of Rennes le Chateau then he may not have cared to note a visit to the "Devil's Seat." While on his trip down the canal Jefferson wrote to his daughter that it was good to be "in the land of corn, wine, and oil." He also noted his presence in southern France but ceased to take notes or make them public on the second leg of his trip to Italy. Some speculate that he was visiting Bonnie Prince Charlie in Rome at that time. Jefferson was Secretary of State at this time. Jefferson may have also visited distant family relations in Monaco descendant of the famous Pirate Peter Easton.

One of the early editions of Poe's "The Goldbug" even includes an illustration that matches the imagery of Mary Magdalene and the mysteries of Rennes le Chateau. This artwork includes a prominently displayed skull in a tree as part of the story. The landscape present in this engraving does not resemble the site of Sullivan's Island where the story takes place. The description of this area in the story resembles the Rennes le Chateau area, which does not resemble the true setting of the story in South Carolina. It is almost as though at this point in the story one has been magically transported to Rennes le Chateau/Bains and had entered the realm of mystery so prevalent there.

The illustration depicts a mountainous scene somewhat reminiscent of the rocky knob seen in Poussin's painting "Et in Arcadia Ego." It also resembles a view of Chateau Blanchefort from the valley near Rennes le Bains. The piece also includes a skull hanging from a branch of a tree with a mountainous backdrop. The skull in the tale is integral to finding the exact location of the treasure. The Death's Head theme is repeated throughout the entire story even relating that the "Gold Bug" itself having this design on its back. The story also relates the importance of the death's head in Pirate imagery and lore. If one that was aware of the imagery of Mary Magdalene did not know this illustration was from the "Gold Bug" then it may easily be mistaken as having the feminine theme.

The main character of "The Gold Bug" Legrand is undoubtedly meant as a metaphor for Thomas Jefferson. This character is an intellectual naturalist who is also adept at reading maps and following the clues on the parchment he finds. Some of the references made by Legrand in the story also suggest he is a student of Alchemy. Legrand is the one bitten by "The Goldbug." Guillaume Legrand was one of the architects that was most admired by the President who inspired the design of the domed portion of the octagon at Monticello. Poe would have likely been aware of Jefferson's admiration of this person. Of course, Jefferson owned a copy of the painting "Magdalene Penitent" by Rivera so he was aware of the meaning of this symbology.

One other possible coincidence may involve the fact that Legrand's employee (freed slave) in the story is named Jupiter. It is commonly known that Thomas Jefferson also had a slave that was a personal servant who was named Jupiter. Here again Poe is presenting us with the scantest of clues that do serve to conjure the image of President Jefferson. One who is familiar with the character and life of Thomas Jefferson may notice these hints right away. We have examined the possibility that Jefferson visited Rennes le Chateau. We know he was in the area and there are many hints he was aware of such mysteries. Is Poe telling us that President Jefferson had once visited or been aware of the secrets of Rennes le Chateau and other mysteries?

It is starting to look as if Poe's knowledge in this realm may have come from Jefferson or those he was closely associated with. Poe may have heard of Jefferson's affinity for what some would term "Personal Meridians." All of this may point to the fact that Thomas Jefferson was put through an initiation which involved sitting in "The Devil's Chair" while he was in France. In personal correspondence, we even see Jefferson discussing how to establish a meridian with Jean-Dominique Cassini. In fact we also see Cassini being made a foreign honorary member of the American Academy of Arts and Sciences. Cassini came to the United States for a prolonged stay. Who knows what mysteries he may have imparted to those in the U.S. that were capable of understanding at that time. Some evidence suggests that Cassini was sympathetic towards the American ideal and a republican form of government in France.

So here is a scenario in which Jefferson and Poe could have become privy to the story of the "Les Bains de Monferan le Cercle" and the associated "Devil's Seat." He was both associated with Cassini and had traveled in the area. In turn this lore made its way to Edgar Allan Poe. This line of reasoning may uncover actual knowledge of both the Rennes le Chateau mystery and the Great Cross of Hendaye on the part of Thomas Jefferson.

The templum of the Great Cross of Hendaye points the way to Jefferson's octagonal estate Poplar Forest. Poplar Forest represents yet another site involving an octagon and a lost treasure or historical mystery. Poplar Forest is located very near to where the Beale Treasure is supposed to be hidden. Jefferson may have been initiated into these mysteries via the octagonal Powder Magazine in Williamsburg. The Powder Magazine is likely associated with the Bruton Parish Church Vault. Later Jefferson would be associated with both Alexander Von Humboldt and Cassini. Both men who were directly associated with the tradition of the Tower of the Winds in Athens.

From Jefferson to Dominique Cassini (Jefferson thanks Cassini for helping to establish a meridian using some new clocks):

"Mr. Jefferson, Minister Plenipotentiary of the united states of America, asked a thousand pardons to Count Cassini, though without having the honor of being known to him, he dares ask him the grace to put the watches he instructed the bearer of this note on the hour average time according to the clock of the Observatory. With that, and using the equation of time, it proposes to start the trace of a meridian line at home, which (despite the small inaccuracy that may occur in the course of returning watches Observatory home) will be fair enough for ordinary use. At solstice however he will ask for permission to use once again the goodness of Count Cassini, because it will be in assembling, by a straight line, then the trait noon he done to the man that

aujourdui it will be compleat his chaise. It has the honor of a thousand apologies for the trouble he dares to give the Count Cassini, and ask him to accept the assurances of his most distinguished consideration."

Edgar Allen Poe even mentions Cassini in one of his short stories entitled "The Unparalleled Adventure of one Hans Phall" (1850). In addition to this reference to the Devil's Chair in "The Gold Bug" there are other geographic associations that may add to the speculation that Poe knew of these tales long before they were made available to the public seemingly 37 years later at the earliest. In turn we may assume that if this information came from Jefferson that he also had knowledge of these secrets. Cassini had come to America before Poe was born (1809) so they did not meet personally.

One of the people who has written a great deal about Rennes le Chateau and other sacred landscapes is author and film maker Henry Lincoln. Lincoln is known for supposing that a pentagonal pattern of landmarks is present in the landscape surrounding Rennes le Chateau. Points that define this star shaped pattern include places of importance in the tale of Rennes le Chateau and the surrounding region. The family history and relations of the owners of places used in this manner may have originally arranged this array as part of a tradition upheld by specific family groups. This pattern of significant points may also be used to form the shape of a pentagon surrounding the pentagram. This shape was originally deciphered from the destroyed Blanchefort tombstone discussed in earlier chapters.

In our analysis here the pentagram identified by Henry Lincoln may also be used as a sighting device that projects arcs on the globe to significant talismanic locations or architecture that is directly related to the people who created the entire scheme or plan being carried out. One such alignment that includes the Rennes le Chateau Chapel and Chateau Blanchefort creates an arc on the globe that leads to Ravenna Italy and the Arian Baptistery of Theodoric. The octagonal Arian Baptistery is somewhat of a millennial monument and exhibits and octagonal plan. Near by Basilica San Vitale was built by Justinian I who was emulating Constantine just as Jefferson would in the octagonal forms of Monticello, Poplar Forest, and Barboursville Mansion.

If one creates an arc on the globe using a line and direction connecting the southernmost tips of Lincoln's pentagram an azimuth on the globe may be extended at this heading that transects the Atlantic Ocean to Sullivan's Island South Carolina. This would correspond to one of the directions suggested by the pentagon surrounding the star. Henry Lincoln's star points to Sullivan's Island South Carolina the location where Poe's story "The Gold Bug" takes place.

Given the association with the Devil's Chair in relation to the date of the Cassini map and this information it may indeed be true that Edgar Allen Poe had intimate knowledge of what the Rennes le Chateau mystery involved long before the exploits of Saunière. Is it possible that Poe knew about the Star in the landscape in 1837 well over one hundred and twenty-five years prior to it being made public by Henry Lincoln? Had he situated the site of his story to reflect this knowledge? Is this why the Devil's Chair is mentioned in "The Gold Bug."

Rennes le Chateau was somehow already valued by a brain trust that Poe had been connected to. Given the chronology of the "Les Bains de Monferan le Cercle" site being present on the Cassini map, the life of Poe, and the exposure of this story to the public we may assume that Poe was privy to all the secrets both Jefferson and the Lee family and had even taken part in the propagation of similar stories as fiction in the view of the pubic. This information was likely known by other Virginia First Families including the Beale's, Moncure's, Washington's, and more.

Via these associations he was also privy to the knowledge of the Cassini's. It seems that Poe was writing these stories into his prose concealing a hidden way to communicate them to those that were aware of how to recognize the hints that something else was being told. This may include the facts that involve versions of a cipher he made popular being used in solutions to the Beale Treasure, Oak Island, and now Rennes le Chateau. For instance, if someone was aware of what the "Devils Chair" was they may then associate the metaphor of President Jefferson as being the main character Legrand in the "Gold Bug." To the trained eye this is what Poe is telling us in his story. Poe may even be telling us that Jefferson had visited the Devil's Chair himself.

In the Gold Bug he may be referring to the Oak Island Treasure, the Beale Treasure, and Rennes le Chateau all in one piece of literature. Along the way he is telling us that Thomas Jefferson as Legrand in the story knew all of this and that he is likely the source Poe used to write this tale. We may also be informed that President Jefferson had solved a mystery of this type just as the main character in the story had.

There are legends and myths existent in Williamsburg that Jefferson was one of the last people to see the contents of The Bruton Parish Church Vault a.k.a. "Bacon's Vault." This means that if true he had solved this mystery long ago explaining why no vault has ever been located in modern times. This still begs the question: "Did Jefferson sit in the Devil's Seat at Rennes le Bains?" Jefferson may have been a cloistered treasure hunter!

This entire scenario is possible but there may be other explanations as well. Here again we have the involvement of the Cassini family associated with other like-minded individuals at the Paris Observatory including Arago, d'Abbadie, Jefferson and even possibly Alexander Von Humboldt. All of these men were members of the same international scientific organizations such as the Linnean Society.

It would have been absolute child's play for these men to arrange such geographic schemes and mysteries during an era when only the elite were aware of the function of a surveyor's instrument, sextant, or astrolabe. Many sources state these skills as being hobbies of rich and influential people. It would have been equally as effortless for these men to decipher other more ancient mysteries that involved the same tradition. It appears as if they had almost in part been trained to do exactly that. It is possible that the star in the landscape of Rennes le Chateau had already been found by these men including Edgar Allan Poe.

It may be that the story of the Devil's Chair is associated with the Cassini's and the Paris Meridian and that the Rennes le Chateau story is a byproduct of their involvement. This tradition had somehow been exposed to Edgar Allen Poe. This is amazing in light of the Cassini story at Perillos and other similar activity associated with the Great Cross of Hendaye and geographer Antoine d'Abbadie. The star of Henry Lincoln also points very close to Perillos so that is notable as well. There are too many common threads in all of these stories to ignore.

It is entirely possible that all of this Poe imagery was added to these mysteries after the fact. At Oak Island this may be exactly what happened if the treasure had been found and a false story had been left behind. It is entirely possible that Poe, Longfellow and others were also aware of the relation between Philip Sindey's "Arcadia" and the Oak Island saga. If at Rennes le Chateau the name of the Devil's seat was actually inspired by Poe's stories then this would make sense as well. Poe was very popular in France.

The naming of the Devil's Seat according to some is the year 1800 37 years before Poe penned "The Gold Bug." It would have been possible for this name to have originated in the Poe story so that should not be ignored either. Some stories about the Devil's Seat even suggest the Cassini's had been behind its placement. It is also possible that Thomas Jefferson had heard of the Devil's Seat during his trip to the area as Secretary of State.

What is suggested also is that Poe did not know anything about Rennes le Chateau but did know about the Devil's Seat via a study of the Cassini family and their famous map. Even this solution is a kind of remote possibility. The only other answer would be that this is all a fluke that displays similar imagery. Given his description of the site of the treasure, the use of the Devil's Seat, the possible association of Sullivan's Island and the Rennes le Chateau Star, and a possible association with information left by Jefferson it appears that he did know about at least some of the factors involved in the Rennes le Chateau mystery as we see it today. So in the end the question still lingers:

"Did Edgar Allen Poe know about Oak Island, Rennes le Chateau, The Beale Treasure, The Bruton Parish Church Vault, The Newport Tower and more?"

All of this infers that the Cassini family had knowledge of the truth of Rennes le Chateau and much more. It appears that they had unlocked some ancient information using astronomical methods that had been employed long ago. Maybe they had solved the same mystery that was later suggested by popular author and Rennes le Chateau authority Henry Lincoln.

There is no hard evidence and only associations and speculation contribute answers to these mysteries but the Poe associations with all of these stories may be true or being applied to them for a reason. For many reasons, all of these tales resemble the work of Poe who may have been inspired by an exposure to the truth of these mysteries. Many standard biographies of Poe state that he never left the United States. Conflicting this view are a few facts including the correspondence of a famous author.

The best evidence that Poe spent time in France includes the fact that famous author of "The Three Musketeers" Alexandre Dumas claims to have met and known Poe in Paris when no records or biographies of Poe state that he ever went there. Dumas goes as far as to say that Poe stayed in his house in Paris during this visit. This claim derives from a letter Dumas wrote to an Italian Police official claiming he knew Poe in France in 1832.

"It was about the year 1832. One day, an American presented himself at my house, with an introduction from ... James Fenimore Cooper. Needless to say, I welcomed him with open arms. His name was Edgar Poe. From the outset, I realized that I had to deal with a remarkable man. Two or three remarks which he made upon my furniture, the things I had about me, the way my articles of everyday use were strewn about the room, and on my moral and intellectual characteristics, impressed me with their accuracy, and truth." –Alexandre Dumas

Alexandre Dumas may have even been researching the famous missing Temple Treasure or Treasure of Alaric in Italy at the time he was corresponding with this Police official. We may also see French and other European writers and artists taking part in the same kind of activities during this era. It is clear that Longfellow and Lord Byron visited many of the same places. Lord Byron has direct family connections to may of the powerful nobles that are involved in this story from start to finish as well. This would all make sense with regard to Rennes le Chateau because one of the fabled locations of the Treasure of Alaric is near Carcassonne somewhere on Montaigne Alaric not far from there.

Here is further proof that Poe had now actually gone to France during an era when Cassini IV was still alive. 1832 is a full thirteen years before Cassini's death in 1845. Given this information if true Poe could have even visited the Devil's Chair himself prior to penning "The Gold Bug" in 1837. Poe was said to have ravenously devoured any information having to do with science and technology so it is no surprise the he would have been aware of and appreciated the work of the Cassini's.

Further evidence suggests that Poe may have been involved in intelligence gathering activities. The entire course of Poe's life was interwoven with characters and organizations that would easily lead one to the conclusion that there was a great deal more to the life of Poe than what is exposed in narratives of his life that paint him as drunkard and tortured artist.

It is likely that his involvement in this sphere of activity started around the time he was a student at the University of Virginia. Some sources do state that at this time Poe and President Jefferson did indeed meet each other, as Jefferson was fond of meeting and speaking with students of his new University. At this time Jefferson was still President of the University of Virginia. It is possible that Jefferson was also aware of Poe's father's service during the Revolutionary War.

Other influences on Poe with regard to intelligence gathering activities would include a possible association with the Society of the Cincinnati. This organization was comprised of United States military officers during the Revolutionary War and their descendants. This would have included Poe whose grandfather was instrumental in providing the Continental Army with hardware and supplies from Baltimore. Poe's grandfather was under the command of the Marquis de Lafayette during this time. The Society of the Cincinnati also included French military officers as well as a few from Sweden and Prussia. This would have also associated Poe with Pierre L'Enfant who who was also an engineering officer under Lafayette at the beginning of the war.

Given his association with Lafayette it is likely that the elder Poe was also associated or knew the Buchanan and Rodgers family of Druid Hill. Nicolas Rodgers was said to have worked directly for Lafayette at this time and it is likely the men knew each other via Baltimore society prior to the Revolution. It is also notable that later while Poe was enlisted in the Army in Richmond that he led an honor guard that welcomed the visiting Lafayette. Some speculate that he was enlisted by Lafayette at this time to do the bidding of the Society of the Cincinnati.

Lafayette as well as other French, German, and Swedish officers of the Revolution were also members of the Society of the Cincinnati.

So this organization also had a strong presence in Europe and was involved in any revolution of the day such as the one in Poland where they were attempting to institute a Republic. This philosophy pitted the Society of the Cincinnati and the American way against the Royal interests of Europe whom also employed spycraft and subterfuge in their efforts to retain power. The Society of the Cincinnati was named for Roman military leader Cincinnatus. Cincinnatus gave up his dictatorial powers and returned them to the Senate of Rome. This made him a good figurehead for an organization dedicated to the preservation of the republican ideal in the United States and beyond.

During Lafayette's final visit to the United States a young Edgar Allan Poe served as part of his personal honor guard. This meant that Poe would accompany the Marquis on his travels and it is likely the two knew each other somewhat. This is an amazing correlation between two individuals who seemed to be aware of many aspects of these mysteries via their family associations.

The aim of this group was in part to preserve the new Republic of the United States of America through time using any means necessary. The Society of Cincinnati was also said to have its own spies and intelligence apparatus on the continent to help further their goals. The Marquis de Lafayette himself led the French branch of the Society of the Cincinnati. The Society in France worked towards the establishment of a Republic there.

Many popular authors and artists of the day may have been sent to Europe to gather data under the auspices of the Society of the Cincinnati. Part of their duties may have been to analyze any cultural activity that may be used for or against them. These men knew that both elements of the European monarchies and the Church would stop at nothing to prevent the ideals of the Constitution from succeeding. During this time it may be that knowledge of many of the myths and legends of Europe became a point of interest for use in a kind of occult psychological warfare. This would apply if a specific caste of royalty valued the placement of talismanic architecture in an esoteric manner as well. Added to the mix would be the Church and its associated organizations such as the Jesuits and scholars of St. Sulpice.

This may be among the reasons that places like Rennes le Chateau and The Great Cross of Hendaye came on to the radar screens of any spies of this nature in Europe at that time. The people and families behind many of these mysteries seem to be rooted in some form of monarchy and associated gentry that would have opposed the concept of a republic for obvious reasons. Knowledge of the family and secret society mysteries of this caste of people would be very useful in crafting countermeasures to combat the elite's efforts to maintain their control on society at large.

Members of this elite group that happened to read the "Gold Bug" would recognize that Poe was aware of something they valued and also be informed where he came across this information. This type of concept is even involved in the politics of Pierre Plantard who seemed to be using the mythology of Rennes le Chateau to claim that he was the true King of France. Given the influence of spies and intrigue in this realm it is no surprise that the famous "dossier secret" may indeed be a fake produced by those wishing to muddy the waters of the entire phenomena intentionally. Spy vs. Spy.

This spy network of the Society of the Cincinnati may indeed be what Californian "Poet of the Sierras" Joaquin Miller would be involved in later in the nineteenth century during his stay in Europe. Joaquin was an early pioneer of Northern California and Oregon. He was an author and playwright who wrote of the American west that was more popular in England than his native country. Miller was from Cincinnati, Ohio and his real first name was Cincinnatus Heine Miller belaying a possible connection to the Society of the Cincinnati. If Miller was a member of the Society that may explain why he chose to change his name to Joaquin prior to his trip to Europe. While in Europe he was said to have hobnobbed with the elite of Europe and even became associated with famous artist's guild the Pre-Raphaelite Brotherhood. In reality Joaquin also known as Cincinnatus was likely spying on them!

Today the main office of the Society of Cincinnati is located in Cincinnati, Ohio. Miller fits the mold of how Poe is described in certain accounts. Joaquin Miller also led a life that displayed an appreciation for arrays of arranged architecture. This included a two year stay living on the White House Meridian in Washington D.C. then returning to Oakland California and developing similar concepts on his estate there in the form of architectural follies. It seems that Miller even built a pyramid on his estate in Oakland that is exactly due south of the peak of Mt. Shasta. Miller once lived at the base of Mt. Shasta for several years. Miller's activities in Oakland associated with Mt. Shasta were likely a response to what had been done at the Frenchman's Tower in Palo Alto earlier.

The life and times of Miller though slightly later than Poe do seem to support the notion that the Order of the Cincinnati did have an intelligence gathering apparatus designed to ferret out the secrets of the elite factions of Europe who were threatened by the notion of a Republic as opposed to the dictatorial regimes of the monarchies of Europe. Part of what the Society did was to infiltrate European society with American artists and writers. Joaquin Miller was likely also a spy for the Society of Cincinnati and ultimately the United States of America.

During the era of Poe France had become a Republic again in no small part due to the efforts of a now elder Lafayette. It is likely that the European branch of the Society of Cincinnati was also working to establish other Republics on the model of the United States and France in other places like Poland. Poland also had a revolution aimed at dethroning a monarchy at that time. Additional evidence that supports Poe going to Europe includes a letter from him to the commandant of West Point to be dismissed from duty so he could seek a commission as an officer in the Polish army. Yet another clue that Poe may have actually gone to Europe at some point.

Other American artists involved in this activity may have included James Fenimore Cooper, Washington Irving, and painter and inventor Samuel F.B. Morse (Morse code, inventor of the telegraph).

Poe was noted by many as having a highly developed sense of analysis and observation. It seems that Poe, due to his intelligence and talent as a writer, may have been recruited via a combination of his association with Lafayette and Jefferson while at the University of Virginia. He subsequently may have been sent to West Point for further training. After this he may have been deployed domestically or sent to Europe under an assumed identity.

It is odd and notable that Dumas noted Poe's presence there even including fact that Poe stayed at his residence for an extended period and that they became friends and took walks together. It may be that Poe's real identity being known by Dumas would also indicate that the French author was also a patriot of France and the Republican ideal.

Opposing this group of truly American artists was another literary faction known as the transcendentalists. This faction included Emerson who may have even had a kind of rivalry with Edgar Allan Poe. It seems that Poe had been none too gentle in his critique of Emerson's work. Here we may be seeing an example of two opposing groups using the media as a battle ground in pre Civil War America. During this era the media was comprised of books and magazines. All of the same techniques used in hiding concepts in TV and music in the modern world were employed during this era via writers and artists. The written word and traditional media still held a great deal of sway on the psyche of the public at this time.

Emerson and some of his other cohorts may have been part of a group of artists that favored monarchies and the "ancient regime" of old Europe. Ultimately the goal of both sides of this literary battle would be to effect the views of the public with regard to their goals and beliefs. Viewed in this context many odd and occult happenings and beliefs may be seen in their true light. These are the same sentiments held by the d'Abbadie's in a longing for a more peaceful well organized time from the past that included monarchies and a landed class of gentry to support it.

Some speculate that the transcendentalist artists were even associated with the Habsburg family or other royal interests in Europe. The same Hapsburg family many point to as having created the architectural follies at Rennes le Chateau via exiled King of France Henri V (Artois). This longing for the "ancient regime" is a sentiment that is repeated by the D'Abbadie family who are associated with the Great Cross of Hendaye mystery in their philosophy and management of Chateau Abbadia.

So in a very real spy vs. spy scenario we have the Republican creators of the United States locked in secret espionage combat against the "ancient regime" of old line monarchies and landed gentry of Europe. It is not clear where Jacobite interests would fall in this conflict though they were instrumental in the establishment of the United States of America. The use of artists and entertainers as spies is nothing new to history. President Lincoln would later be assassinated by an actor. Jusinian I wife Theodora was a "dancing girl." It is possible that Theodora introduced a Coptic form of Christianity into the Byzantine court.

To effectively defeat one's enemy Poe and others would have been looking for the deep cultural roots that drove the psyche of their opponents. This may have included research into the lore and mythology of the many secret societies and family fraternities that existed in the world of the landed gentry. People like Poe and Morse would have been especially adept at understanding any technological secrets that they would have been exposed to during this time.

Poe would have been adept at noting cultural manifestations that would be useful and it appears some of these concepts would also later make a good story. His fascination with science may have led him to a study of the work of Cassini or to even have sought him out to talk personally. The Cassini's may have actually been opposed to the new politics of the Republic given their history and disassociation with the French Revolution. Here again we have more reason to believe that somehow Poe had known about the legend of Rennes le Chateau long before it was exposed later. It is possible that the significance of Rennes le Chateau was known of by Jefferson and this information had been further investigated if not by Poe then by Morse or Cooper and shared with the Society of the Cincinnati for their own uses.

Given all of this information the question of the modern Rennes le Chateau story may be viewed in a different light. What role or which side was Bérenger Saunière representing? The story of his association seems to indicate a break with traditional Catholic beliefs that may have included a belief in Mary Magdalene and a living post resurrection Christ. The introduction of this concept would likely challenge the old line beliefs of loyalists and ardent Catholics alike. Is it possible that this entire scenario was schemed in order to attain a political goal via the manipulation of the truth of history? In other words was it a byproduct of some sort of silent war between factions wishing to spin history in a particular direction? Is the entire story even true? There is likely something to each mystery that contains a kernel of truth. Rennes le Chateau may represent a lost treasure myth that was spun in many ways to resemble the story we see today for political reasons. It appears that Saunière was part of the camp that favored the Ancient Regime which in turn belays a value of the Arcadian theme.

Still many questions and holes in this story exist that can't be ignored. If Poe was a spy then it makes sense that his true exploits would not have been told of until much later if at all. If he had been working for the Society of the Cincinnati then this organization may have chose to withhold these facts for political or security reasons. His profession, intellect, and talents would fit the profile of many of the other artists suspected as being spies here. Undoubtedly there is still a version of this particular silent war going on throughout the entire world.

Notes on Rennes le Chateau Star.

The Rennes le Chateau Star Points to Sullivan's Island

The Rennes le Chateau Star Points to Basilica the Arian Baptistery in Ravenna. .

The Arian Baptistery is a small octagonal chapel built by Theodoric the Great in Ravenna. The Arian Baptistery has symbolic links to forms of Christianity that view Christ as a human being who was inspired divinely but was not divine. This is similar to many of the alternate beliefs said to have been held by the Plantagenets, Arians, and Cathars.

The Rennes le Chateau Star points to Fortress Salvatierra and Montesario Montesion in Spain and Fortress Salvetierra near Perillos

The Star in the landscape of Rennes le Chateau creates an arc on the globe that leads to both Perillos and Fortress Salvetierra near there and another arc that leads to Fortress Salvatierra and the Montesario Montesion (Mount Sion).

This association is interesting in league with the Cassini's operations in Perillos. This part of France was once part of Spain. The fortress of Slavtierra is located near Perillos and is part of the existant lore of the Perillos conundrum. The title of Salvatierra is given to commanders of the Order of Calatrava. The Order of Calatrava is a Spainish Order created by the Cistercian Order of monks just as the Knights Templar were.

It is possible that both of these fortresses were once home to Commanderies of the Knights of Calatrava. It is known commonly that Fortress Salvatierra and Montesario Montesion were indeed controlled and built by the Knights of Calatrava.

This involvement of the term "Salvatierra" is also related to Palacio de Salvatierra in Ronda Spain. Ronda is a location that may be associated with the Great Cyclic Cross of Hendaye. Ronda is included in the templum or places pointed to by the Great Cross of Hendaye.

The Rennes le Chateau Star Points to the Kings Knot

The octagon of the Kings Knot is oriented to point to the Star in the Landscape of Rennes le Chateau and the star points back. This alignment also includes the Tower of the Winds at Shugborough Hall. Shugborough is the home of the famous Shepherd's Monument with its "Et in

Arcadia Ego" inscription. The Shepherd's Monument displays this relationship in theme and its location. Some of the follies at Shugborough may be visible in the altar painting at the Rennes le Chateau Chapel. The alignment of the Kings Knot, Shugborough Tower of the Winds, and the Star of Rennes le Chateau in many ways defines the Arcadian Mysteries.

The Rennes le Chateau Star Points to the Peace Arch.

The Maryhill Stonehenge of Samuel Hill points an arc on the globe to the Peace Arch situated on the border of the U.S. and Canada. The Peace Arch is associated with the International Peace Garden which is also located on the 49th parallel on the U.S. and Canada border. Mr. Hill was also instrumental in building the Palace of the Legion of Honor in San Francisco. This building points an arc on the globe to the octagon of the International Peace Garden. It is notable that the Rennes le Chateau Star also points to the Peace Arch just as Mr. Hill's Stonehenge replica in Washington State does. Mr. Hill is a descendant of the same Washington family as the first President.

The Rennes le Chateau Star Points to Heliopolis, Egypt.

The Brotherhood of Heliopolis is spoken of in Fulcanelli's "Mystery of the Cathedrals." Heliopolis and later its namesake "Heliopolis" now known as Baalbek were the temporal axes mundi of their respective cultures of Egypt and the Roman Empire. The Brotherhood of Heliopolis may be composed during the era of the eighteenth and nineteenth centuries by people like the Cassini's, Jefferson, d'Abbadie's, and Von Humboldt's.

The axis of Heliopolis has many secrets including pointing an arc on the globe that includes Saqarra and many other significant Egyptian sites. The arcs on the globe extending from what is left of Heliopolis may have also contributed to millennial beliefs and the indication that Egypt was somehow related to the development of South and Central American Native cultures. (See "Sacred Towers of the Axis Mundi" for detailed analysis).

An illustration from and early edition of Poe's "The Gold Bug" that seems to depict the environs of Rennes le Bains and Rennes le Chateau and not the landscape of Sullivan's Island South Carolina where the story takes place. This artwork also includes the overtones of the original story of Oak Island as does the story itself.

The following poem by Poe is thought by many to refer to Atlantis. A closer inspection reveals he may be talking about the town of Migdal (Magdala) or original home of Mary Magdalene

175

located on the edge of the Sea of Galilee. Magdala is a Hebrew word for tower that inspired the name of the town. The position of the tower or Magdala next to the sea by Poe may reference this place. This in conjunction with the other Magdalene imagery in the "Gold Bug" may show how much Poe was actually aware of in this sphere.

Poem "The City in the Sea" by Edgar Allan Poe

LO! Death has reared himself a throne
In a strange city lying alone
Far down within the dim West,
Where the good and the bad and the worst and the best
Have gone to their eternal rest.
There shrines and palaces and towers
(Time-eaten towers that tremble not)
Resemble nothing that is ours.
Around, by lifting winds forgot,
Resignedly beneath the sky
The melancholy waters lie.

No rays from the holy heaven come down
On the long night-time of that town;
But light from out the lurid sea
Streams up the turrets silently,
Gleams up the pinnacles far and free:
Up domes, up spires, up kingly halls,
Up fanes, up Babylon-like walls,
Up shadowy long-forgotten bowers
Of sculptured ivy and stone flowers,
Up many and many a marvellous shrine
Whose wreathëd friezes intertwine
The viol, the violet, and the vine.

Resignedly beneath the sky
The melancholy waters lie.
So blend the turrets and shadows there
That all seem pendulous in air,
While from a proud tower in the town
Death looks gigantically down.

There open fanes and gaping graves
Yawn level with the luminous waves;
But not the riches there that lie
In each idol's diamond eye,—
Not the gayly-jewelled dead,

Tempt the waters from their bed;
For no ripples curl, alas,
Along that wilderness of glass;
No swellings tell that winds may be
Upon some far-off happier sea;
No heavings hint that winds have been
On seas less hideously serene!

But lo, a stir is in the air!
The wave—there is a movement there!
As if the towers had thrust aside,
In slightly sinking, the dull tide;
As if their tops had feebly given

Chapter 11: The Frenchman's Tower of Palo Alto and the Legend of J.C. Brown. Arcadia in California reveals all.

Some of what has been examined here to this point suggests the involvement of not only a specific social class or caste of people but of some of the very same families over time. Of course, we are not referring to every treasure legend in existence. Yet those discussed here including Oak Island, The Beale Treasure, The Bruton Parish Church Vault and others all seem to have involved a similar group of related families who may have been working together in business for a very long time prior to the establishment of the colonies and subsequently the United States.

California was originally claimed by Sir Francis Drake and named New Albion on his circumnavigation of discovery. Later a Russian Colony would exist in the same region claimed by Drake owned by the English Royal families Romanov relatives. During the time of the Russian Colony north of San Francisco one of the colonists summited Mt. Shasta. The name "Shasta" may even be a Russian name "Tchastal" or "snowy mountain." So it is interesting in many ways to see the New Age beliefs of Russian people like Madame Blavatsky and Nicolas Roerich being applied to matters of faith in the same region today.

Is it possible that these legends were placed in the mind of the public for some unknown reason? Why are these mysteries more popular and featured in more books and tv shows than others? Part of this is due to the kind of fairy tale like qualities of the folklore surrounding the reality or myth of these treasures or places. Is it possible that these stories were put there intentionally to teach us hidden or neglected aspects of history involving this family group of people? This may be true and may also extend to those that had business dealings with the people that created these mysteries as well. Many of this cast of characters may have been Freemasons or at least had subscribed to a kind of Rosicrucian philosophy.

If the Oak Island Treasure story was somehow copied from Philip Sidney's "Arcadia" then we are looking at a person associated with the premiere writer's guild of Elizabethan England. Other members of the Wilton Writer's Circle of Mary Sidney Herbert Countess of Pembroke included Edmund Spenser, Michael Drayton, Sir John Davies and Samuel Daniel. Note the Drayton named as referred to Charleston South Carolina earlier. Other people sometimes associated with Sir Francis Bacon including Edward de Vere, Ben Jonson, and Inigo Jones were also known to associate with this writers group. It may even be possible that the disputed authorship of the works of Shakespeare had been a group effort that was composed of all the people suspected as authoring these works including William Shakespeare.

If the notion is true that a similar family group had arranged certain aspects of mythology and folklore to in turn communicate valuable information to a select group then it may be possible to see the fingerprints of this philosophy at work at different times and places. In this way we later see Poe and Longfellow taking part in the same activity and even being able to recognize that the original Oak Island story had first been featured in Sidney's "Arcadia."

178

With this in mind there are several common families and themes associated with the myths and legends of Mt. Shasta California that also includes many of the same elements of the Oak Island Treasure and Beale Treasure. Part of the reason for the veiled or metaphorical myths may be to define a real or business domain in the tradition of the Tower of the Winds in Athens. Through time architectural follies such as the Tower of the Winds at Shugborough and West Wycombe may have been put there to tip off those in the know that the structures builder had been initiated into a specific group or had been born a family member of those that valued this philosophy.

Later people would use the concept of the Axis Mundi in relation to the modern view of a Pirates map. If a structure had been used to define property in a legal manner in the past then those wishing to hide or sequester items could use these systems to hide things themselves. This fact alone may contribute to why many legends of treasure are associated. These schemes may be meant to convey a history pertinent to a given secret society or family group that could be easily misinterpreted by others as being meant to hide valuable items. In addition, these schemes are used by religious groups in pilgrimages and quests meant to teach and inform the individual. The Knights of the Golden Circle during the U.S. Civil War used schemes involving cartography and symbol interpretation to lead agents to hidden caches of weapons and valuables so that may serve as a good example of the practical uses of such a plan beyond any tradition or older legal description of property.

Amazingly an examination as to the true origins of the mysterious "Frenchman's Tower" in Palo Alto California may serve to unlock many of the common elements of this overall story into a cohesive and understandable saga. This simple brick tower with crenulations situated on the property that would become Stanford University seems to tell many secrets when one has already become familiar with other similar places such as Williamsburg, Newport (Tower), Star Castle, Aachen Cathedral, and the Tower of the Winds of Athens.

In 1875 a man calling himself Peter Coutts came to Mayfield just north of San Jose, California from France. Mr. Coutts seemed a mysterious figure to the locals and made quite an impression in the south bay area. He bought nearly three thousand acres and established a dairy and stock farm. Coutts also had a residence in "the city" as most bay area folk refer to San Francisco. Rumors swirled that Coutts had escaped France in a banking scandal and had left under threat of legal consequences. He added to this air of mystery by not telling anyone of his past and giving nothing but enigmatic answers to their questions. It did not help that Coutts' real name was Jean Baptiste Paulin Caperon. This man's name alone displays a value of John the Baptist and may belie his true philosophy. John the Baptist is said to be highly valued by different Templar or secret society groups such as the Knights of Malta. Evidence may suggest that Peter Coutts was this man's real name and that Caperon was an alias.

Caperon said he had assumed the identity of his deceased cousin from Switzerland and had actually escaped France in a banking scandal linked more to political alliances than any real wrongdoing. As a coincidence his cousin had been known as Count Peter Coutts. A royal designation. This at least links Caperon to a royal interest. Most accounts do not state where Count Coutts came from originally or what region or domain he was 'count' of.

179

The title of count is usually related to a geographic region or area. This is the origin of the word "county." Interestingly there is a Coutts bank in the City of London.

One of the first structures Coutts built on his farm was a strange brick tower that had an almost Romanesque look to its construction. The top rim of the tower even included battlements just like a medieval castle. This tower was said to have been Coutts' library. He was an avid book collector and possessed many rare early printed books from Europe including many rare editions from the Dutch publishing House of Elzevir. These titles were said to include many hard to find occult documents. Coutts' construction of this feature strangely echoes the uses and purpose of the Tour Magdela at Rennes le Chateau.

Father Saunière also used the RLC tower as a library. Indeed there are many similarities between "The Frenchman's Tower" and the Rennes le Chateau mystery. Seemingly from nowhere these men came and spent relatively large amounts of money not only building their towers but insuring that they would be built in a context in which others would know or be able to decipher their true meaning. It is as if they were acting out the same activity that Dr. John Dee had been involved in with his alchemical tower and involvement in the construction of Star Castle. It is possible that these towers were viewed as places at which the power of their associated alignments may have been used or understood.

The Frenchman's Tower was also said to house a water tank on its upper story. Mr. Coutts also had a series of tunnels dug into the hillside to find a steady source of water for the entire ranch if not the tower itself. Again the local rumor mill ran hot with speculation about what the tower was really for. Though water towers are a common sight in California this structure did not seem suited for that purpose or to be large enough to store a substantial amount of water. It had to be for something else. Here we have a tower associated with what some may term vaults and tunnels just as at Rennes le Chateau.

The tower must have been for him to look out for those coming to arrest him and the tunnels were so he could escape said the locals. In reality, it seems likely that Peter Coutts had constructed an alchemical tower in a tradition he had brought with him to California from France. Coutts' tower was complete with water tank just like the original Tower of the Winds in Athens, which held a clepsydra or water clock. Was Caperon building a clepsydra in the Frenchman's Tower? It seems the towers may have been for both the collection of scientific as well as spiritual data originally.

One could imagine these men late at night casting horoscopes by candlelight sequestered in their towers. There may have been an occult or alchemical belief associated with the towers that led their builders to believe that they could see or control events at a distance. Was Caperon/Coutts placing a talisman in the region for some unknown controller or himself? Was the construction of the tower establishing a certain class or group of people in this region using a seemingly talismanic activity? Was he simply building a tower?

In the end Caperon/Coutts disappeared as suddenly as he had appeared. It seems a regime change in France had cleared his name and he had regained his estate and fortune there and was allowed to return. It is interesting to speculate whether Coutts/Caperon had any link to the Rennes le Chateau mystery. It is possible that he was in some way connected at least to the same group or philosophy that compelled the Tor Magdela to be built. Coutts put his property up for sale and it was purchased by Leland Stanford who eventually developed Stanford University there.

Coutts/Caperon had returned to France by the time the Tor Magdela had been constructed. He certainly possessed the family background, possible Jacobite traditions, including Norman/French associations that he may have valued creating clues to this great mystery. His entire heritage points to him being an adherent of some form of Scottish Rite Masonry or their predecessors. These same associations are present in the more modern versions of both the mysteries of Rennes le Chateau and Girona, Spain. This is only speculation in that it is likely that many different groups value these architectural associations.

The era of the construction of the Frenchman's tower coincided with the Franco-Prussian war. From the descriptions available of Coutts' life at this time the war and his views concerning it may have been part of the reason he was exiled. Strangely the story of a more well known and well connected man matches many of the events and important dates in Coutts/Caperon's life. What we may be seeing in the Frenchman's could be associated with another fallen king.

It is possible that this man was the exiled King of France Henry V also known as the Duc d' Chambord. Henry V was born in 1820. Caperon was born in 1822. Henry V died 1883. Caperon died 1889. In addition the year Caperon returned to France was the same year Henry V passed away. It is entirely possible that these dates are a coincidence. Perhaps Caperon was an associate or relative of the King who had started the farm and invested some of the Kings money in Gold Rush era California. Alternately it is possible that business associate of Henry Artois duc d' Chambord had established the farm for him. Records reveal that Henry V financed the maintenance of Chateau Chambord via the Coutts bank of the City of London.

Is it possible that exiled King Henry V is also somehow involved in the mystery of Rennes le Chateau? Many researchers such as the good people in the Perillos Society of France suggest a connection to Rennes le Chateau and Countess d'Chambord Henry V's wife. A chain of evidence suggesting the d' Chambord's donated the money that was used to renovate the Rennes le Chateau chapel via banking records has been uncovered. Another thread of information even suggests the the heir to their fortune continued to make payments towards further projects in Rennes le Chateau such as the Villa Bethania and Tour Magdala is also suggested.

Though not completely ironclad this evidence does strongly point in the direction of the Duc d'Chambord and his wife having an interest in Rennes le Chateau. The building of the Frenchman's Tower prior to this and their possible involvement in Palo Alto would also lend weight to this argument. It is also clear that Henry V banked with the Coutts Bank of the City of London to finance the upkeep of Chateau Chambord and more. Again possibly a coincidence but we do see this name being introduced into the mystery in Palo Alto. Note again that the Frenchman's tower was built years before any of the mystery in Rennes le Chateau began to develop in its modern form. Renovation of the Rennes le Chateau chapel did begin in 1887 only four years after Caperon/Coutts left Palo Alto to return to France. The Tour Magdala and Villa Bethania's construction did not begin until 1898.

In either case it appears that Coutts had found himself in a similar situation to that of the exiled King of France. This would have put him in opposition to Napoleon III who had also just earlier in history invaded Mexico and set up Emperor Maximillian I.

Henry V, Duc d' Chambord was the owner of one of the most picturesque chateaus in France. The Chateau Chambord is a grand structure that also includes an extensive linear array of aligned gardens and statuary. The linear aspect of the grounds points the way to the northwest and southeast. Chateau Chambord does not point to the Vatican as does Chateau Villette. Chateau Chambord points the way to Palo Alto, California and the Frenchmen's tower built by Jean Baptiste Paulin Caperon a.k.a. Peter Coutts!

An azimuth drawn on the globe from Chateau Chambord to the Fenchman's Tower in Palo Alto matches the angle of the linear grounds there. This may support the notion that the 'Frenchman' of Palo Alto was either Henry V himself or a representative of him. The building of an alchemical tower in relation to a distant axis may be a form of homage and respect towards the central axis. It is possible that Caperon held beliefs that dictated he build his tower in a talismanic manner in order to communicate with Chateau Chambord or to claim this property for the sovereign. Maybe Coutts and the Duc d'Chambord had family in common?

Many parts of this mystery include people seemingly being sent to a specific place to build these towers. In 1883 before he left Caperon sold his property to Senator Leland Stanford who would soon found Stanford University on the site of Caperon's old dairy! Leland Stanford now had control of the legacy of the Frenchman's Tower and some could argue the future of California. Is it a coincidence that one of the most powerful people in California history would take control of Coutts' property? Stanford's involvement in this story may also indicate an association with a person such as Henry V or his associates.

Many things about this entire tale suggest that it may have been all planned and part of Caperon's reason for coming to the San Francisco bay area was actually to build his tower and possibly impart the philosophy that made it a thing of value. It is likely that he searched out and purchased this particular piece of property due to its spatial relationship with Chateau Chambord and Mt Shasta. The true purpose of his visit will likely forever be clouded in time so we are left only to speculate about the truth behind these incidents. Undoubtedly the richness and promise of California's mineral wealth could have been part of this interest as well.

The history and values of Leland Stanford and Caperon's family may reveal some ground breaking clues in this mystery that lead all the way back to Jacobite rebellions in England; their influence in France and the legacy of the Stuarts and clans of Scotland in modern history. It seems that Mr. Coutts/Caperon likely possessed a family lineage that spanned bloodlines including the Stuart family of English Royalty and the family of Napoleon Bonaparte. The lore of the Frenchman's Tower even extends to Mt. Shasta.

The Coutts family name is still a major force in the banking circles of the City of London. This lineage for Mr. Coutts/Caperon would have put him in the same family or Bloodline as Henry V. The story of Henry V does echo the lost king tale of the exiled King of England James II, III and his son Bonnie Prince Charlie who anchored the Jacobite movement in both England and France. The story of the lost Kings of Jerusalem may also fit the line of reasoning in the tale of Henry V. It is possible that Henry V had links to both the Kings of Jerusalem and Jacobites via his royal ancestry. Henry V does share the name of two of the earliest Norman Kings of England. What may be more applicable to all of this intrigue is these families association with the Plantagenet dynasty of France and England.

Mr. Caperon/Coutts was apparently much more connected than the common story of the Frenchman's Tower exposes. Given these facts his family was involved not only in Jacobite sympathies in England but supported the Cultural Revolution while later opposing the policies of Napoleon. In turn all of this may suggest a Norman heritage that would naturally have influence or ties to places like Rennes le Chateau, Shugborough Hall, Williamsburg, and now Palo Alto, California. It also appears that family members took different sides in many of these conflicts and associations. We may also see the involvement of the Coutts family at Oak Island as well.

An examination of the legacy of the names involved in a legend of Mt. Shasta may reveal the truth and also tell us why it is important that the Coutts family are involved in the Frenchman's Tower. In the process we will see strong links between the Coutts family and Bonnie Prince Charlie exiled King of Scotland and England along the way. What we will learn in part is that the Frenchman's Tower may have been built where it is intentionally. The telling of this story will also link the Frenchman's Tower to one of the most popular myths of Mt. Shasta that also has many elements in common with the Oak Island and Beale Treasures.

It is important to note here that the Coutts Bank of London and specifically Thomas Coutts had a very close relationship with Bonnie Prince Charlie and are said to have handled he and his exiled family's finances until his death. Later in the story we will see how some illegitimate grandchildren of Bonnie actually attempted to regain their title and associated riches that Coutts then controlled.

After examining Mt. Shasta and the Legend of J.C. Brown we will return to the genetic legacy of the people involved and how many of these families eventually came to California including the famous Beale family for whom the treasure is named. In the process, the involvement of the same families and caste of people are seen involved in the development of California.

The Legend of J.C. Brown

Though the Legend of J.C. Brown was known of long before Emilie Frank's book "Mt. Shasta, California's Mystic Mountain" was published her rendering of the story contains all the elements that were included in the stories original telling in the Stockton Record newspaper in 1934. If an individual who was aware of their genetic and philosophical legacy somewhat similar to that of an initiate into a mystery school were to have read Ms. Franks book or the Stockton paper of that time a few pertinent facts would have been revealed.

The story tells of how geologist and mining engineer J.C. Brown stumbled upon the hidden entrance to a cave and traveled deep under a mountain thought to be Mt. Shasta and discovered a hidden crypt including mummies, golden tablets, and other riches. At this time J.C. Brown was said to have worked for "The Lord Cowdray Mining Company." After telling crowds in Stockton California wild tales of riches and crypts hidden deep in Mt. Shasta J.C. Brown was said to have disappeared never to be seen again. Prior to this he had arranged an expedition to Mt. Shasta and had talked about it in the Newspaper. J.C. Brown left many people disappointed in Stockton in 1934 never to be seen again. Though the police were contacted it appears J.C. Brown had not been working a confidence scam as he had never accepted any money from those he recruited to go on this expedition. Part of the legend also states that J.C. Brown had left evidence that this was all true in a mysterious bank vault in Texas.

Recently evidence has surfaced that J.C. Brown lived only a few doors away from where the meetings were held to plan the trip prior to his disappearance. (Sindoni)

Many elements of this story resemble the standard Rosicrucian and Enochian stories that include the lost remains of important individuals being hidden in chambers in unknown mountains. Often these stories include the fact that lost information is one of the treasures though many of these stories including the Legend of J.C. Brown feature golden riches meant to lure the seeker in some ways. Elements of both the Beale Treasure and Oak Island treasure include many of the same overtones.

For an initiate of the correct order or family the inclusion of the terms "J.C. Brown" and "Lord Cowdray Mining Company" would have supplied a great deal of information. First of all there are no records of the Lord Cowdray Mining Company having existed at that time. What was associated with the Cowdray name was a construction concern owned by the last Viscount Cowdray Wheetman Pearson who had regained that title after it had been extinct for over a hundred years. Right away someone in the know may have recognized that this story was meant to convey something totally different than the fairy tale elements of the story suggest. In fact if this individual seeker was also familiar with the story of the Frenchman's Tower in Palo Alto some stunning similarities and involvement of the same people would be known right away.

In this case the inference of the Lord Cowdray Mining Company and the Brown name may have rung a very loud bell of realization in the mind of the fortunate seeker who already knew this information. In the end both the story of J.C. Brown and The Frenchman's Tower may have been put there to tell the story of the people who had somehow created these legends.

In the story of the Frenchman's Tower we are told of the involvement of the Coutts family of which Peter Coutts appeared to have some French or Swiss background thus also being known as Paulin Caperon. This line of reasoning will show how Caperon was an alias and that the Coutt's family would have been behind the building of the tower and possibly the propagation of the

Legend of J.C. Brown. The Frenchman's Tower is also due south of Mt. Shasta thus creating a Prime Meridian that includes both places.

Though many relate the tale of J.C. Brown to Wheetman Pearson the last Lord Cowdray a closer examination is needed. If we look further into the legacy of the Lords of Cowdray we will be led to the Viscounts of Montigu Cowdray family. As in many English noble families this name is but a title in addition to their original name of Browne. Is it possible that J.C. Brown himself was a distant American descendant of this family line? This would not be the first time in this study that we have seen American portions of gentry families from England or Scotland carrying on their family legacies. Here again we see the Montagu name just as in the story of Oak Island and the Carolina Corps of Charleston South Carolina.

The last nine Lords of Cowdray were all of the Montagu-Browne family and held many close relations to Kings and Queens beginning with Edward II whose standard bearer was Anthony Browne the 1st Viscount Cowdray. Amazingly the Montague Viscounts of Cowdray would have many interfaces and family relations to the famous Coutts banking dynasty that seemed to be behind the Frenchman's Tower in Palo Alto. The Montacute or Montagu name of the Viscounts Montagu Cowdray had come from a female in the line of Brown that had been a Montagu. The Montagu name also figures prominently in the history of Nova Scotia in the form of Lord Halifax Montigu-Dunk. In the case of Lord Halifax the "Dunk" portion of his name had come from his wife's family at the behest of her father when they were wed.

The 9th Viscount Montagu Cowdray was the last Lord of Cowdray in the late 1700's. This young man was engaged to the daughter of Thomas Coutts of the Coutts Bank of London. Just prior to the marriage the future Lord Cowdray drowned with his Coutts/Burdett cousin in the falls of the Rhine attempting to traverse them in a small boat. Just days prior Cowdray House had burned to the ground thus fulfilling a curse on the Montagu's that included destruction by "fire and water."

".....as we gather from a single ambiguous
sentence in one of Tom Coutts' letters, Fanny, the middle
daughter, had given her affections to Charles Sedley
Burdett, a younger brother of the heir, and Susannah, the
eldest, was openly engaged to be married to Viscount
Montague of Cowdray."

p.4

When Anthony Browne had been given Battle Abbey by Henry VIII after the dissolution of the monasteries a monk had cursed him and his family to perish by "fire and water." In a strange way these two events over three hundred years later had fulfilled that bizarre prophecy. This incident also exposes the close links between the Coutts and Montagu-Browne family. The development of the Coutts family after the sixteenth century also includes many intermarriages with others named Brown or Browne in Scotland.

185

Given this it is even possible that the term "J.C. Brown" is referring to the 9ᵗʰ Lord Cowdray as "IX Brown." Greek letters J and C with of course the Lords of Cowdray given name Browne. The mention of "The Lord Cowdray Mining Company" in the "Legend of J.C. Brown" may be a hidden metaphor tipping one off as to the involvement of the descendants of the Lords of Cowdray in California in arranging both the Frenchman's Tower and J.C. Brown mysteries including the Coutts family. Certain members of the Brown and Coutts family may have been able to recognize such things as a tip off to a family legacy and not any real hidden treasure.

Amazingly the family of Wheetman Pearson may have been related to the Coutts family and via this connection to the Montagu-Browne's. It may be for this reason that after becoming successful Wheetman Pearson was awarded the title Lord of Cowdray without the Montagu portion of the previous title of Cowdray. Wheetman Pearson was definitely in the loop of relations of the Coutts family and this may explain some of his success in construction enterprises the world over and later in publishing.

Here we have a very old and storied family suggesting to us that they were privy to the truths of Mt. Shasta as they had arranged both the Frenchman's Tower and the Legend of J.C. Brown to reference an association with Mt. Shasta. The entire end result may be to suggest that the remains of an important family member are interred at Mt. Shasta. If true this may also mean that there is no hidden crypt but that this individual is buried in one of the known yet older cemeteries in the area. It is clear that no major industries beyond timber and the natural spring water of Mt. Shasta were available to these financiers and titans of the construction industry.

There are however some interesting aspects of the later Wheetman Pearson and his involvement in building railroads and promoting the oil industry in Mexico that suggest some skullduggery afoot in the Legend of J.C. Brown.

Amazingly the entire later story of Joaquin Miller suggests he was aware of the importance of Mt. Shasta to this family and had even travelled in exclusive circles during his time in Europe thus leading him to a greater understanding of this tradition. He later emulated the geographic scheme of the Frenchman's Tower first living on the White House Meridian in Washington D.C. for three years then retiring to Oakland. In Oakland Miller built his "Heights" estate (his intentional misspelling) and building his Pyramid to Moses exactly due south of the peak of Mt. Shasta also aligning with the Frenchman's Tower.

Joaquin Miller had once written a play entitled "First Families of the Sierras." The play's plot revolved around a band of Mormon assassins that were tracking down and eliminating the remnants of the families that had in turn assassinated Joseph Smith. Some of the overtones of the J.C. Brown story also include elements of Mormon belief with even "golden tablets" being suggested in the original tale.

Eventually a Mormon Temple would be built in Oakland right across the street from Miller's "Hights" estate. In turn this structure would also be south of Mt. Shasta as the other structures mentioned here were. There are some strange associations in Mt. Shasta City with a man named

186

H.D. "Curly" Brown who once owned a premiere horse farm near the town. He is even responsible for the town changing its name from Sisson to Mt. Shasta City. Though not established it may be possible this Mr. Brown was also descendant from the Browne Montagu Lords of Cowdray. Very little genealogical information is available concerning Curly Brown but what is seen is him naming each of his children after Mormon Saints including his son Moroni Brown. This Mormon association is possible via the many strange links they seem to have with Freemasonry and the establishment of an alternate faith in the United States.

Other well known individuals associated with Mt. Shasta and its rich history emulated placing their estates in a north to south scheme using Mt. Shasta as the basis for a meridian or Axis Mundi. This includes Dunsmuir House in Oakland (the family namesake of Dunsmuir at the base of Mt. Shasta) and Muir House in Martinez California. John Muir namesake of Muir House would also go on to be close friends with John Bidwell and accompanied he and J.D. Hooker to Mt. Shasta where Hooker assailed them with "stories of the Himalayas" according to Muir's papers. This one small incident may have been the original seed of the kind of New Age lore and beliefs we see being propagated at Mt. Shasta today.

The story of the Legend of J.C. Brown and the Frenchman's tower seems to illustrate a similar tradition to what may be termed "the Arcadian mysteries." It seems that people who were aware of this tradition had valued it by building a series of towers similar to the Tower of the Winds in Athens. This may also lead us to the concept of the alchemical tower or "Magdala." Magdala means "fish tower." And as we see there is a unique link between some of the most emblematic monuments in France leading us to Migdal, Israel and Oak Island.

Repeated from earlier: One of the most identifiable linear arrangements of architecture in Paris is known as the Axe Historique or Historical Axis of Pairs. The Axe Historique began as a linear arrangement associated with French Royalty and their Louvre Palace. The Louvre Museum was once the palace and birthplace to many French Kings including Henri V duc d' Chambord. In later times the I.M. Pei Pyramid and inverted pyramid were added to this array. This more modern feature of the array was featured prominently in the book and movie "The Da Vinci Code." The movie even implied that the crypt of Mary Magdalene was located beneath the Louvre's inverted pyramid which aligns with the "normal" pyramid that serves as an entrance to the Louvre Museum today.

If one examines the linear aspect of the array of pyramid and inverted pyramid at the Louvre some startling associations are made. To the east an arc on the globe created by the direction suggested by this array transects the globe to Migdal Israel said hometown of Mary Magdalene. In the opposite westerly transect an arc extends to Oak Island Nova Scotia. Kind of freaky in relation to the story told in the movie. Does this reflect an actual belief? The Arcadian geography involved is telling us something that was featured in the movie and also pointing us to the largest mystery present in French Acadia.

Again here we have a linear array of architecture seemingly associated even if in fiction with the remains of an important individual. In fact much of the French side of the Oak Island story seems to suggest that whatever is hidden in Nova Scotia is associated with Mary Magdalene or her Royal Blood. In fact the Plantagenet dynasty of families seems to be involved in many aspects of this over all tale all the way from Rennes le Chateau to the Frenchman's Tower of Palo Alto to the lofty heights of Mt. Shasta. It is possible that this family and others associated saw themselves as descendant of Mary Magdalene and Christ.

Is it possible that a further examination of the legacy of the Coutts family and others in theses mysteries will unveil the truth?

Interestingly there is a significant relation between the Coutts, Stuart, and Bonaparte family that may lead us to the true origins of the Frenchman's Tower and beyond.

"Lord Dudley-Coutts Stuart, son of the Marquis of Bute by his second wife Frances Coutts, was born on 4th February 1803. He married in 1824, Chistiana Alexandrine Egypta, daughter of Lucien Bonaparte, Prince of Canino, and by her (died 19th May, 1847) had Paul Amadeus Francis Coutts Stuart, an officer in the army."
From the Coutts and Colt Genealogy.

Here is a direct link not only to the Bonaparte family but to the part of the family that opposed Emperor Napoleon and subsequent other rulers of that name. This fits in a large way the assumption that Peter Coutts a.k.a. Paulin Caperon was directly related to this Stuart part of the Coutts family relations. This also fits the timeframe of Peter Coutts' exile as told in the original story. Lord Stuart's son was even named Paul. During this period of history California would be a perfect place for an exile with money to go and make his fortune and that is exactly what Peter Coutts did. Note also that the farm Coutts established was named the "Ayrshire Farm." This is hardly a name that would be used by a "Frenchman." This would be more aptly applied by a person who was Scottish or of Scots descent.

This relation is also interesting when considering the story of the how the first Masonic charter came to California. The charter was brought to the Ranch of Peter Lassen from Missouri by Lassen, Commodore Stockton, and a man named Lucien Stewart. While there is no record of Lucien Stewart being related to Lord Dudley-Coutts Stuart this may be possible. Lucien Stewart was one of the signers of this first California Masonic Charter. He shares the same name as Lucien Bonaparte the father of Christiana Stuart. The names Stuart and Stewart are indeed the same family with "Stuart" being the European version avoiding the confusion of the "v" sound made in relation to the "w" sound in the original Scottish name of Stewart. Since Lucien was American he would have used the Scottish form of the name using the letter "w." It is entirely possible that Lucien Stewart was related to Lord Dudley Coutts Stuart and was given the name Lucien in response to him being related to Lucien Bonaparte. It is also stated that Paul Stuart was "in the army."

This Charter was brought to Benton City or the Ranch of Peter Lassen. Benton City had been named for Missouri Senator Thomas Hart Benton by Lassen. For a time the ranch was used by Benton's son in law famous western explorer John Fremont as a base of operations. Lassen's town of Benton City would eventually fail causing the first Masonic Charter to be moved to the Western Star Lodge at Mt. Shasta City where it remains to this day.

Later Lassen's Ranch would be owned by Leland Stanford eventually passing to the Monastery of New Clairvaux which occupies part of Lassen's original rancho today. The Hearst family has in part funded the construction of a medieval chapter house from the Monastery of Santa Maria de Ovila in Spain that William Randolph Hearst had shipped over from Spain in the early 1930's. The medieval chapter house at New Clairvaux is composed of the "Sacred Stones" of the original 12th century Spanish monastery and original mason's marks can be seen on some of the stones today.

Could the Frenchman's Tower have been built to "point to" this Masonic charter that had been signed by a member of the Stewart family regardless of his relation to the Coutts family? If true this would certainly fit the entire scheme of events and fit the chronology of those events closely. It is possible that in some small way the Legend of J.C. Brown and the Frenchman's Tower are clueing us into the historical importance of how this charter was brought to California from Missouri so long ago. Still there is likely more to the story but the Frenchman's Tower and Legend of J.C. Brown were both developed past the time the charter had already been moved to Mt. Shasta.

The Frenchman's Tower on what is today Staford University property. By Confr - Own work, CC BY 3.0, https://commons.wikimedia.org/w/index.php?curid=16115812

Chapter 12: Bonnie Prince Charlie's Legacy from Oak Island to the Frenchman's Tower.

An examination of the life and loves of Bonnie Prince Charlie reveals many concepts and family members that had an impact on the how and why of places like Oak Island and even Mt. Shasta. We have already seen how the Alexander family was involved in the development of Scottish Nova Scotia and even Washington D.C. in the United States. The Alexander's had a close link to the Stewart family of Bonnie Prince Charlie and had descended from the same genetic stock.

We have seen how the octagonal Kings Knot of Stirling Castle home to Scottish Kings creates an azimuth or arc on the globe that points to two other places where the Arcadian theme is present. This includes Shugborough Hall and its Shepherds Monument, and Rennes le Chateau with its Arcadian imgery suggested by the same Poussin painting "The Shepherds of Arcadia." Is it just a coincidence that these three places all involve the concept of Arcadia? It seems the Jacobite and Scottish influence may have something to do with all of these mysteries. How would this apply to other mysteries that we have examined such as Oak Island, The Beale Treasure, Williamsburg, The Newport Tower, and even the Kensington Rune?

Towards the end of the seventeenth century the Parliament of England was making a great effort to wrest power from the monarchy that was at that time James II. James' involvement with his Catholic faith also put him at odds with many different groups of people in England, Scotland, and Ireland. The path that James II was trodding had already been traveled by his direct ancestors Charles I, II, and even the Duke of Monmouth Charles I bastard son (onetime owner of Anson's Moor Park estate).

Eventually James was forced to escape England. On his first attempt James was captured but had been assisted in this task according to some sources by "his backstairs page Abbadie." The second escape was successful and this time James II was assisted by a man named "Biddulph." Both of these names are prominent in everything exposed in this book and others produced by this author. Here below we will see the importance of the d'Abbadie family. The name Biddulph over time became anglicized leading us to the Bidwell founders of both Hartford Connecticut and Chico California of which both places illustrate the Arcadian mysteries in art and architecture.

As time progressed both James III and his son Bonnie Prince Charlie would serve as the exiled Kings of England and Scotland. Their exile in part would inspire the American Revolution and creation of the United States of America. This is one of the factors in this story that would lead to families like the Alexander's, Washington's, and Lee's becoming involved in making the U.S. a sovereign nation separate from that of England. Amazingly the family relations of the Stewarts and others over time may lead us to some amazing insights with regard to the Oak Island Legend and other similar treasure stories.

The one-time conspiracy theory that Charles Edward Stewart a.k.a. Bonnie Prince Charlie had a daughter by Clementina Walkinshaw a Scottish woman is now undisputed. Clementina was the daughter of a staunch Jacobite and supporter of Bonnie Prince Charlie's father the exiled King

James II named John Walkinshaw. Bonnie first met Clementina during his attempt to invade Scotland in 1746. After that time Clementina and Bonnie were reacquainted and subsequently lived together for several years. The product of this union was a daughter named Charlotte. Since Charlotte was never accepted by others as a legitimate claimant to the title other relations of the Scottish Royal family over time have also claimed this distinction. This would also include the current Royal family of England who are indeed Stuarts descendant of Elizabeth of Bohemia.

Prior to his liaison with Clementina Walkinshaw Price Charles was said to have had an affair with a woman named Louise de Montbazon de La Tour d' Auvergne. This affair was also said to have produced a child that lived but was never identified and likely grew up in exile. This connection to the de La Tour d'Auvergne name and associated family exposes some interesting and bizarre connections to the development of Nova Scotia later in this tale. Ms. de La Tour was also Bonnie's first cousin. This association will also lead us to Rennes le Chateau!

Interestingly during the period of her life prior to being recognized as Bonnie Prince Charlie's daughter from Clementina Walkinshaw, Charlotte would serve as mistress to Ferdinand Maximilliam Meriadec de Rohan, Archbishop of Bordeax and Cambrai. This man was of the same family as the woman Marie Louise de La Tour d' Auvergne that Bonnie had previously had a relationship with and had fathered a child. Is this an interesting coincidence or were there more connections?

Since the Archbishop de Rohan was not supposed to have a wife or mistress this was of course kept a secret. Charlotte ended up having three children by de Rohan which ultimately were raised by their Grandmother in Paris, Clementina Walkinshaw. So, there is a pronounced loop of direct family relations between the exiled Stewarts of Scotland associated with the Jacobite cause and a very well connected branch of the French Royal family and landed gentry. Again, is it odd that Bonnie's daughter the Duchess of Albany had an affair with and bore the children of this family even if clandestinely. This may also explain why these children are relatively unknown and were kept in semi-seclusion.

Eventually Charlotte would be recognized by her father Bonnie Prince Charlie near the time of the French Revolution (1790). Charlotte would go to live with Bonnie near Paris and attended to him in his final years. It was at this time Charlotte was styled Charlotte Stuart Duchess of Albany in the exiled court of Charles Edward Stewart King of Scotland, England, and Ireland. Though her children were raised in exile they would have been due the titles belonging to them by blood but were denied this for many reasons even though it was known they were legitimate heirs. Through their lives these children would be funded via the generosity of one Thomas Coutts of the Coutts Bank of London who also shared a distant family relation to Clementina Walkinshaw. It appears a loop of family had developed that included many of the major players in the development of Nova Scotia later. It also included one of the most powerful bankers in the world at that time.

At this point we should also remind ourselves of the relationship between James II wife Clementina Sobieska and her sister Maria Korolina Sobieska who was married to Charles

Godefroy de La Tour d'Auvergne. The daughter of Karolina Sobieska and Godefroy de La Tour was Marie Louise de La Tour d'Auvergne. Marie Louise was a first cousin of Bonnie Prince Charlie and they had had an affair with issue of a child as stated above. This is also the family with which the Duchess of Albany had had an affair with Ferdinand Maximilliam Meriadec de Rohan and had children with. So, two Stuarts or Stewarts had had interface with members of this family that had produced children with a similar genetic makeup to that of the union between Clementina Sobieska and James II. As we will see the de La Tours had also had family interface with Sir William Alexander of Stirling's family two hundred years prior. Unfortunately, Marie Louise would be guillotined during the French Revolution.

The arms of de La Tour d'Auvergne include a Tower but also the symbol used today for the Lauguedoc-Roussillon region of France:

This is a vital link in the saga of Oak Island and may expose many hidden aspects of what was going on there prior to and after the Oak Island Legend was exposed to the public near the turn of the nineteenth century. The following may also explain how Nova Scotia was considered to be still the territory of Bonnie Prince Charlie even though it continually passed from French to Scottish to English hands. Here below exposed is why the strange relations between the Stewarts and de La Tours is important to the Oak Island Mystery and the development of Nova Scotia. In a very real way this information also leads us to Palo Alto, The Frenchman's Tower and Mt. Shasta.

In reference to the Marriage of Ernest Judson Clark to Marie Breson de La Tour. Clark was a lineal descendant of both Mary Ball (G. Washington's Grandmother) and the Clarke family of the famous Lewis and Clark expedition member William Clark

" *Mrs. Clark and her sister, Mrs. John Howard Herrick, also of Baltimore, are the daughters of Mr. Louis de La Tour of Lynchburg, Virginia, who was formerly of Paris. They are scions of that famous French family which produced during the Napoleonic period the "First Grenadier of France," Theophile de La Tour d'Auvergne, whose history and romantic interest rival that of the famous Chevalier Bayard. Mrs. Clark is a lineal descendant of the first governor of Nova Scotia, General Charles de La Tour, whose wife's name she bears. General de La Tour was grandfather of the "First Grenadier of France." This was the family name of the Bouillon dukedom, and the great French marshal, Turenne, second son of the Duke de Bouillon bore the name of Henri de La Tour d'Auverngne."*

Men of Mark in Maryland, Johson's Makers of America Series; Biographies of Leading Men of the State, Volume II; by Lynn R. Meekins, A.M. (B.F. Johnson, Inc. Baltimore, Washington and Richmond, 1910) P. 254

Interestingly Louis de La Tour lived in Lynchburg Virginia a town which is also intimately involved in the saga of the Beale Treasure. Though no links are apparent Louis would own a home only a few blocks from Morriss' boarding house which is part of the Beale Legend. Thomas Jefferson's Poplar Forest octagon is also located just outside the city limits of Lynchburg in Forest, Virginia today.

Though the title of Bouillon is held in common with famous Knights Templar and King of Jerusalem Godefroy de Bouillon the La Tour claim to this title did not come until later. Given this there may be blood family links between the two family groups. Later Dukes of Bouillon of the de La Tour title also assumed the name Godefroy de Bouillon including the father of Marie Louise de La Tour d'Auvergne first cousin and paramour of Bonnie Prince Charlie. This is yet another interesting link between the Menteith and the Knights Templar and could be linked to Fitzalan's patronage of the Knights Templar in the twelfth century. These connections may be leading us to broad associations between Scottish nobles and the Knights Templar that do not include the Sinclair family.

This above citation from "Men of Mark of Maryland" establishes the fact that Bonnie Prince Charlie's family is directly related to the first French Governor of Nova Scotia Charles de La Tour as well as the Bouillon family name. This lineage would also of course have stemmed from Charles's father Claude de La Tour who also plays a vital role in this story.

Both Claude and his son Charles went to Nova Scotia. At one point Claude returned to France to obtain credit and supplies for the Cape Sable colony. He was captured by English captain Kirke on the return trip and returned to England. Claude de La Tour then agreed to work in tandem with Sir William Alexander of Stirling and his son Alexander in establishing a Scottish Colony in Nova Scotia. This is the same era during which Sir Alexander had amended part of Sidney's work "Arcadia" and may also be the same time that the truth of the Oak Island saga may finally be discerned. At this time both Claude and Charles de La Tour were made Barons of Nova Scotia by William Alexander.

Strangely many of the biographies and histories of what comes next are vague and somewhat difficult to ascertain. Charles de La Tour was born in 1593 to Claude de La Tour and Marie de Salazar. Ms. de Salazar was said to have been a Brides Maid to Henrietta Maria wife of King Charles I. Both Claude and Charles' Canadian biographies state that Marie de Salazar was a distant relation to Sir William Alexander of Stirling. If true this will supply us with a direct connection and may reveal many unknown things about the development of Nova Scotia. This may explain why both Claude and Charles de La Tour were considered Barons of Nova Scotia no matter if the French, English or Scottish ruled Acadia.

At one point in this story we see Claude siding with the English and Sir William Alexander attempting to convince his son Charles to accept a Baronetcy of Nova Scotia as he had done after his capture. During this negotiation, he likely reminded his son that he was indeed related to William Alexander and his son William the Younger who was also present during these negotiations. Charles steadfastly refused to cooperate and a battle ensued between the forces of the father and son. Eventually Claude lost and a few years later the efforts of William Alexander to found a Scottish Colony in Nova Scotia were halted. Or had they been?

Eventually the winds of war saw Charles de La Tour ejected from Acadia in a fight against a rival faction of colonists. The 1654 English Sedgewick expedition resulted in Nova Scotia being returned to English hands. Via a long string of events we see Charles de La Tour finally being offered the original Baronetcy of Nova Scotia that his father had arranged and returning to help administer Nova Scotia under the original terms set forth. In this way the influence of the Alexander's and other Scottish nobles had been maintained via family ties that spanned the divide between the French and English during this era. As we see the French and Scottish connection may have contributed to France allying itself with the colonies later during the revolutionary war.

So, no matter who controlled Nova Scotia it seems that Bonnie possessed a legacy and interest in what was going on there that may have actually been honored by the French as Bonnie was exiled Scottish royalty that had always had very close ties to the French monarchy and gentry. This right to Nova Scotia by Bonnie and the subsequent Barons of Nova Scotia had come to him via his ancestor James I and all subsequent Scottish Kings. Given this the family relation between de Salazar and Alexander aligned them with the de La Tours via an important marriage.

Much of this information could also be applied to how and why the image of the Knights Templar has been applied to the Oak Island Treasure and Newport Tower. It appears that via a long chain of events and intermarriage that the Stewart family had a much broader association with even the origins of the Knights Templar than the Sinclair family ever possessed. All of the legends of Henry Sinclair being a Knights Templar would have to include the fact that he valued this order long after they had officially ceased to exist. All of the supposed exploits of Henry

194

Sinclair in Nova Scotia may now be explained as later manifestations of the Alexander family. The Stewarts were related to Godefroy de Bouillon the founder of the Knights Templar and first defacto King of Jerusalem.

Here in the personages of Bonnie Prince Charlie, James II, Charles de La Tour and the d'Abbadie's we have an open book that shows us this tradition in reality as it applies to Nova Scotia. The Knights Templar in Nova Scotia were a reality in their descendants the de La Tour governors of Nova Scotia and likely just as much in the legacy of William Alexander Baron of Nova Scotia. The Knights Templar who had a greater impact on the development of Nova Scotia included their real descendants who were more associated with the French and Scots heritage of Sir William Alexander which had extended from the earls of Menteith and subsequently the Stewart family. Among them were many Knights of Malta with William the Younger Alexander possibly being the first speculative Freemason to set foot on Canadian and Nova Scotian soil!

This likely would have not included the Sinclair family during both the time that Fitzalan had sponsored the Knights Templar as well as during the era this was all unfolding in Nova Scotia. This era of Nova Scotia history makes no mention of the Sinclair's nor do any of them hold the family ties that illustrate the connections between the Alexander's, de La Tour's and Bonnie Prince Charlie. At times in Scottish history the more Norwegian Sinclair's found themselves at odds with the Menteith and Stewarts. We also see Anthony Alexander the son of William the 1st Earl of Stirling taking over the reins of Freemasonry in Scotland from the Sinclair's at the time of the advent of speculative Masonry. Despite this there are some later family relations between Sinclair's and Stewarts.

It is clear that Bonnie Prince Charlie and all the other exiled Jacobite Kings had been just as related to the French de La Tour governor of Nova Scotia as they had been to the Alexander Scottish governors of Nova Scotia. This would explain why and how a man named Alexander Alexander was said to have lived in New Ross Nova Scotia "on his estate" after the time the French had taken back Acadia in about 1632. Amazingly the de La Tour's in Nova Scotia were both awarded Baronets of Nova Scotia by the Alexander family with Charles de La Tour even being personal friends with the elder and younger William Alexander of Stirling and marrying Marie Salazar said to be a distant relative of William Alexander's.

The de La Tours were allowed to maintain these titles even during the period they were representing French control of Acadia. Through time this may also explain why the Alexander's interests in the United States would encourage General William Alexander of the Continental Army to attempt to regain his title of the Earl of Stirling thus giving him dominion over Nova Scotia.

Though the story is told that Charles de La Tour was captured and later had to woo his son into supporting the Scottish and English claim to Nova Scotia it is clear that when he was taken to England he had switched loyalties to the English at that time. Instead of this being a product of him being captured we may now consider that he willingly became a Baron of Nova Scotia due to his close family relation to the Stuarts even before the time of Bonnie Prince Charlie! The entire dominion of Nova Scotia was a family affair no matter who controlled it and the Oak Island Treasure Legend may be associated with this dynamic of Nova Scotia history and lore. Now we may also discern that the legacy of the remaining families of former original Knights Templar had also showed a great interest and value of Nova Scotia.

The marriage of Claude de La Tour to Marie de Salazar also shows us another strong connection to Charles I who we have seen in the earlier Shugborough Hall chapter is also strongly associated in the opinion of this author with the Shepherd's Monument there. William Alexander was a childhood friend and tutor to both Charles I and II. He was in the court of James I. We do know there are many sources stating Charles I last words were from "Pamela's Prayer" part of Philip Sidney's "Arcadia" which also seem to include the original Oak Island Money Pit story.

The association with historical figures in Nova Scotia and their descent from original Knights Templar would later even extend to Lord Halifax Montagu-Dunk and resident of Nova Scotia Frederick Wallet des Barres. The Montagu family had during the time of Frederick II Holy Roman Emperor (mid thirteenth century) held the title of Grand Commander of both the Knights Templar and Knights of Malta/St. John of the Hospital. In fact both Grand Commanders were named Pedro Montagu and both men refused to be seen together at Frederick II marriage to Eleanor of England. Des Barres was a direct descendant of former Grand Commander of the Knights Templar Eberhard de Barres. Des Barres was a premier cartographer of his day as we continually see an individual of his skills involved in these questions including everyone from Thomas Jefferson to John Bidwell founder of Chico California.

Also of note here is the associations between the de La Tours of Nova Scotia and the d'Abbadie family who were also involved in the early military and administration of French Acadia. It had been a man named "Abbdie" who had aided James II in his first escape attempt and it would be the d'Abbadie St. Germain family managing the Palace of St. Germaine en Laye where the exiled James II would live for a time.

Some of the d'Abbadie's and de La Tours intermarried with each other and Native Americans in the early history of Maine and Nova Scotia. Eventually after the English had taken Nova Scotia an Acadian Privateer and military figure named Anselme d'Abbadie would return to France with his native bride and children to reclaim his father Jean Vincent d'Abbadie St. Castin's (namesake of Castine Maine) title. As a result, Anselme d'Abbadie was styled the "Count of Norumbega." His title is one of the only references to the entire Norumbega phenomenon or use of that name that can be found documented. It appears that Norumbega had been a term applied to southern Acadia by the French. One of Anselme's daughters would eventually marry into the Bourbon family.

The d'Abbadie's have a rich legacy in geography and cartography via Antoine and Arnuad d'Abbadie's travels in Ethiopia that were in part inspired by James Bruce's sojourns to Ethiopia a century before they had gone there. Strangely both James Bruce and the d'Abbdie's here have links to Nova Scotia. The d'Abbadie family are also the subject of study in alchemy and the mysteries due to their suspected association with the Great Cyclic Cross of Hendaye mystery

196

written of by Jay Weidner and Vincent Bridges. It is no surprise that families like the Alexander's, d'Abbadie's, and de La Tour are involved in a historical conundrum like Oak Island. Antoine d'Abbadie would also build his Chateau Abbadia near Hendaye that is considered by some to be "The Rosslyn Chapel of France."

James Bruce's book about Ethiopia was comprised of letters he had written to the second Lord Halifax Montagu-Dunk. Later the d'Abbadie's also with a link to Nova Scotia would go to Ethiopia. Antoine d'Abbadie even openly stated his journeys to Ethiopia were inspired by James Bruce. This is also strange in relation to the Enochian themes of the real Oak Island Legend and the version of it in Sidney's "Arcadia." James Bruce would return from Ethiopia with three ancient copies of the Book of Enoch and also obtained ancient copies of the manuscripts that comprise the Pistis Sophia from Alexandria Egypt.

Another piece of evidence bringing this all together is an early fifteenth century association between the family group of the Coutts family and that of the de Rohan or de La Tour. The Coutts family is associated with the Frenchman's Tower in Palo Alto California. This involves the marriage of Thomas Colt (Coutts same family different spelling) that married Marguerite de Rohan de La Tour d'Auvergne producing fourteen children. This may explain many things in relation to Thomas Coutts' concern for the children of the Duchess of Albany in the story of Bonnie Prince Charlie. Here is the family name associated with the Frenchman's Tower in Palo Alto intimately involved in the genetic lineage of the Stewart line of Kings and the development of Nova Scotia.

Also note that Clementina Walkinshaw the mother of Bonnie Prince Charlie's daughter the Duchess of Albany did hold a family direct relation to the Coutts family and this may also explain why later she spent a great deal of time with the daughters of both Thomas Coutts and the Burdett family (Lady Burdett Coutts). This does illustrate a very old link between the Coutts' and de Rohan line of de La Tour directly associated with Charles de La Tour of Nova Scotia.

Given what we have learned about "Sancto Claro" and the involvement of the Earls of Menteith and subsequently the Stewart family we may begin to see the importance of the image of the Tower in all of these mysteries. This image had been valued for a great deal of time before our family group here began to build towers thus establishing a meridian and associated domain. Part of the value of such a structure may also refer to the one emblazoned on the arms of the de La Tour family.

Here now we also have a family named de La Tour or "of the tower" intimately involved in the entire progression of the building of these towers in the Arcadian Mysteries. This factor alone also may explain why the image of the tower is also associated with the much vaunted and lauded Knights Templar and may also more accurately explain their legacy in Scotland and Nova Scotia.

If the Oak Island Treasure was some kind of political ploy who had it been aimed at? Given what we have learned above the only conclusion if this is true would be that it was designed to fool

197

and confound the English rulers of Nova Scotia after General Lawrence retook it for the crown. On the other side of the coin we see a clearly allied French and Jacobite concern that seemed to share Nova Scotia no matter which country controlled it. When the Hanoverian English royal concerns retook Nova Scotia as part of their domain their legacy would not have held such a close tie to the history of Nova Scotia. Though the Hanoverians were Stuarts they were not Catholic as the Scottish and French inhabitants of Nova Scotia had been. This part of the story also explains one reason the French allied themselves with the colonists in the American Revolution. They were supporting their family ties to a claim to North America that Scottish interests felt they had more of a right to than the English at that time.

Cargyll, is named as sitting in a consistorial court held in St Giles's Church, Edinburgh, on 13th November 1524.[1]

Blaise, another son, was involved in the Duke of Albany's conspiracy; he went to France in 1482, where he obtained an appointment at court. He married Marguerite, widow of a French nobleman, and daughter of Sieur de Rohan, a cadet of the famous house of that name. Fourteen children were born of the marriage. Several of the children, being Protestants, sought refuge in Great Britain.

Blaise, son of Thomas Colt.

Blaise, son of Blaise Colt, was born at Paris in 1516,

Blaise, son of Blaise Colt.

The above source states that Colt and de Rohan had intermarried at an early date. Colt and Coutts are the same family with the name spelled differently. Colt firearms is part of this family.

This is the point in the story where the legacy of the Sinclair family may be more important. They among all of them were descendants of King Olaf of Norway. It was their family that were more closely related to the sagas and stories of Leif Ericson. In turn, they were more closely related to whomever actually travelled to L'Anse Aux Meadows in Newfoundland and had established an outpost. It had also been the Earls of Orkney who had established a meridian in the Arcadian Tradition using the Orphir Round Kirk of St. Nicolas and Rossyln Chapel to mark this sacred line on the globe. Even though the Sinclair's had not been involved in the development of Nova Scotia it was their family legacy that had supplied Scottish people like James I and William Alexander to envision a Scottish colony in Nova Scotia. The Earls of Orkney would also play an important role in the development of the Hudson's Bay Company.

It is entirely possible that the reality of what Oak Island really represents was known of by the family of Bonnie Prince Charlie including the de La Tours and their associated family legacy. This information may have well fallen into American hands at the time of the Revolution and later the French Revolution. The genetic legacy of William Alexander extending to the Alexander's of Alexandria Virginia and General William Alexander may also lead us to the reasons why later people like Henry Wadsworth Longfellow and Edgar Allan Poe may have been aware of the truth of what had gone on or been left at Oak Island.

The American faction of Nova Scotian's who retained their property in Nova Scotia had included some close relatives of Poe and Longfellow and we even see them involved via the Prescott family in dividing the original lots at Oak Island that Daniel McGinnis and others would own during the period in which the Money Pit had actually been found. This could again infer that other residents of the Truro Parish in Northern Virginia such as the Lee and Washington families may have also been aware of the truth of Oak Island, The Newport Tower, The Beale Treasure and more. Even here so late in the game we have Louis de La Tour descendant of Claude and Charles de La Tour of Nova Scotia residing in Lynchburg Virginia in the very same region of that state where the Beale Treasure is said to be waiting.

Rennes le Chateau, Rennes le Bains, and the de La Tour Auvergne family. Mystery solved?

Amazingly the following information was discovered when looking into the genealogy of the Marquis de Lafayette the French hero of the American Revolution. His daughter married into the de La Tour Auvergne family. His ancestors also included many notable French and European nobility going far back in time. It is somehow apropos that the Marquis would be the avenue by which the entire string of mysteries may now be characterized as a single phenomenon. All of this may also lend credence to the notion that both Bonnie Prince Charlie and Thomas Jefferson had visited Rennes le Bains to take the waters there as many had for millennia before them. Lafayette's involvement also illustrates why and how the Society of the Cincinnati were aware of these mysteries eventually leading to the involvement of associates Poe and Longfellow. While still a young man Poe would be one of the Marquis de Lafayette's honor guard during his last visit to the United States.

It appears as if the de La Tour name meaning "of the tower" is related to some of the treasure myths and associated mysteries we have been looking at. Though there is no proof of their involvement they even seem to be present in Lynchburg Virginia where a great deal of the story of the Beale Ciphers and Papers take place during the period the legend was developing. They are present in Nova Scotia in the very region where Oak Island is located. They had played a hand in the building of the Frenchman's Tower in Palo Alto and likely the Legend of J.C. Brown. It is also obvious that the legacy of the Stuart or Stewart family is intertwined with that of the de La Tours if not the French monarchy itself during the era of Bonnie Prince Charlie and prior. Both of these families in turn are associated with exiled monarchs.

If we examine the arms of one branch of the de La Tour family d'Auvergne we are also presented with the image of a Tower quartered with that of the same symbol or logo used by the Languedoc-Roussillon province of France today. Some people refer to this symbol as the "Cathar Cross." In fact the tower suggested by their arms and name is reminiscent of one of the largest icons of the Rennes le Chateau Mystery the Tour Magdala. Indeed, we have seen a string of towers from the Powder Magazine in Colonial Williamsburg, The Newport Tower, and even the Frenchman's Tower of Palo Alto California seemingly representing a similar philosophy or family group. Later some stunning associations may be made with the arms of the Saunier family of France.

How are the de La Tour's connected to Rennes le Chateau? As we may discern they are attached to all the mysterious happenings at Rennes le Chateau and a brief examination of part of their family may expose many things about Rennes le Chateau while also confirming the geographic connections between the Kings Knot of Stirling, Shugborough Hall, and Rennes le Chateau.

Could there be yet another literary piece that may help us to understand this entire scheme?

*"The Dauphin and the other children of France, going to Avignon to visit Pope Clement VII., Slept at Castelnaudary. On this voyage was concluded at Marseilles the marriage of **Catherine de 'Medici,** niece of the pope, with the second son of the king, who was afterwards Henry II. Catherine bore to her husband, the county of Auvergne and that of Lauragais, which we cross;* **They belonged to him of the head of his mother, Magdeleine de La Tour;** *(French to English translation) It also had a hundred thousand ducats."* (note Lauragais includes Rennes le Bains and Rennes le Chateau)

Voyage a Rennes-les-Bains by Lobouisse-Rochefort, Printed by Labadie (d'Abbadie) a Castelnaudary. P.267.

> 1177 **Labouïsse-Rochefort**. Voyage à
> Rennes-les-Bains, avec des fac-simile.
> Paris, Desauges, 1832, de l'impr. de G.-P.
> Labadie à Castelnaudary. 1 fort vol. in 8,
> reliure neuve genre ancien.   8 fr.
>   Ouvrage rare.
>   Bel exemplaire. Curieux et intéressant ouvrage.

2 vols. MR '61

The above passage is from "Voyage a Rennes les Bains" by Lobouisse Rochefort was printed in 1832. This passage is telling us that the de La Tour d'Auvergne-Lauraguais family are the lords of Rennes le Bain and the surrounding area including Rennes le Chateau. Strangely the Tour Magdala of Rennes le Chateau has a name that matches that of Magdeleine de La Tour. The reference to Catherine d' Medici Magdeliene de La Tours daughter matches a sixteenth century date corresponding with the Elizabethan era in England. Catherine Medici was the daughter of

Magdeliene de La Tour d' Auvergne and Lorenzo de Medici, Duke of Urbino. Of course, Catherine went on to become Queen of France.

Amazingly the book "Voyage a Rennes le Bains" was authored by a member of the family. The mother of the author Labouisse Rochefort was Anne de Bonaffos de La Tour. Also of note is the designation in the above citation for the book naming Labadie as the printer. Labadie is a form of the name d'Abbadie. We see a great deal of interface between the d'Abbadie's and de La Tour in Nova Scotia as well. So, it is of note that someone so closely related to other mysteries that are "of the tower" is involved and interested in writing and printing a book about Rennes le Bains. This may also mean it is no coincidence that the d'Abbadie's are related to the mystery of the Great Cyclic Cross of Hendaye (France).

Could it be this simple? After all the exhaustive examinations by many authors and researchers all producing in depth theories and ideas, could the name "de La Tour" unlock all the secrets of the Arcadian mysteries? It appears that there is a great deal of interaction between the Stuarts, de La Tours, Coutts, and others may point to their influence being behind the Kings Knot of Stirling, Shugborough Hall, Rennes le Chateau, the Frenchman's Tower, and Oak Island.

Many of this cast of characters includes family members that felt they had a right to the crown of Scotland via their relations to the Stewart family of exiled kings i.e. Bonnie Prince Charlie, his father James III, and his grandfather James II. Part of the impetus of these towers and mysteries may have been to keep alive their history among all the skullduggery and regime changes in both England and the continent. Included in this array of fallen kings may be the former Kings of Wales and France.

Even the life and loves of Henri V duc d' Chamord exiled king of France illustrates this concept. His wife Archduchess Maria Theresa of Austria-Este was one of those in succession that may have had a legitimate claim to the Scottish throne via her descent from the daughter of Charles I Henrietta of England. Henri V had married a Stuart! This may make a lot of the theories that Henri V wife had made an effort to fund the construction of the Tour Magdala and Villa Bethania at Rennes le Chateau a real event and not theory. Even though the follies were remembrances of Henri V as a Stuart the Archduchess would have seen the tradition of her Scottish ancestors and their value of "Arcadia" at play as well. Maria Theresa may be the reason the imagery of Poussin and the pentagonal geometry in the landscape were ever introduced to the mystery of Rennes le Chateau.

This may also explain the involvement of the Coutts' who seemed to have funded Henri's exile. Even in Labouisse Rochefort's "Voyage a Rennes le Bains" he is referencing a "The mystery, the mystery" in poetry about Rennes le Bains. This book was published in 1832 just two years after the time Henri V was exiled and Phillipe Orleans was given the crown instead.

Labouisse Rochefort from "Voyages a Rennes le Bain" describing the mineral springs:

Is far from making health:

201

It has no other efficacy, ·
What to call on its shore,
By a well concerted complement,
The procession of banter,
The inconstancy, the idleness,
The boredom, the splendor, the coquetry,
Games, curiosity,
The finesse, the voluptuousness,
The mystery and the mystery ....

Could it be that the entire suggestion of a treasure or intrigue at Rennes le Chateau had started at about the time this book was published so soon after Henri V exile?

What mystery is Rochefort referring to? Here again we have a family member that is as closely related as Philip Sidney and William Alexander of Stirling contributing a literary element to the mystery at hand. It seems that these people want one to read and learn about all of this and they are telling you in a fairly straightforward manner. Unfortunately, many are blinded by the promise of monetary riches and lost treasures that may only be there to attract the seeker and expose them to the truth. The truth of the "treasure" of Rennes le Chateau may be that Father Saunière was funded by these families and had not found a golden treasure.

"Voyages a Rennes le Bains" was written about sixty-eight years prior to the same "mystery" being exposed by father Saunière later near the turn of the twentieth century. The Frenchman's Tower in Palo Alto California was a mystery to the local population about twenty years before the earliest indication from Saunière that anything was afoot at all near Rennes le Chateau. Still Rochefort's cryptic reference to "The mystery, and the mystery" may indicate that Rennes le Chateau was known of at that time (1832) but this was not shared or popularized with the public until later. It is possible that this location was selected due to its proximity to the octagonal Kings Knot at Stirling Castle. All along the way we see not only the influence of the Stewart family but of the descendants of Charles I and II who of course are the son and grandson of James I linking us back to Mary Queen of Scots James' mother.

Is it possible that "Voyage a Rennes le Bains" was written to begin to expose this mystery to the world? Was all of this to commemorate and remind us of the forgotten and exiled kings? This may be possible. In fact the similar mysteries that reference the Stuart family coincide with the dates of their exile. The same could be said of the French and them promoting Rennes le Chateau as a kind of reminder of this forgotten history. Along the way each mystery seems to include a literary or artistic element similar to Sidney's "Arcadia" or Nicolas Poussin's "The Shepherds of Arcadia." Now we may include Rochefort in the list that includes Poe, Longfellow, Dante, Shakespeare and many others. None the least of which would include the finding of riches beneath stones in the Rennes le Chateau Chapel.

In fact the part of the Rennes le Chateau story that has Father Saunière examining and in some cases destroying grave stones leads us to a common thread in many of these mysterious locations. This would include the Service Stone at Stirling Castle, the Bruton Parish Church vault and others. Clues found on headstones at all these places may match illustrations and passages of poetry from a previously published book of symbols. In the case of Rennes le Chateau if such a book exists it was likely published in French.

Many of the images of Rennes le Chateau that are considered to be part of the mystery currently evolved from the Blanchefort family. Even the notion of the star in the landscape that connects to Stirling Castle via Shugborough Hall may have originated from the Blanchefort's via a strange design present on a tombstone. Given this it is interesting that the de La Tour Auvergne's and Blanchfort family did have some relations via marriage.

Here we have an indication that both families are indeed closely related:

- Charles de Blanchefort, prince de Poix, duc de Créquy, seigneur de Canaples, deceased in 1630 - au siège de Chambéry, Ambassadeur à Rome
  Married 31 May 1620 (Sunday) to
- Anne de Grimoard de Beauvoir, Deceased 18 February 1686 (Monday)

Madeleine de Blanchefort *1662-1707 married 3 April 1675 (Wednesday) to* Charles Belgique Hollande de La Trémoille, *duc de Thouars 1655-1709* with issue:

- Marie Victoire de La Trémoille *1677-1717 married 1 February 1696 (Wednesday) to* Emmanuel **Théodore de La Tour d'Auvergne**, *vicomte de Turenne 1668-1730* with issue :
  - Armande de La Tour d'Auvergne *1697-1717*
  - Frédéric Maurice de La Tour d'Auvergne, *prince de Turenne 1702-1723*
  - Marie Hortense de La Tour d'Auvergne *1704-*
  - Charles Godefroy de La Tour d'Auvergne, *duc de Bouillon 1706-1771 (*This appears to be the father of **Marie Louise de La Tour d' Auvernge** who was Bonnie Prince Charlies paramour and first cousin)
- Charles Louis Bretagne de La Trémoille, *duc de Thouars 1683-1719 married 13 April 1706 (Tuesday) to* **Marie Madeleine Motier de La Fayette**, *marquise de La Fayette †1717* with :
  - Charles Armand René de La Trémoille, *duc de Thouars 1708-1741*

(http://gw.geneanet.org/frebault?lang=en&pz=henri&nz=frebault&ocz=0&p=charles&n=de+blanchefort&oc=2)

-Juste-Charles de La Tour-Maubourg….married Anastasie de Lafayette; they had two children…

Many of these mysteries also involve designs or inscriptions present on headstones. The above association not only connects us to Rennes le Chateau and the Blanchefort's but also the first cousin and paramour of Bonnie Prince Charlie Marie Louise de La Tour d'Auvergne and the ancestor and also later a daughter (Anastasie de Lafayette) of the Marquis de Lafayette, Marie

203

Madeleine Moriter de La Fayette! Marie Madeliene Motier de La Fayette was Bonnie Prince Charlie's aunt! It is starting to appear as if the entire string of mysteries does have a unique point of view that is in many ways related to the history of the United States of America! It is looking more and more as if Thomas Jefferson was actually aware of these factors via his association with Lafayette and many other French people who were in the know with regard to this entire phenomenon. During his trip to France Jefferson spent time in Castelnaudary and was known to have travelled within thirteen miles of Rennes le Chateau and Rennes le Bains along the Canal du Midi.

All of this information also suggests that it was also at least the image of Henri V and his Stuart descendant Queen that had been instilled into the construction of the Frenchman's Tower in Palo Alto in 1875. It is clear that the Coutts' were aware of and valued this tradition with elements of their family also related to all the major groups of nobility involved here. All of these mysteries seem to include the legacy of Scottish nobles and how they valued France in a way that England ceased to after the Hanoverian Stuart family was brought in to replace their Scottish cousins. Scotland has always been on close terms with France and this factor may contribute to why they shared the legacy of all these towers and mysteries. The Catholic faith of many Jacobites and French people may also be a factor in this alliance. Many alienated Protestants also side with the Jacobite cause at this time. This may explain why only about one fifth of Jacobites were of the Catholic faith. Even so there are signs that Queen Victoria and other Hanoverian Stuart's were aware of this tradition. They were still family even though separated by a gulf of differences.

This association with the Frenchman's Tower also seems to in many ways solve the Legend of J.C. Brown which is associated with Mt. Shasta. This information also connects us to the Louvre and Oak Island Nova Scotia. Finally we are led to Washington D.C. and Chico California.

When one delves into the origins of these mysteries nothing is told directly. If you follow the path of intrigue and mystery you are led to a historical story that exposes what may have not been told otherwise. These towers expose the legacies of people who were dethroned and made to even leave the countries they once ruled. From the fallen Welsh Kings, the Stewarts, and finally the fallen French Kings we see a legacy where we are being taught via the ancient methods of the mystery school. This in effect is why all of these treasures and strange towers seem to have been promoted and singled out in the minds of the public.

Those that chose the historical context of these mysteries may have been aware of the themes of Merovingians, Arcadia and Arcas that stem back to Ravenna and beyond from Emperor Arcadius and other sources. The theme of the lost Temple Treasure seems to run throughout many of these stories as well as the legacy of the Plantagenet dynasty. In the process, we are also exposed to many elements of the "Man in the Mountain" mythology of Charlemagne who may have gained an appreciation of these dynamics via Constantine the Great and his admiration of Greek, Roman, and Byzantine culture.

For instance, the Oak Island treasure has always been a popular subject over a great span of time. When one researches this treasure an amazing and true history of Nova Scotia is exposed as illustrated in the facts and theories in this book. The same goes for Shugborough, Williamsburg, the Newport Tower, Rennes le Chateau, and many more. Once one becomes familiar with the elements of all these somewhat mythical tales it is easy to see the correlations between them. Here these family ties may expose for the first time a common origin to many of the mysteries we have discussed here. It appears that later literary figures from Dante to Longfellow had somehow been informed of these hidden historical factors and had included clues in their work that would help guide one to an understanding of what was really being told.

As time went on these concepts were made available to interests in the United States. It is clear that Jacobites loyal to Bonnie Prince Charlie and his forebears had helped to create the new country. At one point Senator Gorman even introduced a bill to make Bonnie Prince Charlie "King of America." Though Thomas Jefferson was instrumental in defeating the notion of an American monarchy this was a serious effort that many people were in favor at that time. This admiration and value of Bonnie Prince Charlie may translate later to why people like Dante, Shakespeare, Sir Francis Bacon, Henry Wadsworth Longfellow, Edgar Allan Poe, Emerson, Lobouisse Rochefort, Alexandre Dumas, and James Fennimore Cooper were all aware of the mysteries existent during their lives discussed here. The legacy of the Jacobites and in some regard the fallen French Kings had become an American secret in many ways.

Much of the mystery surrounding Rennes le Chateau is also linked to the Hapsburg dynasty of the House of Lorraine. This in turn links us to Godefroy de Bouillon and the advent of the de La Tour Family Dukes of Bouillon. Interestingly this lineage of the Hapsburg includes the House of Guise which included the mother of Mary Queen of Scots who is central to a value of this entire scheme on the part of Scottish exiled kings and nobles.

In previous work I have noted how Mary Queen of Scots and her mother were schooled at a convent that was part of the Order of St. Clare of Assisi. This included instruction in weaving and needlepoint that may have been a tradition started by Empress Theodora wife of Justinian I as she established convents of nuns that were taught this art. Both Mary Queen of Scots and Theodora have many associated themes that may belay a value of Mary Magdalene or the Plantagenet view of their genetic heritage. This may be the reason why Hapsburg's are involved in the later Father Saunière era version of the Rennes saga. (see chapter about "Sancto Claro" here for more). Of course Mary Queen of Scots is a lineal forebear of James II and Bonnie Prince Charlie. Mary Queen of Scots belongings stashed in what some term a small casket may be part of the Beale Treasure legend of Virginia and may represent the strange casket featured the Poussin bas relief of the Shepherds Monument of Shugborough. An Abbot Beile is mentioned in the Saunière era version of the Rennes le Chateau story as well. A man named Beile is mentioned in the saga of the commissioning of the construction of Washington D.C.

The Marquis de Lafayette and Chateau Villette

Chateau Villette sometimes known of as "Little Versailles" was designed by Francois Mansart (1592-1666) for the Count of Aufflay, Jean Dyell II. The chateau has a distinct linear aspect to the design of the landscaping that includes lavish fountains and two small obelisks. Chateau

Villette is also famous for its inclusion in the movie "The Da Vinci Code." The scenes from the movie featuring the chateau as the home of Grail Scholar Professor Leigh Teabing include the heroine Sophie Nouveux finding out she is descendant of Mary Magdalene at the Chateau. Part of that scene in the movie also has she and Langdon being attacked by a Monk of Opus Dei.

In the late eighteenth century Chateau Villette had come into the possession of Marie-Louise-Sophie de Grouchy (1764-1822). At this time the Chateau became the center of her active social life as she hosted many well known individuals at events there. Some of these gatherings included Voltaire and Rousseau. Thomas Jefferson was even rumored to have been to Chateau Villtette with the Marquis de Lafayette during his time in France. It is interesting that both the owner of Chateau Villette Sophie de Grouchy and the heroine of the film share the same first name! A name that relates to wisdom and sometimes associated with hidden notions with regard to Mary Magdalene. This is also the name of a powerful Byzantine Augusta, who may also be the namesake of the famous document "The Pistis Sophia." Reference also the name of Hagia Sophia in Istanbul (Constantinople).

Sophie de Grouchy also hosted a salon at the Hotel de Monnaies in Paris. Sophie is starting to sound like an echo of Mary Sidney Herbert Countess of Pembroke and her Wilton Writer's Circle. Even Thomas Jefferson was said to have frequently attended events and meetings held by this group of artists and free thinkers hosted by Sophie de Grouchy. This salon as they were known also resembles the Academy degli de Arcadia of the Vatican discussed earlier. Sophie even personally translated works by famous friend of Thomas Jefferson's Thomas Paine and others. Sophie was quite the intellectual who lived up to the meaning of her name "wisdom." Sophie de Grouchy's salon at the Hotel Monnaies seemed to display elements of the Republican ideals of the United States and the French Revolution. With all of this in mind it is no surprise that Ms. de Grouchy was also a tireless advocate of Women's rights somewhat ahead of her time! Note the Hotel Monnaies is located on the Seine only about 250 ft. west of the Paris Meridian.

At this point Sophie engaged in what would be a scandalous affair with the Marquis de Lafayette. Some say this affair was part of the reason that Lafayette went to America and fought for the Americans at that time. Later Lafayette would attend the wedding of Sophie to the Marquis de Condorcet. The Marquis was the chairman of the Academy of Arts and Sciences of France and was known to display great proficiency and knowledge of many different aspects of practical science and philosophy. It seems that Chateau Villtette had become a place of illuminated thought during this time.

All of this is especially interesting when one considers the linear aspect of the chateau and its grounds when viewed on a global scale. The grounds and building of Chateau Villette actually form an arc on the globe that points to the Egyptian Obelisk at the center of St. Peter's Square of the Vatican. This is interesting considering Sophie's husband the Marquis of Condorcet was the liaison between Napoleon and the Vatican at one point!

This is also intriguing in light of Jefferson's travels as Secretary of State in the direct environs of Rennes le Chateau and Rennes le Bains. Jefferson's association with the Marquis de Lafayette coupled with the Marquis connections to the de La Tour family and others makes all of this very interesting indeed. In many ways we are now being led to how and why interests of the Society of the Cincinnati would be aware of historical mysteries like Rennes le Chateau and Oak Island.

Another famous alignment of architecture in "The Da Vinci Code" book and movie is the famous I.M. Pei pyramid that serves as the entrance to the Louvre and the inverted pyramid featured in the movie. At the end of the movie the protagonist Langdon realizes that the crypt of Mary Magdalene is beneath the inverted pyramid that is part of this array.

The linear aspect of the inverted pyramid as it aligns with the pyramid that serves as the entrance to the Louvre may be used to form an arc on the globe that transects to the east to Migdal, Israel the said birthplace and hometown of Mary Magdalene. Archaeologists have recently identified the remains of both a tower and a synagogue there with included Christians symbols.

The westerly arc suggested by the two pyramids of the Louvre transects the Atlantic Ocean to reach or "point to" Oak Island Nova Scotia! Oak Island Legend anyone? This is astounding given what we have learned about the Alexander's, d'Abbadie's, and de La Tour's in Nova Scotia! We are being shown this in the cinema.

What are we to make of these two representations being included in such a popular movie? This movie is showing you the story of two seekers named Sophie Nouveax and Professor Langdon who are initiated into a path of learning on the part of Sophie's deceased uncle Jacques Sauniere. Note the use of the name of Father Sauniere from the Rennes le Chateau mystery. Its seems the movie is also paying a well deserved homage to the real heroine of this story Sophie de Grouchy. Sophie's daughter Alexandrine Louise Sophie de Caritat de Condorcet Married a prominent Irishman name Arthur O'Connor who would serve Napoleon in a military capacity. Their great granddaughter Brigitte O'Connor was the mother of the French poet Patrice de la Tour du Pin.

Chateau Villette "points to" St. Peter's Square of the Vatican.

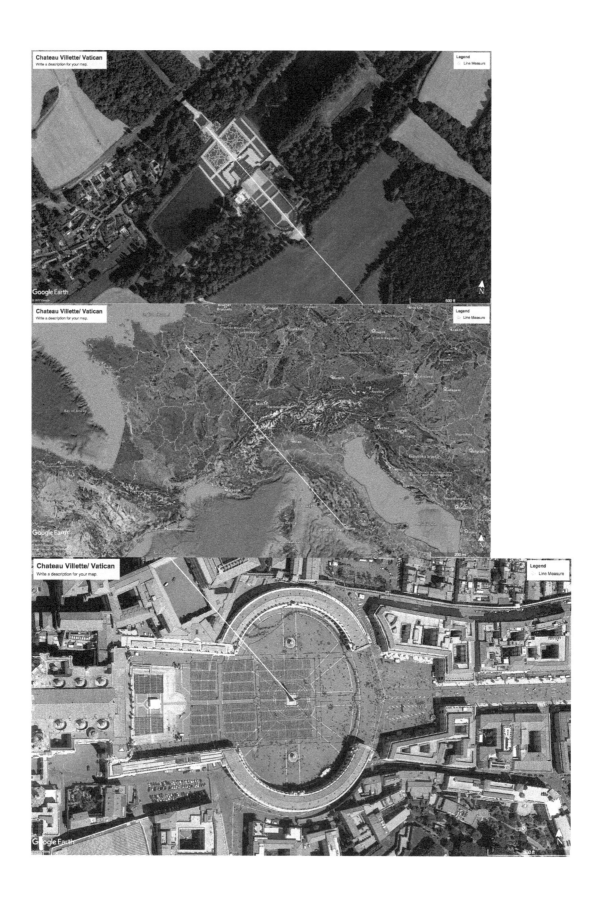

The azimuth or arc on the globe created by the orientation of Chateau Villette "points to"
St. Peter's Square.

Father Saunière and the de La Tour family.

Father Saunière is of course a central figure to the Rennes le Chateau mystery as presented to the public near the end of the nineteenth century. Saunière was the parish priest of Rennes le Chateau. Through a series of discoveries including the Blanchefort tombstone he was said to have found a great treasure. Note that cemeteries and funerary clues are very common in a this seemingly related string of mysteries. Some of these clues were found during an early restoration of the church on the part of Saunière. After this point he paid to have the Chapel in the town renovated in a lavish expensive style and added the artwork and statuary that we see there today. Many people have interpreted this array of artwork in different ways. In past works I have examined the geometric qualities of the chapel in geography which seem to match some elements of the star in the landscape suggested by the tombstone and other clues such as the Pontil's Tomb nearby (Lincoln).

What may be revealed here is that Saunière had been working as part of a family legacy or loyalty in what he had done. Many facets of the story of Saunière also include elements that are present on Oak Island and in Edgar Alan Poe's "The Gold Bug." Part of the original story has Saunière and his workmen finding two stashes of golden objects and parchments sequestered beneath stones. One of the stones has a strange engraving of people on horseback and another wooden pillar hides a parchment with clues. All of this also adds up to be reminiscent of Philip Sidney's "Arcadia" in many ways. The story seems to also infer that there is an important vault involved in whatever the treasure is. The standard story also seems to give us a rationale as to why Saunière had come into so much money. Even the skull in the tree in the plot of "The Gold Bug" reminds one of Mary Magdalene and the many artistic renderings of her in association with or contemplating a human skull.

The way Father Saunière's name is spelled in the mystery presented to us may be hiding some vital information. The name Saunière has many different forms in France including Sonnier, Songy, and Saunier. The latter seems to be the most popular version of the name and matches Berenger Saunière's name minus the "e" at the end. Saunier means "salt gatherer" or "salt seller" loosely translated or "of the salt." This is no surprise since the area near Rennes le Chateau has deposits of natural salt that may even contribute to the healing qualities of the baths of Rennes le Bains valued in the mystery and as shown in "Voyage a Rennes le Bains" by Rochefort. Rochefort also tells us of a value of Rennes le Bains going far back into antiquity including Roman and early Christian times. The origins of the Saunier family in the Auvergne region also associated with the de La Tour possess salt deposits and an associated long standing industry. The salt lines of Europe may be some of the oldest traveled routes of the world.

The book "Voyage" even mentions the treasure of Rennes long before the time of father Saunière in 1832. Saunière did not begin to make his revelations until the late nineteenth century nearly seventy years later. During this time the legends of the Frenchman's Tower and

Shugborogh Hall had already been established using the Arcadian theme as well as of course Stirling Castle and the surrounding region in Scotland. The Frenchman's Tower of Palo Alto, The Powder Magazine in Williamsburg, and the Newport Tower had been built long before anyone knew the name "Rennes le Chateau."

The development of the Academy degli de Arcadia of the Vatican in about 1650 may have also contributed a great deal of imagery and theme that is displayed in the more modern version of the Rennes le Chateau mystery. Nicolas Poussin who Henry Lincoln associates with the Pontil's Tomb near Rennes le Chateau and geometry present in his painting "The Shepherds of Arcadia" was likely a member of this artists and writer's guild. The Academy even met for a time on the Capitoline Hill of Rome and still has a grove dedicated to them in Rome today. This group resembles in many ways a larger group similar to the Wilton Writer's Circle of Mary Sidney Herbert Countess of Pembroke that gave us Philip Sidney's "Arcadia" about sixty years prior to the establishment of the Academy of Arcadia.

The Academy of Arcadia was still very alive and active at the time of Father Saunière. It is possible that this influence as well as others contributed to a mystery school conundrum being established in the late nineteenth century involving Rennes le Chateau and Rennes le Bains as parts of the mystery. The region around these two villages has a rich history including early Christians and Romans who came to take the waters of Rennes le Bains. In this context, it may also be interesting that both names refer to "Reindeer" in the meaning of the word "Rennes."

Another theme of the Rennes le Chateau mystery is of course that of Mary Magdalene and what many speculate was her family including her husband Jesus Christ and their children. This is but one variation of the same theme that even included a non-heretical version having the area visited by only Mary Magdalene. These kinds of beliefs are not out of the question in that even the Latin Church accepts to some degree the stories of Saintes Maries de La Mer that have the three Mary's coming there in tandem with the later story of the Magdalene at St. Maximin et Baum near Marseilles.

Many speculate that Father Saunière eventually found a great treasure sequestered somewhere in the Rennes le Chateau area. This is supported by the notion that Saunière paid to renovate the Rennes Chapel and built the Tour Magdala and Villa Bethania in the village. This display of wealth made many suspicious and led to Saunière being accused of selling his services as a priest for profit which was frowned on by the Church. The inclusion of a treasure in such a situation is not abnormal. We see the same phenomenon associated with Oak Island, Williamsburg Virginia, The Beale Treasure, The Legend of J.C. Brown of Mt. Shasta, and many others.

Is it possible the treasure story was added to attract people to the region in order to solve the mystery? It seems that investigating this strange story reveals many odd connections and aspects of history that were later overlooked. It is almost as if those in the past had created a kind of mystery school that informs one of their neglected role in matters of faith and history. Even so there are many historical hints that riches could be stashed in the area.

The region surrounding Rennes le Chateau and Rennes le Bains was once part of what was termed Septimania by the Roman and Byzantine rulers of the area. Septimania was eventually controlled by Ostrogothic King Theodoric of Ravenna. In my book "The Prophecy of Dante and the New Jerusalem of Ravenna" I discuss the geographic and cultural ties between the two places. Merovingian and Visigothic King Alaric's family was intermarried with that of Theodoric's eventually making the region part of their domain as it had been willed to them by Theodoric himself. Alaric's family connection to Theodoric also supplies us with strong links to the origins of the Arcadian theme in Ravenna which also later hosted a large population of Cathars. The Byzantine hierarchy and some related ecclesiastical figures are also related to Merovingian blood in many cases prior to the time they accepted Christianity.

This in turn may show us a Byzantine or Greek connection to this theme including Emperor Arcadius and his descendants that also had forms of that name including "Arcadia." Byzantine Emperor Zeno who raised Theodoric had a wife named Arcadia. Part of what may being displayed is this Merovingian mingling w/ Byzantine rulers that were later connected to the Plantagenet dynasty and their beliefs with regard to being descendant of Christ. There are many indications that would take another entire book to illustrate that show Charlemagne was aware of this and valued it to a certain degree. Even though he may have repressed this idea it is clear that he likely had knowledge of it and displayed a great value of Byzantine culture in the architecture he funded along with the early schools he established. The d'Abbadie (of the Abbey) family associated with the de La Tour's we discussed earlier descended from lay Abbots that were teachers at Charlemagne's schools. All of these values in part came from Emperor Constantine and his value of Greek culture in the form of the octagonal Tower of the Winds of Athens.

Of course, Alaric is the Visigoth that sacked Rome including having taken control of the famous Temple Treasure from Jerusalem which was being displayed at the Temple of Peace of Rome at that time. There is an existent Temple Treasure myth in Carcosonne just to the north of Rennes le Chateau that many have searched for in the past. This may be part of the mystery suggested in Rochefort's book "Voyage a Rennes le Bains." The reality or myth of the Temple Treasure being part of this mystery is an effective way to also use the theme of alternate Christianity in Christ's Blood as valued by the Plantagenet's over time. This would definitely be a treasure they were interested in. Some Plantagenet genealogies include an association with James the brother of Christ also leading us to a similar value and may also contribute to the culture of Santiago in Spain. The point of this value is not whether these beliefs hold up under historical scrutiny. What is relevant is that these people did believe this was true.

Father Saunière was taking part in what may have been this family group intentionally exposing their history to the world. They may have felt as though they would be neglected or that the truth would be covered up over time. This history seems to be associated with an angry race of fallen kings who wanted to insure their place in history and even remotely provide a pathway they could use to regain their titles eventually. This is how and why much of the imagery and family associations of the de La Tour's has to do with the mystery at hand.

We see the fallen kings of Scotland and France being closely associated via family. This may also include the earlier fallen Welsh Kings that also possess strong ties to the Plantagenet and Norman families. Bonnie Prince Charlie's identification as being part of this family group was likely of more importance after his exile and this would give us a rationale as to why he or his family are involved at Rennes le Chateau. We have already examined the fact that Henri V who many suspect of being the impetus behind the construction of the Tour Magdala and Villa Bethania was married to a Stuart who was actually in line for the fallen title of monarch of Scotland and England.

What if Father Saunière was also part of this family group?

This indeed may be true as elements of the Saunière or Saunier(e) family are intermarried with the de La Tour et Bains branch of that clan. Even the armorial bearings of the Saunier family of Auvergne and Lauraguais include the towers of the de La Tour! Father Saunière was working in a family tradition that is directly related to the "Ancient Regime" of fallen French Kings and also the Plantagenet mythology! It seems he had somehow been made aware of this family legacy and expressed this in solving a mystery he may have been prompted to investigate. This is also suggestive of the possibility that he was simply funded in his efforts by other elements of the family such as the Coutts bank or the de La Tours themselves. This family would have also possessed a readily identifiable Scottish element via associated genealogy that included the Stewarts of Scotland. Henri V wife was a Stewart.

The theme of Arcadia and the Ancient Regime have many values in common. The Ancient Regime is a value of past kings and queens and a view that this provided a more Arcadian simple lifestyle void of the trappings of the Republic and modern business practices. It seems that the efforts of Saunière were to support this old idea and somehow keep it alive via mythology and the application of a treasure story whether true or false. The values of all of these fallen kings were also in line with that of the Latin Church that may in turn lead us to the Academy degli Arcadia and its association with many famous literary figures over time.

This would have in turn led to knowledge of these traditions on the part of Society of the Cincinnati members the Marquis de Lafayette and Thomas Jefferson. Later authors Poe and Longfellow would be exposed to these same concepts via their descent and possible membership in the Society of the Cincinnati. Again, Poe knew the Marquis de Lafayette and likely Jefferson from his time as a student at the University of Virginia. In this manner what appear to be two opposing groups would use this imagery for their own purposes. Alexandre Dumas claims Poe came to France as he hosted him at his house though this fact is disputed by many.

This may have included the use of myth and legend to cloud the waters of truth surrounding subjects like the "blood of Christ" and other heretical concepts. Concepts like freedom of religion and speech are tied to these values that are reflective of the ideals of the Republics of the United States of America and France. In some cases a treasure story may be required to lure those that are interested into following the treads of logic suggested to the real truth. Rennes le Chateau is not about a treasure it is about exposing the truth of history to a forgetful public. Both sides see this as a point of great value and naturally wish to tell their side of the story. This may have resulted in works like the "Gold Bug" by Edgar Alan Poe and other literary pieces from family members Sir Walter Scott, as well as others like Lord Byron, Longfellow, Emerson, and Cooper.

If Saunière was related to the de La Tours this would also link him to a long line of Sulpician Priests of that family. Saunière's own lineage from Mercouer (heart of the sea or heart of Mary) France in d'Auvergne also includes many ecclesiastical figures. Part of the saga of Rennes le Chateau dictates that Saunière had travelled to St. Sulpice and had returned with specific pieces of art including a copy of Poussin's "The Shepherds of Arcadia." Here again we have all the interesting overtones of St. Sulpice and its "rose line" or meridian, linking us even to the Compte de Maurepas and his association with the settlement and exploration of North America. We also see the famous Cassini family who established the Paris Observatory being involved in these questions (Cassini Space Probe).

It appears Father Saunière had been made aware of a family legacy and had been somewhat prompted into solving the mystery. His association later with places like Girona, Spain and its Torre Magdala may be no coincidence as he endeavored to spread this knowledge in its metaphorical form. (See the work of author Patrice Chaplin for more on Girona Spain).

The arms of the Saunier de Bains family. Only one indication that they are part of the family of de La Tour. Note towers in arms.

213

Chapter 13: The Paris and St. Sulpice Meridians

The Paris Meridian or "Rose Line" as some call it seems to cross in and out of the mysteries of both the Paris Observatory and Rennes le Chateau. An examination of the Great Cross of Hendaye reveals a cast of characters with many commonalities between that mystery and Rennes le Chateau. We have seen our family cast of characters all involved in a kind of hidden geography linked with mysteries that are seeming presented to the public as folklore with some truth in the telling. Many of the central figures related to these mysteries were schooled in the arts of cartography and astronomy. Both of these crafts require an understanding of the Arcadian concept of the Pole Star or North Star.

What is it about this imaginary line that is pertinent to these places and their associated airs of myth and history? The Paris Meridian was marked in order to measure time. This location was selected by Louis XIV to be the Prime Meridian of France. The day would be measured by how long the earth took to rotate and return to the same point as measured. This would be the meridian that all French vessels at sea would refer to in both time and location. The Paris Observatory would serve as the temporal axis mundi of France and her colonies.

The Rose Line and the Paris Meridian may actually be different things. The Rose Line may refer to a meridian that was established at the Cathedral of St. Sulpice slightly west of the Paris Meridian and observatory grounds. This is the Rose Line as depicted in the popular book and movie "The Da Vinci Code." This meridian was established by using an aperture in the window of the cathedral to measure a point of light in comparison to a north to south line marked with an inlayed copper strip in the floor of the church. This device can also be used to measure the number of days in the year and displays the track of the sun if each day's measurement is charted. The use of the meridian of St. Sulpice goes beyond simply marking time as the Paris Meridian does.

There is a similar device referred to as the "Tower of the Winds" located at the Vatican. The Tower of the Winds of the Vatican (ca. 1578; Ottaviano Mascherino) is located just above the map room of the Holy See. This part of the Vatican is aptly named for the original Tower of the Winds in Athens. The Tower of the Winds was likely the original Vatican observatory. The star log collected at the Tower of the Winds could be compared with other ephemeris to establish relative locations of both points on the globe. The Tower was equipped with all the latest astronomical equipment of the day.

The Tower of the Winds of the Vatican also includes a device very similar to the one at St. Sulpice in Paris. The structure included a dark room with an aperture that was used to establish the accurate number of days in the year as well as the day of the Spring Equinox. The entire Key Hole-like plan of the Vatican seems to be oriented to sunrise on the equinox so it makes sense that their observatory would have a device that aided them in establishing accurate timekeeping methods. Interestingly this device was also used to establish the correct day for Easter since this was in dispute with the Orthodox Church at that time. Interestingly the entire eastern orientation of the grounds of the Vatican point the way to Hagia Sophia in Istanbul. At the Vatican the obelisk and windrose markers serve as a directional device that indicate place's important to the history and lore of the Church. For more on that see my book "The Sacred Towers of the Axis Mundi."

The gnomon at St. Sulpice was constructed in 1714 to 1748 by Jean-Baptist Lenguet de Gergy. The stated reason for the construction of the gnomon was to accurately measure the correct time to ring the bells on appropriate days. Lenguet would return to St. Sulpice each year to measure the solstices and equinoxes using the gnomon. From this he also made several other astronomical observations including the earth's perihelion (closest point) with the sun and the angle of the ecliptic. It appears that Monsieur Lenguet was a skilled astronomer. After his death members of the nearby Paris Observatory continued his observations using the gnomon he had constructed.

The establishment of a meridian in this fashion may be an age old custom that is displayed in many of the structures and towers through history. More aptly these structures may be referred to as temples since they mark time. Temporal, Temple, Templum, Time. It is possible that even many of the arrays of monolithic stones seen at many Neolithic sites were used in a manner very similar to the gnomon of St. Sulpice and the Tower of the Winds at the Vatican. Interestingly these towers may have also been referred to as Magdalas, which is a Hebrew word for "Tower" and the name of Mary Magdalene.

Given the stated functions of the gnomon of St. Sulpice and the nearby Paris Meridian it appears there is a different function to both lines on the globe. Both the Paris Meridian and the Rose Line of St. Sulpice are oriented to true north. True north is often measured by the use of the pole star to establish a north to south axis on the ground. Is it possible that this meridian was somehow valued in an occult manner before the official establishment of the Paris Meridian by Louis XIV in 1666 when he authorized the construction of the Paris Observatory? It is clear that a value of the North Star or Stella Maris (star of Mary) is valued in tandem with the themes of Arcas being cast into the skies as Ursa Minor whose tail includes the Pole Star. The symbol of the bear is thus a symbol of Arcadia and also representative of Arcas' mother Callisto.

In 1667 members of the French Academy of Sciences traced out the plan of the observatory on the site in what was said to be a north to south orientation. This ceremony is reminiscent of the way Constantine consecrated the royal district of Constantinople using the Spear of Destiny to trace out the boundaries. This ceremony would also be repeated to establish the small California gold rush town of Chico. John Bidwell the founder of Chico was a descendant of Knights Templar Ormus le Guidon who had also adhered to this tradition in 12th century England in his construction of Norman churches in Staffordshire.

When viewing the Paris Observatory on Google Earth globe it appears the members of the Academy made an error in the orientation of the structure. The Paris Observatory and grounds are not oriented to true north even though the common history says this is the way they arranged it. The building and grounds of the observatory as seen today are not oriented to true north or the pole star. They are oriented significantly to the northeast and southwest of true north. In other words the orientation of the grounds of the observatory do not match the orientation of the Paris

Meridian itself or the way the building is described as being originally designed. Was this an error or was this "mistake" intentional? Were the Academy members leaving a message to future astronomers or cartographers? These people would simply not make a mistake like this.

The Pole Star is relatively easy to sight. Its orientation in relation to any position is easy to mark with stakes in the ground. Compasses did exist and the difference between magnetic north and true north was known during this era so this anomaly is very odd.

This "mistake" may be presented to us in the same manner Fulcanelli claims the stonemason who carved the Great Cross intentionally made miss-spellings to tip one off as to the hidden nature of the monument. The finest geographers, astronomers, and cartographers of this era simply would not make a mistake of this nature. The true orientation for the grounds of the observatory was meant to tell you something.

If an arc on the globe is drawn to the south at the heading or orientation of the grounds of the Paris Observatory it traces an arc or path directly to the Monastery of Montserrat in Spain. This monastery is one of the fabled possible locations of the Holy Grail itself! Here displayed in the orientation of the grounds of the observatory may be some of the hidden beliefs of the astronomers who established it. If they were instilling some occult secrets into the establishment of this meridian in this fashion is it possible they had left other mysteries or clues associated with the meridian? The strange sandstone pillars seen on the Shepherds Monument may be referring to those near the Monastery of Montserrat home of the grail.

The entire value of the Devil's Seat, Rennes le Bains, and the story of Rennes le Chateau all occur in a context that is connected to the Paris Meridian both physically and metaphorically. Already discussed is the relationship of the Devil's Seat to the Paris Meridian. This alone may be connected to Edgar Allen Poe and Thomas Jefferson in bizarre fashion as revealed earlier.

The eastern tip of Henry Lincoln's star in the landscape near Rennes le Bains is very near the meridian established by the gnomon of St. Sulpice and also not very far from the Paris Meridian itself (approx. 100m west). It is possible that this tip of the star was meant to indicate the Paris Meridian. Given a margin of error in comparing Google Earth to the Cassini map this may be considered. If so then a value of this longitude would have been existent at the time the arrangement of the Rennes le Chateau Chapel, Bezu, and Chateau Blanchefort were established thus indicating the star. This raises the specter of the possibility that this meridian was valued long before either the St. Sulpice gnomon or the Paris Observatory were established.

The impetus for Henry Lincoln theorizing that the star in the landscape near Rennes le Chateau/Bains was an inspiration from Poussin's painting "The Shepherds of Arcadia." A tip off to this was the discovery of a tomb near Arques and Rennes le Chateau that seemed to be representative of the one in the painting. This tomb is located in "Les Pontils" and is also situated with a few hundred meters east of the Paris Meridian.

Part of the legend of father Saunière states that he bought a reproduction of this painting at the Louvre Museum when he visited Paris and St. Sulpice after discovering whatever it was that he found in the area around Rennes le Chateau. So this painting is intimately associated with the mystery of Rennes le Chateau just as the Paris Meridian and Rose Line are. To this point we are being provided with a great deal of imagery from the Poussin painting being presented in association with the Paris Meridian.

Poussin's painting of "The Shepherds of Arcadia" is displayed in the Richelieu wing of the Louvre Museum on the second floor in room number 14. Room number 14 (1+4=5 penta) is directly located on the Paris Meridian. The Shepherd's of Arcadia are located on the Paris Meridian. Not just the museum but the actual location of the painting itself within the museum is on the Paris Meridian. This is very curious given the context of the painting in association with the modern form of the Rennes le Chateau mystery. "In Arcadia I am" on the Paris Meridian! The same meridian that is geographically associated with a pentagram in the landscape of Rennes le Chateau that was inspired by a geometric analysis of the painting itself! Something more is afoot. This is also interesting in the context of what is revealed in "The Da Vinci Code" and how the alignment of the pyramids of the Louvre point the way to Migdal and Oak Island. Here we are presented with a very real geographic relationship that connects the mysteries of Rennes le Chateau and Oak Island together. This coupled with the family connections we have discussed adds up to some very curious coincidences or more an intentionally left path.

It seems as if all of this was intentionally arranged in association with the Paris Meridian. It is possible that the propagation of the legend of Rennes le Chateau was inspired by this association with the "Rose Line." It has to be more than a coincidence that Henry Lincoln's star is based on the Poussin painting; The star in the landscape seems to be physically registered to the meridian; The tomb in the Poussin painting is situated in close proximity to the Paris Meridian; and the painting itself is situated on the meridian in the Louvre Museum in Paris. In this context it really does not matter if the "Les Pontils" tomb is the one Poussin used in this painting or not. Someone is trying to tell us something here. The Arcadian Mysteries are all linked via the imagery of Poussin and Sir Philip Sidney's "Arcadia!"

This cluster of imagery from the painting was arranged but by whom? It may have been a group of people. Possibly the same group including the family legacies we have discussed that was centered around the Paris Observatory that is also situated on the Paris Meridian. Are we supposed to be led to the Paris Observatory by this string of clues with a "Shepherd's of Arcadia" theme? These intelligent people of the Paris Observatory may have figured out this entire scheme independently of the family groups that had produced it. Still it is possible that they had also been informed of these concepts by that group.

The more developed this story becomes it seems that the involvement of the Cassini's in this scheme is nearly certain. In the murky waters of politics it is not clear where the Cassini's loyalties were. They were appointees to the Paris Observatory by royal decree until the time of the revolution but this did not make them part of the aristocracy at large. Some of the others like Royal interests and Antoine d'Abbadie may have comprised some of the faction that the Society of the Cincinnati opposed. These old families were firmly rooted in the 'ancient regime' or values of past monarchies in France. There is also a distinct overlay of Jesuit involvement at St. Sulpice, Hendaye, and Rennes le Chateau.

In other examinations of the use of geodesy and cartography to encode important locations it became obvious that Thomas Jefferson practiced this art by establishing what were said to be "personal meridians." Jefferson used structures he designed and built to make associations on the globe that were important to him. It is possible that the Cassini's viewed this art in the same manner. It appears as if they used their personal residence Chateau Thury as a datum from which to establish a "personal meridian" of their own. The Cassini Chateau was built by César-François Cassini de Thury. The structure was built on the site of an ancient fortress and includes a moat surrounding. The pediment of this Greek revival structure includes a rendering of an array of astronomical instruments.

Chateau Thury is oriented to true north. This structure is located about 1.23 miles to the west of the Paris Meridian! This property is virtually on the Rose line! If an arc on the globe is extended south to Paris paralleling the Paris Meridian it continues south and reaches the northern tip of the star in the landscape of Rennes le Chaetau.

Chateau Thury "points to" the star of Henry Lincoln. The entire mystery of Rennes le Chateau is exactly due south of the Cassini's Chateau. This small bit of geographic information may indicate that the Cassini's were indeed the first to recognize that there was a star in the landscape of Rennes le Chateau. It also may infer that they were the creators of the entire mystery that involves the star. Their Chateau was built long before the mystery of this place was known of. This either infers that they constructed the entire tale or that they were privy to it beforehand. Either way this association with their chateau may change a few things with regard to the overall scheme of what is and was going on at Rennes le Chateau. In the end if this spatial relationship is intentional it could mean that the Cassini's manufactured this entire story. It is also possible that this point of the star, which is occupied by Chateau Blanchefort, has some other unknown significance in this entire tale. Perhaps the version of the Rennes le Chateau legend that has German miners tunneling near Chateau Blanchefort is true. We now know that the Blanchefort name is associated with both the de La Tour families and that of the Marquis de Lafayette.

Supporting the notion that the Cassini's created this mystery is the association of the star in the landscape with the Paris Meridian itself. It appears that the eastern tip of the star is about 100 meters west of the Paris Meridian and still closer to the meridian of St. Sulpice. It is possible that the tip of the star was intended to touch the Paris Meridian by whoever planned this scheme. We must consider the possibility that two places intimately associated with the Cassini family including their Chateau and the Paris Observatory are due north of two of the tips of the star of Rennes le Chateau.

Other factors associated with the Rose Line and the mystery of Rennes le Chateau also involve characters that others have associated with the story. The birthplace of exiled King of France Henri V was located just meters northwest of where the Louvre Pyramid is located now. Henri V was born on the Paris Meridian at the Louvre, which was once the royal palace. Some research concerns have identified Henri V or his direct relations as the person who financed the building of the Villa Bethania and Tour Magdala at Rennes le Chateau.

In the movie and book "The Da Vinci Code" the I.M. Pei pyramid is a central location throughout the entire movie. At the end of the film we see the main character Langdon coming to the realization that the remains of Mary Magdalene are hidden beneath the inverted pyramid that is now part of the entrance to the Louvre. The inverted pyramid is directly due north of the octagonal fountain to that is part of the grounds of St. Sulpice and its gnomon. The octagonal fountain of St. Sulpice creates an arc on the globe that leads to the Temple Church in London another place featured in the movie and book.

The linear east to west orientation of the inverted pyramid and main larger pyramid at the Louvre can produce an arc on the globe that extends to the southwest to Migdal, Israel. Midgal is the home of Mary Magdalene in the bible. Migdal is another word for Magdala, which is interpreted as meaning "Tower." So the entire theme of Mary Magdalene at the end of the story of the "Da Vinci Code" is a metaphor for Mary Magdalene in a very real way. In the book and movie the resting place of Mary Magdalene actually points to her place of birth. Here we are also being told of the metaphor and importance of the towers in all of these geographic schemes. So the name of the Tour (Tower) Magdala is somewhat redundant. The opposite direction of this aligment points to Oak Island Nova Scotia and the involvement of the same family names there as well.

Other linear associations included in the movie include Chateau Villette. This is the place in the movie where Magdalene scholar Leigh Teabing lives. This Chateau was originally built in the seventeenth century. Its linear grounds point directly to the Egyptian obelisk at the center of St. Peter's Square at the Vatican. Ironic considering the part of the plot of the story that takes place there. Also not how the character of Teabing in the story is caught up in a mesh of intrigue and violence that includes elements of the Church.

The concept of the "ancient regime" may be why spies associated with the United States and the Society of the Cincinnati in France would want to know all the details of a place like Rennes le Chateau or Rennes le Bains. If this mystery was truly valued by elite factions and hid some sort of grand secret then it would be valuable information for any enemy they had. This may be part of the reason the truth of Rennes le Chateau and Hendaye are locked up in so much interpretive historical and anthropological lore. The hidden ways of the occult and ancient secret societies had been guarding secret information for centuries. In response their opponents developed the skills to investigate their values and weaknesses and use any obtained information against them.

It looks as if the mysteries of Perillos, Hendaye, and Rennes le Chateau include the influence of the Cassini's, Arago, d'Abbadie's, and others associated with the French Academy of Sciences and Paris Observatory. Previously noted is the husband of Sophie de Crouchy the Marquis de Condorcet who was the head of the French Academy of Arts and Sciences. Also associated was the salon of Sophie at Hotel Monnaies that included Jefferson and the Marquis de Lafayette. Here we may see how the Cassini family were also involved in the salon of Sophie de Crouchy.

Beyond that the mystery is still not solved. This story undoubtedly has its roots in much older myths and historical events of the region. What may be exposed here is how and why these things were valued by the elite of the nineteenth century. It also exposes how these concepts may have been used against them. This tradition has obviously been valued since antiquity and had also always been associated with the intelligent elite of each culture.

Given this it is difficult to decide who belongs on what side of the fence. There are some scant clues to at least the allegiances of Cassini III and IV. Thus far we have seen some information that indicates that the Society of the Cincinnati were involved in espionage on the continent designed to foster republican democracies in response to the age-old monarchies that still held sway over much of Europe. Via this intelligence network it is possible that Edgar Allan Poe became privy to the secrets of Rennes le Chateau and encoded the story in metaphors in his story "The Gold Bug."

Amazingly the papers of Benjamin Franklin show us a sliver of light in relation to the allegiances of the Cassini's. Among Franklin's papers was a correspondence from one Jean-Baptiste Le Roy.

(The Papers of Benjamin Franklin: Volume 41: September 16, 1783, through Frebruary 29, 1784) Cohn, Dell, Frankel, Anderson, Buenaventura, Cain, Garbooshian, Sletcher: Yale University Press)

"Tuesday morning (December 23, 1783)
My Dear Doctor give me leave to Send you these two petitions......The other is for an Officer who fought in America for your good cause and who is the brother-in Law (Vicompte de Mory) of The young M. Cassini. Accept my Dear Doctor of my best compliments be So Good to Send me The Volue of the Encyclope in which there is the B." (p319) (spelling and capitalization as original)

The index of the book (p 620) also includes the entry:

Cassini de Thury, Ceasar Francois
Cassini fils, Jacques-Dominique; wants brother-in-law to be accepted into Society of the Cincinnati (P 319, 40-1) Acknowledges Libertas Americana medal for brother-in –law.

This communication indicates that Dominique Cassini was appealing to Franklin to assure his brother-in-law's acceptance into the Society of the Cincinnati as well as being awarded the accompanying medal. The medal of the Society of the Cincinnati was designed by none other than Pierre L' Enfant who is also credited with designing the plan for the City of Washington D.C. Dominique Cassini was a contemporary of Thomas Jefferson and Edgar Allan Poe as discussed earlier. This letter to Franklin is interesting and revealing. What does it mean? Most of all why does Le Roy want the "B" encyclopedia? Strange. There must be an explanation but it sounds like a coded message from a B movie spy drama or…..an Edgar Allan Poe story!

This indicates that at least Dominique Cassini may have shared values in common with the Society of Cincinnati. His association with brother-in-law Mory may have given him access to the Society. From the letter it appears that Cassini had implored Monsieur Le Roy to write to Franklin asking for this. We know that Jefferson had written Cassini so these men were all known to each other. It does appear that Dominque Cassini was sympathetic to the Republican cause as noted in some biographies.

Cassini's possible association with this group is surprising given the royal legacy of much of his family's history. The Cassini's were not treated badly after the revolution but were no longer associated with the Paris Observatory in a hereditary manner. Previously the King had ensured that the son of Cassini would inherit the position at the Observatory. Dominique became a respected astronomer and cartographer even though he was not running the Paris Observatory. He had managed despite this to carry on the family legacy of charting the cosmos. Given their royal connections it is notable that the Cassini's survived the Revolution. One of the people who served as director of the Paris Observatory during this post revolution period was Francois Arago. Arago is famous for installing the famous brass medallions in Paris that mark the Paris Meridian. These are also prominently featured in "The Da Vinci Code."

It is also possible that Dominque had retained his loyalist sympathies and hoped to glean inside information from Mory about the exploits of the Society of the Cincinnati. Given the political climate in France during this era it is likely that Cassini was in favor of a more Republican form of government and was not a loyalist though it is clear that his family developed and had been part of the elite of France for four generations. Even so their connections to gentry were via academic pursuits and their skills as cartographers. The Cassini's skills at accurately displaying the landscape in map form became a viable military advantage that aided the accuracy of artillery and troop movements. Even compared with Google Earth today the Cassini map of France is very accurate.

The Society of Cincinnati in France at this time was headed by none other than the Marquis de Lafayette. It is also doubtful that the Marquis would allow any members who were not in line with the goals of the Society. If Lafayette had not wanted de Mory to be in the Society then it is likely he would not have been admitted.

The nineteenth century was a great time of turmoil in France as they struggled to develop a form of government that served the people yet still valued a monarchy. The dispute of kingship between Louis Philippe and Henri Artois for the crown in the post Napoleonic era may serve as an example of this conflict within France at that time. These types of intrigues may be part of why Rennes le Chateau had become of interest to intelligence gathering concerns including the Society of the Cincinnati, Freemasons, and artist's guilds. Henri Artois' (Henri V exiled King of France) possible involvement in financing the exploits of Sauniére as well as the construction of the Tour Magdala and Villa Bethania may serve as a testament to this theory. The influence of Henri V may also be seen in the enigma of the "Frenchman's Tower" of Palo Alto California. Later in the Rennes le Chateau saga we would even see Pierre Plantard using the mythology of this place for political ends among others.

221

In summation the entire Rennes le Chateau mystery may be a memorial to the blood ties of Henri V to Dagobert II. Given Henri V dispute with Philippe and his camp over the monarchy Henri likely had proof that he was more 'of the blood' than his rival for the crown. Whether Christ, Mary Magdalene or Dagobert the entire story may revolve around hidden remains and information that would prove Henri V's royal legacy over all others. It is clear that the Society of the Cincinnati would be opposed to any monarchy. It is equally as clear that Henri V did not want to have anything to do with a republican form of government. The importance of the legacy of Rennes le Chateau to Henri V constituted good inside information to his enemies including the Society.

Given all of the above it is curious that the primary claimant to the French throne in 2015 Louis Alphonse of Bourbon, Duke of Anjou is an honorary member of the Society of the Cincinnati. Louis Alphonse and Henri V are of the same royal line all related to the Habsburgs as well. It is a cloudy and hard to decipher question at Rennes le Chateau. It seems clear that the Society of the Cincinnati once opposed Henri V becoming King.

Perillos

To learn what comprises the mysteries of Perillos go no further than the Society of Perillos in France. These men and women have done exhaustive historical research into the mysteries of Perillos and how it may be associated with Rennes le Chateau. It is thought that Father Saunière of Rennes le Chateau had visited Perillos and had a model of that area built that included locations for places labeled "Christ's Tomb" and "Mary's Tomb." Though many dispute the authenticity of this three dimensional map there is further evidence linking Perillos to Rennes le Chateau as well as the over all scheme of similar places like The Great Cross of Hendaye, Ronda Spain, Shugborough Hall, and Stirling Castle. Evidence included here may help to support the ideas of the Society of Perillos.

The idea of a landscape such as the one depicted in the three dimensional map that Saunière had commissioned is not a new concept in studies of the occult and Christian mysteries. Some places over the centuries seemed to have been deemed a new "Jerusalem" and given the same importance in the eyes of pilgrims and worshipers alike. All of the Arcadian mysteries may have sprung from Ravenna and direct relations to the name and philosophy behind them.

Examples of this would include Lalibela Ethiopia. The famous rock hewn churches of Lalibela are pointed to by the array of obelisk and windrose present at St. Peter's Square of the Vatican. Though some of the churches there are said to be older ruler Mescal Lalibela proclaimed that the complex of Churches would be the Jerusalem of the Ethiopain Orthodox faith. Much of the story of Rennes le Chateau also suggests the surrounding area was also thought of in this way.

Santiago de Compostela may also be included in this group of possible "Jerusalems." The Cathedral there includes the remains of the Apostle James in a Sepulcher there. This holy place became a subject of pilgrimage and veneration more so during the periods when Jerusalem was unavailable to Christian pilgrims. So all of the lore and value of Santiago de Compostela indicate that it held a place of similar interest to Jerusalem.

Many scholars also point to the writings of Sir Francis Bacon in reference to a New Atlantis or New Jerusalem. This concept of Bacon's seemed to have been valued by those who comprised the Rosicrucian portion of the settlers of the early colonies in America. Many point to the early Jamestown settlement and later Williamsburg as having possessed some Rosicrucian influence from an early time. It is no coincidence that Jamestown was also ultimately named for Santiago given the origins of why it is named such. The grounds of Stirling Castle include the Jerusalem Stone Pyramid that is similar to the steep sided pyramid seen on the Great Seal of the United States.

One of the common factors in each of these valued places may include the involvement of the Cassini family and their cohorts at the Paris Observatory. All of the mysteries discussed here include the establishment of a Prime Meridian and the application of esoteric and hidden concepts associated with an array of talismans associated with the axis of the meridian. Anyone can establish a meridian yet in this tradition it seems to be limited to national interests, churches, secret societies, royal interests, and gentry. At many of these sites an octagon serves as a sighting device that indicates other places of importance locally as well as at a great distance across the globe. Some sites use other geometric shapes such as the hexagon or pentagon/pentagram.

From the perspective of the theories in this book Perillos is interesting because Cassini II used the area as a base of operations for several years. During this time he lived in relatively spartan conditions while traveling the region to collect data for the famous Cassini map of France. In addition Francois Arago was born and grew up only a few miles from Perillos and Fortress Salvetierra.

The small village of Perillos is pointed to by the eastern orientation of the Star in the landscape of Rennes le Chateau. An arc on the globe plotted in this way transects or passes only a short distance north of the center of the village. This is yet one other small way that the two mysteries are linked.

One of the other as of yet discussed similarities to this mystery and others involving the Cassini's was unveiled in our studies of Ronda Spain and Palacio de Salvatierra. The Fortress Salvetierra near Perillos was undoubtedly also associated with the Knights of Calatrava as the Palacio in Ronda is. The part of France that includes Perillos was once part of Spanish dominion so it is very likely that the Fortress Salvetierra was once occupied by this Order of Knights that had also been created by the Cistercian Order just as the Knights Templar had been.

In fact the Order of Calatrava had been known as the Knights of Salvatierra for about a fourteen year period before changing their name back to Calatrava. The Order of Alcantara is also associated with Calatrava and the Cistercian Order. During the time Fortress Salvetierra was occupied by the Order they were undoubtedly involved in the expulsion of the Moors from Spain. It is also clear that Charlemagne had also once controlled this region as part of what was termed the Spanish Marches. The Order of Montessa an offshoot of Calatrava was also said to have been comprised of former Knights Templar after the time of their persecution in 1307.

There is indeed another Fortress Salvatierra in Spain. Amazingly Montesario Montesion is adjacent to this castle. The fortress there is also referred to as "The Castle of Five Points" due to the shape of one of its battlements. This shape does not form a perfect pentagram but is interesting due to other associations. It is interesting that the castle has this nickname though the real official name is Castle Salvatierra. So a pentagram in the landscape of Rennes le Chateau points to the "Castle of Five Points." This is an interesting metaphorical association if nothing else.

Very little is known about the ruins of the castle there but the Monastery is still active with only three monks remaining. It is interesting that two Fortresses named the same one in French the other in Spanish are related to the entire scheme or plan we see here. Of course the imagery invoked by the Monastery of Mount Sion and how this may relate to the Priory of Sion and Monastery of Mt. Sion in Jerusalem theme in the Rennes le Chateau mystery is intriguing.

Something is being said with all this imagery. It seems the hub of much of this is in and near Rennes le Chateau and is spread out through other similar mysteries seemingly created by the same people. Each myth or ritual includes a central geometric shaped datum or axis from which measurements are taken that have spiritual and talismanic importance to those who create these systems. It is almost as if everything has to be arranged correctly for the "spell" to work. So, there is an element of superstition and magic that also seems to be believed and applied in these scenarios.

There is one other distant yet possibly important link in the story of Perillos and its connection to other places of mystery. James "The Black" or "The Good" Douglas depending on which side you were on might also have an association with Perillos. Douglas was the right hand man of Scots King Robert the Bruce. Douglas died in the battle of Teba in Spain while carrying The Bruce's heart into battle encased in an enameled locket. Douglas is also directly related to and named for his uncle James Stewart who was in turn named for Santiago or St. James. Sir James Douglas called his castle in Scotland "Castle Perillos" (Perilous). Douglas had even been educated in France so there may be a connection.

While this story is likely a fairy tale concocted to cover the disappearance of Douglas and his Knights from the pages of history James may have a bearing on the Perillos story. Douglas like many members of the Scots nobility was educated in France for several years before returning to Scotland to serve The Bruce. It is during this time he may have come to know the secrets of Perillos. It is also likely that Douglas was a Knight of Santiago though no record of this exists. Records do exist that list him as a "Knight of the Tomb." Many others may make the mistake of assuming this is referring to the Order of the Holy Sepulcher. In fact "Knight of the Tomb" could be just as readily applied to the Knights of Santiago who guarded the Sepulcher of St. James and the Pilgrims that visited it.

224

Douglas' designation as a Knight of the Tomb is interesting in comparison to the portion of Philip Sidney's "Arcadia" that William Alexander had written. The entire portion penned by Alexander revolved around a character termed "The Black Knight" and the passage even terms him "A Knight of the Tomb."

In addition James Douglas is named for Santiago (St. James). Douglas was the nephew of the 5th earl of Stewart whose father Alexander had named him in honor of Santiago. This is the first instance of a Scots or English nobleman being named James. So Douglas had been named "Iago" in honor of his uncle and Santiago. It is likely that the truth of the Battle of Teba is somehow associated with Santiago de Compostela. These associations with the name "James" may reveal a little discussed affiliation of some Scots gentry with the Order of Santiago. William Sinclair the builder of Rosslyn Chapel was also a Knight of Santiago. These men's association with the Order of Santiago and Santiago de Compostela leads ultimately to the reason why Jamestown Virginia was named such as discussed above.

It is possible that Douglas and the other Knights that accompanied him to Teba had decamped in secret to North or South America. (See "The Sacred Towers of the Axis Mundi" for more on that). In Scotland Douglas named his castle "Castle Perillos." Many point to this as meaning "Perilous" or dangerous. But would have an educated Douglas made such a spelling error? Even the way this word is spelled in that era in not the same as the small village in southern France that is part of this mystery. It is possible that Douglas had been initiated into the secrets of Perillos because he was a Knight of Santiago. The Order of Santiago was closely associated with the Knights Templar and both orders of Calatrava and Santiago had taken in many Templars when the Templars were disbanded in 1307. Douglas would have even been the correct age in relation to the disbanding of the Knights Templar to have been taught this information by one of them himself while he was a student in France. This is a long shot but the fairy tale overtones to the story of the Battle of Teba suggest something else happened that did not include Douglas and the others being killed. The same may apply to Douglas' use of "Perillos" as the name of his keep in Scotland

Again for the full story of Perillos and the Lords of Perillos visit the Society of Perillos online or purchase one of the books they have available there.

From South to North on the Paris Meridian:

Rennes le Bains and the Devil's Seat
The Pontil's Tomb
The Paris Observatory
The Louvre
Poussin's Painting "The Shepherd's of Arcadia" is located within the Louvre directly on the Paris Meridian.
Cathedral of Notre Dame (Also featured in Fulcanelli's "Mystery of the Cathedrals)

Chateau Thury the Cassini estate is due north (0 degrees) of the northern tip of the star in the landscape around Rennes le Chateau. The estate is 1.23 miles west of the Paris Meridian. Virtually on the meridian.

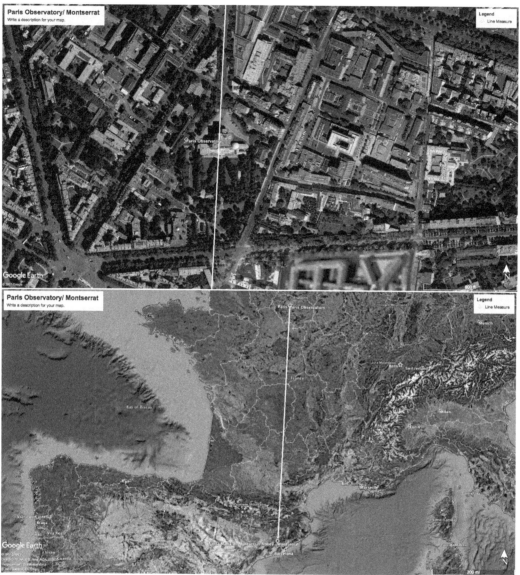

The Paris Observatory "points to" Montserrat Monastery a storied location of the Holy Grail. This orientation is far from the True North orientation of the structure as told in its history. Continued on the next page.

There are many sandstone pillars at Montserrat Monastery (below) very similar to those depicted on The Shepherds Monument at Shugborough Hall.

227

Chapter 14: The White House Meridian

To speculate that the plan of Washington D.C. was inspired by that of Paris is not an unreasonable assumption. The National Mall in Washington D.C. can look to the famous Axe Historique (Historical Axis) of Paris comprised of the Louvre Array and the Place de la Concorde stretching through the city to the Arc de Triomphe. Though Jefferson was in favor of a more conservative plan he undoubtedly recognized the plan of L'Efant as including some of the elements that are present in Paris. This includes the National Mall echoing the attributes of the alignment of the Place de la Concorde and Arch de Triomphe. Jefferson would also contribute an element to the city that was inspired by the Paris Meridian and its array of monuments and talismans.

In earlier works I have noted how the wife of Chico founder John Bidwell was a direct relation of Andrew Ellicott. After L'Enfant withdrew his services Ellicott planned the city and actually laid out the boundaries street plan of Washington District of Columbia with his crew of surveyors and astronomers. John Bidwell of Chico's wife's maiden name was Annie Ellicott Kennedy and she was from Washington D.C. This association led to Chico having a strange street plan and array of monuments that infer that it is indeed a miniature plan of Washington D.C. Ellicott is only one of the amazing family relations of John Bidwell which also include many of the people that seemed to have formed what is termed "New Age" philosophies during the current era beginning in the mid nineteenth century.

Jefferson seems to have been personally responsible for the establishment of the White House Meridian in a very real sense. The White House Meridian is the line of longitude that goes through the center of the White House on a north to south axis. Later the establishment of first the old Naval Observatory and later the new Naval Observatory would fulfill the function as the temporal axis in a similar manner to the Paris Meridian. What Jefferson created in the White House Meridian would become a talismanic monument to great American Presidents as well as an object of mystery and intrigue.

Jefferson established two pier stones or surveyor's markers along this longitude to mark what he considered an important longitude. Pier stones appear as small obelisks that are meant to be set in the ground and provide a datum from which measurements can be taken. The small stone monuments are made of stone and built to last the ravages of time.

The first Jefferson Pier was said to have been located in what today is Meridian Hill Park. This park marks the White House Meridian. Another exists to the west of the Washington Monument. The Meridian Hill stone is missing as is the one near the Washington Monument. There is a replacement marker near where the original Jefferson Pier was located at the Washington Monument.

Pictures and records of a nearby manhole that has a brass surveyors pier beneath it do exist. This is likely the original Jefferson Pierstone that was buried at the time of the grading and filling of the area for the construction of the Washington Monument. Many people are wrongly misidentifying this surveyor's pier as a "miniature Washington Memorial." This pier stone that was placed by Jefferson may have been meant to mark the future location of the Washington Monument. Apparently, the ground in this area was too unstable or wet to place the Washington Monument so its site of construction was moved slightly to the east of where it is now seen.

The establishment of the White House Meridian by Jefferson seems to be a precursor of the tradition he upheld in the plans of his two estates Monticello and Poplar Forest. It is possible that Jefferson was inspired by things he had learned in France during his two extended stays there. He may have been inspired to create such a meridian via his knowledge of the Paris Meridian and the Axe Historique. His associates in France already knew of and practiced the arrangement of monuments on their estates. This is the same group of people who included the Casssini's and Von Humboldt brothers. It is in fact an easy assumption that the entire plan of Washington D.C. had been inspired by the design of Paris. Even the Scots factions of Colonial America would have valued these French inspired designs.

It is clear that over time the spirit of Jefferson establishing this meridian was appreciated and carried on. Several monuments were eventually added to the White House Meridian that paid respect to past Presidents including the Jefferson Memorial, Reagan Airport (Same site as the Alexander's Abingdon Estate), Woodrow Wilson Bridge, Ft Washington, and of course the White House itself. Interestingly the home of the Alexander family whose land comprised about half of the original District of Columbia owned a house directly on what would become the White House Meridian on the grounds of what is today Regan National Airport. Remnants of the home can still be seen next to the main terminal there.

Other important monuments in United States History that are located on the White House Meridian include Meridian Hill Park, The House of the Temple Scottish Rite Masonic Building, and Rose Hill Maryland the estate of one of Washington's physicians Gustavus Brown. Each of these places has a unique and interesting story to tell but what of the Meridian itself? Did this line of longitude have any significance prior to Washington D.C. being planned and placed where it is? Is there a reason that Washington D.C. is placed where it is? This may be true.

The Design of Washington D.C. and the Society of the Cincinnati

Some aspects of the tale of how Washington District of Columbia got its street plan seem to be veiled in secrecy and intrigue. A close examination of the characters that played major roles in the design of the city may reveal some background information that makes it all a little easier to understand. Given this all of the secrets of the City may never be revealed while other mysteries inferred in symbolism and lore may have been meant to be solved and understood. Part of the philosophy behind these mysteries may be that one is supposed to work hard and speculate to find the "treasure" via a path of information that is left to interpret. This vision quest if you will exposes the seeker to the truth of the origins of the United States of America which in turn inspires one as to the uniqueness and equality provided the citizen by the Republican ideal when compared to political systems that have existed through much of earlier human history. Earlier in

229

history Greece, Rome, and much later even England began to develop a system of rule that included input from the population with regard to law and domestic policy.

As noted prior the Alexander family played a key role in establishing both Washington D.C. and Alexandria Virginia. Their family may have been aware of the full gambit of places of mystery during their era including Oak Island, the Newport Tower, and the Legend of Bacon's Vault in Williamsburg.

One hidden influence that may have played a role on the development of possible symbols in the streets of Washington D.C. would include the Society of the Cincinnati. We have already examined this organizations possible involvement in foreign intelligence gathering in France and England. This group must at least be considered when looking at the background of the scheme to build the city and those involved.

Many of the major players involved in the planning and design of the city such as George Washington and Pierre L'Enfant were members of the Society of the Cincinnati. Washington was known to have doubts about the Society but remained a member and leader of the American branch of the organization despite this. Washington felt that the hereditary nature of the membership rules of the Society might be misinterpreted as being a group of gentry controlling things from behind the scenes. Jefferson's name is conspicuously missing from the membership roles of the Society of the Cincinnati. Differences between the Order of Redmen (derived from the Sons of Liberty) and the Society of the Cincinnati were highlighted by a political rivalry between Thomas Jefferson and Alexander Hamilton. Jefferson was a member of the Order of Redmen. This is not to say that Jefferson opposed the ideals of the Republic but that he had some differences with Hamilton and others that were part of the Society.

In addition to Washington the Society of the Cincinnati counted the Marquis de Lafayette, Pierre L'Enfant and Alexander Hamilton as members. L'Enfant had served as a battlefield engineer with both the Marquis de Lafayette and General Washington. Here again we are exposed to the facts that Edgar Allan Poe's grandfather was an associate of Lafayette, Nicolas Rodgers of Druid Hill, and now likely L'Enfant as well. It is almost starting to look as if Poe had been trained for his role since a young age despite the loss of his father. There is a healthy debate within circles of literary historians as to the truth of the life of Poe. His possible association with the Society of the Cincinnati or Untied States intelligence gathering activities adds fuel to the fire to the concept of the unknown qualities of Edgar Allan Poe.

Pierre L'Enfant designed the badge of the Society of the Cincinnati. The Society also had a very strong French branch of the organization that fell in and out of favor as regimes changed in this volatile era of the history of that country. It is clear that the ideals of the American Revolution had made their way back to France with the many soldiers and sailors that had served in that conflict. It may be that this influence combined with that of the English and Scots Jacobites contributed much to the French Revolution, reign of the Napoleon's, and the subsequent Republican experiment we see in France in the nineteenth and twentieth centuries. In any case it is clear that L'Enfant was a supporter of the notion of a Republic in France.

It is not clear if L'Enfant retained his French citizenship as he is referred to as being American in some of his biographies. It is evident that he visited France under the auspices of the Order of the Cincinnati to design military badges for members in France and Sweden. L'Enfant also served on the administrative boards and organization of the Society in France. During his visit to produce the appropriate medals for the order he also helped to organize this group there. The Society of the Cincinnati would go on to play a major role in the politics of France through many regimes. Sometimes it seems the Society was forced to operate as a secret society as in the reign of the Napoleon's for example. Of course many of the members of the Society of the Cincinnati were also Freemasons.

The approval of the wearing of this decoration was originally approved by King Louis XVI himself . The King had also approved the existence of this group in his country prior to that. This is odd in that later the stated goal of the Society of the Cincinnati was to create and maintain republics in the countries that included members. It seems out of place somehow that the King or his intelligence service would not have considered the revolutionary spirit as a threat to the monarchy until it was too late. Similar sentiments as expressed by the republican values of the Society is why and how Poe may have been decamping for Poland when he left West Point later in history.

The development of Washington D.C. and its famous plan included the input of George Washington, Alexander Hamilton, and Pierre L'Enfant all staunch supporters of the ideals of the Society of the Cincinnati. Even arguments about how to use the limited funds that were available at first were argued over party lines that pitted the Society of the Cincinnati members against Jefferson and his camp. Jefferson was in favor of building federal buildings and infrastructure before designing the memorial function of the city in more depth. His opposition which included L'Enfant seemed to have won out in the end though L'Enfant left the project before it was complete in frustration over small changes to the design of the plan. This left Andrew Ellicott and Benjamin Banneker to finish the job.

Even though there appears to be a divide in the ideals of both sides in the plan of Washington D.C. story there are many similarities as well. It is clear that both sides in this argument were aware of the ancient tradition of aligning architecture with talismanic meaning and metaphors engrailed in elements of its construction. At times it is difficult to tell which side is which. It is clear that both sides believed in a democracy or government with representatives of the people. Beyond that their differences were somewhat semantic in the overall scheme of history. It is possible that Jefferson was opposing an attempt by Jacobite factions to arrange the business landscape of the new country in a more favorable vein with regard to their interests. Elements of the Southern Colonies were at that time developing a kind of feudal system based on agriculture and slavery that conflicted with the Republican business style of many northern industries and businesses. New York City was the home to Wall Street while the south was home to plantations and slavery.

Many Jacobite ideals would have dictated the existence of landed gentry and a controlled currency in the United States. These differences would later contribute to the reasons the Civil War occurred. This conflict is still going on today as well with Jefferson's side losing badly. Later this rift in philosophies would be underlined by an actual movement to make Bonnie Prince Charlie or George Washington "King" of the United States! True to the ideals of the Society of the Cincinnati Washington refused to consider this idea. Jefferson was also opposed to the monarchy though rumors persist that he had a clandestine meeting with Bonnie Prince Charlie while Secretary of State (foreign affairs).

Thomas Jefferson's contribution to the plan of the city in part includes the establishment of what is now known of as the White House Meridian. This meridian was laid out by Jefferson himself using a surveying instrument. His survey included the setting of two pier stones along the path of this meridian in the city. This meridian would bisect the plan of the White House perfectly on a north to south axis thus its name "The White House Meridian." Jefferson planned this meridian prior to completing Monticello and Poplar Forest both of which represent personal meridians to the President. The White House Meridian would through time come to be an overall monument to Presidents of the United States.

Jefferson is said to have placed one of these pier stones in what is today Meridian Hill Park. Meridian Hill Park includes a linear array of statuary including a rendering of Joan of Arc that marks the White House Meridian. Later we would see Joaquin Miller building a Cabin on this site in order it seems to intentionally live on the White House Meridian. Meridian Hill Park may mark the northern extent of this alignment of monuments included on the White House Meridian.

Jefferson Placed an additional pier stone where he felt the Washington Monument should be placed. This marker is known as the Jefferson Pier Stone. This location is marked today with a replacement stone that resembles the original. It is located a few hundred yards to the west and slightly north of the position of the Washington Monument today. This pier stone is directly on the White House Meridian. Nearby to this replacement pier stone is a manhole cover that hides what is possibly the original Jefferson Pier Stone. Pictures exist of this surveyor's pier under the manhole.

This marker likely represents what was ground level prior to the grading and construction of the National Mall over the years. At some point someone surrounded it with a brick casement and the manhole to cover it. Main stream sources with regard to the Jefferson Pier state that it is missing and ignore the existence of this second surveyor's pier close to the replacement marker.

From Jefferson's placement of this marker it appears that he may have envisioned the Washington Monument being located at this point on the White House Meridian. This would fit the scheme of places added to the alignment later like the Jefferson Memorial, Reagan Airport, Woodrow Wilson Bridge, and Ft. Washington. To him, at this early stage in the planning of the city he may have also planned for this point to be the middle of the National Mall. In either case he valued this point as being part of the meridian he had established with his placement of two

232

surveyor's piers along what would come to be known of as the White House Meridian. It is also interesting that one of the Alexander's estates Abingdon is located on the White House Meridian.

Is there are reason or historical impetus for why Jefferson would value this longitude and create a significant cultural phenomena to celebrate this meridian?

There are some sources and historical basis for a value of this meridian on the part of the President and other planners of the city. Sir Walter Raleigh was an early figure in colonial history that led expeditions to the east coast of America. He was an investor into the ill fated "Lost Colony" of Roanoke Island, North Carolina. The Raleigh Tavern in Williamsburg was named for this man.

As was common in the Elizabethan era many people held esoteric beliefs that may be applied to their political and practical views of the world. Among the many noted values of Sir Raleigh was a regard of what is termed "The Sacred Longitude" or 77th degree of Longitude. This is very nearly the same longitude as the White House Meridian (77"02'11" E: 7+7+2+1+1= 18 or 3x6 or 666 the Sacred Longitude of Washington D.C.). Is it possible that Jefferson and the other planners of the city were aware of Raleigh's value of this meridian in the placement of the White House Meridian if not the entire city itself? One additional place located on this meridian may serve to support this idea.

The alignment at 77"02'11" W longitude is interesting in that it is located about 370 meters east of the centerline axis of the Washington D.C. city limits as defined by the original ten mile square diamond shape of the city. Logic would dictate that the linear array of monuments would be centered on the axis of the city but this is not the way the city was built. If diagonal lines are drawn from corner to corner on a map of the original city limits then the center of the city would be at D.A.R. Constitution Hall just southwest of the White House. This arrangement may be a nod towards the goddess and the sacred feminine.

After Jamestown had been established one of the notorious Captain John Smith's duties was to explore the Potomac River area. It is possible that part of his mission was to look for places present on the "Sacred Longitude" as valued by Raleigh. In association with his exploration of this area is a myth of Captain John Smith bringing the Holy Grail to the Sacred Longitude.

A legend does exist in Maryland of Captain John Smith coming to what is today Accokeek, Maryland. Accokeek is located directly on the White House Meridian or Sacred Longitude. Part of the legend of Smith coming here incudes the fact that he "taught the Holy Grail" to the Native American population. This tale represents high strangeness given its situation on the Sacred Longitude and the significance that was applied to this meridian previously by Raleigh and later by Jefferson including all subsequent eras of American history. It is possible that some value of this Sacred Longitude had come from Sir Francis Bacon himself.

It is possible that a sacred value of this longitude by people in the past in part dictated the placement of the new Capitol of the United States of America. Somehow Jefferson and others had valued and maintained a belief that this longitude was significant and special in some regard. All of this plain to see long before the city had been planned or its location decided upon. Is it possible that a value of this meridian had evolved from a concept introduced by Sir Francis Bacon? Many of the actions and values of our founding fathers seem to adhere to some Baconian concepts.

Here in these legends as least we have a clear reason as to why the Capitol would be located where it was placed. This area of Northern Virginia and Maryland were settled early and were the home of many powerful families including the Custis', Lee's, Washington's, Moncure's, Mason's, and more. What was known of as Truro Parish in Northern Virginia was an especially powerful base for the landed gentry of early Virginia. As discussed some of these families may have even recovered the famous Oak Island treasure.

Through a long series of events we have examined how some of the land south of the Potomac River that was to become Washington District of Columbia included land holdings by the Alexander and Lee families among other prominent citizens of that region. George Washington also had a desire to include the City of Alexandria which had been named for the Alexander's within the boundaries of the District.

Over time the street plan of Washington D.C. took shape via the efforts of Pierre L'Enfant and others like Andrew Ellicott who had worked in tandem with a committee that had included both Washington and Jefferson. Many people have analyzed the layout of the city with regard to astronomy and astrology and have made many connections that may be valid. The famous D.C. Star itself has inspired many conspiracy theories and occult associations. The entire District itself had been planned as a ten mile square rotated 45 degrees to form a diamond shape that is sometimes compared to a goddess symbol by many. In some forms of geomancy this shape is indeed associated with Puella the goddess and harkens us back to the book about geomancy written by Philip Sidney's sister Mary Herbert Countess of Pembroke. In many ways the entire city is reminiscent of the Arcadian theme and its associated geographic connections.

It seems that a similar cast of characters to those seen or inferred at everywhere from Rennes le Chateau to Oak Island had also played a part in the establishment of Washington District of Columbia. The Alexanders for one are deeply involved in the history and lore of Nova Scotia as we have seen. They seemed to have worked in tandem with the Society of the Cincinnati and many of the same French gentry families we have observed included those of the Marquis de Lafayette and Pierre L'Enfant. L'Enfant (meaning "the infant" in French) is buried at Arlington National cemetery and his cenotaph or tombstone contains a portion of the plan of the city with a nearby obelisk.

Amazingly we even see a Stuart directly involved as one of the first commissioners of the new city. So, all along the way we see a similar cast of names and characters that links us far back in time to the legacies of the angry fallen kings who may have contributed to the creation of the United States and the Republic of France among others. It is interesting to see Stuarts and

Alexanders involved in the creation of the Capitol given their family legacies with regard to the other mysteries examined here.

Thomas Johnson, David Carroll and David Stuart were the original three commissioners of the City. Among their duties was to obtain the property that would become the District of Columbia and administer its design and function. These men had the opportunity to create a grand city from scratch and a member of the Stuart family was directly involved with all the other famous founders such as Jefferson, Madison, and Washington in making this a reality. In the process they had created an array of architecture very similar to the Axe Historique and Louvre array in Paris in conjunction with the Paris Meridian. In Washington D.C. the White Houe Meridian fulfills the same symbolic purpose as the Paris Meridian. This is likely true even though the Naval Observatory to the west of the White House Meridian marks time in the United States. The building of the Naval Observatory happens to closely resemble the plan and appearance of Shugborough Hall which is of course a central theme in these mysteries.

David Carroll's family is the namesake of the hexagonal Ft. Carroll built by Robert E. Lee in the late 1850's when he was still in the Union Army. This structure "points to" Port Royal Nova Scotia and the Dome of the Rock in Jerusalem in single arc on the globe suggested by its hexagonal form with regard to true north. Port Royal is both the site of the first French colony in Nova Scotia or Acadia as well as the site of William Alexander the Younger's first Scottish colony in Nova Scotia. Much of this mystery also revolves around the possibility that Constantine had built an octagonal structure where the Dome of the Rock today. The Dome of the Rock may have even been rebuilt by Emperor Justinian II in a clandestine manner using spolia or older elements from the structure that Constantine had originally built there. To Constantine the site of the Dome of the Rock may have represented what he believed to be the Holy Sepulcher. (Sacred Towers of the Axis Mundi).

Washington D.C. is indeed a wonderland of temporally themed monuments. It seems the most important city to the United States is a place that Templars using Templates had defined Templum that measure the temporal fabric. This indeed would echo the functions of all the towers discussed here and display this legacy in the grandest and most obvious form of all of them. All of the landscaping and architectural clues present in all of these other mysteries are waiting for the seeker who explores Washington D.C. with some knowledge and study of these concepts.

The John Ericsson National Memorial

The City of Washington D.C. is comprised of an amazing landscape of monuments and memorials. Many authors have speculated as to the existence of hidden patterns in the streets of Washington District of Columbia. In this rush to interpret the broad overall scheme of the city and its possible meanings many of the less well known monuments in the city have been overlooked. Among these is the John Ericsson National Memorial just south of the Lincoln Memorial.

The John Ericsson National Memorial is dedicated to the man who invented the screw propeller and designed the famous Civil War ironclad Monitor. This memorial was dedicated on May, 29, 1926. The dedication ceremony was presided over by President Calvin Coolidge with Crown Prince Gustaf Adolf of Sweden in attendance. The Ericsson Memorial is one of thirty in the United States given the designation 'National Memorial.'

John Ericsson was a native of Sweden and worked throughout Europe before coming to the United States. Interestingly it appears that Ericsson also was of partial Scottish descent. This is not uncommon in Sweden as the history of both countries in intertwined even including a strong influx of Jacobite refugees after the 1715 and 1745 Jacobite uprisings in England and Scotland. Ericsson lived during the same era as President Lincoln whose memorial on the National Mall is about 1000 ft. due north of the Ericsson Memorial.

Ericsson's Scottish connections are interesting in light of the hidden function of the monument that commemorates him. There is a strong tradition of Jacobite and gentry factions in the United States expressing themselves in architecture that includes directional attributes. His life story has him associated with some of the greatest inventors of the Industrial revolution. Among his inventions were a heat driven motor and another that ran off of the fumes from burning wood. Also notable is him possessing the same name as famous Viking explorer Leif Ericsson. The Vikings were also masters of the art of navigation at a very early date.

The U.S. Navy ship Monitor was a unique design for the day and was composed of heavy iron plating above the waterline making it appear as a modern tank on the water. Its turret carried two large caliber cannon. The entire design of the ship looked very modern and sleek compared to the sail and steam driven ships that were common at the time. The Monitor inspired the design of several similar vessels and was instrumental in subduing Confederate shipping and naval operations during the war.

Due to his genius in these achievements Ericsson was honored with the Construction of the National Memorial that bears his name. A closer examination of the Ericsson Memorial may reveal some intriguing hidden aspects of the monument that have never been revealed before. The Ericsson monument is a directional device that points the way to places in Washington D.C. like: The White House, Teddy Roosevelt Memorial, Jefferson Memorial, House of the Temple, Naval Observatory, United States Institute of Peace, National Holocaust Museum (hexagon), and Washington Circle Park. The Ericsson Memorial also points the way to Rose Hill, Maryland south of the city. Rose Hill may have played a hidden role in the Lincoln assassination and the placement of the Ericsson Memorial may be a clue as to the truth of this idea.

The memorial itself includes a compass design along its circular outer plan that creates arcs on the globe that direct one on a map to the above locations. Descriptions of the memorial do refer to this design as representing a compass. The compass design is oriented to true north enabling one to measure points in the City of Washington D.C. in relation to this symbolic axis or datum. This attribute serves as a kind of way of indicating places that will teach one something that includes an overall theme or lesson. To understand more about the Ericsson Memorial an

236

examination of the artwork and statuary featured as elements of the monument may also lead to some understanding.

The form of the statue includes a seated Ericsson with three figures behind him that also circle a rendering of the Viking sacred tree known as the Yrrgdrasil tree. The figures are representative of the themes of Ericsson's life including adventure, labor, and vision. This inclusion of the Yrggdrasil tree is repeated at places like the Apprentice Pillar of Rosslyn Chapel and in the imagery of Le Baton Rouge in Louisiana which may even have been meant to represent this sacred tree.

The figure representing adventure appears to depict a Viking figure. This is appropriate in that Ericsson was from Sweden and shares the same name as famous Viking explorer Leif Ericsson. There is no proof that John Ericsson was related to Leif though they share the same name. Ericsson is a very common name in Scandinavia that may only indicate a relation to a man named Eric. This Viking imagery is interesting given the possibilities of early Viking exploration of North America long before other Europeans came and claimed it. The figure of the Viking with the Yrggdrasil tree may give us some metaphor and imagery that goes beyond the heritage of Ericsson. The Vikings were early explorers and expert navigators so it is appropriate that this monument also represents a sighting device used to indicate places of talismanic importance within the city of Washington D.C.

The portion of the statue representative of labor incudes and muscular male figure that does not have any obvious connections to any historical or mythical figure.

The statue of the theme of vision is obviously representative of the goddess or female deity. Given the location of this memorial it may be assumed that this figure is representative of the Goddess Columbia or Goddess of Freedom. This monument points due north directly to the nearby Lincoln Memorial and both monuments refer to the Civil War era of American history. As we may see this monument coupled with the Lincoln Memorial may be telling us hidden secrets of American history associated with President Lincoln.

Prior that that discussion lets examine the other places this monument 'points to' on the map of Washington D.C.

The most impressive or interesting targets of the Ericsson axis are the White House, Jefferson Memorial, National Holocaust Museum, and the House of the Temple. The White House, House of the Temple (Southern District of the Scottish Rite), and Jefferson Memorial all sit on what is known of as the White House Meridian sometimes referred to as the "Sacred Longitude." This is notable in our studies of the Sacred Longitude.

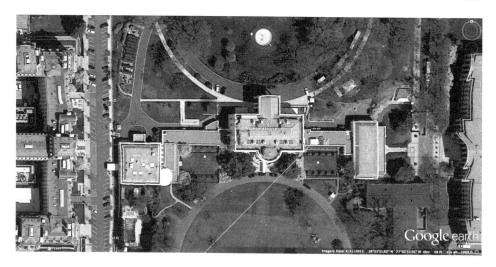

The Ericsson Memorial points the way to three locations on the White House Meridian including: The White House, House of the Temple, and Jefferson Memorial.

239

The White House Meridian including Joaquin Miller Cabin, Meridian Hill Park, Scottish Rite Temple, Lafayette Park, The White House, Jefferson Memorial, Abingdon House, Regan National Airport, Woodrow Wilson Bridge, Ft. Washington, Accokeek Maryland, and Rose Hill Maryland. Each place has an association with important American History and Presidents.

Chapter 15: Chico California and the Arcadian Mysteries

The layout of Washington D.C. may be an important factor in the Arcadian Mysteries of North America. The Alexander family was one of several Scottish families that played a role in the development of the City. Members of the Alexander family owned much of the land that would become Washington D.C. and one of their homes, Abingdon was located on what would become the White House Meridian. Their influence is seen in many historical questions that seemed to have been presented to the public as treasure myths including Oak Island, Rennes le Chateau, the Frenchman's Tower of Palo Alto and more. All of these historical goings on also seem to be related to the Jacobite cause that valued the lost Stewart Kings of England, Scotland, and Ireland including Bonnie Prince Charlie and James II.

Later Californian Joaquin Miller displayed that he was aware of the importance of the plan of Washington D.C. as he seemed to value the White House Meridian. He lived in a log cabin on the Meridian near what is today Meridian Hill Park in northern Washington D.C. He then retied to Oakland and built his estate and pyramid exactly due south of the peak of Mt. Shasta. He may have done this in response to him becoming aware of the entire scheme of important places in America. Joaquin had travelled extensively in Europe due to the popularity of his book "My life Amongst the Modocs." Western stories and culture fascinated Europeans of the pre and post Civil War era in America. Miller may have indeed been one of our Society of the Cincinnati literary agents at that time and many of his activities and associations may bear this out. Joaquin Miller even seemed to have had an effect on later historical trends including the Beat Generation and later Psychedelic and "Hippie" movements in the San Francisco Bay Area.

The Frenchman's Tower story has shown us how the influence of this philosophy even extends to the development of a small town in Northern California named Chico. The founders of Chico John and Annie Bidwell had a profound influence and also likely took part in the same tradition of using representative architecture that we have seen at each place along the way. As it turns out Bidwell and his wife Annie were showing us a great deal about Washington D.C. in the design of the street plan of Chico.

The design of Chico is based on some of the same concepts we see at play in the development of Washington D.C. including the original eight by eight block diamond shape of the original plan of Chico that mimics the ten mile a sided diamond shape of the original boundaries of the District of Columbia. The southern tip of the Washington D.C. diamond is in Alexandria Virginia named for the Alexander family that we have seen involved in the development of Nova Scotia and the United States. The southern tip of the diamond of Chico sits on the latitude of the Mason Dixon Line as do Indianapolis, Denver, and others. These towns and cities may have been intentionally developed on this latitude. What other proof may there be that Chico is associated with Washington D.C.?

John Bidwell ran for President at one time as part of a political party that supported women's rights and the prohibition of alcohol. At that time in history many of those points of view were not widely valued and although Bidwell made an admirable showing in the election he lost. He also ran for governor of California twice and lost. He did serve a single term as Congressman from California and it was during his time in Washington D.C. that he met his future wife Annie Ellicott Kennedy. His time in Washington D.C. may have also exposed him to the inner circle of families discussed in this book that all were part of the D.C. scene at that time. This would include elements of the Beale and Alexander families. It is likely that Bidwell had also met Annie's sister Sarah "Sallie" Jane Alexander (Kennedy).

John Bidwell himself held a family legacy stemming from the first families of Hartford Connecticut. Many of these families including the Hooker's, Beale's, Bacon's, and Bidwell's would go on to play prominent roles in the development of the west as the country grew. Of course much of the middle part of what is today the United States was skipped over by settlers heading to the Gold Fields of California. This is one of the reasons that California developed quickly ahead of many mid-western and western states prior to the Civil War. California played an important role in the Civil War and it is clear that the golden riches of both the Golden State and Nevada were controlled by the Union side of that conflict. This also included John Bidwell who was a General in the California Militia at that time. Robert Beale was also a U.S. Army General and Surveyor General of California during this era.

As we will see even the Coutts banking family had a hand in the development of Hartford Connecticut and its many symbolic connections to Chico. A Coutts or Colt (same name and family documented) accompanied Reverend Hooker in his move to establish what would become Hartford Connecticut. This would solidly link this entire group of early colonist's later families to the establishment of cities and town across the U.S. that seemed to mark special places on the globe that were important to them. This would also include the legacy of descendants stemming from the same Bacon family that Sir Francis Bacon had come from as they are prominently listed on the Hartford Founders Monument with all of these other important families.

The involvement of the Hartford families may have had the goal of helping to establish the New Atlantis envisioned by Sir Francis Bacon. This concept may serve to explain why certain towns and cities seem to have been valued by this group of people who may have established legends like Oak Island at many of these locations. A string of "New Atlanitis'" and "New Jerusalems" had been constructed in this manner that all included representative art and architecture that tells a historical story that may commonly be overlooked.

How is Chico related to Washington D.C. and the Arcadian Mysteries? While it may be easy to ascribe the plan of Chico to John Bidwell who designed it himself it may be that his wife Annie also was a major influence in why the town has a plan that resembles a miniature Washington D.C. Annie Bidwell was from Washington D.C. and had met John while he was a Congressman. At first, she resisted Mr. Bidwell's desire to make her his wife. After John promised to ban alcohol and adapt her Presbyterian faith she relented and agreed to marry Bidwell and come live in Chico. It is possible though unknown that Annie at this time also expressed a desire to represent her family's legacy in the design of the new town.

Annie Bidwell's family legacy links us directly to connections to the Beale and Alexander families who were at that time prominent citizens of Washington D.C. Both the Beale's and Alexander's had played roles in the establishment of the city and served as commissioners who facilitated the establishment of the District of Columbia. This also included a member of the Stuart family. Robert Beale Surveyor General of California also owned Decatur House located on Lafayette Square just north of the White House itself. Lafayette Square is one of the prominent features located on the White House Meridian.

Annie Ellicott Bidwell (Kennedy) is a direct relative of Andrew Ellicott via her father who had, along with Pierre L'Enfant designed the city's plan. It is likely due to this relation that Annie's middle name was Ellicott. After L'Enfant withdrew his services in the design Andrew Ellicott reproduced the plan from memory and actually laid out the pattern of streets and original boundaries of the District of Columbia that are the subject of so much conjecture today. The original plan of Washington D.C. is a ten mile a side diamond. This is also the plan of Chico on a smaller scale.

In addition, Annie Bidwell's younger sister Sarah Jane "Sallie" Kennedy married prominent Washington D.C. lawyer Thomson Hankey Alexander. Thomson Hankey Alexander was a direct lineal descendant of Sir William Alexander the 1st Earl of Stirling who had written a portion of Philip Sidney's "Arcadia" that leads us to Oak Island Nova Scotia. This is almost too much to believe but here we are seeing a thematic and philosophical link that spans all the way from Nova Scotia, to Washington D.C. then westward to the small unassuming town of Chico California and the legacy of John and Annie Bidwell. Et in Arcadia Ego in California.

Eminent and Representative Men of Virginia and the District of Columbia in the Nineteenth Century

Thomson H. Alexander

Thomson H. Alexander is a native of Kentucky and a descendant of the old and well known Scotch family, i.e. Earles of Stirling, an authentic record of which is traced back in an unbroken succession. Among the remote ancestors was Robert Alexander, after whom in regular order are recorded the names of John, Robert and James, the last named of whom was born in the year 1624. The son of James was John Alexander, whose son William was the great-grandfather of the immediate subject of this biography, William Alexander, the grandfather, was a native of Scotland, born in the year 1729. In early boyhood he was taken to France and came to America, settling in Virginia, where he resided until 1811, at which time he emigrated to Kentucky, where his death occurred in 1819 at the advanced age of ninety years. William Alexander was a man of more than ordinary powers of mind and during his life succeeded in accumulating a handsome fortune. He was twice married, his second wife having been Miss Agatha De LaPorte, a member of an ancient and honorable French family which acquired more than a local reputation in France. The ancestral home of the LaPortes is at the town of Montpelier. The eldest son of William Alexander, William Alexander Jr., uncle to the subject of this sketch was created Lord Chief Baron of the Exchequer and prior to his elevation thereto had received the order of knighthood. Charles Alexander, father of Thomson H. Alexander, was born near Staunton, Virginia in 1798 and was by profession a lawyer in which calling he earned a brilliant reputation. He was also a man of fine literary ability and as a linguist stood very high among the scholars of his native state, having mastered the ancient, classical and several modern languages. He removed with his parents, to Woodford County, Kentucky, in 1811, where he resided until 1857, at which time he became a resident of Washington, D.C., where his death occurred in July 1883. **His wife, whom he married in 1821 was Miss Martha Madison, a grandniece of James Madison, fourth President of the United States.**

As already mentioned, Thomson H. Alexander is a native of Kentucky, born in the beautiful blue grass county of Woodford on the 25th day of February 1837. His early educational training was received in the schools of his native county, and after taking a more than thorough course in New Albany, Indiana, he removed, in 1856 to Washington, D.C., where he entered upon the study of the law, which profession he had early determined to to make his life work. After acquiring proficiency in his chosen calling he was admitted to the bar of the District of Columbia, where his abilities soon won for him a very lucrative share of the legal business of the city. The war coming on about this time he abandoned his profession temporarily and responded to the country's call for volunteers enlisting April 15, 1861 in the old national rifles for the defense of Washington City, which was then in danger of being captured by the rebels. Later after all danger to the city was averted by the withdrawal of the Confederate forces from the vicinity he marched with his company to aid in the defense of Harper's Ferry, which at that time was threatened by the Confederate forces organized especially for its capture.

At the expiration of his term of service, Mr. Alexander returned to Washington and resumed the practice of his profession, which he has since successfully continued, being at the time one of the best known and most successful patent lawyers in that department of the profession, in the city.

Mr. Alexander's legal career is a series of uninterrupted successes and his high reputation in the special field of jurisprudence alluded to, makes him an authority on all matters pertaining to patent law upon which he has also written at various times and his opinions relating thereto, have almost uniformly been sustained by the courts. In all relations of life, both in a public and private capacity Mr. Alexander has won the respect and confidence of his fellow citizens and during a long legal career, his many clients have learned to trust him as a wise and judicious counselor. He was united in marriage to **Miss Sarah J. Kennedy, daughter of Hon. J.C.G. Kennedy, formerly Superintendent of the Census Bureau.**

This amazing family relation between the Bidwell's and Alexander's of Washington D.C. is astounding given what we have already learned about the Alexander family. Thomson Alexander has all the important connections to have made him a person of great importance in the propagation of their family philosophy including the themes of Sir Francis Bacon and Sir Philip Sidney. Also impressive is the connections to France and the family's direct relation to the family of 4th President of the United States James Madison. Explained in this short memorial for Thomson Alexander is the reason why Madison's estate is called "Montpelier." It seems the

President valued the French connections in his heritage and had named his estate due to this value. Also notable is the association with the de La Porte family group that has many genetic intermarriages with the de La Tour families including the Marquis de Lafayette's forebear and daughter. Really the evidence is mounting that all of these mysteries have a uniquely American flavor to them as these people and their French cohorts were all aware of and valued the history inferred at all of these places of intrigue. Annie Bidwell had direct family relations to Andrew Ellicott and the Alexander family linking her family's legacy all the way from Oak Island to Chico California where the same concepts are indeed expressed. This of course includes the plan of Washington D.C. as she was undoubtedly aware of the significance of these factors in her heritage.

Other prominent family names that took part in the development of Chico and the surrounding region also include members of the Bacon and Bruce families that are also linked to the Alexander's and others. An early resident of Chico was Wilhelm Bruce who had been a bodyguard of Napoleon himself. Both Baxter de Vere Bacon and Hardy de Vere Bacon were related to earlier Butte County resident Thomas Lafayette Bacon. Even the names used here infer a knowledge of what may be termed the Arcadian Mysteries and all of these people were privy to the importance of places like the Frenchman's Tower of Palo Alto and later myths like the Legend of J.C. Brown which we have examine prior here.

Even the filming of the movie "Robin Hood" in Chico during the 1930's links us to the historical character of a member of the de Vere family that may have been the real "Robin Hood" in English history. Over time modern media has also been used in a similar manner to how literature had been designed to promote the culture and ideals of a given group or organization such as the United States or France.

The use of the Bacon, Lafayette, and de Vere names by a single family may be clues that tell us that these people were actually using the legacy of Bacon's "New Atlantis" in their roles in the development of important places like Washington D.C. and Chico California. In this way we are also looped back to the involvement of Mary Sidney Herbert Countess of Pembroke, her brother Philip Sidney, and her sons William and Philip Herbert. William and Philip Herbert were the subject of the dedication of the famous First Folio of Shakespeare's works that has gained a status in the mysteries similar to that of the streets of Washington D.C. and may also include information leading us to Oak Island and other similar questions in early American and Canadian history.

All of these places of importance in turn link us to the mysteries of Peter Lassen, the first Masonic Charter of California and finally Mt. Shasta itself. All of these places have talismanic mythology and lore that is meant to be properly interpreted given the connections we see here. All of these factors may be considered when reading the below account of how and why John and Annie Bidwell are important people to this family group. It is even possible that John and Annie were brought together in part by their family legacies and that somehow, they were matched due to these associations. Both families had links to the Society of the Cincinnati and the development of the American ideal that in turn was expressed via our cast of authors, artists, and architects which tell us the true story of American history in symbols, allegory, and metaphor.

The Axis of John Bidwell at Chico. The Hooker Oak and the legacy of Hartford Connecticut.

1n 1873 John Bidwell preformed a ceremony very similar to that of Constantine the Great in founding Constantinople to found his town Chico in northern California. The Chico City Plaza stands as an Axis Mundi created by Bidwell. Its modern form even includes a mosaic of the earth in its fountain. The downtown original street plan of Chico seems to have been fashioned after the chessboard as chess was the favorite of the Egyptian goddess Ishtar. In the chessboard layout of Chico the City Plaza sits in the Queens square. An examination of the life and family connections of John Bidwell may reveal why and how he was even aware of such a ceremony.

The Chessboard city plan of Chico is also seemingly intentionally oriented on the latitude of the Mason Dixon line as are the cities of Indianapolis and Denver. Those two cities origins may have had a strong input from members of the Society of the Cincinnati. Indeed some of Bidwell's ancestors were eligible for membership in the Society so some association between that organization and the origins of Chico is possible. Bidwell built his Mansion in line with the northwest orientation of the City Plaza. The City Plaza 'points to' Bidwell Mansion.

This alignment also includes the foundation stone of Chico at the NW end of the city plaza. Over time the array in Chico also came to include a tower that is somewhat of an architectural folly. In addition other groups like the Rosicrucian Order and the Cistercian Order of monks may also have come to be aware of and value what Bidwell had created in Chico. Thickening the plot is the fact that two of the greatest businessmen and builders of California Leland Stanford and William Randolph Hearst also seemed to value what John Bidwell had created. An examination of John Bidwell's ancestry connects him to both First Families of New England and Norman royalty that has a pedigree that includes Charlemagne and all the Latin Kings of Jerusalem.

The entire reason that Bidwell may have been sent to the future site of Chico displays a distinct value of the axis of the International Peace Garden. The Chico City Plaza does not point to the IPG. The International Peace Garden points to Chico! Using the regular octagonal division at a bearing of 247.5 degrees true north an azimuth on the globe may be produced that intersects with the northern boundary of the City of Chico. As this scale in this era this is a direct hit. Bidwell seems to have properly placed his axis. At first this may seem a chance association. On closer inspection it may be revealed that this is the reason Chico was founded where it is.

Later in the 1930's Chico was home to part of Warner Brothers Studios and Warner Street is named thus. Errol Flynn lived in the Chico area for three years around the time he starred in "Robin Hood" which was in part filmed in Bidwell Park in Chico. During this era the Senator Theatre was constructed on the corner of fifth and Main streets just diagonal from the Chico City Plaza. Erroll Flynn had once been interested in investing money in the recovery of the Oak Island Treasure and may have looked for the lost treasure of Peter Lassen while he was in the area. It is thought Flynn did not invest in Oak Island because fellow actor John Wayne already had.

As it turns out Chico has many connections to "New Age" figures from many different eras. Mt. Shasta is only about a three hour drive from Chico though it is visible from just north of town. John Bidwell once made a trip to Mt. Shasta with his wife Annie and an interesting cast of characters both associated with a Harvard intellectual naturalist Asa Gray and another naturalist from English gentry J.D. Hooker who was related to Harford Connecticut founder Reverend Hooeker. These connections to Chico have not been discussed in the past and may reveal some amazing and startling realities that do apply to many of the movements and philosophies of the twenty-first century.

The Senator Theater was designed by Bohemian Club and 'Family' member architect Timothy Pflueger. On the corner as part of the design a large tower was constructed that seems to resemble what is known as the 'staff of Ishtar.' Other parts of the theatre's design include gargoyles and dragons in its motif. Pflueger was also a member of 'The Family' an organization begun by William Randolph Hearst after some disagreements with the Bohemian Club of which Hearst was also a member. The staff of Ishtar is somewhat analogous to the spear of Pallas Athena as well. Athena is interpreted by many to be an evolution of the concept of Ishtar. The theme of Ishtar and Pallas Athena is repeated in another talismanic piece of architecture in Chico as well. The tower of the Senator Theater is also tipped with a large glass diamond finial that represents the premiere symbol of Chico and may also link us back to a value of this symbol in the original plan of the boundaries of Washington D.C.

The tower in Chico is directly diagonal of the city plaza and may have been built in the tradition of an alchemical tower in the form of a folly as well. The diamond is one of the symbols of Chico and later the Diamond Match Company would play a large role in Chico's development. During the nineteenth century a match was known as a 'Lucifer.' Later in Chico history an man named Baxter de Vere Bacon would be a prominent high level employee of the Diamond Match and Timber Company.

Amazingly a symbol is seen in the diamond motif of this tower that is common to many of the mysteries of North America. If viewed from the appropriate distance the large glass diamond atop the tower reveals the Auspice of Maria (Mary) symbol. The auspice of Maria symbol is a combination of the letters A, V, and M. Some forms of this symbol also suggest the letter X. A common interpretation of this symbol would suggest "Ave Maria" thus referring to Mary Mother of Christ. This symbol may have seen somewhat less use later in history due to its similarity to the Masonic Compass and Square symbol. Many important symbols have been used and later neglected by the Latin Church. The symbols of the Phoenix, Skull and Bones, All Seeing Eye, and Auspice of Maria later all saw use by Masonic groups possibly leading to them being intentionally neglected by the Church who sometimes seems to oppose Masonic organizations. The shape of the diamond is also present within the Auspice of Maria symbol.

During the filming of "Robin Hood" The Tower Bar at the base of the tower was closed for Eroll Flynn's use exclusively. This arrangement conjures images of Flynn partying in the alchemical tower. As we may see Flynn's fascination with Chico after the filming was through may be telling. This man stayed in the Chico area near Vina for two years after the movie was done. Flynn was said to have spent a great deal of time at Richardson Springs near Chico. This may fit with the ritual bathing habits of some secret societies. He was known to have been fascinated by lost treasures and Masonic lore. Errol Flynn was rumored to be a member of the Rosicrucian Order based in San Jose. Though Richardson Springs once seemed to be a hot springs resort oriented towards the Masonic and Rosicrucian set today it is owned by a Christian group that uses it for a retreat.

Many things have been added to alignments using the shape and orientation of the Chico City Plaza since the time of Bidwell. The northwest azimuth or line extending from the plaza seems to be the most valued. This northwest side of the city plaza also contains what is likely considered the foundation stone of Chico. This large granite boulder has a plaque affixed, which tells of Bidwell's donation of the space for the City Plaza to the citizens of Chico. This northwest trending azimuth or line next includes a building designed E.H. Minton that used to be a Bank of America building. Minton designed many Bank of America buildings at this time. He was a Harvard educated architect that did not seem to be part of any secret societies or groups. He was Catholic and this may fit into the reason he was involved in designing this structure for a powerful bank also owned by a Catholic American. Adjacent to the old bank building situated directly on this arc on the globe is a large and well executed mural of John and Annie Bidwell.

The old B of A building itself resembles some descriptions of the old Temple in Jerusalem and may well represent a kind of "Rosslyn Chapel" of Chico. The entrances to the building are reminiscent of the Ishtar's Gate of Babylonia. The exterior of the building is decorated by cement relief sculptures of Ishtar/Athena, Prometheus giving fire to man, Hermes, A Masonic character, and two other enigmatic seals one depicting a seal (sea creature) dominating a second seal and another depicting a bear dominating a lion. A large stylized letter "I" decorates the top corner of the building on the corner of Broadway and Second.

The façade of the building also includes an octagon with a sailing vessel within it as well as other elements depicting birds of prey and ears of corn. These are all goddess symbols. Directly across the street today is a Citibank and its octagonal logo. Just up the street the owners of a popular Mexican Restaurant used the same cement molds used in the construction of the decorations on the original Bank of America building to decorate the façade of their business after a fire. The corner of this building now incudes the large letter "I" that is included on the old bank building. The building occupied by this restaurant was once used as a brewery owned by John Bidwell.

The Phoenix Birds included in the band of artwork near the top rim of the structure is a repeated design that alternates with what appear to be ears of corn. Amazingly each Phoenix is rising out of a chalice inferring the "Holy Grail" or Lapis Excillis. Both of these themes again were at one time manifestations of the Church and its followers. Similar interpretations of sculpture at Rosslyn Chapel have been made by many.

The southwest side of the "Ishtar" building includes two strange seals or coats of arms. One of the designs includes a seal (animal) atop another seal as if in domination. The other design includes a Bear dominating a Lion. This second design may represent the California Bear Flag Republic breaking away from Mexico and its imperial overtones. The presences of the Bear may also be indicative of the presence of Merovingian influence in Chico. The Bear in metaphor may represent the theme of Arcadia and the Pole Star as it seemed to be valued by people who believed in the bloodline of Christ and Mary Magdalene. The entire concept of "Arcadia" is laid bare by analyzing the artwork present at both Anson estates Shugborough Hall and Moor Park in England. This array of artwork including the famous Shepherds Monument also reveals a distinct association between Arcadia and the "Wilton Circle" of Countess of Pembroke Mary Sidney extending possibly even to Sir Francis Bacon.

All of these concepts are related to the image of the Bear as seen on the California flag that even includes a star representative of Polaris. It is not certain what the design including the seals represents. The seal was one of the symbols of Alistair Crowley the famous Masonic magi who promoted his faith of Thelema via the Ordo Templi Orientis. An order name that may have one interpretation "Order of the Oriented Temple."

The old Bank of America building in Chico does display a stunning relationship in symbols to many of the other mysteries of North America including the Kensington Rune and Archer reliquary of Jamestown. Both these mysteries are also linked to a kind of relic of the phenomenon of the "hidden Catholic" in colonial America. Many of these people went on to form a Jacobite power base that contributed a great deal to the concept of the American Republic.

Hidden among the Birds that line the upper pediment of the building is the Auspice of Mary symbol combined with the same strange X featured on the Kensigton Rune. This X may be representative of the Chi-Rho symbol that includes the Alpha and Omega symbol. The lower case Omega that is used in that symbol resembles a fisherman's hook. In addition the figure of the bird is seen rising from what appears to be a "Grail Cup" Lapis Excillis. This figure of what may be interpreted as a Phoenix is rising from a chalice with the AVM and X symbols emblazoned on its breast. This is a direct reference to many Jacobite Masonic symbols. The concept of the Holy Grail is suggested in direct association with this motif. It is almost as if this old Bank of America in Chico serves as a twentieth century version of Rosslyn Chapel and Chateau Abbadia. Stories are being told in the artwork included in this grand building.

This motif is seen on the chest of these birds and is meant to suggest an arrangement of feathers on the chest of the bird that matches the art deco style of the entire building. The Auspice of Maria symbol is upside down and appears to be dangling from the beak of the bird. This bird is likely also representative of the Phoenix and American Bald Eagle that many refer to as a metaphor for the Phoenix. Connected to the upside down tip of the letter "A" in the Auspice of Mary symbol is the letter "W." This design both infers the Diamond symbol associated with Chico, The Auspice of Mary, and the strange X shaped font seen in other mysteries.

The letter "W" is discussed in association with Sir Francis Bacon is representative of the number 66. Again the letter "A" with the "V" shaped crossbar also suggests the diamond symbol of Chico. All of these symbols are present in a tapestry that was personally created by Mary Queen of Scots who is also one of the largest Jacobite symbols in the movement. All of this symbology relates directly to her family including Charles I and II, James I, Elizabeth of Bohemia, and even possibly St. Germain himself. It is likely that the inclusion of these somewhat hidden symbols in this art is not a coincidence. These symbols would have also held a special value for the Alexander's, Beale's, Bidwell's, Kennedy's and others stemming from the first families of Jamestown, Plymouth, Hartford, and others.

Most notable is that the bird or Phoenix that is included in this rendering seems to be rising from a "Grail Cup." Birds like this compose the entire upper band of decoration on two sides of the structure. Up until the mid 1990's this structure was not painted and the cement reliefs were harder to see and did resemble stone. A later owner decorated the reliefs in bright colors reminiscent of the Aztec culture since the building was being used as a Mexican restaurant. When the structure was decorated the artist chose to make the cup shaped design blue in a possibly unintentional metaphor that matches the concept of the "Lapis Excillis" or Lucifer's stone. Of course the concept of the "Grail Chalice" has many different meanings including those associated with Mary Magdalene. Again our hidden Catholics and other Jacobites seem to be presenting us with Mary Magdalene as an object of veneration. Or are they really telling us the standard story of Mother Mary that matches the "straight" interpretation of the Auspcie of Mary or Maria symbol. This symbol does indeed resemble the Masonic Compass and Square as well.

The Auspice of Mary Symbol is also hidden in what is considered to be the symbol of Chico. The Diamond has always been a motif popular in local companies including the famous Diamond Match Company that once owned a large timber concern in Chico. The diamond's association with Chico is illustrated by the large glass diamond finial atop the Tower of the Senator Theatre. This tower is diagonal to the City Plaza itself. A sacred tower or Magdala is many times included in such arrays of architecture and art. Within the diamond pattern of facets in this glass decoration plainly visible is the AVM or Auspice of Mary symbol.

The inclusion of these symbols somewhat hidden in this particular building is notable and is directly related to many mysterious events and goings on in Northern California history. This old bank may represent the presence of a group of people that opposed the kind of philosophy held by town founder John Bidwell. It may also be that both side of this struggle were operating with the assumption that they were all in favor of a strong Republic. These squabbles were somewhat based on faith and secular notions that came into contrast with each other at times. The addition of new faith based institutions and concepts such as the Mormon faith and New Age ideas may have been seen as a threat to the part of this American group that still valued the Catholic Church. So while confusing two sides are beginning to emerge.

One side were American idealists who still had ties to family and gentry in the old world that they worked together with in business terms. One part of this group were solidly Catholic if not

Jesuit. This group was opposed by another group that had also played a large role in the creation of the United States who seemed to favor the doctrine of Thomas Jefferson's secular views regarding the role of religion in government. Among this faction were the seeds of what would later become the "New Age." This faction was also tolerant of every form of religion but did not want it to dictate the policies of government. The Catholic faith has seeming at times played a meddlesome hand in politics in the United States at times. These activities would always garner a response from the "other" side. It may be that this side of the coin would have also favored the formation of the Mormon faith or any other that did not adhere to the doctrine of the Catholic Church. Many of the founding fathers though Christian favored a form of government in which no faith played a central role. Among these factions may be seen the early distant rumblings of the Civil War. Along the way a prodigious amount of mudslinging and skulldugerous operations were carried out by both sides that sometimes left the public bewildered in understanding any of it.

It is possible even at times that Jesuits had posed as secular Masons and visa versa. Each side seemed to know the intimate inner workings of the other's symbolic and mythological beliefs and this information was deemed weapons grade at any given time.

The AVM, X, and W symbols are amazing in the context of what has been reveled in past work. Here again is a reference that is also seen in the Rennes le Chateau mystery as well as the strange phenomena of the Great Cyclic Cross of Hendaye and a similar cross in Sara, France. The Auspice of Maria is repeated in Ronda Spain as indicated by the Great Cyclic Cross of Hendaye both in the inscription of Palacio de Monctezuma and Palacio de Salvatierra. We will see all these places linked to California via the interest and influence of William Randolph Hearst. This is all relative to the reasons people associated with Henri Artois would have built the Frenchman's Tower in Palo Alto and why Joaquin Miller, the Dunsmuir's, Muir, and others seem to hold these same values. This style of the letter "A" with the "V" shaped crossbar also seems to have originated in Greece the original land of Arcadia.

Moving north from the center of the City Plaza the alignment includes the old Chico Masonic lodge now the Blue Room (Blue Lodge) Theatre, the World War I memorial, a recently added reproduction of the labyrinth at Chartres Cathedral, Bidwell Mansion, and The Gateway Science Museum and its diamond shaped logo. Bidwell mansion is a grand Victorian structure built in a kind of Italian Renaissance style that includes a central tower over the entryway. This home resembles the caretaker's house at Tower Grove Park in St. Louis that served as a kind of base of operations for the Linnean Society of London.

Next this alignment may include the reason Bidwell oriented the City Plaza the way he did originally. The azimuth now extends about eighteen miles northwest to just west of the small town of Vina, California. On its transect to Vina the line crosses a road named the Cana Highway. Many Gnostics believe that Jesus and Mary were wed at the wedding at Cana. One may suspect this may be the true origin of the name of the country of Canada. To some the Wedding at Cana is also related to the story of Lazarus and how Jesus brought him back from the dead. Some conspiracies dictate that Lazarus had been drugged with a substance that made him appear dead and this is what Christ had done to appear dead at the crucifixion. A closer investigation even reveals a man named Thomas Lafayette Bacon buried in a cemetery included on this alignment. Later his descendants would live nearby including Baxter de Vere Bacon and Hardy de Vere Bacon.

The structure of the Vina School near the Monastery resembles the plan of the Palace of the Legion of Honor in San Francisco. Strangely the orientation of this building points an arc on the globe to Peter Lassen's grave about thirty miles away in Lassen County near Susanville. This is an amazing connection to the story of Lassen bringing the first Masonic Charter to come to California on the same property where the school is now located. The pediment above the doorway to the school even includes two dragons flanking a shield that includes the fleur di lies design of French nobility. Some branches of the de Vere family do indeed include similar imagery. This is quite a coincidence given the other geographic relationships to monuments and architecture in the area. Much of this imagery would come to include the mysteries and legends of Mt. Shasta as well. This design may also further link us to the kind of Scottish and French cultural alliances we see in all the families involved here. Echoes of the Frenchman's Tower of Palo Alto seem to extend to Vina and the well designed and constructed school there.

Next the arc on the globe extending northwest from the Chico City Plaza extends to property that was originally the ranch of well known Californian Peter Lassen who nearby Lassen County and Lassen Peak is named for. Lassen was a Danish citizen that had much in common with Bidwell both publicly and secretly. Lassen originally planned a small town on his property named Benton

City but lost all of his money in a scheme to use large steamboats on the Sacramento River. He lost all his money when the one boat he bought foundered in the river. Prior to that Lassen did bring the very first Masonic Charter from St. Louis to California at his Vina Ranch. Lassen often hosted famous western explorer Captain John Fremont and his troops on his property which he named Benton City. Benton City was named for Fremont's father in law Missouri Senator Thomas Hart Benton.

This fact that he was friends with Lassen and that the first Masonic Charter had come there may have been significant enough for John Bidwell to orient the City Plaza towards that point on earth. All of the subsequent talismans added to this alignment may have been in veneration of this fact. Bidwell may have been aligning his town with that of his friend Lassen. Perhaps the Chico City Plaza would have pointed to a similar structure in Benton City as Lassen planned on naming his town. This alignment of Bidwell's would have aligned him with the only Masonic Lodge in California at that time. Later we will see how, in a very strange way, this Masonic Charter is but one small clue in the mysteries of Mt. Shasta. The original Masonic Lodge in Chico is part of the northwest trending line that points to the site of Benton City.

As a coincidence, a local legend states that Lassen left a large hidden treasure of gold stashed in iron pots somewhere on the property. This may have been what interested Errol Flynn and coaxed him to stay in Chico for so long. Long before Flynn when Lassen died the next owner of this property was none other than Leland Stanford coincidentally the new owner of the Frenchman's Tower in Palo Alto. This fact fits the trend of treasure legends being attached to geographic mysteries. From this point on the same names continually arise in this topology of whimsical architecture in California. These riches were somehow associated with Lassen by some via his Royal Danish connections as well as the "wealthy family" of St. Louis he was supposedly related to.

It may be possible that California Governor and U.S. Senator Leleand Stanford valued this place because Lassen had brought the first Masonic charter there. Bidwell seemed to have taken this into consideration when orienting his City Plaza, which is not plumb with the cardinal directions or with the equinox. Interestingly the city plaza is oriented about four degrees east of true north. This would make the total of each even 45 degree direction suggested by the orientation of the plaza total the number 13 (319 3+1+9=13; 4+9=13; 1+8+4=13 even 3+6+0+4=13). If John Bidwell's "mistake" in not orienting the City Plaza and streets of Chico to true north was intentional then this still displays a distinct value and use of the Pole Star.

If Bidwell had oriented the City Plaza to four degrees east of true north then a value or knowledge of the Pole Star is then a given. In this way John Bidwell was showing us his value of "Arcadia" and how it applied in California as possibly part of his family legacy. Coincidentally one of Bidwell's largest business endeavors is located directly across the Esplanade from Bidwell Mansion. Bidwell was the owner of one of the largest grain mills in Northern California aptly named Northern Star Mills. It is interesting that Bidwell chose to name his business after the Pole Star given his possible ancestral value of this concept. Arcas is the namesake of Arcadia. Arcas is Ursa Minor whose tail includes the Pole Star. Also of note is the name of the

Esplanade that is a major north to south thoroughfare in Chico. An Esplanade is defined as a large open way or plaza associated with an Axis Mundi as represented by the City Plaza. This term may also apply to the linear aspects of many parks and monuments like the National Mall and International Peace Garden.

Chico is also home to an odd memorial that no one is really sure where it came from. When one enquires at the Bidwell Mansion museum what this strange monument is no one can really give you a straight answer. About 50 yards behind Bidwell Mansion is a strange circular arrangement of cut and polished granite set at ground level. This arrangement is about 30 yards in diameter and has four openings in the stone circle that is suggested. In the center of the circle is what appears to have once been a grinding stone from Northern Star Mills about 200 yards away to the east. There are no sources as to what this monument is though it is close enough to Bidwell Mansion to be considered as part of the alignment that also "points to" Bidwell Mansion and the Monastery of New Clairvaux from the Chico City Plaza.

One tour guide at Bidwell Mansion did mention that they thought this was a memorial to the location of the Mechoopda Tribe's Round House. A Round House in the Native culture of the Central valley was a kind of central feature to a settlement where meetings and councils were held. It is remotely possible that this structure reminded John Bidwell of his family legacy that included a value of such places as viewed in Western Culture. The assumption that this memorial represents the Mechoopda Tribe's roundhouse is likely a valid assumption. Some historical notes do mention a Round House somewhere adjacent to Bidwell Mansion to the west. It is notable here that this place was the site of a memorial that mimics the shape or plan of a round house while also being located on a talismanic alignment created by John Bidwell in what appears to have been an ancient family tradition. Today the Mechoopda Tribe is a viable entity in Chico and Butte County that does include descendants of John Bidwell.

After Stanford purchased the Vina property that Lassen once owned he ran what was considered the largest vineyard in the world at that time. Eventually it was decided the climate was too hot to make good wine so production shifted to Brandy. After Stanford's passing the property known as the Great Vina Ranch became the dominion of Stanford University. In addition it is noted that Stanford attempted to buy Rancho Arroyo Chico from John Bidwell on three separate occasions and two of these times the attempts may have been less than cordial. It seems almost as if Stanford was trying to gather all the available game pieces in California during that era. Is it possible that Stanford and Bidwell had different views about what Chico represented?

Why would Stanford value Chico and Lassen's Ranch so highly? Stanford already owned the property of Stanford University where the Frenchman's Tower is located. Like the Frenchman who would come later many things in the story of John Bidwell indicate that he could have been sent to where Chico was founded specifically to attain a spatial relationship with an already established octagonal axis such as the one at the International Peace Garden. In this way they may have been establishing a real or metaphorical domain in the Roman and Byzantine tradition. This may have also been the reason Stanford valued Chico. Subsequent events in the twentieth century would lend credence to the thought that this area was special to a wide variety of people with secret society and occult philosophies; More specifically the Chico City Plaza itself. The Chico City Plaza and Frenchman's Tower were created at close to the same time with the location of the City Plaza having been defined prior to the building of the Ayrshire Farm and Frenchman's Tower in Palo Alto.

Also note the similarity in the name of Chico and the Chi-Rho. Chi is the letter X in Greek and is thought to be a representation of the god and goddess symbolically. The form of the Chico City Plaza from plan view also resembles the letter X inside the letter O. This symbol is also a goddess symbol that many others wrongly associate with Lucifer or Satan. Often the Alpha and Omega symbols are included as part of the Chi Rho symbol with the lower case omega symbol possibly being an interpretation of what a "hooked X" truly means.

In 1955 on land donated by Stanford University once owned by Peter Lassen the Cistercian Abbey of New Clairvaux was established in the vicinity of Lassen's Ranch near the confluence of Deer Creek and the Sacramento River. New Clairvaux is a Cistercian Monastery named after the first Abbey of Clairvaux established in France by St. Bernard himself.

Note here that St. Bernard was originally a member of the Carthusian Order as was St. Hugh of Avalon the Bishop of Lincoln. New Clairvaux is known as a Cistercian Order of Strict Observance. Today the Monastery produces fine wines and is open to the public for tastings and limited lodging for retreats. New Clairvaux is 'pointed to' by the Chico City Plaza. On property where he first Masonic charter in California was established. On property once owned by Leland Stanford and Peter Lassen. In this realm this piece of land seems to have some significance beyond the stated or obvious values.

Today the Abbey of New Clairvaux is undertaking a grand project. In 1931 newspaper magnate William Randolph Hearst purchased the remains of the Abbey of Santa Maria de Ovila near Guadalajara, Spain. The monastery was then disassembled and moved to San Francisco where the stones sat until 1994. The entrance to the monastery was eventually rebuilt on the campus of San Francisco State University. The remaining stones were donated to the Abbey of New Clairvaux where the original Chapter House from Santa Maria de Ovila is being reconstructed. William Randolph Hearst is said to have used additional stones from Santa Maria de Ovila at his home Wyntoon near Mt. Shasta. Hearst also purchased and moved another entire monastery to a place just north of Miami, Florida.

Today the stones that comprise the rebuilt chapter house at New Clairvaux are referred to as the "Sacred Stones." Many of the stones include the original Mason's marks from the 12th century guild stonemason's who created them. William Randolph Hearst was an avid art collector and also had built what is known as Hearst Castle in southern California. This man seems to have had a great appreciation for gnostic oriented Christian artwork from the past. He was known to have had a great collection of classic antiques and even built his homes in the form of medieval and ancient structures. It is possible that Hearst was aware and valued the alignment of these sacred structures as well.

It is possible Mr. Hearst was aware of this tradition. Amazingly Casa Grande or "The Big House" at Hearst Castle was somewhat modeled on the Cathedral in Ronda, Spain. This is an interesting connection to other mysteries that have been exposed here. Some of the artwork present at Hearst Castle displays the arms of the Knights of Calatrava and another carving depicts Saint James or Santiago. Casa Grande of Hearst Castle "points to" the octagonal Powder Magazine in Colonial Williamsburg.

Even though these men were not closely related it is almost as if they were being guided by some unseen and unknown hand. Blind obedience to one's unknown superiors is a trait of the Knights Templar Strict Observance. In fact this tenet of the KTSO's organization is said to be one of the reasons it became an unpopular rite within Masonry. The concept of unknown masters may fit the entire range of the creation of axes through history discussed in this book. It is unknown how this plan came together or was executed. People at later dates in time had a large hand in the planning and realization of this sacred arrangement. This type of blind obedience is also a tenet of many monastic organizations of which the Knights Templar were based on. This concept could also easily be applied to notion's of the "Ascended Master's" referenced in different Theosophical beliefs. More on that coming up.

Now we have the monastery and the eight hundred year old structure of a Cistercian Chapter House being rebuilt at another Cistercian Monastery, which is pointed to by the Chico City Plaza. On Danish Citizen Peter Lassen's Ranch where the first Masonic Charter was brought to California. The Masonic Charter signed by Lucien Stuart now resides at Mt. Shasta once the domain of the Hudson's Bay Company. On land once owned by California Senator and Governor Leland Stanford. Whew. It appears to be an important place in the history of California from many different perspectives that always don't seem to jive with each other.

This is terribly fascinating in that the original location of Santa Maria de Ovila in Spain is pointed to by the array of windrose and Egyptian obelisk present at the center of St. Peter's Square, Vatican. This structure was moved from one sacred alignment to another with the direct involvement of two very influential and prominent California families and another well connected European clan being involved over a nearly one hundred year span of time. Let's not forget John Bidwell and Joaquin Miller in the mix as well. Both the story of the Frenchman's Tower and Chico/New Clairvaux involve Leland Stanford.

John Bidwell also had ties to some other very impressive secret societies and scientific groups. He may have also been a member of the International Order of Odd Fellows (IOOF). It is not clear which rite of Masonry Bidwell belonged to but a preliminary assessment might indicate he was a York Rite Mason. Other aspects of Bidwell's family heritage seemed to guide parts of his life and character beyond his membership in the Masonic organization.

In their 1877 trip to Mt. Shasta John and Annie Kennedy Bidwell were accompanied by famous naturalist and author John Muir as well as Linnean Society of London members Asa Gray, and John Dalton Hooker. The Linnean Society of London was the English arm of an international group of botanists and naturalists that may have partially served as a cover for secret society activity. Both the story of Lewis and Clark and the Astor Party exploration have Linnean Society ties. Former Linnean Society members Pehr Kalm and Alexander Von Humboldt both displayed a keen interest and wrote of relics and the 'Holy Grail.' Some members of the Lewis family were first families of Hartford Connecticut as were the ancestors of John Bidwell.

Hooker is famous in Chico as the Bidwell's had named a huge oak in Chico in honor of him in a ceremony that is reminiscent of a similar Druidic ceremony practiced in ancient times. The Hooker Oak is on the Seal of Chico today. Dalton was Charles Darwin's brother in law. Recently samples that Darwin had collected on his famous voyage of discovery had been found in London where J.D. Hooker had misplaced them over a hundred years prior!

The phenomenon of the Hooker Oak has an aspect to it that has to this point been overlooked in studies of Chico History and John Bidwell. As it turns out the Bidwell and Hooker families were among the earliest founders of Harford Connecticut. These two families have at least three significant intermarriages in early Hartford. John D. Hooker who later visited Chico and had the oak named for him is related to the Hooker's of Hartford as well even though he was from England. Reverend Hooker is actually credited as being one of the leaders of early Hartford.

Though the Hooker Oak has since fallen wood from the tree was used to craft a gavel for the Chico City Council Chambers and benches in City Hall. Other wood from the Oak was also used in the construction of a pipe organ at California State University Chico. Though there is no record of documents having been recovered from the Hooker Oak when it fell this may have been possible as part of the veneration of the Charter Oak of Connecticut.

Amazingly one of the earliest legendary historical occurrences of Hartford involves an Oak tree known as the Charter Oak. This early story of the Charter Oak Tree also has a Hooker family member associated that was a leader in the community during colonial times and one of the main founders of the town. This large Oak tree was said to be the hiding place of Connecticut's Royal Charter of 1662. In 1687 the colonists hid the charter in this large oak so the British could not confiscate it. At this point James II attempted to revoke the charter that had been granted to the colony by James I and included an unusual degree of autonomy for Connecticut. The theme or image of the Oak Tree is a common thread linking the Arcadian Mysteries. From Oak Island to the Sidney Oak in England this image is used. The story of the Charter Oak of Connecticut also includes the fact that the charter was hidden in the tree by a Wadsworth ancestor of poet Henry Wadsworth Longfellow!

This did not suit James II. Because of this dispute The Charter Oak became a symbol of independence and is featured on the Connecticut quarter coin. The Charter went on to become the model for the United States Constitution and as well as a great symbol of freedom during the Revolutionary War thus the state's nickname "The Constitution State." The book "The History of Butte County" does include a wild tale involving "Templar Documents" being recovered from a tree in the nearby Feather River Canyon but no story like this was noted with regard to the Hooker Oak. This does not mean there were no papers there when the tree fell. It is curious such a story exists nearby to where the Hooker Oak is located.

John Bidwell naming what was thought to be the largest Oak in the world at the time after J.D. Hooker is an amazing reference to the Charter Oak from the town that Bidwell's family sprang from. The naming of an Oak for a specific person has some druidic overtones yet it is clear that Bidwell was giving us a clue as to his values and origins with this nod to the concept of the Charter Oak from a continent away in Chico California. It is no coincidence then that some of Hooker's and Bidwell's other exploits during this visit may apply to the mysteries of Mt. Shasta and the silent war at play in the northstate during this era. Many first families of Harford would go on to have an impact on the settlement and development of the west over time. Many of them came to live with John Bidwell later in Chico.

Many local Chico sources dispute John Bidwell's association with Hartford. This story may be hard to explain in relation to Bidwell's origins in any other regard but that his family did originate in Hartford Connecticut. There are many more associations to come shortly that also support this idea in grand fashion. Anyone saying that John Bidwell's family did not originate in Hartford Connecticut is wrong according to many sources.

The Linnean society still exists today and has included past luminaries such as Charles Darwin, Thomas Jefferson, and Alexander Von Humboldt as members. In fact Hooker and Darwin were related via marriage. It is not clear if Bidwell was a member of the Linnean Society or not but he was known to be friends and associates with many of its members as he had a great interest in botany and agriculture. Miller also had a known association and friendship with Muir. Bidwell honored Von Humboldt by naming Humboldt road in Chico and nearby Humboldt Peak for him. Asa Gray's nephew worked for John Bidwell for many years and is a valued person in Chico history. An examination of the genealogy of the Bidwell's and Grey's also shows some intermarriage over the years. The Grays are also an important English and Scottish family that is connected to many powerful people and organizations.

The LSOL may be responsible for the establishment of Tower Grove Park and subsequent Missouri Botanical Gardens in St. Louis. The caretaker's home at Tower Grove is of the same Italian renaissance style as Bidwell Mansion in Chico. Tower Grove Park is also home to a linear park and array of statuary that is similar to the array at the Shönbrunn Palace in Vienna, Austria ("pointed to" by an azimuth extending from the center of St. Peter's via the ENE windrose marker-home of the Habsburgs). The array at Tower Grove includes statues of Aphrodite and LSOL member Alexander Von Humboldt as well as a contrived array of ruins similar to that of the Shönbrunn Palace. St. Louis is in Missouri the same state where Peter Lassen obtained the Masonic charter he brought back to California. Chico is also home to Bidwell Park one of the largest municipal parks in the country. John Bidwell also displayed his value of Von Humboldt by naming Humboldt Road and Humboldt Peak in Butte County for him. John Bidwell's Wife Annie donated land that would become Bidwell Park in Chico one of the largest municipal parks in the country also providing a nature space for the citizens.

Linnean Society Members Pehr Kalm and Von Humboldt had previously written of their interest in the "holy grail" as well as other "relics" that may have been hidden by Europeans in North

America long before Columbus was said to have discovered the continent. These objects may have been hidden using the spatial arrangements of monuments as clues that reveal their location. Indeed part of the hidden knowledge these men valued may have included evidence that these facts were true. The Newport Tower and Kensington Runestone are part of this mystery as well. Amazingly the very relics that Kalm and Von Humboldt were curious about are associated with the same International Peace Garden and its octagon that "points to" Chico.

Chico was likely established in association with a long ago hidden axis that was left in North America the point of the future International Peace Garden. Alternately this axis had been established about the time the Hudson's Bay Company came into being and was used by them to define their territory or domain in an age-old tradition. There are many suggestions that this may be true. Chico may have been founded partly with a family interest at stake.

In veneration of this sacred point the International Peace Garden on the border of the U.S. and Canada was constructed. Today the octagonal Sunken Gardens represents what may be the oldest axis in North America. Using the common octagonal scheme the earlier axis at today's International Peace Garden points to Chico. As at Lassen's property this axis may have been a point which was claimed symbolically in the name of a Masonic order and not for a nationality or imperial power. This is why it may be rational to consider that John Bidwell was instructed to establish a subordinate axis where Chico sits today and why Peter Lassen brought the first Masonic charter in California to his ranch nearby. Both men were close enough to the azimuth from the Peace Garden to be considered 'on the line.' Both of them may have thought they were creating settlements in line with this axis.

Strangely Danish citizen Peter Lassen died in a spatial context in relation to the International Peace Garden axis that is the same as Chico. He died on the same ley line or azimuth on which Chico may have been intentionally situated (Strangely the site of his death is very near the site of the Burning Man festival in the Black Rock desert of Nevada-an axis itself). This axis may have been established by 'Scandinavian Explorers." Lassen's Danish citizenship may point to more of a story than a man seeking gold in California.

The relics that Von Humboldt and Kalm were curious about in association with the Verendrye Rune where also found in a context of being pointed to by the International Peace Garden, as is Chico. The current location of the International Peace Garden on the border of the U.S. and Canada in N. Dakota and Manitoba was likely established as an Axis long before Columbus 'discovered' America or the site was designated a peace garden. The Peace Garden is a linear park with a large octagonal axis that behaves as a directional device on the face of the earth. As such it is valued in a secret manner by different secret societies. The International Peace Garden points to Chico, The Very Large Array, Baton Rouge, Council Bluffs Iowa (City Plaza just like Chico), Georgia Guidestones, Jekyll Island Georgia, Washington D.C./Columbia Md., The Kensington Runestone, Discovery site of the 'Verendrye Rune' and L' Anse aux Meadows Viking Site, Newfoundland.

Given the Scandinavian back-story of the Kensington Rune, and possibly the International Peace Garden it is interesting that Lassen was Danish. Danish Bornholm Island in the Baltic Sea has been identified by researchers Ehrling Haagensen and Henry Lincoln as having a geometrically aligned landscape using the location of Templar Churches to form interesting geometrical patterns. There is a strong tradition of Templarism and secret societies in the Baltic region including the Hanseatic League and others. It is possible that Lassen was searching for a stone or hidden relic when he was ruthlessly gunned down by what was said to be a sniper. He may have also been sent to leave such a stone or relic as opposed to discovering it.

Part of this theory involves the way items like the Kensington Runestone were hidden and how knowledge of the hidden axes or significant places that were valued allowed one to solve the mystery. The monument at each place had to be examined for directional and informational clues in order to solve the mystery or lead to the next clue. In order to solve the mystery one must be skilled in the arts of navigation and map reading among others. A firm understanding of symbology, code breaking, and art history are also needed skills. In this manner adepts of a given order may be sent on a type of vision quest in which they come to understand the world in its "real" context while learning philosophies important to the order.

If Chico was a sacred place then it makes sense that men like Lassen, Hooker, Gray, Muir and President Rutherford B. Hayes would visit Bidwell in Chico. Given the possible Masonic bent of Bidwell and his fellow travelers it is also possible that during a trip to Mt. Shasta they may have been the ones who left the strange petroglyphs at Castle Crags near to where Joaquin Miller once lived. Alternately they may have known that famous explorer John Fremont left them and were simply trying to relocate them. It is possible that the glyphs contained an important clue that would have been valued by members of a given philosophy? What sort of message may these strange symbols impart to those in the know?

It is also possible that on their trip to Shasta the party spent a few days in the Castle Crags area and one or more of them may have taken the time to create the inscriptions before the party moved on to Mt. Shasta itself. Viking runes are sometimes emphasized using red pigment similar to that described originally at Castle Crags. Either way it is interesting that glyphs very similar to these are located at Joaquin Millers estate in Oakland. It seems Miller may be the likely candidate as creator of the glyphs as he once lived very near the glyphs at the Crags though others espouse theories involving Freemont.

Some speculate that these series of symbols were left by the Hmong people who immigrated to the western U.S. after the Viet-Nam war. One of their forgotten alphabets has many similar characters to the Castle Crags petroglyphs but none that match exactly. The Hmong have an interesting legacy that suggests their race may have been of western origin with Catholic ties. The Hmong story resembles the legends of Prester John. More strangeness adding to the mystery. The suggestion that Hmong were involved in these petroglyphs may also suggest the influence of an organization associated with the Catholic Church whom the Hmong are also associated.

The chain of events beginning with Peter Lassen and John Bidwell may have influenced Caperon/Coutts to build the Frenchman's Tower in the Context that he did. Given this the Frenchman was the first to point his tower to Mt. Shasta though the Chico City Plaza "points to" Castle Crags. Later Miller recognized this and paid homage by adding his pyramid and towers. This suggests that Shasta had already been identified as a sacred point on the earth. Shortly we will see how a later relative of John Bidwell's paid homage to him by pointing his octagon at the Chico City Plaza.

All of this in a context that indicates their behavior was in association with some unknown group or entity. These men likely were aware of each other even if they were members of opposing groups. This again may be similar to English and French members of the same order acting beyond national identities to achieve a common goal. This in turn matches the interwoven French and Scottish families that may all in turn be termed Plantagenets. It is possible that the recent acquisition of California from Mexico may have had a great deal to do with this activity. This region was now open to a group that was different than the one who previously controlled it. Is this seemingly some sort of game or do these people's hidden spirituality dictate this activity? Were they in some strange way marking their territory or legally describing it using a Roman or Byzantine tradition? We do see the Hapsburg influence albeit briefly in the form of Emperor Maximillian of Mexico a direct relation to Henri V Artois exiled King of France. Both of these men also hold bonds to the Stuart and Stewart family that includes St. Germain and his family.

Note also that Joaquin Miller was cremated on his property in Oakland by his Bohemian Club brothers as per his wishes. His 'funeral pyre' is an additional stone structure at the Hights. Later we see characters like Leland Stanford and Hearst taking the reigns of this secret system of monuments and places of talismanic importance. Could this be the same concept at work in the distribution of the much earlier Gothic Cathedrals of Europe? The great cathedrals were also built by wealthy men of means possibly to display their own philosophies. Through their works it may be possible to decipher many unknown truths about history and the development of our society and values.

These men may have been using an empty slate to crate a new series of monuments and mysteries that all lined up on the globe with regard to a central axis. This was both a symbolic domain with regard to the Republican ideal and a blessing for business ventures that may take place in this context. Along the way they were valuing what John Muir termed a 'Cathedral of Nature' in the form of Mt. Shasta. All of it possibly linked to France and England via a series of spatial associations such as that noted between the Frenchman's Tower and Chateau Chambord. Each place may be designed to tell us something of the surprising truth of their creation. In response an either real or mythological lore has sprung up around the mountain in the tradition of many sacred places. The lore of Mt. Shasta seems to have a distinctly modern flavor to it and includes many concepts that exist outside of the realm of the Church. This is true though a great deal of the less discussed overtones of the Mountain also suggest a distinct value on the part of those that do value the Church.

Since this scheme or topology of places of importance is easily seen in the relatively recent development of California what may we now infer about places like Rennes le Chateau and Shugborough Hall or even the Great Pyramid? Truly what are these 'alchemical towers' who define themselves through their connection with other places via *__arcs__* on the globe that mean something specific to their creators? The answer to that question is not easy.

What may be clear is the fact that John Bidwell came to California and established Chico as what was at first entirely his domain. Chico was not incorporated into a City until about 1871. Prior to that Bidwell had control over who could even live in the town. With this said Bidwell did appear to be a kind and resourceful person. Some accuse him of enslaving the Natives and he even had a few Native American children himself. In fact the course of Bidwell's life and even praise and criticisms of him remind one of Thomas Jefferson. In fact Bidwell's brother Thomas Jefferson Bidwell was an early inhabitant of Chico as well. Perhaps there were some Masonic connections between the orders that both Jefferson and Bidwell had been brothers of. It almost does appear as if Bidwell were proceeding by attempting to create a legacy similar to that of President Jefferson.

It is notable that John seemed to fill the bill of a Jefferson clone in a more impressive way than his brother who was named for the President. In the course of this study it is clear that certain of the extended family members seem to have used forebears traits and successes as a model for their own. Bidwell is no exception. When he first established Rancho Arroyo Chico he was in effect a kind of feudal lord who owned and maintained his interests in much the same manner Jefferson had. Bidwell had a strong interest in Politics and was a General in the California Militia. He was Senator from California during which time he married Annie Kennedy whom he brought back to Chico from Washington D.C.

During the time during which Bidwell owned Chico he kept several Native Americans to help him work his property. Many later historians have termed these people slaves thus leading us to an unpleasant parallel between Bidwell and President Jefferson. Just as Jefferson had done John Bidwell fathered Native children prior to the time that Annie Bidwell came to Chico. It is said that Annie was magnanimous with regard to the American Western tradition of the "country wife" for pioneers and explorers. Many accounts have her treating the native children of Bidwell well and her and his Native wife getting along well.

Masonic philosopher and mystic Manly P. Hall discusses how characters later in history may be actual amalgams of people from previous times. Hall makes this comparison in a discussion involving the possibility that St. Germain was indeed Sir Francis Bacon who had gone through an alchemical transformation in order to be immortal thus allowing him to later assume the role of St. Germain. In reality what this concept may involve is a living individual recreating himself as an amalgam of an admired figure from past history. Considering all the similarities between John Bidwell and Thomas Jefferson it is possible that John Bidwell had taken part in some sort of process that resulted in his life mirroring that of the President. If true then this would infer that John Bidwell was an alchemist. We do know he was a Freemason and from a family line that may have made this possible. In the end it is possible that Bidwell resembles Jefferson due to his circumstance in history.

In previous work a connection between Jefferson's mother's Randolph family has been established with the Easton family some of whom founded Newport Rhode Island. This is discussed in my last book "The Geographic Mysteries of Sir Francis Bacon." Family relations of the Easton or Norman de Eston family link Jefferson's mother's family to the Easton's who may have even been one of the families behind the fabled Newport Tower also discussed in the Bacon book. It is likely that Jefferson named one of his Sally Hemming's son's Eston in honor of this family connection. In addition Jefferson's octagonal country estate may have been named "Poplar Forest" due to the inclusion of this tree on the de Eston and Easton arms. The de Eston family is also directly descendant of the Mortuo Mari family thus supplying us with a metaphor for "Dead Mary" or possibly Mary Magdalene. Mary Magdalene may represent an alternate interpretation for the AVM symbol seen in Chico, Kensington, as well as Williamsburg and Jamestown.

A quick check of the Bidwell family genealogy entitled "Genealogy of the first Seven Generations of the Bidwell Family in America" reveals at least one intermarriage with between the Easton's and Bidwell's. This means that at the very least there is a family relation. On some level this is all that may be needed to be "in the club" so to speak of these family groups. It is likely that there are many more connections between these families in blood in the way the first families of America first intermingled with each other for long periods of time prior to the development of the colonies in a large way. This led to a close knit group of people who had bonded together in a goal of survival for a long time. This bond was continued through the revolution and beyond and made many of these families the successes they are today. This dynamic is seen in many of the early settlements of the Colonies including Jamestown and Charleston.

Here are some high points that show direct intermarriage between the Bidwell's and other families involved in this over all mystery. Each one of these relations would go on to have a major impact on the mysteries of Mt. Shasta if not North America on the whole as well as Europe.

81 Roger Bidwell, b. 17 14 and d. 28 Dec, 1782; m. Rhoda **Easton**, b. 1721 ; d. 24 Aug., 1782. She was a dau. of Timothy,   They lived, died, and are buried at East Hartford.

30 Ephraim Bidwell, b. 16 Aug., 1686; d. 1753; "^v 3 Nov., 1713, Elizabeth **Lewis**. They were married at Wallingford, Ct., and lived at Glastenbury, Ct,

314 Rachel Bidwell, m. Justus IV **Olcott**, d. Glastenbury or vicinity.

63 William Bidwell, b. 27 Nov
He m., 2d, Hannah **Olcott**.

98 John Bidwell, b. 1740; d. 9 March, 181 7; m. Sarah **Spencer**^ b. 1743, d. I Aug., 1 830. They were born and always lived at East Hartford, Conn., and are buried there. He was a miller and farmer. His father left him a share in the mill.

171 Hannah Bidwell, b. 1747; d. 14 Feb., 1819, aged 72; m. George **Olmsteady** b. 1745, d. 14 July, 1792, ae. 47 years.

22 Thomas Bidwell, b. 27 Dec, 1682; d. 1716; m., 28 March, 1707, Prudence **Scott**, b. 1683, d. 14 Feb., 1763. He was bapt. 31 Dec, 1682. Her father was Edward Scott of New Haven, 20 May, 1739.

Jean-Pierre d'Abbadie d'Arrast born December 1874, Deceased 1 March 1912-Ciboure,64500, Pyrenees-Atlantiques, France age at Death: 37 years old married in 1904 to **Elena Bidwell** born 1876, Deceased in 1930 age at death: 54 years old.
(http://gw.geneanet.org/favrejhas?lang=en&p=robert&n=d+abbadie+d+arrast)

Jean Pierre is the son of Arnaud d'Abbadie:
Parents: Arnauld d'Abbadie d'Arrast born July 1815 Dublin, County Dublin Leinster, Ireland. Deceased November 1893 age at death: 78 years old. Married December 29, 1864 to Elisabeth West-Young, born May 1838-Portsmouth, Hampshire, England, United Kingdom, Deceased March 1923 age at death: 84 years old.
(http://gw.geneanet.org/favrejhas?lang=en&p=jean+pierre&n=d+abbadie+d+arrast)

The above relations of the Bidwell's are all to first families of Hartford Connecticut that would go on to have interface and seemingly even goals in common with later members of this family group. This will be very important here in just a short while in this narrative.

The only exception to the Harford First Families here of import is the last relation to the d'Abbadie family of Arnaud d'Abbadie. Arnaud and his brother were famous Ethiopian explorers. Their family is likely behind the Great Cyclic Cross of Hendaye mystery. The d'Abbdie's are also intermarried with the de La Tour family and have shown some allegiances to the kind of Scottish and French secrecy that was going on in Nova Scotia involving Oak Island and the Arcadian concepts of William Alexander and Sir Philip Sidney.

Again we should note that during James II first escape attempt he was assisted by a man named Abbadie. This escape attempt failed with his second attempt being successful. On James II second escape he was assisted by a man named Biddulph wich is the original English form of the name Bidwell. After James' escape he resided at the palace of St. Germaine en Laye managed aby the d'Abbadie St. Germain family directly related to our Acadia d'Abbadie family. In fact it is likely that both Antoine and Arnaud d'Abbadie had descended from or been closely related to Anselme d'Abbadie the Acadian privateer that returned to France to reclaim his father's title of Baron St. Castin. Castine Maine is named for this family. One of Anselme's granddaughters

264

eventually married into the Bourbon family of Navarre. Every connection in this story has a direct loop back to the same group of families that would come to be associated with the Stuarts and other fallen monarchs.

This relation between the Bidwell family and d'Abbadie family is amazing and is illustrative of a link between two families that had very successful explorers and adventurers as family members. All of this is simpy amazing as we see all the same names and influences being involved in what is uncovered by using Philip Sidney's work "Arcadia" to lead us to all of these connections including Washington D.C. and Chico!

The above intermarriages do seem to show that John Bidwell likely has a distant family relationship by blood to these families. It does establish the notion that these families were part of what they considered a legacy together to some degree. There is also a direct Bidwell to Arnold family of Newport Rhode Island via the Eno family who are descendant from the Bidwell's. It is clear that John Bidwell's ancestry is among this group of Bidwell's in early Hartford. These associations may provide information that will rock the foundations of the New Age world and realms of alternate thought in a fashion as of yet never witnessed before. Even the distant link to the d'Abbadie's is very important even though it comes via a distant Bidwell relation to family from Norwich, England.

John Bidwell even once ran for President of the United States and had served as Congressman from California. The entire pattern of the way Chico developed and evolved fits the notion that it had somehow been designated a special place not only to Mason's but also to members of the bloodline Bidwell had come from. Had Bidwell made himself an amalgam of President Jefferson? Were there others who knew of and believed this due to family traditions and legacies? Is this why Bidwell married a Kennedy? There are some amazing ancestors in the Bidwell line that may serve to tell part of the story:

Excerpt from Benson Bidwell inventor of the Trolly Car, Electric Fan, and Cold Motor. (*P.185 Chicago; The Hennebary Pres 1907*):

"In America lustre has been added to the name not only by Prof. Benson Bidwell, but another of this distinguished family, John Bidwell, during his very active life, was known all over the land. He was born in Chautauqua County NY in 1819. Having acquired an academic education, he began life as teacher, but soon entered politics. He went to California in 1841, and, with the accustomed Bidwell (or biddulph) proclivities for fighting, there entered the Army and served through the Mexican War. During the Civil War he was Brigadier-General. In 1864 he was elected to Congress, and in 1892 was the Prohibition candidate for the Presidency of the United States. He died April, 5, 1900. He was cousin to Prof. Benson Bidwell."

This same volume goes on to tell how Bidwell's forebears established Hartford, Connecticut and corroborates the information from several different sources. This version of Bidwell's family story also seems to have been echoed by Bidwell himself in the form of the story of the Hooker Oak in Chico. This information has been collected from different sources at different times and all points to the fact that Bidwell was from a valued background. It is interesting that his cousin Benson Bidwell was cited as being the inventor of the trolley car. This theme is repeated in the Chico City Plaza in the form of a large mural depicting the trolly cars that had once operated in downtown Chico.

The question still lingers: "Was John Bidwell sent to Chico to find this point on earth to establish a "colony city"? As it turns out John Bidwell had a lineage or ancestry that seemed to include such things. Just as Henri V seemed to have a royal legacy in creating the Frenchman's tower and possibly influencing the Rennes le Chateau mystery Bidwell may have held the same family legacy. John Bidwell's ancestors are among the First Families of New England. Going further back we see that a strong tradition of even the Knights Templar exist in the family tradition of this man. The legacy of John Bidwell does echo all of the attributes of the First Families of New England from which he descended. John Bidwell had been either burdened or blessed with a destiny that would lead him to create Chico, California. Mr. Bidwell also has some strange connections to those that would create an air of mystery and intrigue surrounding Mt. Shasta to this day.

The Bidwell family descends ultimately from the Forrester family of Flanders and central England. Some references state the Biddulph line being known as far back as the fourth century. This bloodline had direct links to Charlemagne and all the Kings of Latin Jerusalem. Bidwell ancestors went by the name Biddulph that translated later to Bidwell. The family arms of Biddulph includes wolves and the name is loosely interpreted as 'War Wolf.' This family established a town in England named Biddulph in Central England near Stafford and Shugborough Hall. This is also the same region we see the Earls of Shugborough coming from as well as the Lee family (Robert E. Lee) and Adams Family (not the tv show but the lineage of both Presidents Adams).

One of the earliest Forrester's (Bidwell's) was known as Ormus le Guidon. "Le Guidon" means 'standard bearer' or flag bearer. In this case it referred to the flag of the Norman Kings of Europe. This position denotes a great deal of value in the recipient in the art of war and combat. The name or word 'Ormus' also has a double meaning in what many consider to be the lost secrets of the Knights Templar and other orders of Knighthood.

Ormus is another name for Monoatomic gold. There are scant hints in the historical record of the era of the Crusades that suggested this substance could heal wounds or prolong ones life. This is a legend that extends back to the time of ancient Egypt. Ormus is composed of powdered white gold of the highest purity. It may be that 'Ormus' held the properties that some people espouse colloidal silver as having. In any case it is very interesting that this forebear of John Bidwell possessed this name. Doubly Ironic in that John Bidwell was the owner of one of the richest gold strikes during the Gold Rush of California. It is connections like this that lend an air of mystery and suspense to Chico and other similar mysteries.

The Biddulph's were very active in the crusades with Ormus le Guidon even bringing back what were said to have been 'Moorish Stonemason's" from his foray's into the Holy Land. These men would go on to build what may be considered the family chapel of the Biddulph family. In fact we see the phenomena of the chapels being sponsored by families in Scotland and England by families that would later be very influential in the development of the United States. These chapels serve to tell the story of the lineage and ancestry of these families while also providing clues as to their political and spiritual alliances.

'*The Biddulphs do derive themselves from one Ormus Le Guidon, the son of Ricardus Forestarius" of the Norman race, who held, as appears by Domesday, ten lordships in the county of Stafford, which were conferred upon him in reward of his services. Biddulph, and other large possession were not included in these.*"

"*One of the tenants in Capite, named in the Domesday Book (1086) as Ricardus Forestarius, one of the Tadeni family, the hereditary standard bearers of Normandy. He became owner of half of Staffordshire.*"

"*The family which had been thus 'constant to the father, were more tender of the son,' and continued their devotion to the race of Plantagenet, in the person of Henry III. They were particularly attached to his brother Richard, Earl of Cornwall, whom James de Audley attended when he was crowned King of the Romans at Aix in Chapelle, in 1257.*"

Both Audley and Thomas would also take part in the battle of Portiers France on the winning English side. They were cousins of the same family. This same family is involved in the story of the "Knights Tombstone" of Jamestown Virginia. They had also taken part in the Crusades:

"*In the 54th year of Henry II. 1270, it seems that Thomas de Biddulph, with his kinsman James de Audley, attended Prince Edward in the Crusade to the Holy Land, which he undertook, accompanied by Eleanor, afterwards his Queen, when Acaon (Ashkelon) was gallantly rescued from the infidels. There is a tradition to this day in the neighborhood of Biddulph, that certain families, whose lineaments betray their Eastern origin, are descendants of some Saracen followers, who attended their master on his return from this crusade.*"
(*A Genealogical and Heraldic History of Great Britain Volume 3 by John Burke; London 1834 pp 280-285*)

The Audley family came from the Eaton family as Audley was first a title of some Eaton's. The arms of the Audley and Eaton are similar designs that include the Auspice of Maria (AVM) and X designs seen throughout this mystery. Eaton Road in Chico is named for the Eaton family that lived in Chico. Of course the Eaton family created Dunseith North Dakota now located 13 miles south of the octagon of the International Peace Garden. The family created this town Dunseith which translates to "Fortress of Peace" in Scots Gaelic. The Town was established fifty years prior to the establishment of the International Peace Garden. Is it possible that the International Peace Garden in part created by the Eaton family "points to" Chico very near Eaton Road for a reason? There are also overtones of the name Eaton in the memorial to the "other" Sir Francis Bacon in Norwich England that also seems to refer to many of the interpretive themes seen in the street plan of Washington D.C.

This legend of 'Saracen followers' with regard to Ormus le Guidon is told as 'Saracen Stonemasons' in other accounts. Evidence supporting the truth of the later is the existence of the Church of St. Lawrence in the town of Biddulph that features sarcophagus covers that have Norman Templar designs carved into them. Adding to this mystery is a church in nearby Stafford that features what is said to be in local mythology Moorish architectural elements as well as burials of Knights Templar. There may be ancestors of John Bidwell who were Knights Templar who fought in the Holy Land interred there. This is the tradition upon which Chico is built.

As it turns out the truth of the 'Saracen Stonemason's' is revealed in an examination of the Church in Stafford known as St. Chad's. St. Chad seems to be somewhat of a local cult figure in Staffordshire at some point with many churches and places being named for him. It is likely that the true architectural heritage of the stonemasons was byzantine in nature and had nothing to do with any 'Saracen's.' In addition the stonework in Stafford they are supposed to have created is clearly Norman in nature with an almost 'Viking' motif to most of it. No sign of any Arabic or Saracen influence is noted at St. Chad's at all.

The legend of the Saracen stonemason's creating the artwork in St. Chad's Stafford likely evolved from the previous legend of these stone mason's arriving at Biddulph Moor to the north with the word 'moor' being part of the name of the small town just adjacent to the larger Town of Biddulph. Inscriptions included in the stonework of St. Chads tells the story of how our Ormus le Guidon had created or sponsored the building of the church and the content of the stonework within. Some sources point out that one of these families of original stonemasons was likely the seed of the famous Ashmole family.

If this story is true then this also marks a point in time during which the entire Masonic concept had come to England. The values and secrecy of the Stonemasons guilds later evolved into Freemasonry. The compass and square symbol of Freemasonry that resembles the Auspice of Maria is comprised of stonemasons tools.

St. Chad's in Staffordshire does include an inscription stating that Ormus le Guidon created the Church. This inscription includes the Auspice of Mary symbol just as the Bank of America building in Chico would about a 750 years later! This symbol is present through the legacy of many strange and interesting places like Chico.

Later in the era of Elizabeth I and King James I we see the emergence of another important Bidwell ancestor.

William Biddulph:

Wrote: "*Travels into Africa, Asia and to the Blacke Sea* (1609). This book was meant to aid pilgrims in their journeys to the Holy Land. William Biddulph had lived in Aleppo Syria for many years. This is an incredibly early date for a European living in the Levant in the post Latin Kingdom era. Each of these gentry families seemed to have one intellectual world traveler explorer in their midst. This tradition is seen in the likes of James Bruce, The Drummond family, and the d'Abbadie family creators of the Great Cross of Hendaye mystery. In the United States this tradition would continue with Jefferson as well as members of the Lewis, Clarke, Spencer, and Pike families. Note also that John Bidwell crossed the wilderness to California in 1841 eight years prior to the 1849 Gold Rush. It is noted also that one of the only books he carried on this journey was a text on celestial navigation.

William Biddulph (same as above);
"... learned divine and topographical writer of the reign of James First. He was concerned in the revised edition of the Scriptures, published in that reign. He was educated in the University of Cambridge."
(American Biography a New Cyclopedia by Richard Cutter. The America Historical Society of New York inc. 1918 P. 225)

Biddulph had actually helped to edit and revise the Kings James Version Bible. This is an amazing connection to John Bidwell. In addition to that many people have insisted the involvement of Sir Francis Bacon in the writing or revising of the KJV and it is entirely possible that William Biddulph had at least met Sir Bacon at some point. Later members of the Biddulph and Bacon families would be among the founders of Hartford Connecticut. It may be that these family groups were enacting their vision of Bacon's New Atlantis in the United States.

Both John Bidwell and a man named Charles Toll Bidwell both include William Biddulph in their ancestry. William became a sort of archetype for later world explorers like James Bruce, William Drummond, and Arnaud and Antoine d'Abbadie. William explored the Levant and North Africa as early at 1600-1608 and wrote his findings up in his famous book. William was the chaplain to the English merchants of Aleppo, Syria at this time. Many facets of Williams life seem to include him in this group of magi that later is emulated by the character of St. Germain. William was a kind of Christian "Merlin" figure who was both an intellectual and accomplished writer.

Charles Toll Bidwell from Norwich England was also descendant of the same Biddulph family that had produced William our Levant traveler of the early 1600's and John Bidwell of the United States founder of Chico California. Charles would go on to become British consul to places like Puerto Rico, Majorca, and finally Malaga, Spain. During his travels he married Colombian national Amalia Hurtado. Eventually in later years this Bidwell family settled near St. Jean de Luz just north of Hendaye France that features "The Great Cyclic Cross of Hendaye" and the "Rosslyn Chapel" of France known as Chateau Abbadia. Amazingly Charles' grand daughter Elena Hurtado Bidwell would marry one Jean-Pierre d'Abbadie d'Arrast the son of none other than Arnaud d'Abbadie famous brother of Antoine d'Abbadie both of them Ethiopian Explorers in the mold of James Bruce. A Bidwell family member was a d'Abbadie related directly to one of the most famous Ethiopian explorers thus making her the niece of Antoine d'Abbadie who had created Chateau Abbadia.

It is highly likely that given their vocation of geographers and explorers of the day that Antoine and Arnaud d'Abbadie would not have only been familiar with who William Biddulph was but would have also read all of his works in their education leading up to their travels. The fact that Jean-Pierre married a Bidwell family member is notable in this family of explorers who proceeded through their lives in a very similar manner to that of William Biddulph who coincidentally was one of the authors associated with the production of the Kings James Version of the Bible.

None of this suggests that the d'Abbadie's even knew of John Bidwell or were acquainted with him. The Bidwell family of Norwich England was far removed by this time to John Bidwell in California but it is possible in this scheme of family values and planning that they were indeed aware of who John Bidwell was. It is even remotely possible that they were part of the same organization. Both Arnaud and Antoine d'Abbadie were members of the same Linnean Society discussed before in association with John Bidwell of Chico. In turn both of these men had an at least passing association with Linnean Society member J.D. Hooker for whom the Hooker Oak in Chico is named.

Here we have come full circle with a connection between two family groups from two different countries that seemed to value the use of talismanic monuments in a geographic scheme reminiscent of the Axis Mundi as applied by Constantine and other Roman and Byzantine rulers. Elena Bidwell d'Abbadie lived at the same time John Bidwell did. Given the d'Abbadie's Linnean Society connections it is very possible that both Bidwell in Chico and d'Abbadie's in France were aware of each other and what this family connection represented in the realm of these geographic mysteries.

This connection between the Bidwell family and the Great Cyclic Cross of Hendaye and Chateau Abbadia is amazing. The association between the two families is but one of many that suggest this group had an interest in creating schemes of talismanic architecture. It may be that a plan had been in place even before colonists came to the New World to execute these plans on an open playing field that was just no longer possible in continental Europe. The d'Abbadie family seemed to be associated with the same kind of intrigue we see developed at Mt. Shasta. This family was associated with the same circle of astronomers and naturalists in Paris that Thomas Jefferson was associated with. These connections are amazing.

Of course we may also proceed with caution. These family ties are only important if they were planned and went on over a fairly long period of history. The fact that Bidwell and Biddulph genealogical sources state that they kept track of their ancestry from the fourth century suggests a value beyond that of a passing interest in knowing whom they were related to. This factor may also bring us into the realm of the Bloodline of Christ that has been debated and written of extensively in the modern age.

Many things suggest a value of the Auspice of Maria as applied to Mary Magdalene among this group of families. Though counter to the doctrine of the Church it seems as if though some of the followers of Mary Magdalene also had a grudging respect and value of the Church. They may have viewed their philosophical differences as being minor in some cases. It may also be that this caste of those who saw themselves as Plantagenet, Merovingian, Christ descendants may have also had an interest in degrading a value of the Latin Church in a still developing United States. An examination of President Jefferson's art collection does seem to reveal a value of the Magdalene concept in both spiritual and revolutionary terms.

Another eighteenth century connection to the Bidwell family is amazing in the scope of the mysteries of Mt. Shasta specifically the legends of St. Germaine. As stated before both the Hooker and Bidwell families were among the earliest of settlers to Hartford Connecticut. A monument there commemorates the group that first came under the guidance of John Hooker. Among those names is the family of Olcott. A quick genealogy check displays at least three intermarriages between the Bidwell and Olcott family in the early stages of the development of Hartford.

Of the descendants of the Hartford Olcott's related to Bidwell at least collaterally if not closer includes the well known figure in Theosophical studies Colonel Henry Steele Olcott (1832-1907). Olcott is one of the creators of the Theosophy movement and Society that in turn contributed greatly to the beliefs surrounding the figure of St. Germaine at Mt. Shasta. Mr. Olcott was not only a close associate of Madame Blavatsky one of the other founders of the movement but was also said to be a paramour of hers. Though Bidwell and Olcott lived during the same era he was a little older and there is no record of the two knowing about each other. Even so this is an amazing coincidence given Bidwell's association to J.D. Hooker and their trip to Mt. Shasta at a time long before most of the New Age lore had been applied to Mt. Shasta. It is clear that many writers and researchers link the myths and philosophies of this lore at Mt. Shasta to the Theosophical Society and their teachings. Interestingly Olcott was also one of the investigators into the Lincoln assassination earlier in his life.

Other impressive relations of the Bidwell's include intermarriages with the Olmstead family who also were among the First Founders of Hartford. The Olmstead's have a strong tradition in landscape and building architecture that echoes many of the tenets of early Freemason architect Inigo Jones who was associated with Sir Francis Bacon. In fact others from the Bacon family were also among the small group of the founders of Hartford as well as Easton family members that were related to the earliest governor of Newport Rhode Island. Please see the list of founders named on the monument in Hartford at the end of this chapter.

It is clear that John Bidwell likely held very few "New Age" beliefs during his life though he may have at least been aware of such concepts. It is more likely that the Englishman J.D. Hooker would have had some of these kinds of beliefs rather than Bidwell. Interestingly out of this entire cast of characters Joaquin Miller appears to have held the most obvious set of alternate beliefs. Joaquin Miller was a spiritually oriented person that had many occult beliefs and secret society associations. If he was a member of the Society of the Cincinnati he may have been conversant and schooled in such concepts for practical reasons that had nothing to do with how much he personally believed these concepts. It is still uncertain in these murky waters who is on which side in many instances. Was Joaquin a real "New Ager" or was he spying on those that wished to introduce these concepts into the lore of Mt. Shasta if not California at large? Was it more associated with the Theosophical movement? Miller was also a member of the Bohemian Club of San Francisco.

It does appear as if John Bidwell had been sent to the place where he would found Chico intentionally to add another site for collecting ephemeris or star charts in the grid established by this group long ago. There has been in fact a small astronomical observatory added to Bidwell Park in 2007. The legacy of Bidwell and the similarities to Thomas Jefferson may be seen by the way others in Northern California viewed the Third Presidents legacy. It is possible that Bidwell intentionally chose a point on earth to establish a town that would be "pointed to" by the International Peace Garden. The Eaton family who are involved in the story of the International Peace Garden were among Chico's early settlers with Eaton Road being named for them. Other Eaton's were among the early mayors of Los Angeles.

There is way more than a thread of possibility that suggests John Bidwell may have been aware of some of the secrets of Mt. Shasta. It is likely that he would have been aware of concepts being associated with Mt. Shasta in the press of the day. It is also interesting to speculate if John Bidwell was aware of whatever significance had been placed or developed in association with the mountain by the Hudson's Bay Company and their associated families. Bidwell was close to many of the family groups of the Hudson's Bay Company who had branches all over New England including Hartford and Newport Rhode Island. Even the family of Ballard is present on the founder's monument of Hartford. As it turns out Bidwell has some amazing connections to other people in addition to Olcott who had a large impact on the kind of modern spirituality we see being developed and displayed in the folklore of Mt. Shasta.

A man named Guy Ballard would eventually claim to have had an encounter with St. Germain on the slopes of Mt. Shasta leading to the creation of the "I Am Activity." An examination of the genealogy of Guy Ballard reveals that it is highly possible that his family did indeed come from Hartford Connecticut and had intermarriage with the Olmstead family related to the Bidwell's as well as other relations common between the two families. The town of Hartford, Kansas named for Hartford Connecticut by the founders of the town is only a few miles from the birthplace of Guy Ballard near Newton, KS a town named for Newton, Massachusetts. The Ballard name is also connected to the mysteries of Williamsburg. The given name of Nathaniel Bacon famous for "Bacon's Rebellion" was actually Ballard. He changed it to Bacon due to a close family relation to the family of Sir Francis Bacon. Note also both Ballard's and Bacon's among the first families of Hartford.

The Ballard family was well represented in Kansas with one family member carrying on the tradition of milling in the family by operating a mill at Ballard's Falls also known as Ballard's Mill. It is entirely possible that Guy Ballard was part of a family organization that came to Northern California during the Gold Rush and founded Chico and other places in association with John Bidwell even though he did not come until the 1930's. The family and original connection between Bidwell, Ballard, Olcott and others is too much to ignore in a possible scheme that involved the development of different myths and legends at Mt. Shasta. The

272

phenomenon of these three people coming from the same first family community echoes the involvement of many First Families of Virginia that were involved in similar activities. In Minnesota we may see these families associated with the Kensington Rune that may have been a symbol for what was known of as the Norumbega political movement that was popular in the era in which the stone was recovered. The Kensington Stone also includes the AVM Auspice of Mary and the X symbol valued in these other places of intrigue and mystery.

If Ballard was somehow aware of this family tradition and what had been developed at Mt. Shasta then it is not hard to imagine that there may have been some reasons in this realm that he was sent to California just as it appears John Bidwell was. The Bidwell family has many close associations with other prominent New York families such as the Coopers and Van Buren's.

There are records suggesting that John Bidwell and Daniel Bidwell knew future 8th President Martin Van Buren in Eastern New York as they both held public duties at the same time and place. There are also many records of the Cooper and Van Buren family intermarrying. This connection is very interesting given the twentieth century involvement of Elizabeth Van Buren in the famous mystery of Rennes le Chateau. Indeed it appears as if the two mysteries may have even been developed in the same era with the Frenchman's Tower of Palo Alto and Joaquin Miller's estate being built many years prior to the mystery at Rennes le Chateau even taking place in its original form.

There are two Bidwell family members during the era or generation proceeding John Bidwell that are eligible for membership in the Society of the Cincinnati. It is clear that James Fennimore Cooper was a member of this organization as well as other famous authors Morse and Edgar Allan Poe. The Bidwell family connection to both the Society and Martin Van Buren are interesting. Abram Bidwell the father of John Bidwell of Chico ended his days in town called Van Buren Ohio. Martin Van Buren was President when John Bidwell undertook his early journey to California a full seven years prior to the gold rush. Some of these associations make it almost appear as if Bidwell had been sent west to look after the interests of the United States and his family organization.

We also see John Bidwell producing a map of "gold country" including the location of specific deposits in 1847 two years prior to the official "kick off" of the 1849 Gold Rush of California. Like the Beale family of Virginia and Pennsylvania it Appears the Bidwell's and other Hartford First Families had brought their family tradition of working together for a common goal in Northern California at an early date in that great state's history. The Lewis, Spencer, Montague, and Ballard families all had an impact on the mysteries of the First Families of Virginia. Many individuals from these family groups went on to be scions of industry and commerce through many phases of American history.

Is it possible that John Bidwell had been sent to California in association with Martin Van Buren and some secret plan? Did this scheme involve the intentional propagation of myths and legends at Mt. Shasta? Why did later Royal interests and the Church also seem to be interested in Mt. Shasta in this context? Finally, was the association between St. Germain part of an intelligence ploy created to spook early Royal interest in California or was that faction privy to some other truth at the mountain?

So far we see the Bidwell related to Ballard (I Am Activity), Olcott Theosophy, and William Biddulph (Explorer and King James Version contributor). While these relations aren't directly associated with John Bidwell it is clear that his genetic makeup included input from many of the Hartford First families including the Olcott, Spencer, Hales, and Lewis family that in turn married to Ballard's. In turn all of these families also intermarried with the Bacon family of early Hartford. Though this family of course did not descend from Sir Francis Bacon those that held this name may have been viewed in high esteem by their fellow colonists.

Names on the Founders' Monument, Hartford, Conn.

On the East Side of the Monument:

John Haynes Thomas **Hooker** George Wyllys Edward Hopkins Matthew AUyn Thomas **Wells** John **Webster** William Whiting John Talcott Andrew Warner William Pentrey William **Westwood** James **Olmsted** Thomas Hosmer Nathaniel **Ward** William **Wadsworth** John White John **Steele** Thomas **Scott** William Goodwin Thomas **Stanley** Samuel **Stone** Stephen **Hart** William **Spencer** John Moody William **Lewis** William Rusco Timothy Stanley Richard **Webb** William **Andrews** Samuel Wakeman Jeremy **Adams** Richard Lyman William Butler   Thomas Lord Matthew Marven Gregory Wolterton Andrew **Bacon** John Barnard Richard Goodman Nathaniel Richards John Pratt Thomas Birchwood George Graves John **Clark** William Gibbons John Crow Edward Stebbing James Ensign George **Steele** Stephen Post George Stocking Joseph Mygatt Nathaniel Ely William Bloomfield

On the North Side of the Monument:

Thomas **Judd**, William **Hill** Richard Lord William Hyde William Kelsey John **Arnold** Richard Butler Arthur **Smith** Robert Day John Maynard Seth Grant William Heyton Thomas **Spencer** Thomas Stanton George Baysey John Hopkins William Pratt Nicholas Clark Thomas Bull John **Marsh** William Holton Edwin Elmer Francis Andrews Richard Church James Cole Zachariah Field John Skinner Joseph **Easton** Thomas **Hales** Richard **Olmsted** Samuel **Hales** Richard Wrisley Thomas **Alcott** Robert Bartlett Thomas Selden Thomas Root William Parker John **Wilcox** Samuel Greenhill Benjamin **Burr** Ozias Goodwin Richard Seymour Thomas Bunce John **Bidwell** Clement **Chaplin** Thomas **Bliss**

The above names in bold type are from families who have displayed a tradition of hidden artwork and architecture. Each of these families were among the first in New England and contributed a great deal to the untold and standard history of the colonies and the United States.

Many industrious family groups would station a family member in each major port in the colonies including Maritime Canada and the West Indies. This provided a ready made network to take advantage of any business opportunities that may have arisen in each place. In some cases these family groups would still have allegiances with their families in the old country. If one married into this family group then they may now be considered part of the group and would be rewarded as per their contributions. In many ways these families seemed to value the success of their group over their loyalty to their new country. This was not always the case but there seemed to be a few of these families who did not always act in the best interest of the country. This survival strategy is a normal affectation of the day and likely of the modern age as well.

The names on this monument read like a who's who of this saga in the United States. Easton, Bacon, Adams, Olmstead, Webster, Webb, Scott, the list goes on and on including many families suspected of taking part in this tradition of hidden symbols and messages including those in artwork and architecture. All of those named were prominently featured in my last book about Sir Francis Bacon as well. Their English, Scottish and French families were all active in similar pursuits.

In many cases the Bidwell's are intermarried with these other influential and landed families from the old country. The Biddulph families from which the Bidwell's derive were clearly a storied and royally connected family of great note in Staffordshire. Biddulph means "War Wolf" and some attribute even the origins of the saga Beowulf to the Biddulph family. Some such as the Webb and Scott families have a tradition of intricate artwork including the ownership of one of the better-known potteries in England. Many Scotts have been famous poets and artists in this tradition. John Webb was the assistant to Inigo Jones in the Elizabethan and James I eras as stated above.

The list of founders of Hartford holds a great deal of significance in showing the legacy of John Bidwell. Some of the families mentioned on this monument actually later end up settling near Chico the town the latter John Bidwell founded. Members of the Bacon, Hooker, Kennedy, Bidwell, and Campbell families would all contribute to the history of Chico and the surrounding region including Mt. Shasta.

Though unverified other amazing connections between the mythology of Mt. Shasta and the first families of Hartford includes the author of the book that seemed to have kicked off the entire idea of a city and race of beings existing beneath the mountain. Frederick Spencer Oliver was the author of this book entitled "A Dweller of Two Planets." The use of Spencer as Oliver's middle name may apply given the following information. Oliver's book seemed to have been the first to document many of the associations with Mt. Shasta that would be used and referred to by subsequent lore. Oliver seemed to have been the first to document this in a book though other earlier magazine and newspaper articles also seemed to have suggested a similar story. There is also a documented trail of the use of false names and anagrams of names being used in the authorship of books with regard to the myths of Mt. Shasta. Given this it may be that Oliver was connected to an interest associated with a specific group or order.

One of the other major books that contributed to the legends of Mt. Shasta was printed by the Rosicrucian Order of San Jose (AMORC) entitled "Lemuria: The Lost Continent of the Pacific" by Cerve Wishar Spenle which is widely considered to be a pseudonym for a leader of the Rosicrucian Order (AMORC) at this time named Harve(y) Spencer Lewis. Is it somehow possible that the Spencer name from author Oliver is also related to Lewis?

Mr. Lewis' name may represent two first families of Hartford including the Lewis' and Spencer's. Is this really possible? The same may be said of Mr. Oliver's middle name Spencer though this is a more tenuous connection. The use of the middle name Spencer is very common in groups of this family that descended from these early families of Hartford. Had a group of people who all originated in early colonial Hartford Connecticut have really created the entire mythology and lore of the mountain we see today? The only influence at work in the lore of Mt. Shasta not directly influenced by this family would be that of the Frenchman's Tower and its imperial and Church oriented connections.

The plot thickens even more. It is clear that Harvey Spencer Lewis is from New Jersey putting him solidly in a geographic area that may also associate him with this particular family group. There are a few hidden suggestions that Lewis was aware of his relation to John Bidwell of Chico. Very little in depth information is available with regard to Mr. Spencer's genealogy. It is clear that many Hartford First Families later spread to New Jersey, Pennsylvania, New York, and ultimately points west as the country began to expand. Members of this family group still seemed to work together as new opportunities became available as the West began to be settled throughout the nineteenth century.

Mr. Lewis is also the founder of the Rosicrucian Order in the United States (AMORC). Lewis is also responsible for the complex known as the Rosicrucian Museum near San Jose also known as "Rosicrucian Headquarters." This complex includes a world class Egyptian Museum, The Sir Francis Bacon auditorium, and an array of obelisks and other Egyptian inspired statuary. A small pyramid serves as a memorial and marks the resting place of Harvey Spencer Lewis. Adjacent to this pyramid is a small octagonal fountain.

Using the northern orientation of this octagon an arc on the globe can be plotted that transects Central and Northern California leading directly to the Chico City Plaza that had been established by John Bidwell. Indeed this direction matches the entire north to south orientation of the city block on which the Rosicrucian complex is located. It may be that Lewis was aware of his relation to John Bidwell and the Axis he had established in Chico. This may indicate that Lewis was aware of this family tradition and was paying homage to his distant relative Bidwell in Chico. This geographic relationship uncannily seems to mimic the themes and family relationships we see in this family group from Hartford Connecticut. It may be that Bidwell's status as a descendant of Charlemagne and Ormus le Guidon gave him a higher position in the hierarchy of this group. Bidwell did once run for President. Is it possible Lewis arranged this array at his gravesite to point the way to an axis mundi created by his distant relative John Bidwell? It appears this may indeed be possible if not probable. If not it is a cosmic coincidence featuring men with origins in the same colonial city along with the other magi Olcott and Ballard.

It appears that Three members of this family group were intimately involved in the formation of organizations that were concerned with spiritual matters. Olcott, Ballard, and Lewis were associated with the Theosophical Society, I Am Activity, and American Rosicrucian Order respectively.

Honestly. What are the odds that three people from this group would all be involved in spiritual movements that seemingly degraded the philosophy and influence of the Catholic Church if not Christianity on the whole in the United States? Of course, this would be a view dictated by political concerns and would point to an organization that believed this type of social engineering would help the country break the bonds of the old world faiths and form a New Atlantis in the spirit of Sir Francis Bacon. All of these families are related to Bacon family members that may not be directly related to Sir Francis but do stem from the same family that produced many brilliant individuals. This would comprise any part of a critical analysis of what is suggested here. The presence of Bacon family in many early colonial efforts is reflected later in their involvement in the development of the west. Is it possible that even these later Bacon family members were invested in the concept of the New Atlantis?

What does this story mean for the Theosophical Society, the I Am Activity, and Rosicrucian Order? It appears that there could have been an effort to create a faith that would degrade Christianity if not Catholicism directly. The I Am Activity seemed to have included a member of a prominent Royal dynasty as its object of worship. It is entirely possible that if John Bidwell were related to Charlemagne then he was also related to the Stuarts and other branches of St. Germain's real family. Given the status of the Biddulph/ Bidwell family in English history it is also likely that other intermarriage links them to the sphere of Stewart influence and political intrigue. What we may be seeing here is a more modern value of these people's Merovingian blood or at least the belief that they held this legacy. If true this may have given them the impetus and liscense to create new ways of viewing spirituality. These dynamics have led many of their enemies to label them as "Satanists" and Heretics.

Among these three groups the Rosicrucian Order has the most directly identifiable connection to the kind of mythology we see at Mt. Shasta. The philosophy that dictated the construction of the Frenchman's Tower also seemed to adhere to the same dynamic. The Rosicrucian Order valued a "Man in the Mountain" myth in association with the central character of their doctrine Christian Rosenkreuz.

The central part of this myth is that Rosenkruez' remains are hidden in an unknown mountain along with other precious documents and information. This myth not only echoes the same type of mythology as applied by Charlemagne, Otto II, Frederick Barbarosa, and Frederick II, but is also similar to other popular sagas such as the Oak Island Treasure, Bacon's Vault in Williamsburg, The Beale Treasure and more. The Charlemagne Man in the Mountain mythology had been established long before the Rosicrucian's seemed to have adapted this facet of folklore as their own. Rosicrucian beliefs also dictate the existence of "lost stones" that are inferred in the mystery of three strange stones that seem to mark the border of the Hudson's Bay Company holdings and French Louisiana. This includes the Kensington Rune and two sandstone pillars that are said to have once included stones in alcoves carved into them. The stories of these boundary markers have taken on a mythology of their own including an association with "Vikings" and "The Stone of Destiny."

It is starting to appear as if many of these stories concerning stones and cities in Mt. Shasta may have been meant to have been viewed from an allegorical perspective and were not meant to be interpreted literally. Those that had been trained to recognize the earmarks of Masonic and Rosicrucian metaphor would instantly recognize these tenets at play in the stories of Mt. Shasta and other places like Rennes le Chateau. In fact many sources state that Pierre Plantard who is central to the modern myths of that place had indeed taken a correspondence course from the Rosicrucian Order at some point prior to him exposing either a scam or the truth or both mixed. Many of the more modern myths and theories associated with Rennes le Chateau do seem to echo similar concepts to the Rosicrucian mythos.

Next even the notion that St. Germain appeared on the mountain to Guy Ballard and a city beneath the mountain is inferred also resembles this kind of Enochian metaphor and allegory at Mt. Shasta. Even the legend of J.C. Brown mentions mummies and crypts as part of what the intrepid explorer finds beneath Mt. Shasta. All of these myths seem to feed a kind Masonic or Rosicrucian view that was later modified by the Theosophical concepts popularized by Olcott, Blavatsky, and others. Perhaps the Rosicrucian involvement in printing books that suggested these legends of Lemuria were true were meant as a metaphor that initiates would understand and relate to their own doctrine of Christian Rosenkreuz.

Let us reiterate here also that an ancestor of John Bidwell had been an editor of the King James Version of the Bible. This family groups involvement in spiritual matters is very interesting and suggests many things that are surprising.

Just because all of these people are related does not prove any conspiracy nor detract from the ideals of the Theosophical Society, the I Am Activity, Rosicrucian Order, or even Christianity. If this story is true then the same or something similar could be said about all the major religions of the world. Many researchers have linked Theosophy to Russian intelligence and the Nazi's though it seems to be a faith or way of belief that does not include the negative aspects of those organizations. Via these associations Theosophy has been given a bad name. To assume that such a new and powerful way of faith could take hold anywhere on earth and not come on to the radar of rival factions, national interests, and imperial intrigue is simply naïve and impractical to consider.

If these family groups had intentionally created some basis for a new belief system this does not mean they control it in total. It is clear that throughout history spiritual movements have been coopted and derailed by infiltrators that wished to use them for their own political or social ends. This does include individuals maliciously and intentionally creating a faith or religion in order to use it for intelligence gathering or social engineering purposes. Many people speculate this is true about the Mormon faith and this theme was even explored by Joaquin Miller in his play "First Families of the Sierras."

Among all of this possible creation of faith and spirituality may have been a rationale held by these families. It is possible that the Bidwell's, Ballards, Olcotts, Lewis', and Spencer's all actually saw themselves as having descended from the Merovingian Dynasty thus being of the Holy Blood of Christ. Whether is true or not it is possible that these people's actions and associations with regard to matters of faith and religion were guided by this belief. They may have seen themselves as having the right to propagate these beliefs in any way they saw fit. Coupled with this may have been a sociopolitical desire to degrade the status of the Christianity in the new country. With this in mind it is no surprise that the church may have silently created their own mythology at Mt. Shasta that the Frenchman's Tower is likely a part of.

With that said it is difficult to find anything bad said about the "I Am Activity" or their adherents in Dunsmuir near Mt. Shasta. The group puts on a popular pageant every summer that many people in the area attend. So there are no signs of English spies in Dunsmuir or anyone attempting to twist the morals and values of unwilling participants. It is the U.S.A. and many may pray any way any day. There have been a few minor rumblings about the "I Am'ers" as some refer to them but relations with the local population that are not part of their group seem to be very good with members of the Activity taking part in local commerce, jobs, and schools.

Mt. Shasta displays both a traditional and modern or "New Age" folklore that is reflective of the silent political and spiritual war that was carried out in many different places during this era. This conflict may have been more pronounced and had more emphasis in California due to the importance of the riches recovered in the Gold Rush. The presence of so much wealth would have attracted interest from the Royal or Gentry class that seemed to value the concept of the "Ancient Regime" or more pastoral simple life of the feudal system in past ages ruled by monarchs. Many elements such as those that likely built the Frenchman's Tower were representative of this side of the coin in tandem with their value of the Catholic Church. It may be disappointing to contemplate that these spiritual ideas seem to have been intentionally applied to a place that really has nothing to do with them other than the fact it is a place of natural beauty. The fact that the first Masonic Charter to come to California is located in Mt. Shasta City and signed by a Stewart may hold some extra value with regard to those who view St. Germain in a spiritual manner. I am sure it is a point of pride to local Freemason's who don't necessarily adhere to the New Age concepts we see promoted from Mt. Shasta.

Along with this value came an appreciation for the "Man in the Mountain" myths of Charlemagne and other historical figures. This imagery was intentionally instilled at Mt. Shasta and may have even resulted in the installation of the more modern "New Age" imagery we see there as a response to this talismanic system being set up in early California. Over the years both sides have added to the pertinent architecture and have included elements of additional lore and mythology along the way. It is in this spirit that Joaquin Miller may have built his follies at the Hights in Oakland. He was countering the geomantic energy of those that had built the

Frenchman's Tower and shared values different than he and his Society of the Cincinnati and Bohemian Club cohorts.

From the College of the Sikiyous Mt. Shasta Bibliography:

[MS954].   Blavatsky, Helene Petrovna 1831-1891. **Isis Unveiled: A Master Key to the Mysteries of Ancient and Modern Science and Theology**. Theosophical University Press, 1960. First published 1877.   Not seen. Reported to contain the first metaphysical interpretation of Lemuria. Many of the esoteric legends of Mt. Shasta, including those about Saint Germain, have indirect links to the writings of Madame Blavatsky.   16. Legends: Lemuria. [MS954].

[MS153].   Cerve, Wishar Spenle 1883-1939. **Lemuria: The Lost Continent of Pacific**. San Jose, Calif.: Supreme Grand Lodge of AMORC [Ancient Mystical Order Rosae Crucis] , 1974. Fourteenth edition. 'With a special chapter by Dr. James D. Ward.' First published 1931. Additional subtitle on dustjacket: 'The Mystery People of Mt. Shasta.' Wishar Spenle CervŽ is the pseudonym of Harve Spencer Lewis. First paperbound edition published in 1997.   Contains only one short chapter about the legends of Lemurians in northern California. The chapter is entitled "Chapter XI: Present-Day Mystic Lemurians in California" and the Mt. Shasta portions are based in large part on the Selvius 1925 article about a Lemurian Village on Mt. Shasta (see Selvius 1925).

It appears that the Bidwell family and the other First Families of Hartford had somehow developed a legacy that included the creation of new faiths. This is a broad accusation that seems only to be backed up by the association of family members all linked in one way or another by blood to the family of John Bidwell the founder of Chico, California. This is comparable to the legacy of the First Families of Virginia but expressed in a much different way. The Virginia families did include some families in common with the Hartford group including the Lewis family. The population of Colonial America was not large at first enabling many of these relations between family that may have been sent by their main groups to establish a kind of beachhead for their interests in the new land.

The first families of Virginia seemed to have created initiatory mysteries that included many Masonic and family concepts based on a rich heritage valuing both the Cavalier and Jacobite ideals of the state's history. Some of these early Virginians and Maryland citizens were Catholic at a time when they could not necessarily advertise this fact. Part of the ethos of some regions of Colonial America was staunchly anti Catholic. Some of these other groups valued a freedom of faith independent of the Church or any of its influence. It may have been this dynamic that led these early Hartford colonists to later form alternative faiths to that of old line Christianity. This is a theory. The early "hidden Catholics may have formed a kind of mystery school apparatus to maintain their faith and be recognized by others without giving away their values to the population at large. This may have contributed a hidden network that was used long after it was necessary to hide ones faith in the United States. Still we do see many instances of Catholic and Secular disagreements even extending to violence in many cities as the United States expanded westward. St. Louis especially has a legacy of this type of conflict that seems to have cooled to cordial relations between these two groups in the modern United States. American Catholics have proven many times their ability to do what is right for the Republic despite any obligations they have to their faith.

Though the Hartford families established mysteries similar to those originating in Virginia they may have attached more of a spiritual value to this tradition in the form of educating the public about different cultures and belief systems. This idea may not have been part of these families' ideals until later but they seemed to have conflict with many of the forces that the Virginians had allied themselves with. Even the story of the Charter Oak of Hartford has the colonists at odds with James II who is a Jacobite icon. This difference between the ethos through time of the Hartford group versus the Virginia group may have also led to conflicts like the Civil War later. There are also many instances of Jacobite loyalties not being based on faith but a given family's status with the exiled Stewart Kings of England and Scotland. Even may protestant families had business dealings that had benefitted from their support of the Stewarts. This led to them being loyal to the Jacobite cause later in America. In addition only about 20% of Jacobites were thought to have been Catholic.

It is among this group that the symbols of the Auspice of Mary, Octagon, and Chi Rho ("Hooked X") were valued. In this way these symbols also became associated with Mary Magdalene by Jacobites that had some alternate Christian beliefs. These beliefs may have been persecuted in the old world and likely contributed to many of these people's desires to come to the colonies as well. The United States was a relatively safe place now for people of many alternate beliefs. This dynamic led to upstate New York being known as the "burnt over area" during a period during which many alternate faiths including Mormon were being developed. This is also by coincidence where the family of John Bidwell had migrated to from Hartford Connecticut in the 1790's.

So far people from these first families of Hartford were involved in the creation of the King James Version of the Holy Bible, Rosicrucian Order (AMORC), The I Am Activity, The Theosophical Society, The Mysteries of Mt. Shasta and Chico, The d'Abbadie family and the Great Cyclic Cross of Hendaye mystery and others. These are impressive associations that kind of leave a trail of metaphorical and allegorical hints that this theory may be true. True many of these connections are tenuous and distant. They would only mean something if planned in a scheme that valued intermarriage within a specific group somewhat like what Royalty does. This group seemed to value specific families beyond any imperial association. Even given the smaller population of North America during early colonial times it is odd that these family names linked to origins in or near Hartford are continually associated with these phenomenon in Northern California.

Are there any more associations of this type that may be linked to the Bidwell family and the apparent creation of a new form of belief or faith out of thin air?

Hannah Smith formerly Bidwell. Born: May, 6, 1716 location unknown. Wife of Richard **Smith-** Married May, 2, 1754 in Glastonbury, Hartford, Connecticut.

(http://www.wikitree.com/wiki/Bidwell-195#Biography)

Note here all the associations we have made between the Hale family, Smith family, and other first families of Hartford. Two Hales appear on the Founders Monument in Harford along with John Bidwell (original) and Rev. Hooker. The next Hales and Bidwell connection noted below is very impressive. One of the daughters of Issac and Elizabeth Lewis married Joseph Smith the founder of the Mormon faith. It is clear that the Smiths and Bidwell's were at least related via the marriage of Hannah Bidwell and Richard Smith in Glastonbury Connecticut.

> HALE, Isaac *b:* 21 Mar 1763 New Haven, New Haven, CT *d:* 11 Jan 1839 Harmony, Susquehanna, PA *#:* HALE32
> +LEWIS, Elizabeth *b:* 19 Nov 1767 Litchfield, Litchfield, CT *d:* 16 Feb 1842 Harmony, Susquehanna, PA *#:* HALE5 *m:* 20 Sep 1790 Wells, Rutland, VT *Mother:* Esther TUTTLE *Father:* Nathaniel LEWIS

Elizabeth and Issac's daughter:

Hale, Emma b: 10 Jul 1804 Harmony, Susquehanna, PA d: 30 Apr 1879 Nauvoo, Hancock, IL. Married: **Smith, Joseph, The Prophet** b: 23 Dec 1805 Sharon, Windsor, VT d: 27 Jun 1844, Carthage, Hancock, IL; killed by a mob. m Jan 1827. Mother: Lucy Mack, Father; Joseph Smith.

(http://freepages.genealogy.rootsweb.ancestry.com/~dav4is/ODTs/HALE.shtml#~HALE-WARD)

So there you have it. Not only is there a clear yet limited connection to the Bidwell family of founder of Chico John Bidwell there is a solid connection between Joseph Smith and relatives of Bidwell and all the other first families including the Lewis family and Hale family. A direct link between the Bidwell's and Smith family of Joseph jr. may exist in the relatively unreliable documentation of Hannah Bidwell married to Richard Smith above. There are many more links than those listed above. It is clear that the family of Joseph Smith was solidly connected to the First Families of Hartford and the Bidwell family.

All of these families are interwoven and in ways it would be difficult not to have found them all blood related well into the nineteenth century if not beyond. They even seemed to associate with each other as groups of them moved west as part of normal settlement patterns. This family group includes a Smith that was the first lady of President Zachary Taylor as well as other important families like the Olcott's, Scott's, and Hales. In this group we see Presidents Taylor and Van Buren with John Bidwell having been a Senator from California and a Presidential Candidate that did make a legitimate run.

Bidwell was also visited by a list of dignitaries over the years that included John Muir, General Sherman, and President Hayes. It is also possible that Bidwell had at least met first California Surveyor General and Director of Indian Affairs Edward Beale. Edward was of course associated with the Beale First Family of Virginia the namesake of the famous "Beale Treasure" legend. The Beale family is also intimately involved in the "Mystery of Bacon's Vault" in Williamsburg Virginia. The Beale's are part of the colonial group that ultimately would be aware of or create the mysteries of the Powder Magazine in Williamsburg, The Newport Tower, Kensington Rune, International Peace Garden, Maryhill Stonehenge, and the Palace of the Legion of Honor in San Francisco. The legacy of this group of colonists from Virginia is very similar to the evolution of the family group we see coming from Hartford founders.

These associations would seem to go beyond a mere connecting of the dots and may suggest the fact that all of these new forms of faith were part of some sort of family legacy of this group that included their most successful experiment to date the Mormon faith. This also points to a kind of silent war between this faction and a small group of gentry from Virginia who hid their Catholic faith in some way yet were involved intimately in the creation of many symbolic and political American ideals. This will be discussed further in association with President Jefferson who is again a distant relation to the Easton family included on the Hartford Founders Monument.

The Mormon faith is a uniquely American form of spirituality that has a large following. The Mormon's established Utah and Salt Lake City as integral parts of the United States after enduring some conflicts with the Federal Government and other settlers in the early phases of settlement. No matter the details of the origins of this American religion it endures and seems to be here to stay for a very long time.

Partial Contents: Ancestry of Joseph Smith: included are the families of Bagley, Baker, Bennett, Bodfish, Brocklebank, Champion, Colby, **Crocker**, Curtis, **DeWolf**, Dutton, Duty, French, Fuller, **Gates**, Gould, Hidden, Howland, Hunt, Huntley, **Lee**, Look, Loomis, Lothrop, Mack, Meriam, **Olmsted**, Palmer (John), Palmer (William), **Redding**, Rowley, **Smith**, Strickney and Tilley -- Ancestry of Emma **Hale**: included are the families of Barnes, Beach, Bogworth, Bradley, Buckland, Bunnell, Chedsey, Chipman, Cobb, Denslow, Frost, **Hale** (Heald), Hodge, Hotchkiss, Howland, Huckins, **Hurst**, **Lewis**, Lord, Mallory, Maltby, Meigs, Nash, **Paine**, Platt, **Powell**, **Preston**, Prichard, Royce (Rice), Sherman, Spinning (Spinage), Talmage, Thompson, Tilley, Towner, Tuttle, Vinton, **Ward** and Wilmont -- **Posterity of Joseph Smith and Emma Hale.**

Overview of the street plan and significant components of Chico architecture.

The original street plan was designed by John Bidwell and some sources say he helped to actually lay out the plan. At first Bidwell was owner of Rancho Arroyo Chico which had been granted to him by the Mexican government. An examination reveals that during the early years of Chico Bidwell may have even invited like minded people and families from his family to settle in Chico.

His 8x8 block plan is based on the Chessboard. A game sometimes associated with the Knights Templar. The City Plaza today includes Elm Court a tree associated with Leland Stanford and other secret values on the Broadway side of the City Plaza includes chessboards built into tables.

Ishtar was also known to enjoy chess very much in some mythology. She or in her guise as Athena is displayed on the Bank of America Building. The city plaza includes a bandstand that resembles ancient Roman architecture. The center of the City Plaza includes a now faded mosaic of the earth thus demonstrating its value as a temporal tool and Axis Mundi.

The old New Daughters of the Golden West building on Salem and Second streets is where this group used to meet. It is now a restaurant. The basement grate covers are inverted pentagrams thus possibly associated also w/ the Eastern Star. The NDGW was originally a hereditary group comprised of descendants of California Pioneers. They dedicated the plaque on the foundation stone of Chico that is located on the Fourth Street side of the City Plaza. This is the direction that "points to Benton City now known as the Monastery of New Clairvaux. The Main Street side of the City Plaza is home to a Veteran's Memorial that is very aesthetically pleasing and includes many of the integral symbols of the United States that have their origins in the same family group that values the symbols on the old Bank of America building. The Fifth street side of the City Plaza includes a building used for public restrooms. The side of this structure that faces the bandstand includes a very nicely executed mural of the electric trolley cars that used to operate in downtown Chico. John Bidwell's cousin Benton Bidwell was considered to be the inventor of significant portions of the electric motors included in these cars. So apropos.

Discussed earlier is the Senator Theater built by Pfleuger.

The Carnegie Library of Chico. This structure on the corner of Salem and second streets across from the old New Daughters of the Golden West building was once the Chico public Library and is today the Chico Museum. The building has a vaguely Romanesque look to it to match the architecture of Chico State which is also part of the legacy of Chico. The renovation of this building into its current form is one of the greatest blunders of Chico architectural history. It originally included an octagonal tower on its Salem Avenue side. This was removed leaving us with the boxy and far more simple looking structure than what was originally there. It may be the tower was removed to make parking on Salem Street more plentiful. Very sad.

The base of the Chico diamond shaped chess board street plan of Chico may have been intentionally arranged to sit on the latitude of the Mason Dixon Line. This may also be true of Indianapolis Indiana, and Denver Colorado. This may represent a kind of planning effort by the Society of the Cincinnati or other groups.

The newly constructed labyrinth in "Children's Park" (?) is also on the alignment from the northwest orientation of the City Plaza that includes the Old Bank of America building, The WWI Memorial, The Labyrinth, Bidwell Mansion and strange circular feature behind it, The Gateway Museum and its Diamond shaped logo, and the Monastery of New Clairvaux.

Northern Star Mills. Originally owned by John Bidwell and directly across the Esplanade (street name) from Bidwell Mansion. Of course an Esplanade is a large open linear area associated with an Axis Mundi. In this case the City Plaza. The use of the imagery of the Pole Star in one of Bidwell's businesses also may be connected to this value of navigation in the context of Arcadia and his likely Merovingian and Plantagenet ancestry. It is amazing this name was chosen by the man who established the Axis Mundi of the City Plaza by ploughing a circle in the tradition of Constantine founding Constantinople. Given what we have learned about the Byzantine and Arian royal relations to the Merovingian dynasty coupled with Bidwell's ancestry stemming from Ormus le Guidon this is entirely possible and explains many things about Chico that at first glance do not make sense.

California State University Chico was originally the Chico Normal School (for teachers). It was indeed founded by many early Chicoans who were also members of the Freemason's and Knights Templar. The administration building (Kendall Hall) on campus is especially interesting and includes similar cement relief art to that seen at the old Bank of America building. This structure is a very nice building done in the Romanesque style that matches the other older structures around it including Laxson auditorium. Art included in the façade of this structure depicts the scene of the founding of Rome including Romulus and Remus suckling from a She Wolf. The image of the wolf is interesting here in relation to the Bidwell's original old English name of Biddulph or "War Wolf." Some scholars even associate this family line with "Beowulf." The image of the wolf is also parallel in many ways to the mythology of Arcas the namesake of Arcadia who in turn in metaphor is Ursa Minor containing the Pole Star. The California flag even is telling us "Arcadia." An interesting array of time capsules and pavement is located in front of the Kendall Hall that also may be there to infer the millennial and temporal concepts valued by this philosophy. The lentil over the doorway to Kendall hall vaguely resembles the kind of pyramidal doors of some Mycenaean "beehive" tombs.

Other spots of interest downtown are the Diamond Hotel, Old International Order of Oddfellows building, The Phoenix Building, and United States Post Office (on the Fifth Street side of the city plaza).

Chico is also home to a home designed by famous architect Julia Morgan that is also owned by Chico State. Morgan helped William Randolph Hearst to design many of the structures at Hearst Castle and their Wyntoon Estate near Mt. Shasta. The Hearst family also donated the "Sacred Stones" to the Monastery of New Clairvaux as well as donated significantly to the construction of the Chapter House there. The Chico area is home to many impressive Estates that were built by the original "Nut Baron's" of the region.

Chapter 16: The Knights Tombstone of Jamestown Virginia, The Beale Treasure, and the Mysteries of North America

One of the most interesting legends of Williamsburg comes to us from the 1930's Golden Age of mysticism and intrigue in the form of the Legend of the Bruton Parish Church Vault or what some may term "Bacon's Vault." This legend seems to have been inspired in part by the wife of Masonic Philosopher Manly P. Hall, Marie Bauer Hall as well as folklore surrounding the original church at Jamestown. Ms. Hall used the artwork on headstones at the Bruton Parish Church in Williamsburg and related them to Wither's Book of Symbols (1635) to infer that there was indeed a hidden vault of what may have been the personal papers of Sir Francis Bacon located there. This legend dictated that a distant relative of Sir Francis Bacon named Nathaniel Bacon had brought a stash of Bacon's personal effects and papers to the New World in order to preserve them. Though Ms. Hall was involved in certain areas near the Bruton Parish Church being excavated no vault was ever found. Even people as late as the 1990's had undertaken illegal excavations in the Bruton Parish Church yard searching for this lost vault.

Amazingly this author discovered another similar mystery at Stirling Castle in Scotland involving "The Service Stone" and another book of symbols by Quarles also printed in 1635. Some even speculate the hand of Bacon in the production of both of these books that include elaborate engravings accompanied by poems related to the artwork. This stone was named for stonemason John Service who signed the second stonemason charter with the Sinclair family in Scotland.

The Service Stone is covered with Masonic symbols and an illustration from the Quarrels book. This is a similar mystery that existed long before Ms. Hall identified the same phenomena at the Bruton Parish Churchyard that in turn led her to her conclusions about the vault there. Amazingly the Service Stone at Stirling even includes bullet holes that were caused during Bonnie Prince Charlie's attempt to retake Scotland and his crown in his failed Jacobite invasion. No one had linked the stories of the Service Stone and Ms. Hall's theories about Williamsburg prior to the publishing of "The Geographic Mysteries of Sir Francis Bacon."

Both of these books and the appendant mysteries at both Stirling and Jamestonwn/Williamsburg took place at about the same time the sons of Sir William Alexander of Stirling, William and Anthony became the first speculative Freemason's in Scotland. William the Younger would go on to possibly be the first speculative Freemason to set foot in Nova Scotia or Canada as he served as the first Scottish Governor there. If we were to consider the hand of the Alexander family in the Legend of the Bruton Parish Church Vault it would make sense given their connections to Stirling Castle and the Service Stone located there. Echoes of "Arcadia" and William Alexander Earl of Stirlings partial authorship may be seen in both the mysteries of Williamsburg and Stirling Castle.

This story also includes the fact that Nathaniel Bacon had originally hidden valuable items in a vault in the original church in Jamestown Virginia and that they had later been moved to Williamsburg's Bruton Parish Church when that was designated the colonial capitol later. The story of the vault legend then even goes on to suggest that later individuals such as Thomas Jefferson and Franklin Delano Roosevelt were the last two to see the contents of the vault as they may have found it themselves. Of course many elements of this story may simply add up to folklore and local legends though there may be a thread of truth to this entire story. Some of these stories may have developed in tandem with the Rockefeller family's involvement in the reconstruction of the the colonial capitol array in Williamsburg in the 1930's coincidentally the same era in which Ms. Bauer Hall made her assumptions.

Both Jefferson and Roosevelt also have family connections to this saga. Jefferson may be related to the Easton's of Newport while Roosevelt has all the same connections to Nova Scotia that poet Longfellow possessed including the Society of the Cincinnati. We all know that F.D.R. once as a young man invested in the recovery of the Oak Island Treasure. Amazing that here another President of the United States was involved in such activity possibly signaling that he indeed have some inside information with regard to the truth of Oak Island and other places.

In my book "The Geographic Mysteries of Sir Francis Bacon" I discuss how the legend of the Bruton Parish Church vault may indeed add up to being the same phenomena later termed "The Beale Treasure." The dynamics of the story of California Surveyor General Edward Beale and his son Truxtun have many elements that may point us to the truth of the Beale and Vault legends. The fact that Californian Truxton Beale chose to have himself interred at the Bruton Parish Churchyard on his passing links him to his famous colonial forebear Thomas Beale and his role as one the first Virginia Cavaliers, Sheriff of adjacent York County, and commander of the fort at Old Point Comfort in Hampton Virginia.

Truxtun included a memento mori to his ancestor Thomas Beale on his own headstone in the Bruton Parish Churchyard. Here we may see how Thomas Beale may have been privy to the exploits of still another earlier important member of his family whose secrets he may have been hiding. This story may also reveal the object of other important mysteries at Shugborough Hall of the Anson family in England.

Thomas Beale had been a Cavalier bodyguard of Charles I and had fled to Virginia after the demise of the king. We have also seen in past works how the concept of Arcadia is associated with Charles I beheading as his last words were from the work of Phillip Sydney entitled "Arcadia." Of course, Philip Sydney was the brother of Countess of Pembroke Mary Sidney Herbert whose sons funded the First Folio of Shakespeare's works that has also inspired many mysteries and code decipherments.

That factor also leads us to the notion that the famous Shepherd's Monument of Shugborough Hall in England is a Memento Mori for Charles and even Mary Queen of Scots. What may actually be the Beale Treasure is likely displayed as part of the rendering of Poussin's "Et In Arcadia Ego" in reverse bas relief on the Shepherd's Monument itself. This rendering of Poussin includes the addition of a strange casket atop the tomb from the Poussin Work. Otherwise the piece is similar to the original Poussin yet in reverse mirror image. What is in this strange casket? Here this story harkens back to an earlier member of the Beale family that may explain the presence of the strange casket atop the tomb in the Shugborough Poussin rendering.

An earlier member of the Beale family played an important role in the intelligence gathering activities of Queen Elizabeth. Robert Beale was closely associated with many people who would later be identified as spies or "spy masters" of the era of English history. It is likely that Robert Beale knew Philip Sidney. Robert Beale is famous for having been the liaison between Mary Queen of Scots and Queen Elizabeth during their dispute. Mary Queen of Scots had looked to Elizabeth for refuge from difficulties in Scotland. Eventually it was decided to behead her to eliminate any competition for the crown of England as many felt Mary Queen of Scots had more of a right to the title than Elizabeth I. At this time Robert Beale's duties led him to having somewhat of a friendship with the condemned Queen as the story even includes her gifting Beale an expensive necklace.

Beale was actually present at the beheading of Mary Queen of Scots. This part of the story may lead us to what the strange casket is atop the tomb in the Poussin rendering at Shugborogh while also explaining what the famous Beale Treasure of Virginia actually is. When Mary Queen of Scots was beheaded her personal belongings and diary were said to have been placed in what is described as an elaborate casket that resembles in description the strange reliquary or casket seen in the Poussin rendering at the Shepherds Monument at Shugborough Hall. Robert Beale is one of the only people who may have originally had access to this casket of Mary Queen of Scot's belongings so it is not out of the realm of possibility that he had taken this and hidden it.

This casket would represent a symbol to later Jacobite and Cavalier sensibilities aligned with Stewart Kings who were later beheaded including the Anson family of Shugborough. This may have been a symbol of Jacobite sentiments later regardless of the truth of this legend. Is it possible that the later Cavalier bodyguard of Charles I Thomas Beale had possession of this important Jacobite relic? After his original exile after the death of Charles Thomas Beale returned to England to serve as bodyguard for Charles II when he was made king. At the time of his return to serve Charles the II Beale was commanded in his bodyguard duties by none other than Prince Rupert of the Rhine who also served as first governor of the Hudson's Bay Company. This is but one of many links between Virginia and those that would own and run the HBC including Earls of Orkney and their extended family.

These series of events do suggest Thomas Beale's involvement with those that may have even possessed these items of Mary Queen of Scot's. As a bodyguard of the King Thomas Beale had great responsibility and associated with those in the highest echelons of power. Note also that other bodyguards of Charles I and II had come to Virginia and had part of the "Cavalier culture" of colonial Virginia.

All of this adds up to Jamestown and Williamsburg being a place of importance in all these legends of the quest. It seems that the story of the Bruton Parish Church Vault, Mystery of Shugborough, and the Beale Treasure Legend may all have a common origin and purpose in the folklore of early Colonial and American history. It seems that the involvement of Sir Francis Bacon is also inferred as being associated with many of these stories and is backed up by the

288

presence of Bacon family members that are part of the extended family of Bacon in Jamestown and later though out the development of the United States.

So where does this leave us with regard to the Legend of "Bacon's Vault" even if elements of this story have a kind of fairytale quality to them?

We may see some help in understanding these questions in the form of what we are supposed to find inside this hidden vault. These stories infer a great treasure hidden that is worth a great deal of money. What if the treasure is indeed something else? What if the treasure is what is revealed when someone actually searches the original location of the vault in the foundations or environs of the original Jamestown Church? In fact this is actually what has been happening as archaeologists have been excavating the church for the last three years and have found some amazing artifacts and clues that may lead us to the truth of the Bruton Parish Church Vault and many of these other treasure stories.

To date two amazing finds at the Jamestown Church could also comprise what may have been inferred in the intentional development of the Vault and Beale treasure legends. Both the Archer Reliquary recovered in the grave of Captain Archer and the Knights Tombstone of early Governor Sir George Yeardley may be the items we are supposed to find. Both of these objects include symbols and clues that in turn may be linked to the sensibilities of Sir Francis Bacon and later people who meant to continue his legacy while also preserving the Jacobite and Cavalier notions that would later contribute to the American Revolution and associated concepts of liberty and personal freedoms. Both the Archer Reliquary and Knights Tombstone were found at the original location that was said to have included whatever was brought to Virginia by distant Bacon relative Nathaniel Bacon also famous for "Bacon's Rebellion" in early Virginia. Part of the intrigue of Nathaniel Bacon may also include his association with what is known of as "Bacon's Castle" near Jamestown.

The Archer Reliquary was discussed in detail in my book "The Geographic Mysteries of Sir Francis Bacon." This small simple silver reliquary tells the tale of how Captain Archer may have been a "hidden Catholic" in Jamestown. During this era Catholics were persecuted in England as they were slowly given more rights and tolerance under King James I whose mother was Mary Queen of Scots. Previously Elizabeth I had dictated a great deal of persecution and intolerance of Catholics in her realm. This dynamic would continue through history to cause a great deal of turmoil in England that would also extend to the colonies. For the next one hundred years after Elizabeth England would go through a struggle between parliamentarians and the traditional Scottish Kings of England and Scotland that were Catholic. This would lead to the beheading of Charles I and II and the later exile of James II and his sons James III the "old pretender" and Bonnie Prince Charlie. Many of these so called Jacobites would revolt in England and Scotland and after losing many would be sent in exile or escape to Scandinavia and the Colonies. These lost attempts to regain the throne on the part of the exiled Stewarts would lend a great deal to the later American Revolution and provide us with a somewhat overlooked role of the Catholic Church in that struggle.

The short story of the Archer Reliquary is that it may even lead us to the strange and enigmatic Kensington Rune in Minnesota later in History. There is a clear trail of the symbols seen on the reliquary later being present on the Kensington Rune. The symbols etched on the small silver reliquary resemble those later seen in part on the Kensignton Rune. This pathway is marked by a clear trail of the descendants of the first families of Jamestown spreading through the North American continent including Minnesota as the United States expanded westward. Along the way newer references to the older mysteries discussed here were likely left and the Kensington Stone may be one of these symbolic markers left to tell you that a mystery is afoot. Coincidentally the Kensington Stone marks the border between French Louisiana and Rupert's Land of the Hudson's Bay Company along with two other "missing stone legends" that seem to also mark this same border at different points.

Even the modern logo of the College of William and Mary seems to include the same symbols that the Archer Reliquary displays including the letter X and the Auspice of Maria symbol which in other forms resembles a Masonic Compass and Square design. The Archer Reliquary may even be associated with a little discussed earlier Jesuit Mission that had been attempted by the Spanish near the site of what would be Jamestown later. It is even possible that Archer knew this reliquary had been one of the missing votive objects from this failed mission that had been eliminated by the local Native Population. This is even backed up by the fact that Archer's cousin at Holy Cross Monastery in Ireland received a strange communion chalice not long after Archer visited England just before he passed and was interred in the yard of the Jamestown Church where legend tells us "Bacon's Vault" was located. Could the Archer Reliquary and the clues left by the Beale family at the Bruton Parish Church be the actual treasure we are supposed to find or is there still more to the story?

Yes there is.

Recently archaeologists at Jamestown have been recovering and preserving the amazing "Knights Tombstone" burial slab of that they suspect to be that of early Virginia Governor Sir George Yeardley. Sir Yeardley's headstone may reveal some surprising links to things I had written in the book about Sir Francis Bacon I wrote mentioned before. The story of Governor Yeardley is worthy of a book of its own as he was an amazing man who took part in military operations against the Spanish in Queen Elizabeth's struggles against them. It is possible that Yeardley took part in the sacking of Cadiz Spain that seemed to also include other naval and military personnel that would later be instrumental in the early administration of the Virginia Colony and Virginia Company. Note also that Sir Francis Bacon was an investor in both Jamestown and the Cupid's Colony of Newfoundland. It may be that many of these men were rewarded for their service by being given powerful positions in early Virginia. This would also include others such as Lord De la Warr.

One of the elements of Sir Yeardley's burial slab will provide us with amazing links to the symbols on the Archer Reliquary, the logo of the College of William and Mary, and finally the Kensington Rune. The burial slab itself is an amazing artifact though it has broken into several pieces at this time.

The slab is an approximately 3' wide by 8' long crafted piece of stone. One mystery would include how this monument was even brought to Jamestown. It is unlikely that it was produced locally at the time of Yeardley's passing in 1627. This was still an early date for the colony and suggests that great effort was undertaken to even get this stonework to Jamestown. It must have been brought aboard a supply ship. All of this adds up to what an important person Yeardley was. Governor Yeardley was even made a Knight of the Realm by King James I himself on his last visit to England before he passed.

The burial slab itself was once decorated with elaborate bronze plate decorations that are now missing. These decorative elements displayed a border as well as the Knights Head design that is associated with Sir Yeardley. Past records indicate that Yeardley's burial slab once included his family arms and this factor may lead us to some amazing connections to the symbols of William and Mary, Archer Reliquary, Kensington Stone, and other families I have discussed in my theories of how all this is connected together in a continuous treasure hunt with possibly no end in sight.

The arms of Sir Yeardley are very revealing. They are quartered with or include the armorial bearings of the Audley family of Staffordshire who have some amazing associations with the mysteries of the Newport Tower, Oak Island, The Kensington Rune, Beale Treasure, and even the mysteries of Chico and Mt. Shasta California. The Audley family developed from the Biddulph family of Staffordshire who inspired the name of Biddulph Moor in Staffordshire. Later the Biddulph's would be known by the more anglicized name of Bidwell. All of the Biddulph family were said to be the spawn of one Knights Templar Standard Bearer Ormus le Guidon who had served with distinction in the first Crusade. The name Biddulph means "war wolf" and many even credit the Biddulph's for inspiring the literary classic "Beowulf."

This Biddulph family group would include the Audley's whose arms are included in Yeardley's arms. The Audley's are famous for Knight James Audley. In turn the famous Eaton family would develop from the Audley family and include the same design in their arms with a change of colors from red and gold to green and gold. The design included in the Audley, Eaton, Yeardley, and Spencer arms includes a diamond shape with an X overlaid. This design infers both the "hooked X" and Auspice of Mary or AVM symbols seem on the Archer Reliquary, logo of William and Mary, and later inferred on the Kensington Rune.

As it turns out Sir Yeardley's name and family descended from the Audley family thus also making them descendants of Ormus le Guidon and the Biddulph group of families. This is why the arms of Audley are included within Yeardley's arms. Amazingly Ormus le Guidon is credited with bringing the first "moorish" stonemason's to England after the Crusade. Ormus was also known to have built two churches in Stafforshire that include the strange Auspice of Maria in inscriptions there. The stonemason's he brought from the levant went on to build a series of fortresses in Wales to assist King Richard I in his conquest of that region aided by James Audley. This story leads us to distant echoes of some of the themes of Shakespeare's Richard III that seems to tell hidden truths associated with how Richard subdued Wales and created a series of fallen Welsh Kings. It is amazing that Yeardley's burial slab is such a well crafted item for this period of history and may reflect his families association with the first real stonemason's in England.

It appears that Yeardley has a direct family association with a group of families in Staffordshire that would have a hand in many mysteries of the colonies and future United States. This would also include the Stafford family of Newport Rhode Island, The first families of Hartford Connecticut, The Boston Brahmins, and First families of Virginia. The mysteries of Northern California including the strange street plan of Chico and Mt. Shasta are also directly associated with John Bidwell who is descendant of the Biddulph family of England. The connections are also endless to the early settlers of Minnesota from Virginia who may have had knowledge of or even created the Kensington Rune. Kensington incidentally is named for Kensington Palace in London whose first occupants were King and Queen William and Mary. Many of these conundrums also seem to include the influence of the Earls of Orkney with both their Scots and Scandinavian influences.

So how does all this connect us to Sir Francis Bacon?

First of all this entire mystery was framed later as involving a hidden vault of Sir Francis Bacon's papers. This same legend has been applied by others to the Oak Island treasure legend as well. It is important to note that the association of Sir Bacon was applied to both Oak Island and Williamsburg at later dates in history. None of the Bacon associations with these places seemed to have come to light until the twentieth century and Ms. Hall's assumptions about the Bruton Parish Church. What is amazing is that in these mysteries and others through different phases of American history is that a member of the Bacon family seems to have been present during their development. The original stories of Oak Island and Jamestown do not include these suggestions until later in history. It may be this association at Oak Island is even much more recent than any Bacon associated "treasure" at Williamsburg.

There are connections to Sir Bacon via the Eaton family that were split off from the Audley's. This is why their armorial bearings are similar yet with different colors. I have written of the Eaton's influence in being a Mayflower family, developers of the International Peace Garden, Founders of Yale University, and later early Mayors of Los Angeles. Bacon's wife was closely related to the Eaton family. In addition we see "the other Sir Francis Bacon" of Norwich England displaying the arms of Eaton on his burial monument.

The Knights Tomb of Jamestown.

The arms of Sir Yeardley

The arms of Audley

The arms of Eaton

William and Mary, The House of Orange, and Mary Magdalene

Williamsburg Virginia is named for William III of the House of Orange and his wife Queen Mary II daughter of James II the first exiled King of Scotland and England. In past works I have related the logo or symbol of the College of William and Mary to a value of Mary Magdalene. (For an in depth look at the possibility that the House of Orange valued Mary Magdalene as an ancestor please see the great work of author Ralph Ellis). The symbols included in the College of William and Mary's logo display both the "X" sigil and the Auspice of Mary symbol that resembles the Masonic Compass and Square design. One interpretation of this arrangement of symbols may include St. Andrew and Mary Magdalene. As we have seen the French and Scottish families involved in this story would value both of those in a very real way. Even the collar of the Order of the Thistle includes both symbols.

The House of Orange evolved in southern France in a small part of what is now the Provence or Cote' d' Azure province of France. The small area known as Orange is not far north of Avignon and also in the same region as St. Maximin et Baum where the remains of Mary Magdalene are said to rest. Given these connections is it possible that the House of Orange along with all of the de La Tour connections we have found are associated? There are some important mingling of the House of Orange and the de La Tour d'Auvergne family that we see also related to the Marquis de Lafayette and Bonnie Prince Charlie! In turn related to the Blanchefort's of Rennes le Chateau!

In fact Queen Mary II was an aunt of Bonnie Prince Charlie. We do see Henri de La Tour d'Auvergne marrying Elisabeth of Orange-Nassau in 1594. Elisabeth's mother was none other than Charlotte Bourbon of the French Royal family. The connections to influential people who may have believed they were descendant of Mary Magdalene is probable even leading to this imagery being included in Williamsburg and Jamestown Virginia during the same era in which Henri and Elisabeth lived.

The mysteries of Williamsburg include a chapter with a much more modern story that seems to reflect the same kind of intrigue we see at Rennes le Chateau, Shugborough Hall, and Stirling Castle which all include Arcadian imagery in their history and lore.

In 1934 wife of Masonic philosopher and mystic Manly P. Hall, Marie Bauer Hall had speculated that a vault of Sir Francis Bacon's papers were stashed on the property of the Bruton Parish Church in Williamsburg. Williamsburg is home to the Powder Magazine which may serve as a symbolic clue in this saga in much the same way the Tour Magdala and Frenchman's Tower of Palo Alto were meant to represent. All of these structures refer to time and space in the tradition of the Tower of the Winds of Athens and were likely used to establish a prime meridian that in turn identifies a domain of an important individual or philosophy.

As part of this mystery Ms. Hall had identified specific art and poetry located on headstones in the Bruton Parish Churchyard that were also present in Wither's Book of Emblems published in 1634. Amazingly this matches an inferred mystery at Stirling Castle in Scotland that utilized the symbols and poems in yet another Book of Emblems written by Quarles. Some have speculated that both books had been produced by Sir Francis Bacon or one of his circle at that time. Quarles Book of Emblems has symbols and one passage that are included on the famous Service Stone of Stirling discussed earlier in the chapter on Stirling Castle.

Both the Bruton Parish Church and Williamsburg Powder Magazine are part of what is likely the first linear park in North America. This linear array composed of the College of William and Mary to the west and the House of Burgesses or Virginia Capitolto the east and between includes the Governor's Mansion, the octagonal Powder Magazine, and the Bruton Parish Church. It was during the 1930's restoration of this linear park by the Rockefeller family that Ms. Hall was able to excavate in the Bruton Parish Churchyard yet came up empty handed. This is no surprise in that the actual "treasure" being referred to in this scheme evolved into what may be termed the Beale Treasure today. The National Mall in Washington D.C. would later emulate the array of the Colonial Capitol in Williamsburg.

Through a long series of events the Beale family came to include native Californian Truxton Beale named both for the famous Beale family of Washington D.C. and Revolutionary War Admiral Truxton who was a direct ancestor of Truxton Beale. Truxton even though he hailed from California insisted on being interred in the Bruton Parish Churchyard. His headstone includes a memento mori for his Colonial Ancestor Thomas Beale who had been part of the bodyguard of Charles I and subsequently came in exile to early Virginia about the same time both books of emblems had been produced. The dynamics of the stories of both the Beale Treasure and the "Legend of Bacon's Vault" in Williamsburg also include many of the overtones of the famous Oak Island Treasure legend. The exiled Cavaliers or bodyguard of Charles I and II would later be the inspiration for all University of Virginia sports teams being named "Cavaliers."

Williamsburg or more specifically Jamestown is a place that evolved during the time of Bacon and many speculate that his family relation Nathaniel Bacon had brought Sir Bacon's papers to Jamestown and later they had been moved to a vault in the Bruton Parish Church in Williamsburg. This story also speculates that this vault had been originally located in the original Jamestown Church which, in recent years is being excavated by archaeologists. Already discussed is the importance of the Archer Reliquary and Knights Tombstone in this story as both artifacts reveal a great deal about the history of Jamestown and Williamsburg with all of our connections to the same groups of families involved in the Arcadian mysteries at Rennes le Chateau, Shugborough, and Stirling.

Is it possible that the legend of Bacon's Vault was promoted to lead one to finding what the archaeologists are now finding in Jamestown? (Please see director of Jamestown archaeology Dr. Kelso's recent book about their findings!) Even the Archer reliquary seems to include incised designs that resemble those in the modern logo of the College of William and Mary and similar symbols seen on the Kensington Rune in Minnesota.

It is starting to become obvious that these stories in Williamsburg are coming from the same source as the questions at these other locations and indeed at a date much earlier that either Shugborough or Rennes le Chateau. Even the story of the Frenchman's Tower in Palo Alto had been established long before any follies such as the Tour Magdala were built at Rennes le Chateau.

It is clear that much of this story may have been preserved in literature and artwork that only one initiated in these concepts could understand. With the resources available in the twenty-first century it is still difficult for the novice to collect enough information to put two and two together yet a coherent and easily understood story can emerge with some patience.

Of course, the imagery of Mary Magdalene would be important to this cast of families that would also come to include many of the first families of Virginia including that of George Washington, James Madison, and Thomas Jefferson. Thomas Jefferson owned a painting of "Magdalene Pentinent" by Rivera. Famous artist Georges de La Tour of the already discussed family was a well accomplished artist who also produced several renderings of Magdalene Pentinent that are very well known and popular pieces. Mr. Ralph Ellis discussed in his work how Georges de La Tours Magdalene Pentinent was included in the Walt Disney film "The Little Mermaid." This is interesting in that Disneyland is located in Orange County California. In addition, James Madison's Montpelier is located in Orange County Virginia. A mural at the George Washington Masonic Memorial in Alexandria Virginia includes a pensive Martha Washington situated behind a large orange colored banner thus clueing us into these connections.

Washington's great grandfather was Nicholas Martiau was a Huguenot refugee from France at the same time the House of Orange had adapted this faith. Martiau was from the Isle de Re near La Rochelle France where he is memorialized today with statue of George Washington and a rendering of Nicholas himself. Nicholas was an important figure in Jamestown of the early seventeenth century who even rebuilt the stockade fence at Jamestown when he came there in 1620. Nicholas would go on to be considered the founder of Yorktown Virginia at about the same time that Thomas Beale was Sheriff of York County.

All of these connections are interesting and may illustrate how a Protestant faction would come to value Mary Magdalene in a way that would seem heretical to the Church and the story of Mary Magdalene at St. Marie's de La Mer and St. Maximin et Baum. Is it possible that the entire image of Mary Magdalene had now taken on political overtones associated with the exile of James II and the installation of Monarchs like William III and Mary II as King and Queen of England and Scotland? Its seems a battle was brewing that would show us values in the literature and art of the era associated with both sides of this coin.

We have artists like Georges de La Tour, Nicolas Poussin, and many others referring to this imagery that in turn may support their philosophies with regard to Mary Magdalene. This value in European art had been important for hundreds of years prior to the establishment of Jamestown Virginia. If this line of reasoning is correct then de La Tour was championing the alternate version of Mary Magdalene and her children while Poussin, a member of the Vatican's

Academy degli de Arcadia had produced art that supported the Church's view of the Magdalene. The Church would of course deem the fact that Mary Magdalene may have had children as heretical. It is likely that even prior to the advent of Protestant and Huguenot faith that this belief was still a well kept and secret part of these family's values even at a time when the condiered themselves good Catholics. Some of this belief may have come to the Knights Templar via their close association with these French families.

A belief on the part of the Plantagenet dynasty and House of Orange that they had descended from Mary Magdalene would be a true Protestant belief that would not jive with the beliefs of the Church of Rome in these matters. In turn this concept became a political football between Jacobite factions associated with the church and those that had replaced them such as William and Mary. It is almost without a doubt that early American factions would promote the idea of Mary Magdalene in contrast to her value on the part of the Catholic Church. This philosophical dispute would have then also been transported to the colonies by both sides. These same values may have been appreciated by the Knights Templar and other Knighthoods associated with the de La Tour Dukes of Bullion. Had the some Knights Templar strayed from the fold of the Latin Church influenced possibly by Arian and Cathar values of Christ that disputed his divinity? May this have also led to rumors that they spit on the cross because they did not believe Jesus had been crucified?

Many of these beliefs may have been preserved and promoted using the age old tenets of the Mystery Schools that had preserved the faith of Christianity in its early days in Rome when Christians were persecuted. Mystery Schools always seem to be used by persecuted groups of people in a clandestine manner that sometimes come to resemble intelligence services. It is out of this conflict that differing forms of art and literature were produced to promote and preserve the views of both sides. The end result of this may be both a Church version and heretical version of all of these myths and legends from Oak Island to the slopes of Mt. Shasta in California. Eventually the United States would come to promote their views on these matters by also utilizing metaphorical works of art and literature.

Please see my books "The Sacred Towers of the Axis Mundi" and "The Geographic Mysteries of Sir Francis Bacon" to see how all of this even resulted in the placement of the famous Kensington Rune in Minnesota. Note the name Kensington in that mystery as William and Mary were the first English monarchs to reside at Kensington Palace in London. It is even very likely that a group of first families that had extended from Jamestown eventually moving to Minnesota had been responsible for the Kensington Rune. Associations between Williamsburg and the Hudson's Bay Company via the family of Virginia Governor George Hamilton had been responsible for the placement of the rune near Kensington Minnesota using this line of reasoning. This is why the "X" and Auspice of Maria imagery is present both on the Kensington Stone and the logo of the College of William and Mary. It is likely that the Eaton family and Hill families of early Virginia mentioned in association with the Knights Tombstone of Jamestown were involved in the saga of the Kensington Stone.

298

Both the Eaton's and Hill's had family in Alexandria Minnesota at the time the Kensington Stone was first discovered by farmer Olaf Ohman. Both these families were in turn associated with the establishment of the International Peace Garden on the border of the United States and Canada. The International Peace Garden seems to represent a "New Jerusalem" that was inspired by the Temple of Peace of Rome and its linear association with the fora of Trajan, Julius Caesar, and Augustus (Octavian). The linear array of these fora with the Temple of Peace of Rome (built by Emperor Vespasian) forms an arc on the globe that transects the globe thus "pointing to" the International Peace Garden. A portion of the landscaping at the International Peace Garden actually resembles the plan of the Temple of Peace of Rome. The Shepherds Monument of Shugborough also seems to "point to" both the International Peace Garden and the crypt of Admiral Anson of Shugborough. Still another funerary clue in this grand plan.

Many of the facets of the mysteries of Williamsburg point to its Arcadian themes just as the overtones of Oak Island, Shugborough, and Rennes le Chateau do. The development of Jamestown and Williamsburg even involves the same conflicting family legacies we see in all of the stories of Mary Magdalene that are suggested by this imagery. All of this again harkening back to the Marquis de Lafayette and Thomas Jefferson visiting Chateau Villette the estate featured in the movie "The da Vinci Code." It is likely that Thomas Jefferson had been initiated into these secrets via an examination of the Powder Magazine in Colonial Williamsburg that was there when he was a student of land surveying among other subjects at William and Mary.

As we will see much of this imagery is referred to in the momento mori of the other Sir Francis Bacon from Norwich England. This thread of mystery will also include the arms of the Eaton family as discussed prior in this tale.

The modern logo of the College of William and Mary shows the X of St. Andrew which refers to Arcadia and the Auspice of Maria symbol that resembles the Masonic Compass and Square design.

299

Jamestowne, the Browne family, and Frenchman's Tower of Palo Alto?

There are many ghost stories and tales of Pirates in Williamsburg. The story of how pirate Blackbeard's skull was fashioned into the base of a silver punch bowl is both interesting and does include some credible documentation. Prior to the existence of the punchbowl Blackbeard's head was placed on a pike at the entrance to Hampton Harbor known as Blackbeard's Point not far from Williamsburg. This talisman was displayed at the Raleigh Tavern in Williamsburg and disappeared with its last sighting in the early 1920's.

The story of the Bruton Parish Church vault may have also been developing at around this time. Many of the first families of Virginia had ties to the regimes of monarchs Charles I and II or later James II and Bonnie Prince Charlie. Each time the fallen Catholic Kings attempted to regain the throne they were defeated. Many refugees and exiles from those conflicts came to Virginia and the rest of the colonies where their Jacobite spirit helped to create the United States and gain independence from Britain.

Some of these families were well known and connected to the Jacobite movement both in the colonies and Great Britain even though they were Protestant. The regime of the fallen Stewarts included many who depended on them for supplying the government and military with goods and services and those that had also benefitted in their commerce due to the approval of the monarchy. Among these early families to Colonial Virginia were the Browne family.

A man named Henry Browne established one of the first plantations on the south side of the James River known as "Four Mile Tree." It is likely that Four Mile Tree was established in the 1620's and was the seat of the Browne family for over two hundred years. As in other colonial families the Browne's are related to an impressive array of well known and famous early Americans.

Amazingly Colonel Henry Brown was of direct descent of Sir Anthony Browne 1st Viscount Montagu Lord of Cowdray that we have examined in our earlier look at the Frenchman's Tower of Palo Alto and the Legend of J.C. Brown(e). This is without a doubt the same family later involved with the Hammer family of Stockton California that were in turn related to Bacon family members also present in the development of Chico California. Though this may be a coincidence our earlier studies of the Browne family also links them via family to the Coutts Bank and the said creator of the Frenchman's Tower Peter Coutts.

The Browne family had intermarried with the Spencer family of early Virginia. This is the same Spencer family that is also directly related to the family of George Washington. The Spencer's even facilitated the Washington's acquisition of Mt. Vernon of which they originally owned half of. This is the same Spencer family of the famous Lady Diana. Their Althorpe Estate in England even includes a Washington Crypt. So just as in the story of the Maryhill Stonehenge and Art Museum and the Palace of the Legion of Honor in San Francisco we see connections to the Frenchman's Tower and mysteries of Mt. Shasta related to the Washington family via the association with the Browne family. Samuel Hill who was part of the Hill family that owned the

300

Great Northern had been involved in building both the Stonehenge and Art Museum as well as the Palace of the Legion of Honor in San Francisco. Sam Hill was descendant of both George Washington and Reverend Jones of the Bruton Parish Church. It may be that the Hill family is privy to the truth of the Kensington Rune in Minnesota as well.

There are no outward signs or direct family links between the Browne family of Jamestown and the Beale and Bruton Vault stories. While this may be true it is known that their family was later involved in the very same tradition that may have involved their descendant Sir Wheetman Pearson Lord Cowdray who may have had some peripheral influence on the legends of Mt. Shasta including the Legend of J.C. Brown. It is interesting to note that one Edward Browne of this family is interred at the Jamestown Fort burial ground. This site has recently revealed many things bout early Virginia via the Archer Reliquary and Knights Tombstone. Many of these men had been given a stake in the Virginia Company or were sent as agents of those who did have a financial interest. As such many of these family's wealth over time developed into significant industries in the United States including railroads of which the Browne family were later involved in.

The Bruton Parish Church and the Page Family

It appears that the mystery presented to us in Williamsburg, even if in the early 20th century fits the template of the other Arcadian mysteries we have examined here. Even if there are some relics or treasures stashed in association with these places none have been found to date that are known of. Many aspects of the kind of mythology and folklore that surround these places may indicate that a distinct pathway had been left to expose verifiable historical happenings that may cast a different light on commonly told history. If this is true then what are we left to think about the Legend of the Bruton Parish Church Vault in Virginia? It may be that this story had been left to tell the true origins of the United States and that later the Beale Treasure Legend had been crafted as an extension or modernization of the same concept.

An examination of some of the dates and individuals involved in the development of Williamsburg may reveal some clues. The early gentry of Williamsburg was added to with another wave of immigration to Virginia associated with the deposition and beheading of Charles I. We have seen how that event relates to Sidney's "Arcadia" with Charles' last words having come from that work of literature. Charles' death was in 1649. At that time many of his supporters including several of his bodyguard made their exile in Virginia and other Colonies.

This exodus would include Sheriff of York County Thomas Beale who came somewhat before the persecution of Charles in 1640. Beale's wife was Alice Reade. The Reade's of course made up a major part of the family of George Washington as time went on. Thomas Beale may be important to the story of both the Beale Treasure and the Bruton Parish Church Vault legend. Just a generation prior to Thomas Beale and his residence in York County his forebear Robert Beale had been a kind of spy who had served as the liaison between Queen Elizabeth and the doomed Queen Mary of Scotland. Discussed earlier is how Mary Queen of Scots had gifted Robert Beale and expensive necklace and how he may have come into possession of her personal effects after her execution. Her possessions may have included a number of different relics of saints and biblical items. It may be that these items are what is included in the Beale Treasure.

Many of the symbolic overtones of the Bruton Parish Church seem to harken back to a church in England known of as All Saints in Maidstone England. This church includes a memorial to the Beale Family and documents its early origins in the region. All Saints also includes a memorial to a Lawrence Washington who is the original Washington family member to have been named via their relation to the Lawrence family of England. Even more interesting is a third monument known of as the Puritan's monument that includes a reference to a "Franklyn" family.

Later we see a brass plaque marking the life of Thomas Beale in the Bruton Parish Church with many Washington's and their colonial forebears having worshipped there. Subsequently we see the development of a treasure mystery that in turn informs us of many details that are left out of the common history. The memorials at both Maidstone and Williamsburg also continue the trend of each of these mysteries having a funerary or memento mori theme attached to them just as we saw in the case of the "other" Sir Francis Bacon. These conundrums are meant to make you remember things you may have otherwise forgotten.

Now fast forward to the twentieth century during the early 1930's when Marie Bauer Hall wife of Masonic mystic and philosopher develops a theory that a vault of Sir Francis Bacon's papers is hidden in a Vault in the Bruton Parish Church. She documented her theory in her book "Foundations Unearthed." Ms. Hall had based her observations on symbols and poetry seen in Wither's "Book of Emblems" that matched themes and designs seen on headstones in the cemetery of the Bruton Parish Church that in turn told the story of how and why the vault was located there.

There are many gaping holes and leaps of faith in Ms. Hall's theories yet they seem to have attracted a great deal of attention and speculation over the years. Part of the Vault Legend states that the treasure or vault was originally located in the Jamestown Church were recently some startling discoveries have been made. According to Ms. Hall's story the vault was moved to the Bruton Parish Church. As stated earlier in this book it is odd that a seemingly identical use of another book of emblems by Quarles on a headstone at Stirling Castle mimicked what Ms. Hall had proposed. In addition the Service Stone of Stirling had been carved by John Service who was a signer of the Stone Mason's Charter of Scotland with the Sinclair family. Had she known about this headstone and book of symbols at Stirling or had someone else steered her into thinking what she had found applied to Williamburg? It is very suspect and strange that a similar theme is at play in Scotland and that both books had been published the same year of 1634.

The Bruton Parish Church we see today was built in 1715 about sixteen years after the official establishment of Williamsburg and about 41years after the establishment of the Bruton Parish. The original Church had been demolished at that time which was built in 1683. 1715 also marks the year of the construction of the Powder Magazine not far from the Church. This year is also the year of the first Jacobite rising in Scotland. Incidentally the octagonal array of the Powder Magazine also forms an arc on the globe that "points to" the Bruton Parish Church and its cemetery. The use of the Powder Magazine as a clue in the Bruton Parish vault legend may later apply to Jefferson's Poplar Forest and the Beale Treasure.

Our link from Virginia to Scotland may come in the personages of Lt. Governor of Virginia Alexander Spotswood and official governor George Hamilton the Earl of Orkney. Spotswood had come from a very old and influential family in Scotland. The Earls of Orkney had through time engaged in the building of talismanic architecture in the tradition of the Tower of the Winds of Athens that in turned defined a domain by measuring time and space to plot points on the earth. Earls of Orkney had built both Rosslyn Chapel and the Orphir Round Kirk which form a prime meridian as discussed earlier.

Given this we may view the Powder Magazine in Williamsburg as having been built to fulfill this tradition in the new land. The family of George Hamilton would later come to control the Hudson's Bay Company. The Kensington Rune sits in a geographic location which may indicate it was placed as a boundary marker between Rupert's Land of the Hudson's Bay Company and French Louisiana.

This is very apropos as Thomas Jefferson, James Madison, and other prominent early Virginian's were educated at the College of William and Mary and may have been exposed to the true mysteries of the Powder Magazine during their time there. Both men as well as future President Monroe and the family of future President Harrison had attended the Bruton Parish Church while attending William and Mary. Jefferson had even studied land surveying and map making or cartography while a student there. Jefferson was also said to be a member of the secretive Flat Hat Club at William and Mary.

Both the Beale Treasure and Legend of the Bruton Parish Church Vault promise a hidden subterranean chamber full if hidden information and golden riches. Interestingly both hidden vault mysteries seem to include references to the Declaration of Independence penned by former William and Mary student and third President of the United States of America Thomas Jefferson. Some even claim that Manly P. Hall, Ms. Bauer Hall's husband had information stating that Thomas Jefferson had examined and resealed the papers of Sir Francis Bacon thus suggesting he had also examined the vault. If true then this may also explain why the Rockefeller family had donated so much money towards the resurrection and restoring of the Colonial Capitol throughout the 1930's at the same time Ms. Hall had developed her theory.

Eventually Ms. Hall obtained permission to have the foundations of the first Bruton Parish Church (ca. 1683) excavated by part of the Rockefeller team under her direction. As the story goes nothing was recovered at the time. Still the question that keeps nagging at this author is that if there was a vault in the old church why hadn't they built a vault in the new church and moved the contents there? Alternately they may have at that time moved the items to a still more secure location? Even Ms. Hall's theory states the vault was once in the Jamestown Church and had been moved. Why would they leave a vault in that location after demolishing the old Church? Maybe we should all simply forget about this and binge watch the movies "National Treasure" parts one and two? There are some strange truths being told in both of those films.

How does the Declaration of Independence fit into Ms. Hall's theory? She certainly did not speculate as to this connection but a close examination of the Page family of early Virginia and beyond may help to answer some questions in this realm. The Page's are closely related to many of the premier known families of early Virginia. They have ties to the Hill family that I have discussed in other works linking Williamsburg to the Kensington Rune. They are directly related to the Nelson family of Founding Father Thomas Nelson, the Harrison family, Washington family, Lewis family, Lee family, and many other's. Their family serves as a virtual who's who through the era of the Revloution and earlier.

John Page came to Virginia in 1650 in what may have been an exile due to his association with Charles I who had been beheaded the year before. Mr. Page would own most of the Property that would become Williamsburg and the College of William and Mary. His holdings were known of as Middle Plantation at that time. The Page's had a long and storied history in England beginning with the Norman Invasions extending through the period of the Crusades and now in early Colonial America. John Page's wife Alice Lukin had come from an important gentry family in England and her father had owned stock in the Virginia Company.

Page donated the land that the first Bruton Parish Church was built on in 1683 and contributed 20 English Pounds towards its construction. If a vault had been included in the church than John Page presents us with a person that would have all the correct ancestors and political connections to have known about it. Later along with James Blair he helped to establish the College of William and Mary on land that he owned. Mr. Blair holds family ties to the Hill family of Minnesota also related to George Washington. The Hills would eventually settle in Minneapolis and Alexandria which is home to the Kensington Rune Stone Museum. Later in the eighteenth century Thomas Jefferson was also closely related to the Page family via his mother's Randolph family and there are many records stating he visited them at many different times in his life.

The Page family had also created what was said to have been the finest pieces of architecture in the colonies at the time at their Rosewell Plantation in Gloucester Country Virginia. Rosewell was a fine brick structure with two octagonal turrets and a copper roof. Rosewell was located on the York River's northern bank not far from Yorktown. Yorktown had been founded by some of the Page's closest relatives the Nelson family as well as the grandfather of George Washington Nicolas Martiau. Martiau had come to Jamestown in 1620 and helped to rebuild the stockade fence there. Later he had settled in the area of York County that would later be Yorktown.

The name "Rosewell" alone conjures images of hidden secrets and mysterious goings on. The rose is in some cases a symbol of secrecy and even comprises part of the name of the Rosicrucian Order. In these days prior to the American Rosicrucian Order the term "Rosicrucian" denoted a follower of a lossely defined philosophy and not the doctrine of any specific group. The Wilton Writers Circle of Mary Sidney Herbert Countess of Pembroke and the Academy degli de Arcadia may have also displayed some Rosicrucian overtones. Taken literally the phrase may mean "secrets of the cross."

The Rosewell Plantation today is in ruins and only a brick hull of its former glory remains. The grounds are the subject of many strange ghost stories and other happenings. Some local rumors even state that the "Holy Grail" was hidden at Rosewell. The plantation of Rosewell is located on the York river on the east side of Carter's Creek. Interestingly the west side of that creek was the home of a large Powhatan Native American Village that some speculate was the home of their leaderPowhatan himself at one time. This location is also the site at which Pocahontas saved the life of Captain John Smith! Rosewell has many historical overtones that may somehow relate to the legend of Bacon's Vault in Williamsburg as well as the Beale Treasure. The Page's did have one intermarriage with the Beale family but held many other families as common relatives of the Beale's as well. The also held some family ties with the Bacon family in England. The story of Smith's capture and salvation there is interesting in light of his "bringing the Holy Grail" to the Native American's legend in Accokeek Maryland on the White House Meridian.

One of Thomas Jefferson's close friends during his time as a student at William and Mary was none other than the great great grandson of John Page also named John Page. The Page family were also closely related to the Randolph family of Thomas Jefferson's mother with one member even later being named Colonel Thomas Jefferson Randolph. Jefferson's daughter would also marry into the Randolph family which in turn may hold some ancient family ties to that of Sir Francis Bacon and other storied families of English gentry. As Jefferson was friends with this later John Page he was said to have visited and stayed at Rosewell several times.

In fact many aspects of what may be read about Rosewell suggest that a thriving literary salon was active at the estate. One of the descendants of John Page was a well known poet. Gatherings of artists and writers were well known events at Rosewell and it may have been that Thomas Jefferson had enjoyed the company of these free thinkers during his era. In fact Rosewell is beginning to resemble descriptions of Chateau Villette in France where Jefferson had associated with the Marquis de Lafayette and Villette's owner Sophie de Grouchy! Echoes of the Wilton Writers Circle of Mary Sidney Herbert and her brother Philip Sidney may also apply here. It seems that Jefferson had some attraction to this crowed of artistic creators and thinkers.

Even Mrs. Page was a staunch women's rights activist just as Sophie de Grouchy had been while hosting her salon! It is clear that during the era of Jefferson the Pages were staunch Patriots of the Independence movement and many were members of the Society of the Cincinnati after the war along with the Marquis de Lafayette, Pierre L'Enfant, and other American heroes such as General William Alexander and George Washington. It seems that art and literature had helped to foster the spirit of freedom and liberty in more than one country during this era of history.

The Page family even supplies us with a link to the life of author Edgar Allan Poe who we have seen possibly having inside knowledge of many of the concepts and treasure stories discussed here. Poe had documented significant interphase with many members of the extended family of the Page's. His roommate at the University of Virginia was Zacheus Lee first cousin of Robert E. Lee. Poe attended the University of Virginia for only one year yet during a period when Jefferson was still alive and known to have met with students.

In 1824 the Marquis de Lafayette made his last trip to the U.S. At that time he was hosted by President Jefferson at a dinner at the Rotunda of the University of Virginia which was attended by many members of the Page family that had also served in the war. This gathering and others like it on Lafayette's visit were comprised of many members of the Society of the Cincinnati. The Society was composed of Revolutionary War officers or one of their male lineal descendants. The Pages also received General Lafayette in their home in Williamsburg after a celebration in memory of the Battle of Yorktown nearby. Even more impressive is that a Page had served as General Lafayette's aide-de-camp during the siege of Yorktown. It seems the Page family were just as close to the Marquis de Lafayette as their family member Thomas Jefferson had been or even George Washington.

The involvement of the Marquis de Lafayette is very compelling and interesting due to his family relations to the mysteries of Rennes le Chateau as discussed earlier. Here he is now with the Page family whom are somewhat associated with the myth or truth of the Bruton Parish Church Vault and the Beale Treasure. All of this is interesting and impressive but one other factor may serve to introduce a later player in this drama. Enter stage left Edgar Allan Poe!

During General Lafayette's visit he was served by an honor guard that attended all his events in Virginia including one in Richmond in addition to the other mentioned above. A member of this special honor guard was none other than budding author at that time Edgar Allan Poe. Poe served as a member of Lafayette's honor guard just before attending the University of Virginia and was likely also present in Charlottesville when Lafayette and Jefferson had their dinner. Jefferson is also listed as a guest in an account of the event in Richmond prior. Poe was eligible to be a member of the Society of the Cincinnati tough there is no record of this. His father had served as a supply master in the Army during the war as an officer. Here we may have the source of Poe's knowledge of Rennes le Chateau and why he included both the imagery of Jefferson, Oak Island, and Rennes le Chateau in his writing. Somehow it may be that this association is the avenue by which this information came to him and possibly other authors and artists that were working in league with the Society of the Cincinnati.

So how does the Declaration of Independence factor in to this intrigue?

Many of the family histories of the Page's state that Thomas Jefferson had been assisted by his friend John Page in writing the first draft of the Declaration of Independence at the Rosewell Planation. So here we have come full circle leading us back to the use of the same Declaration of Independence that is used as a cipher key in the Beale Treasure Legend. It would be terribly interesting if the Declaration had been created at a location that had also served as a literary salon. It is possible that many important subjects vital to the Revolution were discussed at Rosewell long before the war actually started. If the Page family's legacy had included being exiled due to their association with Charles I then this would also align them with the later Jacobite movement that included their exiled progeny James II and Bonnie Prince Charlie. Jefferson spent time in France after the American Revolution and before the French Revolution.

He may have continued his activities at the Salon of Sophie de Grouchy at that time while visiting with the Marquis de Lafayette.

It may be that both the Bruton Vault and Beale mysteries were another extension of the same Arcadian themes that left us information historically applicable to Stirling, Shugborough, Rennes le Chateau, The Frenchman's Tower, Chico and many other places. These people had left us a virtual hard drive of information encoded into the landscape, visual art, literature, and music that may actually lead to verified historical sources that will confirm this scheme of history. At the same time much of this disputes the political spin applied to historical aspects of this story that may not hold up to closer scrutiny if one is led in the right direction so it seems. Many of these mysteries of Arcaida are screaming to us "don't just believe it, check yourself.....history is neglecting us and has kept us a secret....LOOK." Some of the structures they built may actually literally steer you in the right direction to the next clue or concept needed to understand the whole.

Thomas Jefferson's octagonal country estate Poplar Forest us located just to the southwest of Lynchburg, Virginia. Lynchburg was the home of Louis de La Tour later in the nineteenth century. Louis' daughter had married into the family of William Clark of the Lewis and Clark expedition. The Clark's were also lineal descendants of Mary Ball Washington. It appears Jefferson had built Poplar Forest in the very same tradition that the Powder Magazine in Williamsburg had been created. Coincidentally Poplar Forest sits right in the middle of the region of Virginia where the Beale Treasure and Vault is said to be located. In the past I have speculated that the octagonal form of Thomas Jefferson's Poplar Forest could be used as a directional template that may help to solve the Beale Treasure. Amazingly as discussed earlier in this book both Jefferson and Poe seem to have family ties to the Arnold and Easton first families of Newport Rhode Island both possibly involved in the myth or truth of the Newport Tower.

Adding to this suspicion is the fact that there are indeed stories of how Thomas Jefferson's papers had been lost enroute to the Library of Congress from Poplar Forest where he had kept a library. Though information is hard to find on that subject it is interesting that another stash of important lost papers are referred to in conjunction with an octagonal structure whose form has been used in many other similar mysteries from Aachen Cathedral of Charlemagne to the Kings Knot and now the Arcadian setting of the Piedmont region of Virginia so loved by the Third President. Each of these mysteries infer lost documents or libraries including the original "Man in the Mountain" myth of Charlemagne.

It seems that many of the symbols and themes of other mysteries were added to Williamsburg. How had it happened that no one suspected anything going on there until the time the Rockefellers had helped to restore Williamsburg? Had it all been a kind of made up scam to inform one that the Beale Treasure and Legend of the Bruton Parish Church Vault were the same thing? What we may be seeing is how as someone is led from place to place and mystery to mystery a strange kind of inside view of American history emerges? May this have been the reason for the entire scheme. If all of these people were so rich why would they leave a treasure? It is far more likely they would have left information behind and used the treasure story as either

307

bait or a tip off to those who were already in the know to study the history of a given place or person.

Another theory concerning all of this high strangeness may mean that successive generations of the same families had propagated newer versions or extensions of each mystery either to further inform or confuse other seekers. It may have been in this manner that the Beale Treasure had been the impetus for someone to have later created or surmised leading to a similar mystery afoot in Williamsburg. There are many things about the story of Ms. Hall supposing a vault was in Williamsburg that are suspicious and may have been meant to show us something else. Here in the legends of the Bruton Vault and Beale Ciphers we have learned all about the Page family and how the Declaration of Independence had been created. The same concepts were at play during Thomas Jefferson's time in France where he indeed enjoyed the salons and views of his French compatriots.

The dynamics of the intermingling of the first families of Virginia shows how many of these families sided with the Confederacy in the Civil War. Some of these traditions may have taken on a value of the Confederacy at this time. The tradition of using a central axis seems to have been used by Confederate intelligence agents such as the Knights of the Golden Circle. The collapse of the Confederacy may have also contributed to the Beale Treasure Legend. There are many instances of great hordes of gold being hidden somewhere in Virginia to help fund a Confederate revival that never really took hold. There are many stories of train loads of gold and art passing through the region where the Beale Vault is supposed to have been located. A region which also includes Jefferson's Poplar Forest.

Interestingly despite some of their family being Confederate large parts of the Beale Family had sided with the Union as well. This includes Edward Beale who may be the origins of the Beale Treasure Legend. Beale had traveled the parts of New Mexico and Colorado where the original Beale Treasure myth states the treasure was recovered. Ed Beale had traveled across country to Washington D.C. with the first samples of California gold to reach Washington D.C. He was later appointed a General in the U.S. Army and served as Surveyor General of California after it became a State of the Union. The inclusion of California and Nevada on the Union side was a large financial advantage to the Northern side in the Civil War.

As a result of Edward Beale's residence in California his son Truxton was raised in San Francisco. Many members of the Page, Bacon, Bruce, Bidwell, Marsh and other first families of Hartford Connecticut would help to settle California as the 31st State. One of the factors that links the Beale and Bruton Vault stories is the burial place of Truxton Beale. Despite the fact that he was from California Truxton decided to have himself buried in the Bruton Parish Churchyard in Williamsburg. They very site of mystery that would only about seven years later be identified by Californian Marie Bauer Hall as the site of "Bacon's Vault." Was Truxton trying to tell us something? Interestingly Truxton's tombstone includes a memento mori to his colonial ancestor Thomas Beale. Truxton is inferring that both mysteries are indeed one.

It is also possible that the same template could have been used at Oak Island anytime after the Legend was placed into the minds of the public. Originally it may have been a lark or part of some Masonic imagery meant as a learning tool. As the political winds changed in Nova Scotia someone may have used this tradition to hide something real just as the Confederates had done. In light of many of the discoveries in this book it may be that each of these legends did not originally include a real treasure but were meant as learning tools for an initiate of a family fraternity or an organization such as some orders of Freemasonry. Later some initiates may have recognized the similarities of these plans to those of pirate's maps and stories of lost treasure and used them to hide things. Sometimes places like the Newport Tower and Kensington Rune may have been political footballs meat to fool or misinform opposing sides of a given argument such as those that believe there was a Viking colony named Norumbega in New England long ago.

Some of this imagery was later applied to the Bruton Vault saga regardless of the legitimacy or truth of Marie Bauer Hall's claims. Also hidden in the labyrinth of places, people, books, and maps is the specter of Sir Francis Bacon and the tradition of encoding important concepts into literature and art that could then be taught to subsequent generations. From the use of Greek myths in the story of Arcas to the works of Edgar Allan Poe and Dante this concept has endured and proved itself a useful way to add to the secret overtones of any organization that is persecuted or attacked.

Is there a vault or repository of Sir Francis Bacon's papers somewhere? We certainly see this being theorized at Oak Island, The Wye River in England, and now in Williamsburg Virginia. The papers of the real Sir Francis Bacon are available to us all and no treasure hunt is needed. In addition, the works of many others such as Philip Sidney are also there to inform us using the age old technique of metaphor and myth. The process of solving these mysteries compels one to read the works of Shakespeare and Philip Sidney, examine the work of Georges de la Tour, while listening to folklore that may read like fairy tales. True the quest is worth the candle but the treasure you find may not be the one you were seeking.

Chapter 17: The Other Sir Francis Bacon and Washington D.C.

For many years authors and free thinkers have pondered the significance of the street plan of Washington D.C. Many obvious patterns are suggested by the neatly laid out plan of the city. Features such as the "D.C. Star," and the "Federal Triangle" are pointed to as having significance.

Author's David Ovason and Dr. Robert Heironimus agree that much of the symbolism of the city refers to the constellation Virgo and her associated myths and metaphors. Ovason points to the many astrological associations present with Virgo in the city such as the dedication of monuments and buildings.

Many of the same analysts that point to this association with Virgo also agree that the influence of Sir Francis Bacon is present in the planning of Washington District of Columbia as well as other monuments and State Capitols in the United States. Over the years scholars have exhaustively pored over everything ever written by Sir Francis Bacon and many also attribute the works of Shakespeare to at least including his influence if not his work alone. As exposed in this book the influence of the Arcadian theme and the works of Philip Sidney were likely known to Sir Francis Bacon and others including William Alexander of Stirling and all his descendants who made such a large impact on American history.

Washington D.C. also in many ways may be a representation of both the concept of a New Jerusalem and its Baconian analogue the "New Atlantis." In truth the layout of the first capitol of Virginia, Williamsburg may have been the first New Jerusalem or New Atlantis in English North America. The array of architecture present in the colonial capitol had a linear aspect to it that repeated the designs of landscape architects such as Inigo Jones and Alex de Caus who had planned many royal and estate landscapes in the British Isles and Europe. Both men have written openly of including secret concepts into their designs that many times were dictated by those who commissioned their design. This may be a similar tradition at play to those who sponsored the building of the great cathedrals of Europe.

Jones for example designed many of the structures and grounds that were used by King Charles I and II of England. Both de Caus and Jones were also instrumental in the design of the landscape of Heidelberg Castle home to both Elizabeth of Bohemia sister of Charles I and her son Prince Rupert of the Rhine. De Caus and Jones as well as others such as Webb undoubtedly were influenced by the development of other famous city alignments such as the Axe Historique of Paris, Williamsburg Colonial Capitol array, and ultimately the National Mall of Washington D.C. Even though these English representations are being discussed here it is clear that these type of alignments are repetitions of more ancient arrays of architecture such as the Fora of the Romans or the elaborate alignments of monuments seen in dynastic Egypt and others.

A great deal of speculation and evidence suggests that many times astronomical and astrological significance was given to many of these monuments and arrays of architecture. It is clear that a value of the pole star is seen over a vast period of time through many different cultures in association with orienting oneself on the globe in both a physical and spiritual manner. In order to measure any additional astronomical events or observations the pole star or true north must first be determined as a base line to further measurements. In this way a prime meridian is created such as the Greenwich or Paris Meridian for example.

In this search for the secrets of Washington D.C. has anything been overlooked that may associate the spirit of Sir Francis Bacon to the theme of Virgo in the streets of Washington D.C.? Are the theories of Ovason with regard to Virgo and a value of her mythology in the plan of Washington D.C. valid or without merit?

As it turns out we may see some very obvious clues in this realm in the burial memorial or momento mori to Sir Francis Bacon himself. This memorial is located in St. Gregory's Church in Norwich, England.

But Sir Francis Bacon's memorial is at St. Michael's Chapel in St. Alban's you say? As it turns out the memorial to the "Other" Sir Francis Bacon seems to refer to the theme of Virgo and how it may apply to the talismanic meaning of the plan of Washington D.C. Though this value at the time it was produced included the fact that Washington D.C. had not even been thought of yet we may still see a similar value being applied to the creation of the city later in time.

There was an additional Sir Francis Bacon of the same family that was younger than our famous Bacon but their lives did have some overlap. The second Sir Francis Bacon of this era also emulated his famous kin's profession as a lawyer and judge in the City of London at Gray's Inn. For our purposes here we will refer to him as Sir Francis II.

*"(**BACON**, Sir FRANCIS (1587–1657), judge, was son of 'John Bacon, of King's Lynn, Norfolk, gentleman' (Francis, Admission to Gray's Inn), and grandson of Thomas Bacon, of Hesset, in Suffolk, As Hesset belonged to the immediate ancestors of the lord-keeper. Sir Nicholas Bacon, it seems probable that Francis was sprung from the same stock as his illustrious namesakes, being therefore the fifth of that family who attained judicial rank. Born about 1587, he commenced his legal studies at Barnard's Inn, and was admitted a member of Gray's Inn in Feb. 1607. He was not called to the bar until eight years later in 1615. His name as counsel not being found in any contemporary reports, it has been inferred that his practice must have been either in chancery or in the provinces. In 1624 and 1626 he is mentioned as having contributed considerable sums towards the repair of the font and east window of St. Gregory's Church, Norwich (Blomefield, Norwich, ii. 274). In 1634 he was autumn reader at Gray's Inn (Gray's Inn Books); two years later the king granted him the office of drawing licenses and pardons of alienations to the great seal during his life in reversion (Rymer, xx. 123); and in 1640 he was admitted to the degree of serjeant-at-law. In October 1642, the king, being then at Bridgnorth on his way to London, appointed Bacon to a seat in the King's Bench (Dugdale, Chron. Ser. 110), and at the same time knighted him. This appointment seems to have given satisfaction to the parliament, as we find among the pro- positions tendered by parliament to the king in Feb. 1643, demands for the dismissal of several of the judges, but 'that Mr. Justice Bacon may be continued ' (Clarendon, vi. 231). While Charles was at Oxford, Bacon was one of 'the sworn judges still at Westminster, of*

which there were three in number,' and presided alone in the King's Bench, as his 'brothers'
Reeve and Trevor did in the Common Pleas and Exchequer (ibid. vii. 317).

He continued to sit on the bench until the execution of Charles, but after that event new sions
were issued to the judges, and they were required to take the oath in the name of the people
instead of in the king's name. Bacon and five of his brethren 'were not satisfied to hold ' on these
terms, and had the courage to resign their seats. The other six judges, after some hesitation,
agreed to hold office, 'provided that by act of the commons the fundamental laws be not
abolished' (ibid. 378). After his resignation Bacon lived in retirement until his death on 22 Aug.
1657. Over his grave in St. Gregory's Church, Norwich, a handsome monument was raised by
his eldest son Francis, who became reader in Gray's Inn in 1662. By his wife Elizabeth, daughter
of William Robinson, he had several children, but the family has long been extinct (Wotton,
Baronetage, i. 2).

(Dictionary of National Biography, 1885-1900, Volume 02, Bacon, Sir Francis (1587-1657)

The above clearly shows how Sir Francis II was from the same illustrious family that the more
famous Sir Francis had sprung from. This family had included many geniuses and influential
people stemming from the Bacon's Norman roots. It is even possible that the Bacon's had
developed from the Norman family of Bacon de Molay possibly even linking them to Knights
Templar Grand Commander Jacques de Molay that had been the order's last leader. We may also
see how this illustrious family's association with judicial matters over time could have lent to a
value of the many concepts associated with the constellation Virgo including the scales of Libra
or justice. Virgo is often portrayed as holding these scales aloft emulating the arrangement of
Virgo and Libra in the heavens.

The above passage from the Dictionary of National Biography also displays Sir Francis Bacon II
dedication to Charles I. Charles I is said to have quoted "Pamela's Prayer" from Philip Sidney's
"Arcadia" as his last words. The connections are endless and meaningful as this saga unfolds. It
seems that SFB II had resigned his position and retired after the deposition and beheading of
Charles I. This may have then put him in league with similar sentiments existent in the colonies
at that time as many of Charles bodyguard had fled to the colonies and had subsequently created
what may be termed the "Cavalier Culture" of early Virginia. Among these refugees comprised
of the Body Guards and others loyal to the deposed king was one Thomas Beale related to an
earlier Thomas Beale giving us the legacy and lore of the Beale Treasure Legend we see today.

Given all the speculation and study of Sir Francis and his secrets what may have Sir Francis II
left for us in the way of clues as to the entire family's legacy? We do know that Sir Francis
Bacon was a kind of intelligence operative and associated with many famous artists, writers,
architects, and politicians. It would not be out of the realm of possibility that Sir Francis Bacon II
had been privy to some of the secrets of his namesake. It appears that he left some clues for us on
his memorial at St. Gregory's Norwich his hometown. Sir Francis II's momento mori may also
give us some hints as to why the imagery of Virgo is later valued and included in the mythology
and planning of Washington D.C. and other exotic locations such as Chico California.

The Bacon memorial in Norwich includes the following imagery and suggestions that may in turn link us back to Baconian influence in the planning of Washington D.C.

The Wall Memorial portion of the piece is especially revealing. Here from the Norwich Churches .org website:

"The wall monument pays eulogy in Latin to Sir Francis which basically says he was a worthy judge who deserves to be mourned. There are also references to his refusal to abandon his allegiance to the crown and his subsequent return to Norwich. All of these facets are illustrated by references to biblical and mythological figures:

Niobe *: A mortal woman in Greek mythology whose fourteen children were killed by the Gods and whom is often a symbol of mourning.*

Solomon *: Solomon was the builder of the "First Temple of the Lord" in Jerusalem. In the bible he is described as being great in wisdom, wealth, and power.*

Astraea *: In Greek mythology Astraea ("star-maiden") was a daughter of Zeus and Themis. She and her mother were both personifications of justice. As mankind became wicked, she was the last of the immortals to stay on earth, ascending to heaven to become the constellation Virgo. The scales of justice she carried became the nearby constellation Libra. (note this is a direct reference to Virgo)."*

The final paragraph makes reference to another Francis Bacon and to St Albans. This is believed to be a reference to Francis Bacon, Viscount St Alban (1561–1626), lord chancellor, politician, and philosopher

The translation reads:

"Who comes here, may I ask, who seeks Niobe who has been turned to stone and whose tears dry up the sea? No one can run away from such tears unless they are part of the sea. Be not silent men of stony speech. Equality is indeed just when making laws. He came here burdened, wasted and weighed down. You do not know the unknown. He heard like the Etruscan soldier not wanting to bend to the law for whom is this hymn-like monument of law a mediator, a judge, a reference point, a touchstone, a Solomon here on earth impartial (if anyone is) like the judge in heaven.

At last he is at rest and lies here although he but lies in wait impervious to sand and decay who scolded the world with oratorical attacks and the select few abandoned this good discoverer for the multiple unholy gods justice unsaid on earth. The justice of the angry heavens left the earth to flee to the stars, following Astraea restored at home with holiness, the newest light of legal business.

Rather when the name of great St Albans is spoken and in blood and in name on both sides, he hears worthy Francis Bacon."
(http://www.norwich-churches.org/monuments/francis%20bacon/francis%20bacon.shtm)

It is possible that Sir Francis II is telling us here to study the aspect of Virgo that is related to Astrea the "star maiden" or virgin? In turn this perspective of Virgo could then relate to the New Atlantis or New Jerusalem of Washington D.C. thus linking us to further concepts that may be both related to Sir Francis Bacon and the legacy of the name Bacon in United States history over its entire span. It is possible that the influence of Sir Francis Bacon is seen throughout the westward development of the United States in places like Washington D.C., Indianapolis, Denver, and Chico California. We may also see his influence in "mysteries" such as the Beale Treasure, Oak Island, and the Kensington Rune mystery. This simple memorial or memento mori could show us many of the values of families like the Alexander's, Bidwell's, Beale's, and Bacon's who may have valued the imagery seen in Washington D.C. today. Though it requires some study and understanding it may be that they also intended all of us to value it as well.

As we may see it is possible to view the legacy of Sir Francis Bacon and his ideas via the legacies of two important groups of early American colonists of Hartford Connecticut and Jamestown Virginia that included members of the Bacon family of England that chose to carry on the legacy of both Sir Francis' as well as the other distinguished members of this storied family. Strangely the story of the Bacon family includes both the development of Washington D.C. which is then again echoed a continent away in the tiny town of Chico California and its central role in the Gold Rush of 1849. In this way we also see the Alexander's and other families having an interest in the development of the country as it expanded westward. This activity also matches some of what is speculated about the Society of the Cincinnati and how they promoted the America ideal via the arts and literature.

It may be that specific family groups related to Sir Francis Bacon and his circle of friends in England valued his philosophy and took steps to see that it was included in the architecture and mythology of the developing country. In tandem the secrets of the Wilton Writer's Circle of Mary Sidney Herbert Countess of Pembroke, her sons, and their uncle Philip Sidney may also be considered.

The mineral riches of California were attractive to European and royal interests that are interwoven in the story of how California became part of the United States. Members of the Bacon family as well as elements of the Society of the Cincinnati may have helped to ensure that the west would be part of the new country. The involvement of the Bacon family in the development of Denver Colorado and Chico is a reality. Had they in part went there to insure these messages would be told in some cryptic form at each location?

Along the way one may discern a trail of imagery that harkens back to both Sir Francis Bacon and his vision for the New Atlantis as seen in the plan of Washington D.C. and now possibly Chico California. Along with these other influences a series of mysteries that included many Rosicrucian, Enonchian, and Solomonic overtones may have also been left in direct association with the values of Sir Francis Bacon with regard to his impact on the culture of the United States of America. These mysteries may have included information or "clewes" that would also teach one the underlying meanings of the Republic using mythology and legends as metaphors and allegory. Though many may jump to the conclusion that these quests had been left for Freemason's alone the evidence available shows that this simply is not true.

"The Chief parts that are now still standing of the remains of Temple House Gorhambury, are the ruins of the hall, which constituted the inner side of the court, and a lofty octagonal tower……"

The "other" Sir Francis Bacon's Memorial at St. Gregory's in Norwich England. Note the arms of Eaton on the right central portion of the statue. The famous Sir Francis Bacon's wife was related to the Eaton family.

Chapter 18: St. Paul's Chapel and Pierre L'Enfant. The Mystery of the Montgomery Memorial.

The story of the development of New York City is a true American Tale. Elements of many different colonial powers contributed to its origins and history. The Dutch and English held control of the area that would become New York City in the early stages of colonial settlement in New England and the other colonies. New York was for a short time the Capitol of the United States of America prior to the capitol being moved finally to Washington District of Columbia.

Since the tragic events of September, 11, 2001 many have examined the possible hidden history or occult overtones associated with this disaster. One of the structures that has been discussed in biblical prophecy by some is St. Paul's Chapel just to the east of the World Trade Center Towers that collapsed on that day. Regardless of the truth of how these events unfolded it is clear that the Trinity district of Manhattan, New York City had already been steeped in Masonic and Royal mythology and lore in ways that few understand. Part of this value had to do with what may considered "hidden" messages left in some of the structures that were valued at this time. Is it possible that someone had created a "New Jerusalem" or "New Atlantis" out of the rubble of this tragedy?

Rabbi Jonathan Cahn links the survival of St. Paul's on September eleventh to a chain of events that matches the prophecies of Isaiah. A lone Sycamore Tree is said to have spared the Chapel from destruction on that day by blocking the fall of debris from the collapsing buildings. The remains of the tree have now been made into a bronzed memorial that also reflects the telling of this prophecy by Isaiah. Amazingly the same Sycamore Tree seems to be referred to in the Bob Marley song "Time will Tell" where the "song of freedom tree....Sycamore Tree" is mentioned. It appears Marley was also referring to the Prophecies of Isaiah when this song was written.

We will examine here how St. Paul's Chapel fits into an architectural scheme of places in early America that both tell a story of their own and represent a valued point on the earth from which to measure. St. Paul's has some interesting geographic associations with other colonial era structures that have already been identified by this author as having been important to a specific caste of movers and shakers in Colonial and early American times. Other structures such as the Newport Tower, The Powder Magazine in Williamsburg, Monticello, Poplar Forest, and most of all the strange street plan of Washington D.C. seem to beckon one to use their powers of interpretation, art appreciation, and history to interpret correctly.

The history of St. Paul's itself reveals many links to important figures in American history that have family ties to the premier Jacobite and Scottish families that actually in a large way created the United States or helped to fund its creation in hand with others who held different views. At this time many likely felt they should band together with those of a different view of the new Republic in order to break the chain of colonial domination that had been enacted by the Hanoverian and Parliamentarian factions of England at that time. It was not only George I that wanted to keep control of the colonies but the English Parliament also voted to continue to control and tax the colonies. Within the English Parliament and political system were many who

317

did sympathize with the Exiled Stewart Kings of England in tandem with the goals of the colonies in forming a new Republic.

Many who held this view of a Republic in the colonies were adhering to a kind of "New Atlantis" or "New Jerusalem" concept that had been defined by Sir Francis Bacon in many of his writings including his work "The New Atlantis."

In our examination of St. Paul's we will see distinct historical and familial links to many other strange questions that seem to have been presented to the public such as Oak Island and even the famous mystery of Rennes le Chateau in France. True to form the story of St. Paul's includes alternating English and French influences just as the story of Oak Island does. The phenomena of St. Paul's may have also spawned other contrived grail quest legends and mysteries meant to foster a uniquely American view of spirituality in association with the Republican ideal in early America. Along the way a cadre of American artists and writes attempted to forge an American mythology and identity that extended beyond the old world values of those that had first occupied North America while displacing the Native population.

St. Paul's is located at 209 Broadway in lower Manhattan Island in New York City. Note from a numerological point of view 2+0+9=11. This string of numbers matches other important interpretive information we will examine later in this story. It is strange that these numbers coincide with the date of the destruction of the World Trade Centers on 9/11. St. Paul's was built on land donated by Queen Anne of Great Britain. St. Paul's does include a small centrally located octagonal tower that is topped by a replica of the Choragic Monument of Lysicrates (335 B.C.) This theme or use of classical monuments and even the sculptors of them in transmitting allegorical or hidden information is a common theme throughout history. St. Paul's of the Trinity district of Manhattan is no exception. Here at this small simple chapel one of the greatest moments of United States History occurred and this was not on 9/12/01.

Famous American founding father Alexander Hamilton drilled the troops of "The Hearts of Oak" Military Militia on the grounds of the chapel early in the war. Hamilton would later command the artillery division that would defend New York City from the British. His involvement here at this significant piece of talismanic American architecture echoes his direct family relation from the past George Hamilton Earl of Orkney's involvement in the creation of the octagonal Powder Magazine in Colonial Williamsburg.

At that time the personnel that made up the Hearts of Oak were all Kings College students. Kings College would later be known as Columbia University thus reflecting some of the mythical or folklore views of the new country. It is no coincidence that this institution of learning gained the same name as Washington District of Columbia and Columbia South Carolina. The image of the Goddess Columbia and that name's association with the Columba or dove of peace is a potent symbol through different ages of Catholic belief in Scotland and Ireland and is also associated by some with Saint Columba.

318

Most importantly George Washington along with the other present members of Congress attended services at St. Paul's on the first inauguration day of any American President on April, 30, 1779. At this time Washington literally consecrated the creation of the country of the United States of America. This small chapel was indeed in many citizens eyes the point on earth where the United States was actually born. Washington had a personal pew at the chapel and it is marked by a period painting of the Great Seal of the United States. Washington's pew was indeed adjacent to the pew of early New York Governor Clinton. This painting of the Great Seal is one of the earliest representations of the new design that had recently been decided upon.

Washington's association with this structure in light of the later events of September eleventh is intriguing and adds to the mysterious overtones of both that day and the creation of the new country. George Washington had also of course come from Virginia and had studied at the College of William and Mary in Williamsburg where the octagonal Powder Magazine was located. Again this structure had been erected by colonial Lt. Governor of Virginia Alexander Spotswood under the auspices of Governor George Hamilton the Earl of Orkney. George Hamilton represents an direct relation to Alexander Hamilton of the "Hearts of Oak."

Amazingly an arc on the globe created using the north to south orientation of St. Paul's chapel leads directly to the octagonal Powder Magazine in Colonial Williamsburg in Virginia. In past works we have examined the octagonal Powder Magazine for its directional values and had seen how it was associated with the Hudson's Bay Company also of the Hamilton/Douglas family of Scottish gentry. This is an amazing association that likely was planned and extends far beyond the probability of a chance association given our previous studies of the use of the Axis Mundi in colonial era architecture.

Above: The orientation with regard to true north of St. Paul's Cathedral may be used to create an arc on the globe that transects the East Coast of the United States leading to or intersecting with the Powder Magazine in Colonial Williamsburg. See next two images below.

It is possible that St. Paul's Cathedral was planned to point the way to the Powder Magazine in Colonial Williamsburg which had been built in 1714 significantly prior to the construction of the Chapel in 1766. This may also mean that Broadway also points in this direction. As we will see as this saga develops there are specific aspects of the development of St. Paul's Chapel that may also back up this assumption.

In particular, two of the monuments located at St. Paul's tell a story of the amazing association this structure may hold to European mysteries such as Rennes le Chateau and the "Man in Mountain" mythology of Charlemagne and possibly Constantine himself. The influence of the Hamilton's and Montgomery's of Scotland may be obvious in both the creation of the new country but also in their roles as Jacobite supporters of the exiled royalty of England and Scotland the Stewart family. The Stewart family's involvement here though peripheral may have served as the primary impetus for the installation of a "mystery" at St. Paul's that involves American concepts in tandem with the country's Jacobite origins. As prominent Scottish families

319

the Hamilton's and Douglas' also had many direct associations with relatives and associates in France. The nobility of Scotland has always held close ties with the French people with a Douglas even holding the French title of the Duke of Tourraine at one point. This tradition also includes the French origins of Marie of Guise and her daughter Mary Queen of Scots education at the St. Clare Monastery near Paris.

The story of the Montgomery Monument at St. Paul's will link us back to France and Rennes le Chateau while also establishing a mysterious chain of events in the young United States that may contribute to the American overtones of many mysteries in Europe where this influence has never been considered. This simple yet elegant monument will link us to the intelligence gathering activities of two patriots that in large part defined the intelligence gathering capabilities of the United States in their struggle for independence and also during the early years of the country.

General Richard Montgomery was one of the greatest fallen heroes of the American Revolution. Later famous English General Montgomery of World War Two fame was from the same family that always held a grand military tradition. Richard Montgomery was no exception and led the invasion of Quebec during the Revolution at which he lost his life. Even before the Revolutionary War was over Congress had agreed to build a monument to General Montgomery thus becoming the first monument ever commissioned for construction by the United States of America. General Montgomery had earned in death a very large appreciation and distinction among the founders of the United States. He would be the first American Patriot to be immortalized in the United States of America.

Congress allotted 300 pounds sterling towards the creation of a monument fitting the service of such a great patriot. Benjamin Franklin himself commissioned famous French Sculptor Jean Jacques Caffieri to sculpt a fitting memorial to the General. Originally this piece had been intended to be included at Philadelphia's Independence Hall which was technically the first capitol of the United States. Later when it was decided to make New York the capitol it was decreed that this memorial should be included at St. Paul's chapel in New York where Washington had also consecrated the young country for the first time.

The Montgomery Memorial was indeed created by Caffieri in France and included a very rare form of variegated and pinkish colored marble from the Pyrenees Mountain region of southern France. This is also the region of Basque country, The Great Cyclic Cross of Hendaye, and the famous mystery of Rennes le Chateau. Interestingly Thomas Jefferson also purchased a bust of Benjamin Franklin from Caffieri at a later date that is still on display at Monticello. Jefferson was quite the appreciator of classic forms of art. His collection also included a painting by Rivera (Ribera) of Mary Magdalene Repentant pictured with the inclusion of her contemplating a human skull.

Here via Caffieri we see the influence of our French Allies of the Revolution assisting Franklin and Jefferson in memorializing their fallen comrade in way that had been done for thousands of years. Montgomery would be given a lasting and prominent memorial that would assure his name and actions were never forgotten. Or is there more to the story?

As it turns out another prominent Frenchman would also contribute a great deal to the decoration and hidden themes of St. Paul's Cathedral. None other than the famous architect of the streets of Washington D.C. Pierre L'Enfant took part in the redecoration of St. Paul's after the war. His contributions to St Paul's reflected the decorative concepts seen at many chapels in France that have Masonic overtones. To understand this in more detail we must return to the story of the Montgomery Memorial in order to place the overall hidden context of St. Paul's Chapel correctly.

Beyond the fact that the Montgomery Memorial was created by a French Artist whose work is reflective of the French view of the notion of Republic with all its ancient and classic themes represented it is clear that some degree of intentionally applied mystery and intrigue accompanied the story of the monument from its time of creation to its final installation at St. Paul's nearly ten years after the end of the American Revolution. Upon completion of the sculpture it is said Caffieri had its separate pieces all sealed in lead caskets in order to be shipped to the United States. This is a very elaborate form of packaging for stonework that may raise some red flags in our story to this point. Is it possible that other items had also been included in these lead lined caskets? Why seal stonework that is fairly durable in such containers? Was it because the American's considered it an important first symbol of their victory in the revolution or was Caffieri sending other talismanic items that were more fragile than the large stone segments of the monument as well?

Surely even if a ship sank with such pieces of statue they could possibly be recovered with little damage even without a "lead lined casket" protecting them. To an individual familiar with these concepts the shipping of this memorial may have introduced many strange objects and themes to the colonies and future country for the first time. In addition, this mystery would also suggest that Jacobite Englishmen had also been aware of and supported the efforts of the French. In the end this all may tie into the development of "Scottish Masonry" in France that was intimately associated with the exiled Stewarts and their efforts to forge a new country in the colonies.

Other aspects of the saga of the Montgomery Memorial also indicate that this object was the subject of the geographic mysteries we have studied in the past.

The saga of the memorial includes it being stored unbeknownst to Benjamin Franklin (supposedly) in Edenton North Carolina. Edenton is very near the famous "Lost Colony" of Roanoke near the Outer Banks of North Carolina. Edenton was one of the few places said to have been left accessible at that time due to a British blockade of all shipping on the East Coast. It is said that this is the reason this strange memorial was stored in Edenton. At this point all of our lead lined caskets containing portions of the monument laid in Edenton until they were found after the war. Edenton also holds the distinction of being the first capitol of North Carolina.

Two other strange parts to this story may be pertinent later. First of all the sculpture was shipped via a British ship to Edenton! Records indicate from Franklin's own hand that this sculpture was shipped via an English ship that was associated with missionaries in Labrador. Franklin even expresses thoughts that the memorial would be returned to the Colonies if it was captured by the English. It is possible that this was the only shipping method available at that time. Most of the east coast was blockaded by the British navy at this time thus making it an especially perilous voyage for any French merchantman or ship of war. Franklin's ties to this "missionary vessel" may have been associated with any American intelligence gathering that was in operation at that time. This may have also included many families in the Maritime region including Nova Scotia that were loyal to the Colonial cause against the British.

These Nova Scotians who were loyal to the Colonies during the revolutionary war had been brought to Nova Scotia by the English after General Lawrence had expelled the French Acadians (Arcadians) from the Maritime region of Canada. This included family members of of Henry Wadsworth Longfellow and Edgar Allan Poe. During the war many of these Nova Scotians fought on the side of the Colonies in Maine and some even became members of the Society of the Cincinnati after the war. This dynamic including Americans in Nova Scotia associated with the Society of the Cincinnati may have contributed to the mythology of the famous Oak Island Treasure later.

The other amazing fact left out in the saga of the Montgomery Memorial involves the urn that sits atop the pillar on the piece we see in front of St. Paul's Chapel today. After the war when the fate of the memorial was finally decided the urn and its packaging were nowhere to be found. The urn is missing! The one we see included on the sculpture today is a replacement that was obtained after it was discerned that the original was no longer present with the rest of the sculpture when it was finally located in Edenton. This in itself is intriguing in that the representation of an urn in a cenotaph may suggest that there are remains within it. If there were other relics or talismanic objects sent with the memorial from France what better place to hide them than in the ritual urn as included in the design of the sculpture?

Above we saw how the structure of St. Paul's Chapel itself points the way to the Powder Magazine in Colonial Williamsburg. The Powder Magazine is a structure that I have supposed operated in the tradition of Constantine and Charlemagne as an Axis Mundi based on the Tower of the Winds of Athens. The octagonal form of the Powder Magazine actually points to places on the globe that had significance to its builder thus establishing a real physical or spiritual domain. This may have been exactly what George Hamilton was doing when the Powder Magazine was built under his authority as Virginia Governor in 1714. This is also coincidentally the year just prior to the first Jacobite uprising in 1715. Many of the refugees from this conflict would immigrate to Scandinavia and the Colonies thus forming pockets of Jacobite sympathizers in both regions.

Given all of these mysterious associations it is no surprise then that the southern orientation of the octagonal Powder Magazine in Colonial Williamsburg can be used to form an arc on the globe that transects directly to Edenton North Carolina. This entire geographic scheme suggests that someone had even used the octagon of the Powder Magazine to hide an item they knew was going to be installed at a structure that in turn "pointed to" the Powder Magazine in Colonial Williamsburg. Is it possible that the memorial was stored in Edenton so that someone could discern its location using the octagonal form of the Powder Magazine in Williamsburg? It is even possible that the location of Edenton had originally been decided due to this geographic association.

If this is more than a coincidence this scheme may indicate that there was something more to the Montgomery Memorial than is being told in the standard story. This object had been hidden using an age old method that had been applied in the past to biblical relics and mysterious treasure quests left by fallen kings. Was some sort of geographic ritual being carried out that involved the monument itself or any other associated items that had been shipped in these strange lead lined caskets? Even so there is absolutely no recorded evidence beyond the missing urn from the sculpture that anything is not as the story states in the historical record. Still it does make one wonder.

Among the other information revealed here is the fact that an almost intentionally contrived mystery had been applied to this memorial using geographic points on the earth at which structures had been built to indicate a solution to the mystery. Each of these points on earth played a significant role in American colonial and revolutionary war history. If not a solution, then this may have at least represented a way to find this object after the fog of war had lifted at a later date. It is said that Franklin did not know the location of this memorial sealed in lead caskets until several years after the war when it was finally installed at St. Paul's in the Trinity neighborhood of Manhattan now known as Tribeca.

Also intriguing is this object's origins in France where such mysteries had already been valued in the form of the "Man in the Mountain" mythology of Charlemagne that used the octagonal Aachen Cathedral in the same way. Evidence revealed in my last few books also displays how Constantine may have used his octagons in a similar manner and may have even clandestinely built the Dome of the Rock himself. There may be an unspoken of mystery similar to what Charlemagne had valued in association with the missing remains of Constantine who may have actually been entombed beneath the Temple Mount in Jerusalem. Later many aspects of the famous Rennes le Chateau mystery would echo similar concepts including allusions to the Temple Treasure that once may have been controlled by Constantine.

An arc on the globe plotted at the angle of the north to south orientation of the Powder Magazine in Colonial Williamsburg "points to" Edenton North Carolina. Remember; From the previous photos we saw how the orientation of St. Paul's "points to" the Powder Magazine in Williamsburg.

One of the places in Edenton where the memorial may have been stored during this time was in St. Paul's Chapel there! St. Paul's may have been a prime choice for Governor Hewes or whomever decided on a place to store the monument during at this time. There is an additional

Episcopalian Church in Edenton built in 1736 named St. Paul's. If the geographic association of St. Paul's in New York City and the Powder Magazine is a grand coincidence, then this phenomena is about to get that much more unbelievable.

The north to south orientation of St. Paul's Church in Edenton North Carolina may be used to form an arc on the globe that transects directly to the Powder Magazine in Colonial Williamsburg. These two structures actually point to one another on the globe! Again the Powder Magazine was built somewhat prior to St. Paul's in Edenton making this a distinct possibility. Given the other association with another St. Paul's in the saga of the Montgomery Memorial this is almost too much to believe. It is starting to appears as if this group of patriots had used a technique they may have learned in association with old world traditions such as the mysteries of the "Man in the Mountain" of Charlemagne and possibly the many quest legends associated with The Holy Grail, Temple Treasure, and other biblical relics. The angular association between the Powder Magazine and St. Paul's Church in Edenton also matches the north to south orientation of the original street plan of Williamsburg. This association may have marked the spatial relationship of two early colonial capitols and may have been known of during the Revolutionary War era.

It is noted that Benjamin Franklin displayed an unusual interest in finding the Montgomery Monument after the war and wrote many letters as part of his search for its whereabouts prior to it being found in Edenton and shipped to New York City to be installed at St. Paul's Chapel. St. Paul's place in United States history as being where George Washington was first inaugurated subsequently consecrating the new country in the eyes of god served as a fitting location for the final destination for Montgomery's Memorial. Eventually his remains would be returned from Quebec and interred in a crypt beneath the monument. Thousands of people a day walk past this simple yet elegant monument never suspecting the true history that is revealed in its creation.

Obviously someone was aware of the location of the memorial and its associated lead lined caskets. Again it is very odd that this memorial was shipped via an English ship during this time of war. Is it also possible that it had been hidden in a place that may have become suspect no matter who won the conflict? It is clear that individuals from both sides of the war whether they be French/American or English were capable of using geography and the globe to decipher the hidden location of such an important object. Alternately this same kind of information was used to hide the memorial.

As part of earlier mysteries in history many of these quests, possibly using a structure as a clue or place from which to measure had included biblical relics and concepts to be understood by the initiate in order to solve the mystery. A similar quest may have been arranged by Charlemagne leading to the truth or folklore of at least three subsequent Holy Roman Emperors opening his vault and removing mysterious objects including the Coronation Gospels. Even if these stories were complex folklore they still may have been created for reason and purpose.

It is also highly possible that both Benjamin Franklin and Thomas Jefferson had been initiated into these mysteries either while in France or as some point in their early education in the colonies. It is clear that Jefferson may have been made aware of these connections by being initiated into this concept via the octagonal Powder Magazine in Williamsburg which was present during his tenure as a student at the College of William and Mary. George Washington and James Madison may have also been subjected to the very same initiation or course of study that Jefferson had undertaken. All three men had included land surveying as part of their studies at William and Mary. These men's knowledge of the use of the Powder Magazine as a place from which to measure using its geometric shape with regard to true north seems to have contributed to the way the Montgomery Memorial was hidden until after the war. Jefferson would also carry on the tradtion of the Powder Magazine in his design of Monticello, Poplar Forest, and Barboursville Mansion.

Had a mystery been created in association with St. Paul's Chapel in New York, The Powder Magazine, St. Paul's Church Edenton, and the Montgomery Memorial? If one were writing a novel at this point it would indeed make a good story. Somewhere in the gray area between truth and imagination something very fantastic is become unraveled that leads one to the True History of the United States. The entire saga reads like a plot from a fantastic historical novel. Strange monuments, historical churches, modern disasters, and the suggestion that something had been brought to the new country and hidden using the age old tenets of the "Man in the Mountain" mythology as used by Charlemagne in association with his octagon at Aachen. In addition, it appears that one of the lead lined caskets is missing and has never been found. A mystery lover's dream or contrived initiatory quest?

Here at this point we are led to the involvement of Pierre L'Enfant the man responsible for the design of the plan of Washington D.C. that has intrigued and confounded so many people since it was designed. In turn L'Enfant displays all of the Society of the Cincinnati connections we have seen at play in other similar historical mysteries. L'Enfant's use of the traditions of European landscaping in the realm of famous seventeenth century Freemason, Architect, and Bacon associate Inigo Jones is apparent in his plan for the city that in turn suggests many geometric and conceptual shapes and arrays of architecture. Reams of material had been written speculating as to the true nature of the arrangement of Washington D.C. It is fitting that L'Enfant's grave at Arlington National Cemetery overlooks the city and also includes a portion of his famous plan on the included cenotaph.

Since New York City was the first Capitol of the United States it is no surprise that L'Enfant had a hand in the refurbishment and redesign of St. Paul's Chapel in New York at the time of the post war installation of the Montgomery Monument. Here again is a figure who is heavily associated with geographic mysteries in America lending a hand to a building of great talismanic and symbolic importance to the country at large. Surprisingly a legacy that is little discussed by the public at large whether they be historians, patriots, or blissfully ignorant of any such phenomena.

Pierre L'Enfant the author and inspiration for reams of speculation and countless books supposing a purpose and intent to the design of the plan of Washington D.C. is directly involved in a geographic mystery involving St. Paul's Chapel, The Powder Magazine in Williamsburg, St. Paul's Edenton North Carolina, and several strange lead lined caskets that held the pieces of the sculpture. Something is up with this. Here we will see how French sources influence early esoteric beliefs in the United States in opposition to similar lore valued by British sources.

After it had been erected on the east porch of St. Paul's Chapel the Montgomery Memorial's reverse side was visible from inside the chapel and it was decided that this was somewhat unsightly. In response L'Enfant was charged with redesigning the interior of the Chapel to hide this unsightly feature. L'Enfant created a large wooden sculpture he termed a "Shekinah" or "Glory" to cover this area of the altar of St. Paul's. Amazingly his motif and design of many elements of St. Paul's reflects the sensibilities of specific chapels in France that were created under the auspices of French Freemason's including the Chapels in Sare and Hendaye France associated with the d'Abbadie family and the Great Cyclic Cross of Henday. The personal family chapel of Antoine d'Abbadie known as Abbadia also resembles how L'Enfant had arranged and decorated St. Paul's Chapel after the war.

L'Enfant's design included the tetragrammaton in Hebrew situated in an equilateral triangle with thirteen rays projecting from the triangle. The tetragrammaton is the unspoken name of god in this case written in Hebrew. This motif is repeated at other places in the chapel and matches the same designs in Hendaye and Sare (Sara) France associated with the d'Abbadies. The "Light of Glory Altarpiece" as it is known also includes a rendering of the ten commandments in what appears to be black Marble. This too is a potent symbol for both the ten commandments and the mythical stories of black stones that often were situated in an omphalos at the center of an axis mundi. This may also infer that a belief existed that the remains of the original ten commandments were present in the long lost Ark of the Covenant that is also valued symbolically by Freemason's.

The d'Abbadie's are a very powerful French family that may have descended from the lay Abbots that served as the instructors in the schools that Charlemagne set up for his family and close associates. Both the early Governor of French Arcadia and last governor of Louisiana were d'Abbadie's. The legacy of the Great Cross of Hendaye does include its use as an axis mundi or place from which to measure. There are even many clues and hints that Thomas Jefferson was aware of the Great Cross of Hendaye. It is clear that he associated with many people who were later associated with Ethiopian explorer Antoine d'Abbadie such as Dominique Cassini and other personnel from the Paris Observatory.

Jefferson actually corresponded with Cassini as how to establish a prime meridian using some of the newer nautical clocks that had been developed. In turn a letter exists from Cassini to Ben Franklin asking him to admit his son in law to the Society of the Cincinnati as he had served as a French officer in the American Revolution. We will see through time Society of the Cincinnati members being mentioned or involved in many "mysteries" form Oak Island, the Newport Tower, Beale Treasure, and now St. Paul's Chapel. Pierre L'Enfant was also a member of the Society of the Cincinnati. St. Paul's through many different eras of American History had been anointed a place of great talismanic and symbolic importance. Had it also had an initiatory quest

326

applied to it that in turn told one of all the different aspects of its origins including the Montgomery Monument?

It is possible that the Freedom Tower that took the place of the twin World Trade Center Towers is meant to be a representation of the Dome of the Rock in a scheme or plan that illustrates the concept of a "New Jerusalem." The plan of the Freedom Tower reveals that it is a sort of twisted octagon as it rises from street level. At various altitudes in its height a perfect equilateral octagon is formed. These octagons serve to point directly to St. Paul's Chapel only a short distance away to the southeast. In turn the orientation of St. Paul's creates an arc that extends to the Freedom Tower and the north side of its octagonal form. This layout would mimic the plan of the Temple Mount we see today that illustrates how the Dome of the Rock and Al Aqsa Mousque align with each other. If Constantine had built an octagon where the Dome of the Rock is today then it would have aligned with the Church of St. Mary Justinian built by Justinian I in the sixth century now known as the Al Aqsa Mosque. All of the "New Jerusalems" in the world may be a copy of the plan of the Temple Mount we see thee today. The first "New Jerusalem" may have been Ravenna Italy whose history in turn sheds light on many of the Arcadian overtones of the modern Rennes le Chateau Mystery.

Though the line extending from St. Paul's to the Freedom Tower does not match the octagon of the Tower it does intersect with the building and is very close to being a perfect match. It may be that the form and position of the Freedom Tower dictated that this area had been designated a "New Jerusalem" long ago and that this plan of arranged architecture was only able to occur after the destruction of the Twin Towers of the World Trade Center. It may also be that the Twin Towers served the same symbolic purpose in this representation of the New Jerusalem and this is why they were attacked on that day (possibly). Many feel that the Twin Towers were representative of the pillars of Boaz and Jachin and their Enochian overtones. No matter the reasons for the attacks of September eleventh it appears someone had responded by building a New Jerusalem to replace the array that had been there previously.

In past works we have examined the geographic and spatial relationships of some important monuments in New York City that help to define its New Jerusalem status. These monuments include Cleopatra's Needle, an Egyptian obelisk in Central Park, and its surrounding octagonal Plaza. If one extends or plots an arc on the globe from Cleopatra's Needle to the hexagonal Jewish American Museum in south Manhattan this arc passes the site of the Freedom Tower and matches the angle of the octagon hidden in its plan. This arc also matches the position and direction of sixth avenue or "The Avenue of the Americas" which serves as one of the major corporate business districts of New York City. Amazingly this angle is measured at 209 degrees true north from Cleopatra's Needle to the Jewish American Museum. The arc also matches both the facet of the Freedom Tower's octagon and the hexagonal form of the Jewish Museum. The Jewish Museum "points back" to the Freedom Tower and Cleopatra's Needle. This array may include a crossing element similar to a medieval church extending from the U.N. facility to the U.S.S. Intrepid Museum on the Hudson to the west.

It is amazing that the angular association between Cleopatra's Needle, the Freedom Tower, and Jewish American Museum is 209 degrees thus matching the same numerology present in the address of St. Paul's Chapel as 209 Broadway. 2+0+9=11. 209 Broadway "points to" the Freedom Tower which appears as a diamond or rotated square from plan view after its completion. This diamond shape of the Freedom Tower is also oriented at the same 209 degree angle as the association from Cleopatra's Needle to the Jewish American Museum.

In short the entire array of architecture including the fallen Twin Towers and New Freedom Tower represent a New Jerusalem in a metaphorical sense. It is even fitting that the Twin Towers fell in this story in that the Temple in Jerusalem was also destroyed and rebuilt many times. Indeed, this is what the prophecy of Isaiah is speaking of in its telling. The Temple was destroyed but we will rebuild with dressed stone. The concept of the New Jerusalem in turn has great symbolic importance to not only Jewish Americans but their Jacobite and Gnostic oriented Masonic brothers and Sisters. Again the specter of Bob Marley looms via his song "Cornerstone."

Finally, this arrangement of planned architecture includes a geographic association with the Egyptian Obelisk at the center of St. Peter's Square of the Vatican. The octagonal plaza surrounding Cleopatra's Needle in Central Park may be used to form an arc on the globe that extends to the Egyptian Obelisk at the center of St. Peter's Square. The Heliopolitan Obelisk of St. Peter's in turn functions as a classic example of an Axis Mundi with its included surrounding "Windrose" markers. All of these plans in effect mimic the true function of the original Tower of the Winds in Athens.

In this understanding we may note that Pierre L'Enfant, Benjamin Franklin, and Thomas Jefferson had been taught these concepts more from a French point of view. Any mystery associated with the altar of L'Enfant and Montgomery Monument at St. Paul's would naturally reflect a French point of view in presenting any information that may help one to discern the truth about this talismanic scheme. In the end all of this may be to compel one to examine the facts and heritage being displayed in this famous place in order to understand this hard to decipher historical conundrum. All of this explains why St. Paul's interior resembles in many ways the interior of a Masonic lodge and is decorated in a similar fashion to other chapels in France used for the same purpose. This may also lead us to the assumption that many researchers forget how the French controlled the region where the famous Oak Island "Treasure" is said to exist.

In the end none of this really sheds anymore light on the truth of September eleventh, two thousand and one. It does reflect the story from the old testament in which the Old Temple on the Temple Mount in Jerusalem was destroyed with the Jews being cast into exile in Babylonia. The "Second Temple" now occupies this valued point on the earth with St. Paul's occupying the position of the Al Aqsa Mosque on the Temple Mount.

Al Aqsa was originally built by Justinian I and was named the Church of St. Mary Justinian. This fact among many others covered in other work points to the hidden conclusion that Constantine had once built an octagonal structure where the Dome of the Rock stands today and that Justinian II had manipulated even this newer octagon into existence. This ancient intrigue and hidden scheme on the part of Roman and Byzantine rulers may reflect some of the motivations and reasons for this ordered plan of talismanic architecture in Manhattan and why it was attacked on 9/11.

This story in total may be broken down into terms we can understand if we consider that St. Paul's may have served as a Masonic Hall in addition to its ecclesiastical functions. The motif added by L'Enfant would foreshadow many of the themes that would later be said to also be visible in the street plan of Washington D.C. Many of the figures involved in the decision to place the memorial at St. Paul's in New York City were indeed members of the Society of the Cincinnati including Montgomery's brother in law Livingston who played a major role in the placement of the monument. The fact that St. Paul's "points to" the Powder Magazine may have been the real reason this place was both used during the war as a meeting place, why the monument was placed there later, and why in the end it survived the terrorist attacks of September eleventh. Both St. Paul's Chapel and the Powder Magazine in Williamsburg are associated with George Washington.

So where does this leave us with the nine lead lined caskets and the memorial was shipped in? What of the seven copies of his bust Franklin had commissioned from Caffieri the artist who had designed the memorial? We do know that Thomas Jefferson came into possession of one of these busts but the whereabouts of the remaining six are unknown. The saga of the Montgomery Memorial both before and after the war also supports the notion that the location of St. Paul's was predetermined and may have always served as the place the monument was supposed to have been placed. When viewed from afar the entire scheme seems planned and contrived and centers in many ways on the octagonal Powder Magazine in Colonial Williamsburg that was built long before St. Paul's Chapel was even thought of.

If one were to let one's imagination run wild we could imagine a wide range of relics or valued objects that could have been sent inside these lead caskets that contained the memorial. Here is a direct and documented example of a strange shipment coming from France to the United States during the war in which an older array of talismanic architecture may have been used to establish a ritual as well leave an easy way to decipher the whereabouts of the memorial should it have been lost in the fog of war. Franklin showed an unusual amount of interest in making sure this monument was erected as well as its safety and security in the time prior to it being sent to St. Paul's Chapel. There is more to this story that is begging to be uncovered.

One solution to this mystery may involve the first governor of North Carolina. Edenton was the first capitol of North Carolina. Today the center of the town is marked by the old courthouse that includes a memorial to early governor Joseph Hewes. Hewes also served as first secretary of the Navy and supplied many of the ships used in the Revolutionary War from his own shipping concerns. This may also add information as to why somehow the Montgomery Memorial was created in France yet shipped via and English ship to Edenton. Mr. Hewes and his shipping connections may have made this much easier than anyone would suspect during this era. In short

329

Hewes may have had inside connections in England at that time that sympathized with the America cause. Hewes is also one of the first signers of the Declaration of Independence. He is a very well respected and significant first American Patriot.

As is fitting of his status Hewes is the subject to a memorial cenotaph of his own situated in front of the courthouse in Edenton. This wonderful memorial is an upright rectangular structure that is elegant in its simplicity and style. This memorial is topped by a large decorative stone urn that does in fact appear to have been created from a different hue of marble than the rest of the brilliant white stone used in the rest of the piece. Is it possible that somehow this is the missing urn from the Montgomery Memorial? If so there could be no more fitting use for such a storied piece of art than to commemorate the accomplishments of this great American. Still the question remains; Is there anything of note hidden within this stone urn?

Is it possible that the urn atop the Hewes Monument in Edenton North Carolina is the missing Urn from the Montgomery Monument in New York City at St. Paul's Chapel?

What had become of the Urn that was supposed to have originally been included on this piece? Did it contain anything or was it empty. Is it still lost somewhere in Edenton North Carolina or is it now hiding in plain sight somewhere else as part of the same mystery we see already? What would be in the urn if the French had decided to send something of talismanic importance to their brothers in arms in the Untied States? Had the fact that the memorial passed through English hands meant that they had ended up with the urn and its possible contents?

One almost obscure clue with regard to the origins of the Montgomery Monument may link us back to some of the more well known geographic mysteries of France including Rennes le Chateau and the Great Cyclic Cross of Hendaye.

In previous works we have discussed the possible involvement of the Cassini Family and others in the formation of a Republic in France. This may have also included François Arago famous for the bronze "Arago" medallions that grace the Paris Meridian in that city. Via these connections intimate knowledge of the mysteries of France as valued by the Royal class may have made their way to the Socitey of the Cincinnati who in turn used these concepts in a clandestine manner against their enemies of the time. This included both English and French Royal interests as well as those from the rest of Europe. If this information could be useful towards the establishment of a Republic anywhere in the world then the Society may have deemed it wise to use this information in this way. In short this age old tradition had always had intelligence services uses and this era was no exception.

It may be that American authors such as Poe, Cooper, Longfellow, and others who may have been associated with the Society of the Cincinnati had been privy to this information and had been instructed to craft stories and tales that may convey these concepts to initiates and novices alike. Metaphor in Allegory it seems had been used in the past as a way to communicate what may be considered "top secret" information. In this way the story of Rennes le Chateau may have been known of and intentionally distorted as an intelligence ploy by people like Poe, The Cassini's, Arago, the d'Abbadie's, Jefferson, Franklin, and even Alexander Von Humboldt.

These men's involvement explains almost every "Mystery" in every country that fascinates the public. I ascribe this groups involvement to many modern views of the following conundrums: Rennes le Chateau, Ravenna Italy, The hidden concept of Arcadia, Oak Island, Bacon's Vault in Williamsburg, The Beale Treasure, The Newport Tower, The Westford Knight, the Archer Reliquary of Jamestown, and the Kensington Rune. All of these phenomena were either contrived or expanded upon by the Society of the Cincinnati and their cadre of artists and writers who supported the Republican ideal around the world.

When taking the above into consideration we may now even consider information that seems arcane and unimportant in terms of this type of interpretation. We have already noted the importance of the Paris Meridian in many aspects of this tradition and lore. The Paris Observatory marks the Paris Meridian but its grounds are oriented slightly west of true north thus creating an arc on the globe that leads directly to Montserrat Spain the said resting place of the holy grail itself. The Cassini's simply did not make mistakes of this magnitude leading us to the conclusion that this was an intentional arrangement.

Fitting this scheme of appreciation for the Paris Meridian as it defines the mysteries of Arcadia; The Bear; or the Pole Star is Jean Jacques Caffieri the sculptor of the Montgomery Memorial that rests on the east porch of St. Paul's Chapel in New York City. The quarry from which Caffieri obtained the rose marble that makes up the central pillar of the piece comes from the Languedoc region of France from a point on the Rose Meridian or Paris Meridian just 25 miles south of Rennes le Chateau at the base of Mt. Canigou. Given what we have learned to this point is it possible this is simply a coincidence? Here is a direct link between the region of mystery and intrigue that had been there since the time of the Visigothic Merovingian Kings who were indeed the descendants of the Byzantine rulers of Ravenna and Constantinople.

It is starting to look more and more as if my grand speculation from many years ago involving Jefferson having actually visited the direct environs of Rennes le Chateau is a distinct and real possibility. The same could be said about Benjamin Franklin and possibly James Madison. All of these men displayed these decidedly French Masonic values in many things they did including their intelligence gathering activities. Ultimately all of this would lead to the creation of the Scottish Rite of Freemasonry in Charleston South Carolina in 1804.

Appendix 1 Illustrations and Photos

Note that these associations may only be compared to the navigational technology of the era in which they occurred. Given that some of these directions may have been valued by later people who only suspected that a given location was associated. So the techniques used to make these associations were not as accurate as Google Earth even given the small margin of error present in Google Earth. In addition, the use of methods of astronomy and the use of the associated tools could account for what appears to be small differences between Google Earth and older navigation. Due to this a small margin of error is given. Geographic Information Systems analysts may put a small buffer zone around each target. This buffer zone may take into account the distance from the mother axis etc. Even with the above parameters some amazing and accurate associations were made later as geodetic skills improved through history. Those who added later Temples that aligned with St. Peter's Square for instance could do this in North America more accurately than their earlier predecessors. Note that many plan view drawings of older structures are not oriented correctly. Many artists oriented their drawings by eye or with a magnetic compass. I have found several older plans of ruins and ancient structures that were not oriented correctly. So that is not a reliable source of information in many cases.

The hexagonal port of Portus built by Trajan points to Oak Island and more.

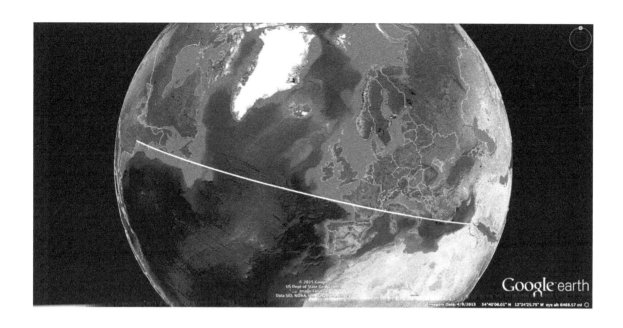

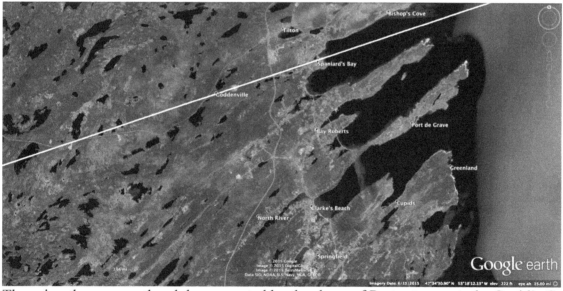

The azimuth or arc on the globe suggested by the shape of Portus transects the Cupid's Colony partly funded by Sir Francis Bacon.

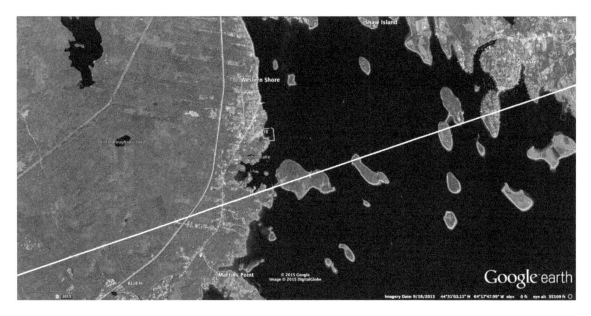

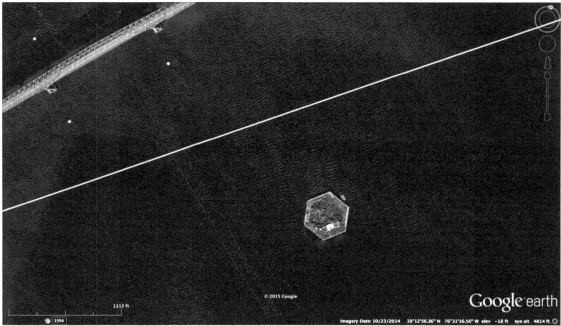

The arc from Portus continues to Baltimore and this hexagonal Fort Carroll built by Robert E. Lee who may have known about Portus. Below we see the arc reaching the Naval Observatory in Washington D.C.

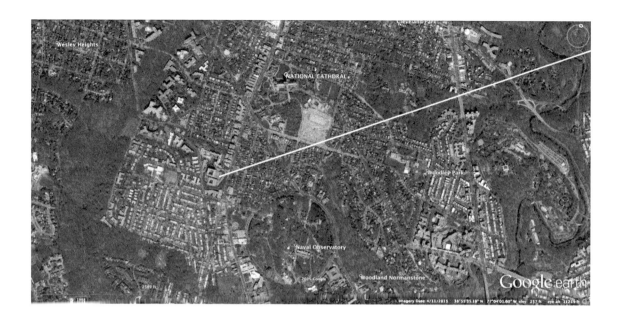

The Daphne Octagon of Constantine was oriented the same was as the Hippodrome of Theodosius and the Egyptian Obelisk in the plaza. This array points to Oak Island and the Powder Magazine in Williamsburg in one arc on the globe.

The array of Obelisk within the Hippodrome array points to Oak Island and the Powder Magazine in Williamsburg in a single arc on the globe.

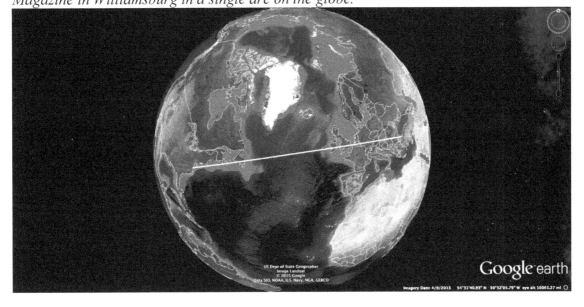

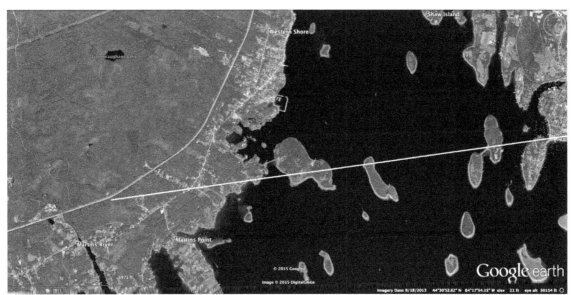
The arc reaches Oak Island and the Powder Magazine.

337

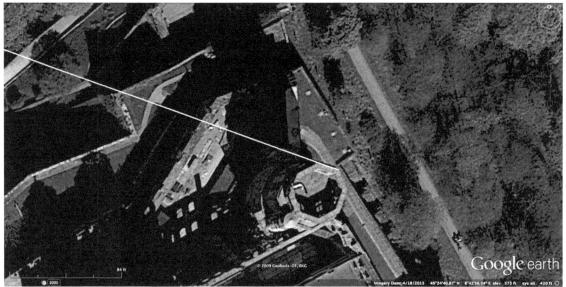

The octagon of Heidelberg Castle points to Oak Island and the Powder Magazine in Williamsburg in one arc on the globe just as the obelisk array of Constantine in Istanbul does.

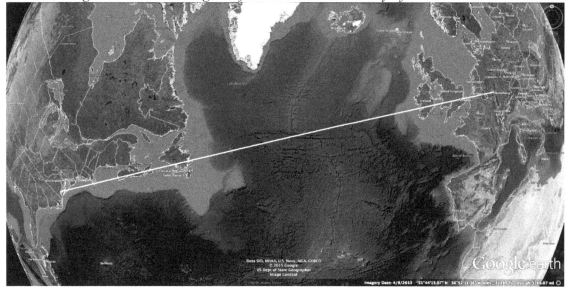

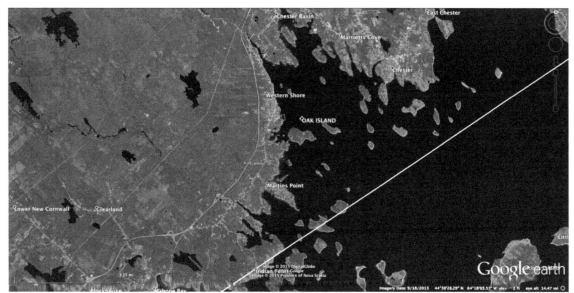
The arc from Heidelberg reaches Oak Island (near) and the Powder Magazine.

The Heidelberg Castle octagon points one arc to Oak Island and the Powder Magazine and another to the International Peace Garden. The Cassini family also built an octagonal structure that "points to" both places.

The octagon at the Cassini Estate north of Paris is directly north of the northern tip of the star identified in the landscape of Rennes le Chateau. This tip of the star is marked by Chateau Blanchefort. The Cassini estate is due north (0 degrees true north) of Chateau Blanchefort.

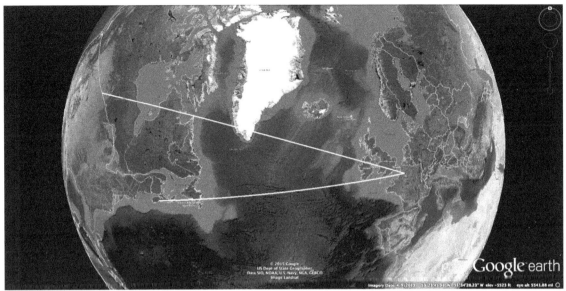

Arcs generated from the Cassini octagon reach Oak Island and the International Peace Garden on the Border of the U.S. and Canada. It is possible the site of the IPG was used to claim North America as early as the time of Charlemagne.

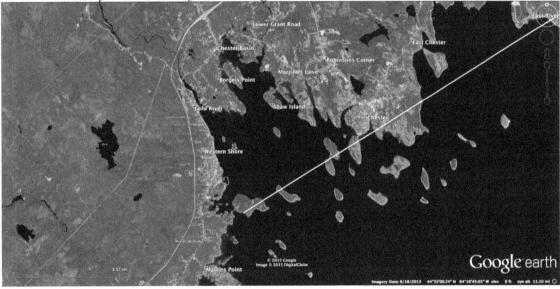

341

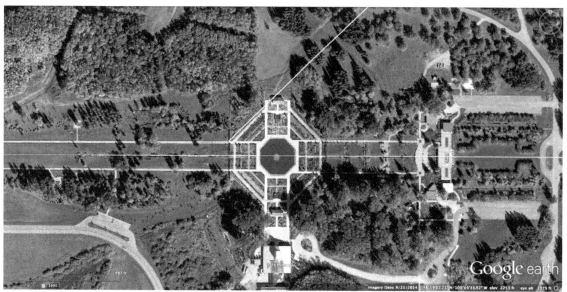
The arc from the Cassini octagon reaches the International Peace Garden.

Below: The array of I.M. Pei Pyramids points to Midgal Israel, the hometown of Mary Magdalene to the southeast. To the northwest this array points to with an mile of Oak Island, Nova Scotia.

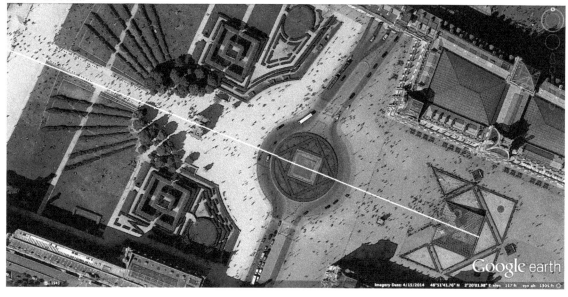

342

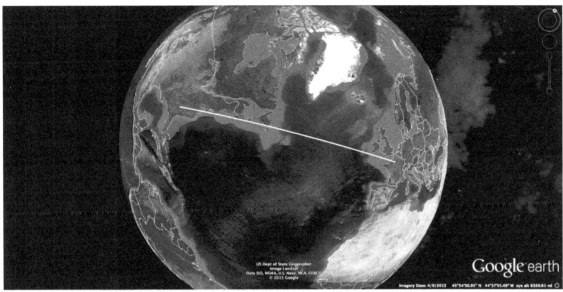

The arc spans the globe reaching Oak Island.

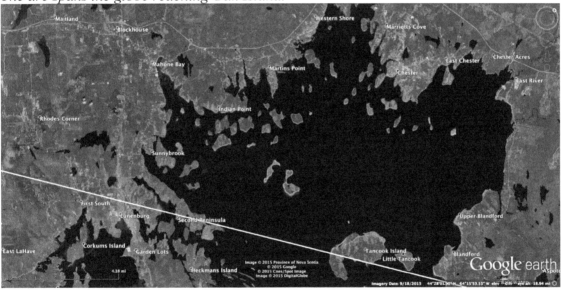

The Array at the Louvre points to the home of Mary Magdalene. This matches the ending scene theme of the movie "The Da Vinci Code."

Structures and arrays of architecture associated with the International Peace Garden.

Saint Michaels Tower octagon at Monte 'Sant Angelo Italy points to the IPG and Tower of the Winds in Athens in separate arcs on the globe. The tower was built by Frederick II Holy Roman Emperor.

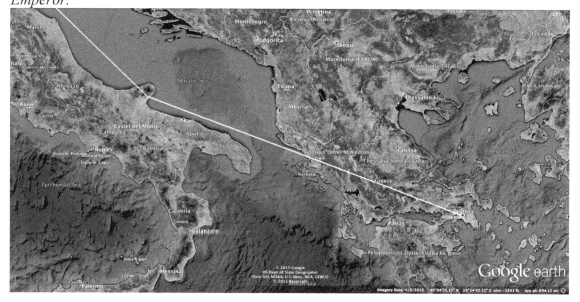

Arcs pointing to the IPG and Tower of the Winds in Athens.

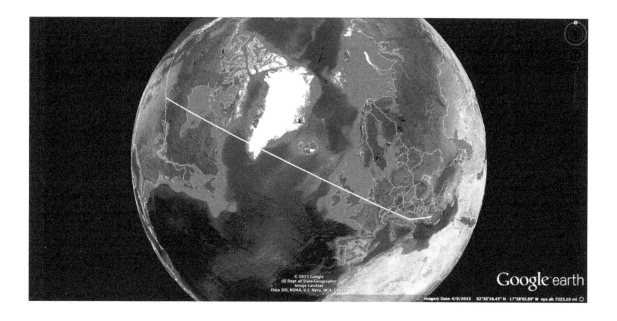

The arc from St. Michael's Tower reaches the International Peace Garden.

Below: Castel Del Monte also built by Frederick II HRE also points to the International Peace Garden.

346

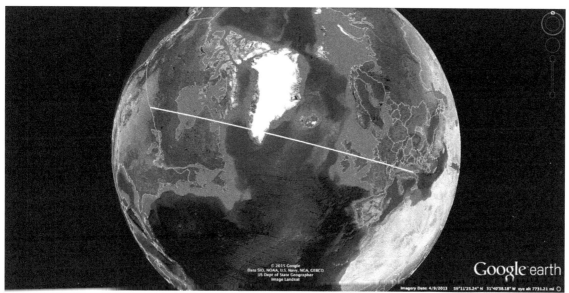

The arc from Castel del Monte reaches the IPG.

347

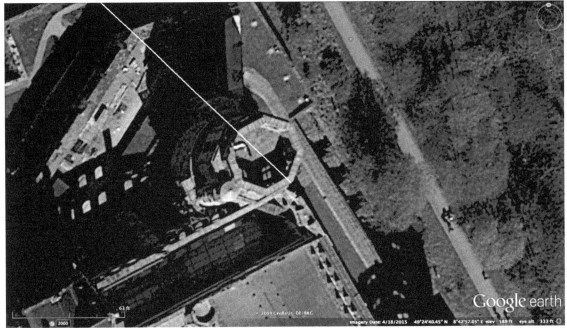
An arc suggested by the octagonal form of this tower at Heidelberg Castle points to the IPG. As we saw an additional arc suggested by this structure points to Oak Island.

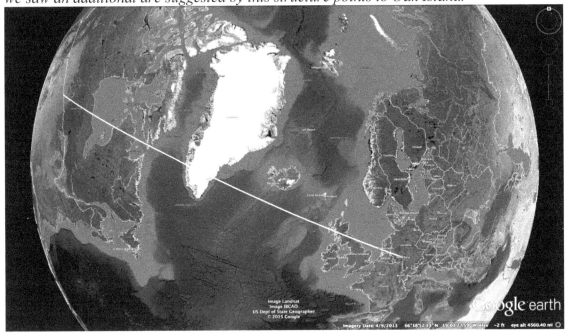

The arc from Heidelberg reaches the IPG.

Below: The octagonal form of the Powder Magazine in Colonial Williamsburg points an arc on the globe to a Masonic Compass and Square shaped building at the IPG. This building is oriented to point back to the Powder Magazine.

349

350

Amazing. Intentional? Likely.

Below: The Shepherd's Monument at Shugborough Hall points to the IPG. This statue or memorial includes a bas relief rendering of Poussin's "Et in Arcadia Ego."

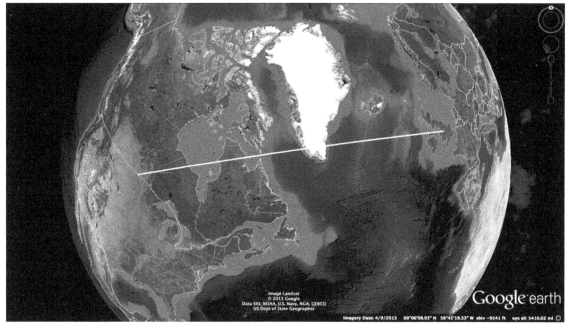

The arc suggested by the Shepherd's Monument reaches the IPG. Shugborough Hall also includes a reproduction of the Tower of the Winds that points to some amazing places including Stonehenge and Avebury Circle's in a single arc suggested by its form and orientation.

This map an others show the location of the Kensington Stone, Minot Stone (suspected), and sandstone pillar w/ Ogham inscription all being located at the margins of Rupert's Land (Hudson's Bay Claim) and what would become the Louisiana Purchase. It makes sense the marker would reflect the political divisions of these groups of people. This map shows the 49th parallel marked within a different scale than the map was drawn suggesting someone added it later. Below: The Williamsburg Powder Magazine built in the tradition of the octagons of Constantine the Great.